WITHOUT THE BOMB

Without the Bomb

THE POLITICS OF NUCLEAR NONPROLIFERATION

Mitchell Reiss

COLUMBIA UNIVERSITY PRESS   New York   1988

A gift from Corliss Lamont, friend of Columbia University Press, has helped in the publication of this book.

Columbia University Press
New York   Guildford, Surrey
Copyright © 1988 Columbia University Press

Printed in the United States of America

Library of Congress Cataloging-in-Publication Data
Reiss, Mitchell.
Without the bomb: the politics of nuclear nonproliferation/
Mitchell Reiss.
p.   cm.
    Revision of author's thesis (Ph. D.)—Oxford University.
    Bibliography: p.
    Includes index.
    ISBN 0-231-06438-1
    1. Nuclear nonproliferation.   I. Title.
JX1974.73.R45 1987
327.1'74–dc19   87-17395

Clothbound editions of Columbia University Press are Smyth-sewn and printed on permanent and durable acid-free paper

Contents

Contents

Foreword

Lincoln P. Bloomfield

One of the persistent concerns of both American and Soviet policymakers is the spectre of nuclear weaponry spreading from the present five nuclear weapons powers to other countries, particularly those located in the world's most crisis-prone regions.

In the United States, nonproliferation policies have varied in detail with administrations. But, in general, U.S. policy has sought to inhibit nuclear spread ever since President John F. Kennedy forecast a world of fifteen to twenty-five nuclear powers by the 1970s. During the Johnson years the United Nations, with a strong U.S.-Soviet lead, consummated the Nuclear Nonproliferation Treaty, which over 130 countries have signed since 1968. A decade later Congress passed the Nuclear Nonproliferation Act, which denied American economic and military benefits to weapons proliferators. The Carter administration gave nonproliferation a high priority, while the Reagan administration at least initially sought to downgrade official moralizing on the subject. But, at root, nonproliferation has been high on the scale of official concerns.

President Kennedy's prediction was not illogical. Today there are in fact six and a half nuclear weapons powers, if we include Israel's widely assumed clandestine nuclear capacity and India's detonation in 1974 of a "peaceful" nuclear device. Other highly industrialized countries such as Japan, Germany, Canada, Italy, Sweden, or Switzerland always had the potential to develop their own arsenals of deliverable nuclear weapons; Britain, France, and China in fact did so.

A major stimulus to concern has been the acquisition of broad technological and engineering skills by developing countries such as India, Pakistan, Brazil, and Argentina, plus such economic achievers as South Korea and Taiwan. All of these have in fact traveled significantly down the road toward a domestic nuclear production capability. And in a turbulent age of incessant crises, it has been natural to agonize over the possibility of even one deliverable nuclear explosive in the hands of a reckless or fanatical leader.

In light of these developments the conventional wisdom has always assumed that proliferation is inevitable, the only relevant questions being "Who's next?" and "When?"

The widespread expansion of nuclear weaponry may yet take place. But it has not yet happened, and the forecasts made during the 1950s and 1960s have uniformly proved wrong. It is instructive to ask why they were so far off. If nothing else, these predictions illustrate the fallacy of straight-line extrapolation. There would be 15, 20, or even 30 nuclear weapons powers, so the reasoning ran, because that many states could build a bomb, based on technological capability as the decisive measure.

But among Western industrialized nations, one after another simply decided not to do so. Canada was a collaborator on the US Manhattan Project, and thus arguably could have fabricated a deliverable nuclear weapons by the 1950s; but it chose not to. (Britain, which also shared the secrets, in fact did so, as did the USSR, which acquired them by a less laudable route). Sweden and Switzerland, after considering the matter, opted in the negative. West Germany was forbidden to build such weaponry, and Japan to this day nurses her nuclear allergy.

Other countries have not publicized their decision processes. But the extraordinary fact is that as of the late 1980s, the *avowed* nuclear weapons powers remain the original five which, by accident or design, happen also to be the five Permanent Members of the UN Security Council already endowed by treaty with special privileges and, presumably, responsibilities.

Why is this so?

That is the vital question Mitchell Reiss explores in this book, with highly enlightening results. In the spirit of Sherlock Holmes' famous inquiry into the dog that did not bark, he asks why six key "threshold countries"—Sweden, South Korea, Japan, Israel, South Africa, and India—did not openly and unambiguously go nuclear when they were capable of doing so.

After investigating the varied histories represented in these very different cases, Dr. Reiss finds that they have in common four distinct sources for nuclear restraint, ranging from domestic constraints to international and bilateral pressures. His analysis, both methodologically elegant and politically sophisticated, yields a conceptual structure that can be fruitfully applied to other instances of "nuclear-capable" powers that have not yet crossed that fearsome barrier.

One of the great values of the Reiss analysis lies in his approach to the cases of Israel and South Africa—both so-called "pariah states" whose very existence is under threat but who have opted, at least so far, for what he calls "an uncertain nuclear posture." In the process the author clarifies a little-understood phenomenon: the value of *threatening* to go nuclear, but without actually doing so. The threshold this suggests that we focus on is thus not between a weapons capability and none. It is the threshold of *nondetonation*, regardless of how far along a national program may be.

In other words, one may know how to reprocess spent fuel rods from power reactors; one may possess a small stockpile of plutonium plus technicians who can fabricate a bomb; one may even have dual-capable aircraft that could drop something incredibly destructive in the general vicinity of one's enemy. But it is the *threat* to do so that is "bankable" in the sense of being convertible to a flow of *conventional* armaments that Israel, India, and Pakistan believe they need to stand off their adversaries.

Paying for nondetonation with lethal nonnuclear weaponry has been called the Dove's Dilemma. Is it also blackmail? Perhaps. But it is a species of blackmail that helpfully keeps multiple local conflicts at a level of low intensity, rather than placing global peace at risk.

Having said this, the author reminds us that would-be proliferators also cannot ignore the international political climate, or the exigent pressures on the part of neighbors and allies. He usefully reviews the major international efforts to construct a proliferation-resistant regime; indeed, one of the book's original contributions is to redefine that regime to include not only the NPT of 1968, but also the whole range of domestic constraints, diplomatic efforts, and world public opinion.

I find particularly appealing his strong emphasis on political motivations alongside technological capabilities. This supplies a helpful corrective to the classic fallacy of basing policy primarily on technical capabilities.

No armchair researcher, Mitchell Reiss spent time in five of the six countries he studied. His own background gives this book special weight: few analysts of his age have served in both the National Security Council and the London-based International Institute for Strategic Studies, in the process gaining a doctorate from Oxford University as well as formal legal training. This important book gives fresh confirmation to Macaulay's observation that "on all great subjects, much remains to be said."

M.I.T.
Cambridge, Massachusetts

Acknowledgments

Writing a doctoral dissertation, and subsequently revising it for publication, resembles in many ways a personal odyssey, and it is therefore not inappropriate to say that "I am a part of all whom I have met." Many people provided assistance during my work at Oxford University and later with preparation of the final manuscript. Bertrand Goldschmidt and Margaret Gowing critiqued the early drafts of Part One. Lionel Bryer, Hedley Bull, Kurt Campbell, Ashok Kapur, Donald Kerr and Tomas Ries provided useful comments on individual chapters in Part Two. Dietrich Schroeer verified the information in the Technical Note contained in the Appendix. My dissertation examiners, John Simpson and J. A. A. Stockwin, offered many helpful suggestions. David Fischer's careful reading of the entire manuscript proved invaluable. I am especially grateful to my supervisor at Oxford, Adam Roberts, for his constant encouragement and support. I would also like to thank Warren Donnelly, Farooq Hussain, Robert O'Neill, John Stremlau, Gregory Treverton, and Charles Van Doren, for their interest in my work. Needless to say, I remain responsible for any errors of fact or interpretation.

I was able to visit five of the six countries discussed in Part Two. Donald Gregg, Yukio Satoh, and Scott Thompson kindly provided introductions for me in these countries. The following people consented to interviews: Sven Andersson, Nils Andren, Romesh Bhandari, Chong-ki Choi, Pran Chopra, Priscilla Clapp, Morarji Desai, Tetsuya Endo, Tage Erlander, Inder Malhotra, Olof Palme, Nils Skiöld, Raja Ramanna, G. K. Reddy, Stig Synnergren, and A. B. Vajpayee. I wish to thank them and also those interviewed who requested that their names not be mentioned.

My research in Sweden was made possible by a grant from the Cyril Foster Fund, and by the assistance of Lars Killander and Dag Linder in Stockholm. The Bradley Foundation paid for my research in India and for my expenses while I revised the manuscript. The Rockefeller Foundation also provided financial assistance for my work. The International Institute for Strategic Studies in London generously allowed me the use of their facilities during the summer of 1986 while I performed my revisions.

The librarians, archivists, and staffs at the following libraries were invariably helpful with my many requests: the Old Bodleian Library, Rhodes House, St. Antony's College Library, the Lamont and International Legal Studies libraries at Harvard University, the British Library, the International Institute for Strategic Studies, and the Royal Institute of International Affairs. In addition, Paula Dobriansky, Ihor Fedorowycz, Thomas Graham, James Marshall, and Renee de Nevers provided material I had difficulty in obtaining. I could not have asked for a better editor than Kate Wittenberg at Columbia University Press.

For their hospitality and generosity, I am indebted to the Bryer, Albert, Royle, and Anselmi families. For her forbearance and friendship, I thank Lisa. Finally, for all that they have done, I am grateful to my family. It is to them that this book is dedicated.

Abbreviations

AEB	South African Atomic Energy Board
CANDU	Canadian-deuterium-uranium
CEA	Commissariat à l'Energie Atomique
DOSB	U.S. *Department of State Bulletin*
DSFB	*Documents on Swedish Foreign Policy*
ENDC	Eighteen Nation Disarmament Committee
Euratom	European Atomic Energy Community
FBIS	*Foreign Broadcast Information Service*
FRUS	*Foreign Relations of the United States*
IAEA	International Atomic Energy Agency
IISS	International Institute for Strategic Studies
INFCE	International Nuclear Fuel Cycle Evaluation
IAEC	Israel Atomic Energy Commission
NPT	Nonproliferation Treaty
NSG	Nuclear Suppliers Group
PTBT	Partial Test Ban Treaty
PNE	Peaceful Nuclear Explosion
SIPRI	Stockholm International Peace Research Institute
UNAEC	United Nations Atomic Energy Commission
USGPO	United States Government Printing Office

Introduction

Over the past forty-two years, six countries are known to have detonated nuclear devices, while five of them have constructed sizable inventories of nuclear weapons. During this same period, a much larger number of technologically capable countries consciously refrained from acquiring nuclear arms. For these countries, the pressures against acquisition outweighed those in favor. To be certain, many countries have not possessed the industrial base, technological expertise, or economic resources to build nuclear arms. In these cases, no choice was involved because the hurdles to acquisition were insurmountable. On the other hand, there have been a substantial number of countries which have not been prevented by these obstacles and yet still have refrained from constructing nuclear weapons. While there have been numerous studies on the motivations of the United States, the Soviet Union, Britain, France, and China toward development, there has been far less focus on why countries have abstained from acquiring nuclear weapons.

This study will examine the extent to which six of these technically competent countries—Sweden, South Korea, Japan, Israel, South Africa, and India—decided not to develop nuclear arsenals, and the reasons for their decisions. It will also determine whether the nuclear restraint exhibited by each country was exclusively, or even largely, the product of the international nonproliferation arrangements which have been established, or whether it was the result of other factors. Finally, the implications of these findings for nuclear nonproliferation and the international nonproliferation regime will be discussed.

The book is organized in three parts. Part One provides a brief historical overview of the international nonproliferation regime since the Second World War, with special attention to how perspectives on the spread of nuclear weapons have altered during this period. A great deal of information has unavoidably had to be condensed in this section for the purpose of keeping the manuscript to a manageable length, but the interested reader is directed to the notes for further literature on the specific issues discussed.

Part Two consists of six country case studies: Sweden, South Korea, Japan, Israel, South Africa, and India. Undoubtedly, other countries merit attention and could have been included in a study of this kind. Argentina, Brazil, and Taiwan could all be able to construct nuclear bombs some time in the near future. Pakistan may well already possess this capability. These and other candidates may even be more likely to fabricate nuclear weapons than the six countries under examination here.

Yet these six countries have been selected for a number of reasons. Each has long possessed the technical competence required to build nuclear arms and has still proved impervious, in various degrees, to the pressures in favor of acquisition that have existed over some period of time. The choice of these countries has also been governed by the desire to illustrate the broad spectrum of persuasive and dissuasive factors for acquisition. The security situation of each country has varied widely. The political legitimacy of South Korea, Israel, and South Africa has been actively contested. Japan and South Korea have maintained a de jure security alliance with the United States, while Israel has had an extensive security relationship with the U.S. Sweden has studiously attempted to pursue a path between East and West. India, too, has remained nonaligned, but has signed a Treaty of Peace and Friendship with the Soviet Union. South Africa has been an international pariah because of its racial policies, but has had limited military and strong economic ties to the industrialized West. The likely adversaries of four of the countries have been nuclear weapons states; the other two have suffered from an inferiority in military manpower compared to their opponents. One country has itself been the victim of atomic attack. Also, the differences in the nuclear status of the six countries indicates the complexity of the subject. The nonnuclear stance of Sweden, South Korea, and Japan has been formalized by their accession to the Nonproliferation Treaty (NPT). The position of Israel and South Africa is more equivocal, not only because neither has signed the Nonproliferation Treaty, but also because of the ambiguity which has surrounded their possible surreptitious development of national nuclear forces. India has also not signed the NPT, but has not tested a second nuclear device.

In addition, these countries were chosen because it was possible to undertake research on them from open source materials. This choice was facilitated by my being able to travel to five of the countries and to talk at length with government officials, politicians, and academics.

Part Two also devotes special attention to possible political motivations for nuclear weapons acquisition. In criminology, there are three elements needed for a crime: means, opportunity, and motive. Our six countries have all possessed both the means and the opportunity to construct nuclear arms. The only variable has been the motive. For each of these states, then, what motivations have favored acquiring nuclear weapons? What factors have militated against acquiring nuclear weapons? Did domestic concerns play any role in the decision? What influence did government leaders exercise? Was the viewpoint of the scientific community significant? What were the attitudes of the military services? Were there any historical or cultural factors that had an impact on the decision? Did public opinion make itself heard? To what extent did foreign policy objectives condition the final determination? Would a nuclear arsenal have enhanced or diminished national security? How would the development of nuclear weapons have affected relations with neighbors, allies, and adversaries? What advantages would a nuclear stockpile have bestowed? What disadvantages would it have brought?

The uncertain nuclear status of Israel and South Africa raises additional questions. Regardless of whether or not they have acquired nuclear weapons, why have they deliberately promoted an ambiguous nuclear posture? If these two countries have indeed developed national nuclear forces, why were they developed covertly? With respect to India, how can its idiosyncratic position best be explained? Why did New Delhi conduct a self-proclaimed peaceful nuclear explosion (PNE) in 1974? Why has it not subsequently conducted any others?

Various benefits have often been attributed to the possession of nuclear weapons. They have been viewed as a means of preserving the security of the state, of influencing an ally or creating greater independence within an alliance, of conferring international prestige, of bolstering domestic political support, and of fostering economic development and scientific progress. Yet while our six countries have sought alternative means to promote their interests, their technological capability to construct nuclear weapons has nonetheless granted some of them the opportunity to realize policy objectives in exchange for eliminating, or at least alleviating, the anxiety which this expertise has provoked in other countries. These objectives might well have been unobtainable by other means, including the actual development of nuclear armaments. In other words, the threat to develop nuclear arms, or alternatively, the promise to refrain from building nuclear weapons, has sometimes been a more effective method of scoring policy successes than the deployment of a nuclear arsenal. The manipulation of this "nuclear option" has been one path by which some of the six countries have sought to secure their national interests and advance their purposes.

Moreover, the more credible the threat to go nuclear, or the more sensitive the international community to the possible ramifications for regional and global instability of a certain country acquiring nuclear weapons, the greater the benefit to be won in return for assurances that nuclear weapons are rejected. Proliferation concern can be stimulated by a single unsafeguarded civilian nuclear power reactor. Assuming some level of nuclear sophistication, a country's nuclear credibility can be augmented by a wide range of actions: purchasing or manufacturing nuclear-capable delivery vehicles, refusing to sign or ratify the Nonproliferation Treaty, issuing statements alluding to a possible nuclear weapons program, detonating a peaceful nuclear device, or developing but not testing nuclear weapons. Part Two examines the decisions of the six countries on nuclear weapons acquisition, and, in addition, how some of these countries have attempted to manipulate the threat to acquire nuclear arms in order to better achieve their policy goals.

A Technical Note explaining some of the basic physics of nuclear reactors and reactions can be found in the Appendix. A knowledge of the terminology and of the numerous steps involved in nuclear energy and nuclear weapons development is useful for understanding how the international nonproliferation regime discussed in Part One has evolved. It is essential for evaluating in Part Two the technological sophistication of each country's nuclear program, and how this contributed to the credibility of its threat to acquire nuclear weapons.

After the evolution of the nonproliferation regime in Part One has been discussed, and after the determinants for and against nuclear weapons acquisition for the six countries have been ascertained in Part Two, Part Three will evaluate the effectiveness of the nonproliferation arrangements in confronting the underlying causes of nuclear weapons acquisition. Were the nonproliferation arrangements responsible for suppressing the motivations to develop nuclear arms? Did they provide the main inhibition to acquisition? Or were they useful but essentially supplementary measures? Did the credit for nonacquisition primarily reside with other factors? Part Three will suggest how the responsibility for countering the incentives and reinforcing the disincentives in the six countries should be apportioned. From an analysis of these countries, some general conclusions on the subject of nuclear nonproliferation and the international nonproliferation regime are distilled.

Any discussion of a subject as complex as nonproliferation, which combines elements of international relations, law, economics, technology, and national security, will contain its own priorities and assumptions, and hence its own limitations. The most important qualification concerns the definition of proliferation: when does a country become a nuclear weapons state? Under the terms of the Nonproliferation Treaty, a state is considered to have acquired nuclear weapons only if it has unambiguously convinced the world by detonating a nuclear device. To be sure, the issue of proliferation is not quite so simple. A single test is not very significant militarily; more threatening might be a country which has stopped short of testing but which possesses the ability to construct rapidly a number of deliverable bombs. Also, laboratory simulation techniques and computer modeling can now give a country high confidence in the characteristics and reliability of its nuclear arms without recourse to overt testing.[1] And historically, every initial test of a nuclear device has succeeded, thereby conferring greater assurance to any state with a proven, even if untested, weapons design.

Yet exploding a nuclear device will no doubt remain a politically significant act, a measure of what Raymond Aron has termed "symbolic violence"—a symbol of the capacity and resolution of armed force.[2] It has been, and will continue to be, an unmatched political signal. Moreover, the nondetonation of a nuclear device can be seen as implicit recognition of the effectiveness of the nonproliferation regime. A test by a non-nuclear party to the Nonproliferation Treaty would violate international law and, by a nonmember, would contravene a widely accepted international code of conduct. For the purposes of this book, then, a nuclear weapons state is one which has publicly acknowledged its exploding a nuclear bomb.

The international nonproliferation regime is more diverse than the agreements and institutions mentioned in Part One. Domestic legislation and bilateral accords complement international arrangements. Security alliances like NATO and the Warsaw Pact, security commitments such as the American relationship with Japan, the so-called negative security guarantees in which nuclear weapons states pledge not to use or threaten to use nuclear weapons against countries not possessing nuclear arms, and multilateral cooperative enterprises like Euratom, all form an integral part of this regime. These factors will be discussed when they are relevant to the country case studies.

In addition, any survey of these countries will necessarily encounter the hazards inherent in writing contemporary history. This problem is compounded by the nature of the inquiry: the only task more difficult than determining why an event occurred is to try to discover why it did not. Furthermore, when interviewing participants and interested observers, one must recognize that memories can be both selective and fuzzy, or worse, willfully misleading. In order to avoid these potential pitfalls, the methodology used for this book relies on the literature which has been published on the subject, government reports, official statements, and journal articles and newspaper accounts. Wherever possible, all personal interviews have been checked against the written record, or other interviews, or both.

Finally, in seeking to understand why these six countries have to various degrees refrained from acquiring nuclear weapons, this book assumes that each must operate in a competitive international system where certain actions are rewarded and others punished, some tolerated and others condemned. These countries have deliberately calculated where their best interests lie, and have carefully adjusted their policies and tailored their diplomacy to where they can most benefit. In our six countries, this has ranged from pledges of nuclear abstention as codified in the Nonproliferation Treaty to not declaring or demonstrating an assumed nuclear weapons capability. It may be legitimate to criticize this study on the grounds that it portrays the behavior of these countries as being more logical, consistent, and intelligent than can ever actually be the case. Yet despite this criticism, it is such enlightened behavior that remains the best hope of preventing the spread of nuclear weapons.

The past four decades have witnessed an unceasing nuclear armaments race between the United States and the Soviet Union, a growth in the number of independent states and the level of military power they have at their disposal, and the outbreak of armed conflict on virtually every continent. With the wide dissemination of scientific knowledge, engineering skills, and civil nuclear technologies during this same period, it has become both easier and less expensive to build nuclear weapons. Yet contrary to almost all predictions, the rampant proliferation of nuclear weapons among states has not occurred. Historically, as indicated by test explosions, the pace of nuclear weapons spread has actually declined. In the first ten years of the nuclear age three countries exploded their initial nuclear weapons. In the next decade two countries made their maiden nuclear tests. The third decade saw only one country detonate its first nuclear device. The fourth decade did not have any new members of the nuclear club. Or, expressed differently, India has been the only country which has decided to explode its first nuclear device during the last twenty-three years. The sources of nuclear restraint have been stronger, more durable, and more adaptable than previously recognized.

Yet while the spread of nuclear weapons has been far slower than anticipated, there is no guarantee of future nonproliferation success. Concern over proliferation has evolved during the past forty years—from talk of halting proliferation in the 1950s, of controlling it in the 1960s and 1970s, and of living with it in the 1980s and beyond. If we hope to do any of these things—halt, control, or live with proliferation—we must first increase our understanding of its nature. With many countries holding the requisite technological capability, it becomes essential to examine the motivations that might activate or deter nuclear weapons acquisition. For those countries in a position to contemplate a national nuclear force, calculations will involve a determination of domestic and foreign policy objectives, and the degree to which nuclear weapons will facilitate or frustrate their achievement. To the extent that the key to wisdom is the knowledge of past events, it is hoped that this study on the politics of nonproliferation will contribute toward a greater understanding of this complex and important subject.

PART I: HISTORICAL OVERVIEW

1.

Changing Perspectives on Nuclear Proliferation

Nuclear proliferation has been a constant concern of states during the nuclear age, but the problem of nuclear weapons spread has been viewed differently over time. The first evidence of proliferation concern actually occurred during the development of the first atom bomb, prior even to its being tested. The impetus behind the early efforts to control information on atomic energy was provided by a unique set of circumstances: the conjunction of the basic scientific discoveries of atomic fission with the rise of Nazi Germany and the outbreak of the Second World War. Wartime secrecy shrouded the development programs in the United Kingdom, the United States, France, Canada, Germany, Japan, and the Soviet Union. In each country restrictions were placed on publishing information on atomic energy. A modification of this early example of countries unilaterally denying information on atomic energy to others was the subsequent limited wartime collaboration on atomic energy matters between the United States and Britain, and, to a lesser degree, among them and Canada.[1] It was the fear of a German atomic bomb that originally stimulated and later solidified this partnership.[2]

Yet as the war progressed, and the possibility of a German atomic bomb became more remote, the fear of a Germany armed with atomic weapons was replaced in the minds of a collection of scientists working on the Manhattan Project by the vision of a postwar competition in atomic armaments. The preeminent position which the Allies now held, due to their acquisition of raw materials, their scientific expertise, and engineering skills, could not be maintained indefinitely. The "secret" of the atomic weapon could not long be kept confidential. The Manhattan Project was an anomaly in the sense that it severely restricted free scientific inquiry; in peacetime the same constraints would not be possible. One only had to look at the number of different nationalities among the Manhattan Project scientists, with names like Bohr, Bethe, Fermi, and Szilard, among others, to realize that no single country could long retain a monopoly on scientific talent. Indeed, the Manhattan Project itself reflected this multinationalism, being a cooperative venture on the part of the United States, Britain, Canada, and scientists from France. As preoccupation with Germany receded and questions of postwar control of atomic energy loomed larger, the first proposals for international control were advanced. Where previously concern had centered on denying information to outsiders, gradually attention shifted toward sharing specialized knowledge with other members of the world community. In contrast to the early years of the war, national security interests now seemed to require a plan for the international control of atomic energy.

Scientists involved in the Manhattan Project took the lead in formulating possible postwar control arrangements.[3] Their suggestions were aimed at discarding much of the secrecy which characterized the wartime effort on atomic energy research, and establishing instead a supranational control authority. The premises upon which these proposals rested were fourfold. First, the American monopoly on atomic weapons was only temporary. Second, and deriving from this, since other countries were certain to acquire nuclear arms, the risks entailed with international control were less than those which would result from the unrestricted competition in national atomic arsenals that was certain to follow the war, and with it the threat of atomic attack. Third, the peaceful benefits of atomic energy could best be realized under a supranational authority to conduct research and development. And finally, the logic of these propositions would be persuasive to the other members of the world community. Common ingredients in these proposals were the free exchange of scientific information and unhindered access by the supranational body to activities relating to atomic energy within countries. The objective was the elimination of all atomic weapons in national hands. These proposals offered the prospect of a fundamental revision of international affairs.

All these plans for international control were founded on the hope that the qualities which had characterized scientific inquiry before the war—the free exchange of information and international scientific cooperation—could reassert themselves after the war in a manner that could promote the peaceful benefits while precluding the military applications of atomic energy. Interestingly, however, none of the proposals was particularly detailed, no doubt reflecting the unprecedented nature of the proposed undertaking and the uncertain complexion of the postwar environment. Rather, the proposals implied that the advantages of some form of international control arrangement—the absence of an arms race and relief from possible atomic attack—were so obviously worthwhile that the means to realize this goal would somehow be found. When compared with the perceived consequences of a refusal to cooperate, obstacles to agreement would certainly be overcome.

In addition to this optimism, these suggestions offered an interesting commentary on conceptions of national security and the spread of nuclear weapons. Plans for postwar control were rooted in the view that the national interests of the United States would be better served by the creation of some supranational control authority than by reliance on the ability of an American nuclear arsenal to prevent attack by the threat of retaliation, i.e., by reliance on a policy of deterrence. All the multilateral control schemes offered during the war rejected the strategic doctrine that Washington has followed in practice from 1945 to the present.

Furthermore, most of the plans for international control implied that the problem was global in scope, and could not be resolved by independent action or purely bilateral means. Specifically, emphasis on multilateral measures suggested that many if not all countries would want to imitate the United States and undertake the enormous scientific, engineering, and financial effort required to build atomic weapons. The original impulse to the British and American atomic energy programs— the spectre of an atomic-armed Germany in time of war—was extended to apply equally to all other countries during times of peace. Since the problem was deemed to be worldwide, only a remedy universal in scope would suffice. The preferred solution called for the creation of a supranational body with discretionary powers over all states in the realm of atomic energy. Each proposal envisioned that the countries of the world would acquiesce in surrendering a slice of their sovereignty in return for the prospect of safety from atomic attack and access to atomic energy technology for peaceful purposes. Efforts along these lines were accelerated after the bombing of Hiroshima on August 6, 1945, and of Nagasaki three days later.

With the successful conclusion of the war, plans for international control of atomic energy were discussed by the United States, the United Kingdom, and Canada at a conference in Washington in mid-November 1945.[4] A month later, at a Council of Foreign Ministers meeting in Moscow, the consent of the Soviet Union was procured for the creation of a United Nations Atomic Energy Commission (UNAEC) to consider the problem further.[5] In March 1946, the State Department proposed *A Report on the International Control of Atomic Energy*, better known as the Acheson-Lilienthal Report.[6] The key to the Report lay in its labeling of atomic energy activities as either "dangerous" or "nondangerous." Those which were deemed inherently dangerous due to their potential for diverting materials for subsequent development of atomic weapons would be assigned to an Atomic Development Authority (ADA). On the other hand, activities classified as nondangerous would be permitted for all countries, subject to minimal inspection. Oversight would be less intrusive while violations would be easier to detect, thereby instilling confidence and attracting greater participation in the plan. The qualities which distinguished the Acheson-Lilienthal Report from earlier efforts, however, were not just its greater thoroughness and attention to detail, but also its affirmation that a control and inspection system for atomic energy was technically feasible.

A modified version of the Report became the Baruch Plan, which was presented at the opening session of the United Nations Atomic Energy Commission in June 1946.[7] Bernard Baruch, the American representative to the UNAEC, borrowed heavily from *A Report on the International Control of Atomic Energy*. Yet while the Baruch Plan was derivative of the Acheson-Lilienthal Report, it was not a mere repetition of all its conclusions. Where the Acheson-Lilienthal Report outlined a plan to prohibit atomic weapons, Baruch more ambitiously forecast a world without war. More significant still was the difference in emphasis between the two. Above all, the Acheson-Lilienthal Report was an argument for the multinational management of atomic energy; it concentrated firmly on international control. The Baruch Plan undoubtedly caught something of this tone, but added the more dissonant note of retribution. Baruch's desire for an "international law with teeth in it" produced a penalization scheme which would sanction "immediate, swift, and sure" punishment against any transgressors. Yet because the proposed new agency would be administratively linked to the United Nations, any talk of penalization raised the issue of the veto power wielded by the five permanent members of the Security Council under Article 27 of the Charter. Penalties could only be meted out with the agreement of nine members, including the concurrence of all five permanent members. Arguing that the terrible consequences of the military use of atomic energy justified an alteration in this system, Baruch insisted that "There must be no veto to protect those who violate their solemn agreements not to develop or use atomic energy for destructive purposes."

The position of the Soviet Union was outlined five days later.[8] Stressing the potential peaceful benefits for mankind to be derived from atomic energy, the Soviet representative, Andrei Gromyko, maintained that this objective would best be realized if states no longer devoted their talents to producing weapons of mass destruction. The first step was an international convention which would prohibit the employment, possession, or manufacture of atomic arms. Six months after the convention's entry into force, the parties would pass legislation providing "severe penalities for violators of the statutes" of the Soviet Union's "Draft International Convention." This convention contained no reference to a control scheme, and indeed, the word "control" appeared nowhere in the text. In his remarks introducing the proposal, Gromyko mentioned that only after the convention was set up should there be "the establishment of a system of control over the observance of the convention."

The basic distinction between the American and Soviet positions was the timing of the control scheme's implementation. The Baruch Plan called for the imposition of an international system of inspection and control, with safeguards, before the divestiture of the U.S. atomic arsenal. The transition period to a control organization would take some years. Only then would the United States have to relinquish its fissile material. The Gromyko Plan, on the other hand, was based on an opposite sequence of control and prohibition. It advocated the elimination of atomic weapons as a first step, to be followed at some later date by a control scheme. Under this proposal, the United States would be obligated to destroy its stockpile of atomic weapons within three months. A method of control to ensure compliance by other states might or might not then be established. In other words, the United States was more interested both in the establishment of effective safeguards to prevent violations and in the control of atomic energy for peaceful purposes. The Soviet Union placed greater weight on the abolition of atomic weapons and on the exchange of basic scientific information.

A second Gromyko Plan, presented in June 1947, offered little to resolve these differences.[9] With the rejection of this second Soviet proposal, further progress in the U.N. Atomic Energy Commission ground to a halt. The initial optimism of the United States for a possible agreement had gradually given way to despondency, and then resignation.[10] By the spring of 1947, the U.S. had turned its attention in the Commission to stressing that the responsibility for failure in the negotiations was due solely to Soviet intransigence.[11] On September 11, 1947, the commission issued a report to the Security Council outlining the gulf which divided the two sides, and the differences that remained outstanding.[12] Reasons for failure in the United Nations included the lack of trust and goodwill between the United States and the Soviet Union, which, if it ever existed, had been dissipated first by the wartime secrecy surrounding the Manhattan Project and later by the postwar competition for power and influence in Europe and around the world, and perhaps more importantly, the asymmetry in nuclear capabilities due to the American lead in the field. With movement not forthcoming from either party, in May 1948 the commission suspended its work. Moscow's detonation of an atomic device in August 1949 dampened any remaining enthusiasm and stilled talk of "one world or none."[13] Meanwhile, until some feasible arrangement of international control could be assured, official secrecy on all aspects of the U.S. atomic weapons program had been legislatively mandated by Congress by the Atomic Energy Act of August 1, 1946.[14]

Technological advances in the early 1950s all but eliminated any remaining hopes for an agreement on comprehensive nuclear disarmament. In October 1952, Britain became the third member of the nuclear club with its detonation of a nuclear weapon off the coast of Australia.[15] Later that same month the United States tested a ten megaton hydrogen bomb (equivalent to ten million tons of TNT), thereby introducing an order of destruction quantitatively different from the earlier fission devices. The Soviet Union exploded its first hydrogen weapon ten months later, in August 1953.[16] At this time, the "Doomsday Clock" of the *Bulletin of the Atomic Scientists* was moved to a mere two minutes to midnight. This new phase in the arms race inaugurated by hydrogen weapons indicated not only the enormous scientific and financial investment in nuclear armaments by both sides, but also that any international control scheme based on the accountability of nuclear materials was no longer feasible, because any margin for error would carry too great a risk. Thus, due to a combination of diplomatic paralysis and technological momentum, international control of atomic energy faded almost completely from public discussion.[17]

While the successful completion of the Manhattan Project had led American policy-makers to believe that it would be possible to retain the U.S. monopoly for some time to come, advances by the atomic energy programs of other countries soon proved this American vision illusory. By the end of 1953, twenty countries had independent nuclear research projects.[18] This development raised fears in Washington that the inability of the United States to compete for overseas markets would result not only in lost commercial contracts, but would also reduce American prestige and influence abroad.[19] In the military sphere, the inability to fulfill the Lisbon force goals led America's NATO allies to request tactical nuclear weapons information for its military forces. By this time, much of the original rationale for America's policy of atomic secrecy had lost its persuasiveness.

The need to adapt U.S. policy to these changed circumstances prompted the "Atoms for Peace" initiative. On December 8, 1953, President Eisenhower addressed the United Nations General Assembly.[20] The president depicted the dangers posed by rampant nuclear proliferation, warning that "the knowledge now possessed by several nations will eventually be shared by others—possibly all others." More positively, he declared that atomic energy could immediately be channeled for mankind's benefit. In order to direct atomic energy activities away from military pursuits and toward promoting "peaceful power," Eisenhower called upon "the governments principally involved" to "make joint contributions from their stockpiles of normal uranium and fissionable material to an International Atomic Energy Agency." This agency would function as an international nuclear materials depository, and would be responsible for the impounding, storage, and protection of contributed fissionable and other materials. Since Eisenhower's plan was essentially a promotional scheme, it could be undertaken "without the irritations and mutual suspicions incident to any attempt to set up a completely acceptable system of worldwide inspection and control." Previous points of contention between the United States and the Soviet Union would no longer be an impediment because they were absent from the proposal.

From Washington's perspective, the Atoms for Peace overture succeeded on a number of levels. It was excellent public diplomacy; before an international audience, the United States cast itself in the role of global benefactor of atomic energy. It was reassuring to the domestic audience; it presented a benign face to something which had hitherto been primarily identified with wholesale destruction. It was supportive of U.S. commercial interests; its advocacy of atomic power led other countries to want nuclear technology. And it was beneficial to the cohesion and defense of the Atlantic Alliance; it paved the way for a modification nine months later of the Atomic Energy Act to permit greater integration of nuclear weapons information into NATO's military planning.

In addition to satisfying Washington's objectives, the Atoms for Peace initiative was significant for a more fundamental reason. For the first time in a proposal for international atomic energy control, the mutual determination of the nuclear weapons states to guard their sovereign prerogatives in the nuclear field was implicitly recognized. In this sense, it signaled a departure from earlier plans. Initially, the fear of an atomic-armed Germany had stimulated efforts during the war to curtail the spread of specialized scientific information. As the war progressed, the fear of a general spread of atomic weapons to many states assumed greater importance. Proposals were then forwarded which aimed at radically revising the international system to ensure that atomic energy was used for peaceful purposes. Eisenhower's plan, however, meant that the idea of a supranational control authority invested with a mandate to prohibit all independent nuclear arsenals was now formally viewed by the United States as unattainable. With Atoms for Peace, proposals for international control would henceforth emphasize *partial* nuclear disarmament. In other words, the notion of a two-tier international system, with one level consisting of those countries with nuclear armaments and the other comprised of countries without such weapons, was now promoted. Efforts would subsequently be directed toward codifying the nuclear status quo. Primary emphasis would be placed on stopping horizontal, rather than vertical, proliferation.

By this time some countries had already renounced any intention to build nuclear weapons. The peace treaties which the Allies and the Soviet Union had signed with Bulgaria, Finland, Hungary, Italy, and Rumania in February 1947 legally barred these countries from the possession, production, or testing of nuclear arms. In October 1954, a decision had been reached to allow West Germany to join NATO and rearm itself with conventional weapons in return for Bonn's officially relinquishing its right to acquire nuclear armaments. The terms of the 1955 Austrian State Treaty were more severe regarding nuclear arms, prohibiting their possession, production, or testing. In addition, the mid-1950s were marked by fears over the radioactive fallout from hydrogen weapons tests, which in turn prompted calls for a halt to all nuclear weapons testing. Nevil Shute's 1957 novel, *On the Beach*, describing the radioactive contamination of the atmosphere and the extinction of the human race, became an international bestseller.

During the latter half of the 1950s, the spread of civil nuclear technology was vigorously promoted through a combination of subsidies, grants, low-interest loans, and cut-rate prices offered as "loss leaders" to gain entrance into what was presumed to be a future high-growth and lucrative market. Civil uses were divulged at the Geneva Conference on the Peaceful Applications of Atomic Energy in August 1955, and later through a series of scientific conferences. Promises of "energy too cheap to meter" were eagerly believed by countries with a growing energy demand; an attraction to the most modern technology also played a part in expanding the market. Bilateral safeguards between supplier and recipient countries to prevent any diversion of fissile materials for military use were only unevenly applied. With a number of nuclear suppliers already in the international marketplace, there was the fear that competition would force safeguard standards down to the lowest common denominator, if not eliminate them altogether. The risk was that the unsupervised dissemination of nuclear power facilities could lead to what Secretary of State John Foster Dulles characterized as "the promiscuous spread of nuclear weapons throughout the world."[21] Not incidentally, Washington realized that countries which had entered into bilateral nuclear agreements with the U.S. would eventually chafe at having their nuclear programs inspected solely by the United States. Further, the U.S. did not at this time have an adequate number of technical personnel to perform inspections. Diverting scientists from other tasks would have been a drain on limited manpower resources.[22]

The solution to these difficulties was to establish an international organization which could provide a uniform set of safeguards and undertake inspection duties. An international safeguards system would be more palatable to recipient states, and a single international body could avoid redundancy and therefore better utilize scarce scientific talent. Discussions between the United States and the Soviet Union concerning an atomic energy agency were initiated in January 1954. Negotiations over the next few years took place in the U.N. General Assembly and in meetings with those countries having a special interest in atomic energy matters.[23] At the conclusion of an international conference on the subject in October 1956, the Statute of the International Atomic Energy Agency (IAEA) was unanimously endorsed by the eighty-one countries attending; it entered into force in July 1957.[24]

Slightly different in conception from Eisenhower's original plan, the IAEA was designed to apply safeguards to nuclear activities with which it was associated in order to ensure that only peaceful benefits would obtain. Safeguard mechanisms consisted of a combination of on-site inspections, audits of nuclear material accounting and inventory procedures, and later, a variety of surveillance techniques and physical barriers to inhibit diversion. These measures were not a foolproof remedy for stopping nuclear weapons spread. They were not intended to provide absolute assurance that any theft or diversion of nuclear materials would be detected. The IAEA was not responsible for physical protection of nuclear materials and installations against attack or sabotage, it could not pursue and recover stolen nuclear materials, nor was it designed to detect development of nuclear weapons in clandestine facilities.

Despite these shortcomings, the IAEA was seen as a valuable supplement to previous bilateral efforts to retard nuclear proliferation. The Agency ensured that nuclear supplies would be made through an international body, under safeguards, rather than bilaterally, without safeguards. As a result, it was less likely that the peaceful applications of nuclear energy would be diverted to military ends. Diversion of fissile materials was deterred further by the threat of public exposure and the IAEA's "direct curtailment or suspension of assistance." By signaling in a formal manner to the international community that nuclear installations would be used for peaceful purposes, IAEA safeguards also removed a potential incentive to acquire nuclear armaments by reducing concern over the intention of nuclear programs in neighboring states.

The IAEA safeguards system was voluntary, and therefore could exert no influence over those countries which balked at placing restrictions on its nuclear program. One such country was France, which became the fourth nuclear power with its test in the Sahara Desert in February 1960.[25] France's detonation was consistent with the trend established to that point;

aside from Canada, every country technically and financially capable of achieving nuclear status had done so. Moreover, previous hurdles to acquisition, such as scientific expertise and engineering competence, were being lowered. As early as 1947, the German physicist Werner Heisenberg had commented that the production of atomic bombs should be regarded as "no longer a problem of science in any country, but a problem of engineering."[26] While Heisenberg had exaggerated how widely new applications in nuclear physics were understood at the time, it was clear by the end of the 1950s that scientific ignorance could no longer be a reason for not developing the bomb.[27] And the fact that engineering skills and technical expertise were being developed in tandem with the spread of civilian nuclear facilities stimulated concern over the possible proliferation of nuclear weapons among many states.[28]

Many observers shared this apprehension. Sir Charles Snow, extrapolating from the rate of nuclear proliferation by 1960, predicted that "Within, at the most, ten years, some of these bombs are going off.... That is the certainty."[29] More analytical examinations were only slightly less gloomy. In 1958 the National Planning Association had published a study entitled *1970 Without Arms Control*. The authors predicted that by their target year nine countries would acquire nuclear weapons through independent development, twelve if they diverted materials from power reactors, and sixteen if given military assistance. They concluded that "a rapid rise in the number of atomic powers can be expected by the mid-1960s. By 1970, most nations with appreciable military strength will have in their arsenals nuclear weapons—strategic, tactical, or both."[30] Two years later, in another report on the spread of nuclear weapons, the National Planning Association defined three categories for evaluating the proliferation potential of twenty-six countries. The twelve countries in Group I were "able to embark on a successful nuclear weapons program in the near future." The eight in Group II were "economically capable, fairly competent technically, although perhaps some-

what more limited on scientific manpower than the countries
in Group I." The six countries in Group III were described as
being "not too likely" to achieve a successful nuclear weapons
program within five years, although they were "probably economically capable."[31]

The responsibility for international peace and stability
made many government officials acutely sensitive to the threats
conjured up by such predictions. The 1962 Cuban Missile Crisis increased fears. It served as a reminder that conflict between
the United States and the Soviet Union could embroil the entire
world in a nuclear war, and suggested the hazards of the spread
of nuclear weapons. The sense of anxiety and urgency expressed by Eisenhower before the United Nations was echoed a
decade later by President Kennedy:

[P]ersonally I am haunted by the feeling that by 1970, unless we are
successful, there may be ten nuclear powers instead of four, and by
1975, fifteen of twenty. . . . I see the possibility in the 1970s of the
President of the United States having to face a world in which fifteen
or twenty or twenty-five nations may have these weapons. I regard
that as the greatest possible danger and hazard.[32]

The instrument with which President Kennedy hoped to ex-
orcise this spectre was a nuclear test ban treaty. Conventional
wisdom had long held that a way to inhibit the momentum of
continuous weapons innovation, recognized as one of the driv-
ing forces behind the arms race, would be to prohibit weapons
testing. Not only would this slow the arms competition, it was
also asserted that it could reduce international tensions, prevent the contamination of the environment, and discourage the
spread of nuclear weapons to other countries.

Government efforts to negotiate a test ban agreement had
been initiated in May 1955 in the Subcommittee of the Five (the
U.S., Britain, Canada, France, and the Soviet Union) of the
United Nations Disarmament Commission. During the next
eight years the discussions took place in a number of forums
and with a variety of participants.[33] In early 1962, the Soviet
Union consented to a partial test ban treaty (PTBT) which

would outlaw nuclear tests in the atmosphere, outer space, and under water, while permitting underground testing. Washington and London concurred, having proposed the idea the year before. A nuclear test ban treaty encompassing these three environments was signed in Moscow on August 5, 1963, and entered into force two months later.[34]

The Partial Test Ban Treaty did not explicitly prevent countries from acquiring nuclear weapons. Indeed, as Secretary of Defense Robert McNamara admitted during Senate hearings on the agreement, "The treaty does not cover the subject of proliferation. That is clear."[35] Nonnuclear weapons states party to the treaty were not barred from developing nuclear explosives as long as they were tested underground. Nonmembers could of course conduct nuclear tests in all environments. In addition, nuclear weapons states could continue testing underground, and could continue to increase their stockpiles of nuclear arms.

Yet the agreement was viewed as exerting some influence on stopping nuclear proliferation. In his address to the country announcing the signing of the treaty, President Kennedy claimed that one of its benefits was its contribution "toward preventing the spread of nuclear weapons to nations not now possessing them."[36] Specifically, its advocates alleged that "the potential cost of a nuclear weapons development program would increase sharply for all signatory states . . . [T]esting underground is not only more costly but also more difficult and time-consuming."[37] While this opinion was seriously questioned,[38] other less tangible advantages were said to derive from the agreement. Its impact was best assessed on the psychological level. Within this context, the Joint Chiefs of Staff, and Generals Maxwell Taylor and Curtis LeMay, all maintained that the Partial Test Ban Treaty would exert a positive influence on retarding proliferation.[39] Noting that within ten years about eight additional countries would be technically capable of building nuclear weapons, the Director of the Arms Control and Disarmament Agency, William C. Foster, and Secretary McNamara also argued that at least some of these states would go nuclear in the absence of a test ban treaty.[40] This view that the treaty created a general consensus against nuclear proliferation was supported by the enthusiastic worldwide reception with which it had been welcomed. Within two months after it was opened for signature, the PTBT was initialed by over 100 countries.

Events during the next few years continued to focus attention on the issue of nuclear weapons spread. In 1963, during a United Nations General Assembly session, the Soviet Union criticized for the first time the NATO plan to create a multilateral nuclear force.[41] Moscow's long-standing anxiety about a nuclear-armed West Germany prompted the accusation that the multilateral force would constitute an officially sanctioned American policy of nuclear proliferation. At the July 1964 summit conference of the Organization of African Unity, the African countries adopted a resolution for the denuclearization of the continent and expressed a willingness to accede to a nonproliferation treaty. At the second summit meeting of nonaligned countries in early October, the participants declared their readiness "not to produce, acquire, or test any nuclear weapons." A week later, on October 16, 1964, China became the first nuclear power to use enriched uranium (U-235) for its initial test.[42] In the United Nations, in June 1965 the Eighteen Nation Disarmament Committee turned its attention away from general and complete disarmament to the specific subject of the nonproliferation of nuclear weapons. In January 1967, the Treaty on Principles Governing the Activities of States in the Exploration and Use of Outer Space, more commonly referred to as the Outer Space Treaty, was signed. It outlawed the stationing of nuclear weapons in outer space and declared that all celestial bodies should be free for exploration and use for only peaceful purposes.

The following month the countries of Latin America signed the Treaty of Tlatelolco, which sought to prevent the introduction of nuclear weapons to the region.[43] Parties pledged to forswear "the testing, use, manufacture, production or acquisition by any means whatsoever of any nuclear weapons." They further agreed not to receive nuclear armaments in their territories or to provide assistance in nuclear weapons manufacture. For verifying compliance with these obligations, Article 12 established a control system with permanent organs of supervision. This system required that each party negotiate agreements with the IAEA for the application of safeguards to all its nuclear activities (i.e., "full-scope" safeguards). In addition to IAEA inspections, one of the organs of the treaty's governing body was empowered to perform "special inspections" whenever requested by a member who suspected that some activity proscribed by the treaty had been or was about to be performed. This method was known as "verification by challenge."

The following year, on July 1, 1968, the Treaty on the Nonproliferation of Nuclear Weapons was initialed.[44] Considering that the negotiation process had spanned almost a decade, the NPT itself was a relatively brief document. Its primary obligations were contained in its first six provisions. Article I concerned the nontransfer of nuclear armaments. Nuclear weapons states party to the treaty promised not to transfer "to any recipient whatsoever nuclear weapons or other nuclear explosive devices" or to "assist, encourage, or induce any nonnuclear weapons states to manufacture or otherwise acquire nuclear weapons or other explosive devices." Article II imposed a complementary obligation on nonnuclear weapons states. They pledged "not to manufacture or otherwise acquire nuclear weapons or other nuclear explosive devices, and not to seek or receive any assistance in the manufacture of nuclear weapons or other nuclear explosive devices."

Article III discussed safeguards. Nonnuclear weapons states party to the treaty were required to conclude a safeguards agreement with the IAEA to verify compliance "with a view to preventing diversion of nuclear energy from peaceful uses to nuclear weapons or other nuclear explosive devices." Further, IAEA safeguards would be applied "on all source or special fissionable material in all peaceful nuclear activities" carried out by the state ("full-scope" safeguards). As a manner of compensation for safeguard restrictions, Article IV guaranteed the "inalienable right of all the Parties to the Treaty to develop research, production and use of nuclear energy for peaceful purposes." It also promised "the fullest possible exchange of equipment, materials, and scientific and technological inform-ation for the peaceful uses of nuclear energy." In theory this meant that there would be no limitations on the transfer to NPT members of nuclear technology, even of such "sensitive" nu-clear materials and equipment as separated plutonium and highly enriched uranium, reprocessing plants, and uranium enrichment facilities.

Since the technical characteristics of nuclear detonations for peaceful and military purposes were indistinguishable, Ar-ticle V stipulated that only nuclear weapons states were permit-ted to conduct peaceful nuclear explosions (PNEs). Yet because there were claims during the 1960s that PNEs could be helpful in civil engineering projects, and oil and natural gas extru-sion,[45] this article ensured that "potential benefits from any peaceful applications of nuclear explosions will be made avail-able to nonnuclear weapons States Parties to the Treaty."

Article VI required the nuclear weapons states party to the treaty "to pursue negotiations in good faith on effective mea-sures relating to cessation of the nuclear arms race at an early date, and to nuclear disarmament, and on a treaty on general and complete disarmament under strict and effective interna-tional control." The United States and the Soviet Union have engaged in negotiations to control nuclear armaments. On the day that the Nonproliferation Treaty was signed, the White House announced that the two countries would begin strategic arms limitation talks (SALT). In May 1972 Washington and Moscow initialed the SALT I accord, which was composed of a five-year Interim Agreement and an antiballistic missile (ABM) treaty of unlimited duration.[46] After further negotiations, the SALT II Treaty was signed in June 1979.[47] The U.S. did not ratify the treaty, which, except for its disarmament provisions, was nonetheless unofficially observed by the parties until November 1986. To date, Soviet-American discussions on strategic arms reductions and on intermediate-range nuclear forces (INF) have failed to reach agreement. The two superpowers currently have about 50,000 warheads in their arsenals.

Although there have been numerous criticisms lodged against the NPT,[48] the large number of countries party to the treaty indicated that nuclear proliferation was viewed as a serious problem by many states, and that to some degree the treaty addressed this concern. Articles I and II on nontransfer and nonacquisition recognized that stopping nuclear spread was in the interests of both nuclear and nonnuclear weapons states. While the full-scope safeguards mandated in Article III might be an imposition, most countries already had IAEA or bilateral safeguards governing their nuclear activities. These three provisions provided legal and technical obstacles to the possibility that neighboring countries would acquire or develop nuclear arms. The knowledge that rivalries among nonnuclear powers would not escalate to the nuclear level was thought to relieve one cause of regional tension and thus remove an incentive for proliferation. Moreover, viewed as a whole, the Nonproliferation Treaty advertised the belief that barriers to proliferation could be constructed, that general concern on the subject would attract a broad measure of support, and, by implication, that the spread of nuclear weapons could be prevented.

However, a number of unforeseeable events in international relations, along with some unsettling developments in the nuclear industry, combined in the 1970s to diminish confidence in the international nonproliferation regime. India's nuclear detonation of May 18, 1974, administered the largest shock. The international unease which followed this event was largely due to the particular route by which New Delhi progressed to its nuclear test as compared to those of the previous five nuclear powers, and what this augured for the future. The U.S., the Soviet Union, Britain, France, and China had all manufactured the weapons-grade material for their initial tests from "dedicated" facilities specifically constructed for this purpose. India, on the other hand, had obtained the plutonium for its nuclear device by irradiating an indigenous source of natural uranium in an unsafeguarded, Canadian-supplied research reactor operated with American-supplied heavy water. India, a non-NPT party, maintained that it had not violated its contracts with either supplier as its nuclear test was for peaceful purposes. Still, for the first time, nuclear assistance provided for peaceful uses was adapted for a nuclear explosion, thereby obscuring the previous, if artificial, distinction between the peaceful and the military atom which had formed the underlying basis of international nuclear trade. Viewed along a continuum, the derivation of a nuclear capability seemed to have progressed from (1) dedicated facilities, which had served five nuclear powers, to (2) research reactors and civilian nuclear energy programs, which had served one nuclear power, but which, more significantly, contained the potential for breeding many more nuclear weapons states.

Complicating matters further was the increasing factionalism in the nuclear marketplace. By the end of the 1960s, a number of countries had decided to partially fulfill their energy requirements by installing or ordering nuclear power plants. To meet this demand, some of the more advanced industrialized countries had resolved to compete aggressively against American domination of the nuclear fuel, reactor, and fuel cycle services markets. In the mid-1970s, French and West German willingness to sell plutonium reprocessing and uranium enrichment facilities in particular aroused anxiety. This "second tier" of nuclear suppliers was joined in the latter half of the 1970s by a "third tier" of supplier countries, some of whom were not bound by any restrictions on nuclear exports.

Concurrent with this confusion in the nuclear marketplace were expectations, especially in the Third World, for nuclear power growth.[49] These had been stimulated in part by the fourfold price rise in petroleum instituted by OPEC in late 1973. Insecurity over oil supplies appeared to enhance the attractiveness of nuclear power as an alternative energy source, and led to a flurry of national calls for greater "energy independence." In addition, President Nixon's June 1974 offer of nuclear reactors to Egypt and Israel (neither of whom were parties to the NPT), along with Washington's decision the following month to suspend indefinitely the signing of any new uranium fuel contracts with overseas clients because of a shortage of uranium enrichment capacity, and an international uranium price-fixing scheme in mid-decade, further undermined confidence in the previously existing pattern of international nuclear trade. The proliferation risk deriving from these developments was that countries uncertain of nuclear supplies would ensure their energy security by developing autonomous, unsafeguarded, nuclear programs which might later be used for building nuclear weapons. The dimensions of this threat were considerable; by the end of the 1970s, nuclear research or power programs existed in over forty-five nonnuclear weapons states.[50]

Furthermore, exaggerated forecasts for increased energy consumption through the end of the century led to recommendations that plutonium be introduced earlier than had been planned as fuel for nuclear power reactors. If implemented, this commercialization of plutonium would have resulted in the dissemination of fissile material which could have been directly exploited for nuclear bombs. And the upsurge in international terrorist activity at this time made such a move even more ominous, leading some analysts to warn of possible nuclear terrorism or blackmail.[51]

Individually, any one of these developments would have stirred concern; collectively, they raised questions about the entire nonproliferation regime. In particular, these developments brought into doubt the efficacy of the IAEA/NPT safeguards system and its ability to cope with the unexpected increase in demand of reprocessing plants and uranium enrichment facilities. The adoption of a "plutonium economy" would have vastly complicated, if not made impossible, "the timely detection" by the IAEA of diversion of significant quantities of nuclear material for nuclear weapons manufacture. This prospect led some analysts to comment that even perfect safeguards would not prevent countries from coming within weeks, days, or even hours of possessing a nuclear bomb. It was now declared, primarily by American critics, that nuclear proliferation could only be checked if nonnuclear weapons states were not permitted to own fissile material suitable for military purposes or facilities capable of producing such material.[52]

Greater cooperation among nuclear suppliers toward the end of the decade somewhat mitigated these fears. In an attempt to restore some order and discipline to the marketplace, a group of nuclear suppliers had initiated negotiations on safeguard arrangements in late 1974.[53] Their objective was to arrive at an agreed-upon list of items whose transfer would automatically "trigger" the application of safeguards. Meetings of this Nuclear Suppliers Group (NSG) were held secretly in London between 1975 and 1978.[54] In January 1978 the NSG delivered a set of guidelines to the IAEA.[55]

Although adherence to the guidelines was voluntary, as a consequence of the NSG deliberations safeguards were no longer an area of such severe commercial competition. The NSG guidelines incorporated the items listed previously by the IAEA-sponsored Zangger Committee, and added to it heavy water and heavy water production plants; all these items would prompt the application of safeguards if they were transferred. As a reaction to India's nuclear detonation, the guidelines enjoined suppliers to obtain "formal government assurances from recipients" prohibiting any nuclear explosions. Further, they requested that exporters "exercise restraint in the transfer of sensitive facilities, technology and weapons-usable materials." They also included controls on the retransfer of trigger list items and a provision barring the replication of any transferred item. In addition, the guidelines outlined physical security measures to reduce the chance of loss or theft of nuclear materials in transit.

The Nuclear Suppliers Group did not directly consider the question of the plutonium economy, which was still a matter of contention. Opponents of a move to plutonium as the basis of nuclear energy programs argued that there was no need to recycle plutonium in thermal (light-water) reactors, or to engage in reprocessing of spent nuclear fuel to obtain plutonium for fast breeder reactors or to ease spent fuel management problems. These critics, largely from the United States, maintained that there were adequate reserves of uranium for nuclear power reactors, that the efficiency of the "once-through" fuel cycle could be improved to generate greater savings, that reprocessing was not essential to handling nuclear waste products, and that fast breeder reactors were a technology of the future whose development could be deferred indefinitely without upsetting national energy programs. Most importantly, they emphasized that the use of plutonium would result in the widespread distribution of a weapons-usable material. It would overburden the existing safeguards system and risk destabilizing international relations by fostering reciprocal fears of nuclear weapons development in neighboring countries.[56]

On the other hand, proponents, largely from Europe, the Soviet Union, and Japan, pointed out that reprocessing for recycle and waste disposal had been considered both logical and appropriate for nuclear energy programs since 1955. Plutonium research and development was also necessary for states to acquire a working knowledge and practical experience in anticipation of a move to fast breeder reactors in the late 1980s. Fast breeders were viewed as a basis for achieving some degree of energy independence, and were already under way in seven countries, including the United States. Moreover, unlike the United States, the lack of readily available alternative energy resources in most countries engendered a greater willingness to seek the fullest possible benefits from nuclear power, even if this appeared in American eyes to tolerate some proliferation risk. Finally, it was contended that the threat of additional nuclear weapons states derived more from the construction of nuclear research and clandestine dedicated facilities than from diversion of civilian nuclear power reactors, which would be both more expensive and more conspicuous.

Meanwhile, as a reaction to the Indian explosion and the French and German sales of sensitive nuclear technologies, some nuclear vendors, primarily the United States and Can-

ada, had unilaterally altered or renegotiated criteria for supplying nuclear fuel and equipment. Legislation enacted by the
U.S. Congress included the Symington amendment to the International Security and Arms Export Control Act of 1976,
which required the United States to cut off all economic and
military assistance to any country which imported sensitive
nuclear technologies without first accepting full-scope safeguards; the Glenn amendment to the International Security
Assistance Act of 1977, which revised the Symington amendment as well as added a provision terminating American
funds to any nonnuclear weapons state party to the NPT who
detonated a nuclear explosive; and, above all, the 1978
Nuclear Nonproliferation Act, which placed additional constraints on foreign nuclear energy programs that were dependent on American-supplied nuclear technology and materials.[57] All these actions created resentment among recipient
countries and were interpreted as U.S. attempts to unilaterally
regulate the nuclear marketplace. The Carter administration's
nuclear policy, outlined by the president in April 1977, was
seen by foreign critics as further evidence of American hostility toward the full exploitation of nuclear energy.

In order to moderate this debate, to enlist the views of those
countries which had not taken part in the Nuclear Suppliers
Group, to prevent any hasty national decisions on nuclear technologies, and to arrive at some consensus on how best to minimize the possibility of nuclear proliferation while at the same
time not jeopardize nuclear energy supplies or the peaceful
development of nuclear energy, the Carter administration suggested convening an international conference. The International Nuclear Fuel Cycle Evaluation (INFCE) was initiated on
October 19, 1977. There was no voting and no country was
officially committed to any future course of action by the proceedings. It was essentially a multilateral exercise to exchange
views on the proliferation risks that countries assigned to different stages of the fuel cycle. Eight working groups were established to examine the different stages, and at the end of two
years final reports were issued.[58]

In general, INFCE's major contribution was that it created a greater sensitivity to the link between proliferation and various types of nuclear technologies. Specifically, the conclusions of Working Group 4 ("Reprocessing, Plutonium Handling, Recycle"), Working Group 5 ("Fast Breeders"), and Working Group 7 ("Waste Management and Disposal"), contained the most significance for national decisions on nuclear technologies. In brief, Working Group 4 found that plutonium recycle in light-water reactors would not offer substantial economic advantages. Working Group 5 concluded that fast breeder reactors were justified only for the most advanced industrialized countries with large electrical grids. And Working Group 7 found that reprocessing was not essential for the safe storage of nuclear waste. Still, these findings had no effect on the French, German, Japanese, British, and Indian nuclear programs. And INFCE was careful not to state that any one nuclear fuel cycle was safer, from the perspective of preventing proliferation, than any other.[59] Like the Nuclear Suppliers Group, INFCE was essentially a technical approach to nonproliferation. It was not intended to present initiatives or establish institutions that would address the political motivations of those states contemplating nuclear weapons acquisition.

As the perceived need for the Nuclear Suppliers Group guidelines and the INFCE exercise suggest, worries over the type and number of potential nuclear weapons states altered during the 1970s. Where concern had earlier centered on some of the more industrialized states, such as West Germany and Japan, and a few specific developing states, such as India and Israel, by the mid-1970s proliferation fears were fueled by the prospect that thirty to forty less developed countries would have nuclear programs. This shift was evidenced by a change in the states that were examined in studies on nuclear proliferation. Of the twenty-six countries considered in the 1960 National Planning Association report, only five could be labeled as coming from the Third World. By contrast, a 1977 study by the United States Office of Technology Assessment looked at eight states, only one of which, South Africa, was not a developing country.[60] Being situated in violent regions and often possessing unstable political systems only heightened speculation over the proclivity of these states for developing nuclear arsenals.

Exacerbating this concern were a number of developments during the 1960s and 1970s which, taken cumulatively, made it progressively easier for a nonnuclear weapons state to construct a bomb. Much of the scientific skill, training, and technical expertise needed for weapons manufacture could be acquired from nuclear research programs. The knowledge of how to build a fission device had been available since 1964 in a report printed in the United States. As for fusion weapons, the November 1979 issue of *The Progressive* contained an article explaining how to construct a hydrogen bomb.[61] Moreover, any country of moderate industrial stature was capable of building its own sensitive facilities for reprocessing or uranium enrichment, assuming that the requisite technologies were not readily available on the open market.[62] In addition, because nuclear programs initially intended for peaceful applications could be channeled to military purposes, the financial cost of acquiring nuclear weapons, a not insignificant obstacle for some countries in the past, declined. For a country already committed to nuclear research and development, only the extra cost and effort of obtaining weapons-grade material and preparing nuclear explosives would be relevant. And even this price tag steadily decreased. In contrast to the over $2 billion spent on the wartime Manhattan Project, a 1968 United Nations study estimated that designing, building, and testing a plutonium-based nuclear device would cost $100 million.[63] A similar analysis conducted for the United States Arms Control and Disarmament Agency (ACDA) in 1976 discovered that this cost had virtually been halved, to $51 million.[64] If the country in question already possessed the fissile material (whose acquisition constituted the major expense), these figures would be reduced still further, to $30 million at the time of the United Nations study and $1 million for the ACDA report. Aggravating concern was the fact that even relatively high levels of plutonium-240 mixed with plutonium-239 could be used to construct workable fission explosives; while less predictable and more difficult to work with than weapons-grade material, it nonetheless could be used to produce yields in the kiloton range.[65] The direct result of all these developments was a shrinking "critical time"—defined as the time required to build a nuclear explosive once the decision was made.[66]

The entire process of concerted action toward actual possession of a nuclear device that fell short of diversion of nuclear materials from civilian nuclear facilities was termed "nuclear drift" or "latent proliferation."[67] The civilian nuclear programs located throughout the world guaranteed that a number of nonnuclear weapons states had advanced a long distance down the road to a nuclear weapons capability. In the words of the ACDA study:

The real problem of proliferation today is not that there are numerous countries "champing at the bit" to get nuclear weapons, but rather that all the nonnuclear nations without making any conscious decision to build nuclear weapons, are drifting upward to higher categories of competence. This means that any transient incentive, in the ebb and flow of world politics, which inclines a country to build nuclear weapons at some point in the future will be just that much easier to act upon.[68]

And adding to the danger that an international event might "trigger" nuclear weapons acquisition was the possibility that a country might be motivated in this direction by domestic political reasons less easily susceptible to influence by outside actors.[69]

It was this potential for widespread and rapid proliferation that many observers found so alarming. The revealing statistic was the number of countries that possessed the capability to acquire nuclear weapons and how close they could come to acquisition without violating any bilateral or international agreements into which they may have entered. As a reaction to these changed circumstances, some of the more sophisticated

analysts modified the previous benchmark for defining proliferation—the detonation of a nuclear device—to a "ladder of
capabilities" more accurately expressing how close a country
was to possessing a bomb.[70] A few observers found comfort in
the prospect of nuclear proliferation, arguing that the gradual
spread of nuclear weapons would "promote peace and reinforce international stability" by introducing greater prudence,
deliberation, and restraint in the conduct of foreign affairs.[71]
On the other hand, more traditional analyses stressed the difficulties that additional nuclear weapons states would present
for international management, regional tensions, and control
over the weapons themselves.[72] The underlying assumption of
both these schools of thought was that nuclear proliferation
was in fact likely to occur in the near future. New predictions of
a world with thirty, forty, or fifty states that could acquire
nuclear weapons upon short notice could be found.[73] Not surprisingly, some recent studies on proliferation have examined
how best to manage in such an environment.[74]

As perspectives on the problem of nuclear weapons spread
have changed, so too have perceptions of the nuclear weapons
themselves. In part, this has been due to the nonproliferation
institutions that have been constructed over the years, and in
part to the example offered by those countries that have decided against acquiring nuclear weapons. But, in addition,
there has been a gradual awareness that nuclear weapons are
largely inappropriate instruments for achieving tangible foreign policy objectives. Despite the American nuclear monopoly
enjoyed immediately after the Second World War, Washington
was unable to force Moscow to relinquish its control over
eastern Europe. The bomb also proved difficult to apply to
military affairs; the United States exercised nuclear restraint
during the Korean War, and later in Vietnam. Furthermore,
other nuclear powers also refrained from using nuclear weapons: the United Kingdom at Suez and in the Falklands War;
France in Algeria; the Soviet Union in Hungary, in Czechoslovakia, during the border conflict with China, and in Afghanistan; and China in its clashes with Vietnam. Reflecting on this

"tradition of non-use," former Secretary of Defense Robert McNamara has written that "*nuclear weapons serve no military purpose whatsoever. They are totally useless—except only to deter one's opponent from using them.*"[75] Reinforcing this conviction have been the writings of military strategists, who maintain that nuclear armaments are generally ill-suited to resolving problems in world affairs; the views of legal scholars, who argue that the use of nuclear weapons would violate international law; the sermons of the clergy, who question the morality of possessing nuclear arms; and the warnings of scientists, who predict global catastrophe in the event of a nuclear war.

CONCLUSION

From the early efforts during the Second World War to the International Nuclear Fuel Cycle Evaluation, how was the problem of nuclear proliferation perceived? Recommendations for comprehensive disarmament argued that nuclear weapons be abolished, and that control over nuclear activities be assigned to a supranational authority with discretionary powers. These plans envisioned a fundamental reordering of international affairs. The lack of success which greeted these proposals, however, gradually transformed the goal of universal nuclear disarmament into the more modest objective of preventing the acquisition of nuclear arms by any additional countries.

Ironically, only when international control schemes attempted to do less was it possible to achieve more. The widespread approval which subsequently greeted the international nonproliferation arrangements and institutions (as evidenced, for example, by the number of PTBT and NPT parties), suggested that this regime has been viewed by most of the non-nuclear weapons states as being in their own best interests. If the nuclear weapons states have conspired to deny nuclear arms to all other countries, then it can be stated with equal justification that the great percentage of nonnuclear weapons states have tolerated this restriction willingly. In other words, nuclear proliferation has been perceived as being detrimental to the policy objectives of both the nuclear and the nonnuclear countries. The international status quo of a few nuclear and many nonnuclear weapons states has therefore been created and preserved not only because it has been imposed from above, but also because it has been supported from below.

Contrary to this evidence of a widespread consensus against nuclear weapons acquisition was the enduring belief that only global arrangements could retard the spread of nuclear weapons. Despite the many differences between the comprehensive and partial approaches, common to both was their preference for nonproliferation measures universal in scope— the Acheson-Lilienthal Report, the Baruch Plan, the IAEA, the Partial Test Ban Treaty, the NPT, the Nuclear Suppliers Group guidelines, and INFCE. While the Treaty of Tlatelolco was an exception to this rule by applying only to Latin America, it nonetheless sought to include all the countries in the region. This bias toward universality could be explained in large measure by the persistent perception that the problem of nuclear proliferation was a global one—in short, that there were a large number of countries which would seize the earliest opportunity to acquire nuclear arms. In fact, this assumption has always been open to question. Surprisingly few countries have developed nuclear arsenals, while many technically competent countries have refrained from building nuclear weapons. Part Two will examine six of these technically competent countries.

CHRONOLOGY

1945   The United States drops two atom bombs on Japan (August)
        The Truman-Attlee-King Conference discusses postwar control of atomic energy (November)

1946   The United Nations Atomic Energy Commission (UNAEC) is established (January)

            The Acheson-Lilienthal Report is released (March)

            The Baruch and Gromyko Plans are presented in the UNAEC (June)

1948   The UNAEC suspends work (May)

1949   The Soviet Union detonates its first atomic device (August)

1952   Great Britain explodes its first atomic device (October)

            The U.S. detonates a hydrogen device (October)

1953   The Soviet Union explodes a hydrogen weapon (August)

            Eisenhower announces "Atoms for Peace" (December)

1957   The International Atomic Energy Agency (IAEA) comes into being (July)

1960   France tests its first atomic device (February)

1962   The Cuban Missile Crisis (October)

1963   The Partial Test Ban Treaty is signed (August)

1964   China detonates its first nuclear explosive (October)

1967   The Treaty of Tlatelolco is signed (February)

1968   The Nonproliferation Treaty (NPT) is opened for signature (July)

            The U.S. and the Soviet Union begin the SALT talks (July)

1974   India detonates a self-proclaimed peaceful nuclear device (May)

1974–78   The Nuclear Suppliers Group (NSG) agrees upon guidelines governing nuclear exports

1977–80   The International Nuclear Fuel Cycle Evaluation (INFCE)

PART II: COUNTRY CASE STUDIES

Part One discussed the evolution of the international non-proliferation regime. Part Two will investigate the ostensible cause of this proliferation concern: the nonnuclear weapons states. Specifically, six countries—Sweden, South Korea, Japan, Israel, South Africa, and India—will be examined in order to discover the extent to which each refrained from acquiring nuclear weapons, and the reasons for their behavior. At various times, there was speculation that each country would develop nuclear weapons. For a few countries, political motivations, such as national security considerations, appeared to argue in favor of developing nuclear arms. For some, it was primarily the pace and sophistication of their nuclear energy programs that aroused proliferation concern. And in other cases, the combination of technological capabilities and political factors rendered their nuclear activities suspect. Still, Sweden, South Korea, and Japan decided not to acquire nuclear armaments. India did not advance beyond its 1974 peaceful nuclear explosion, while Israel and South Africa decided not to publicly articulate their nuclear status.

In this section, the major policy objectives of each country will be outlined in order to provide a framework for analyzing the decision on nuclear weapons acquisition. The nuclear programs in each country will next be discussed, in order to assess the level of technical competence and the different avenues available for nuclear weapons development. The various pressures for and against constructing nuclear arms will then be considered. In the cases of Israel and South Africa, why these countries decided to maintain ambiguous nuclear postures will be studied. Why India stopped after testing one nuclear device will also be addressed.

2.

Sweden

Since the end of the Napoleonic Wars in 1815, Sweden has managed to avoid involvement in armed conflict. An important reason for these years of uninterrupted peace has been the country's geographic location, situated in northern Europe and separated by the Baltic Sea from the main areas of contention and confrontation on the European continent. Domestic political stability, racial, ethnic, and religious harmony, and the absence of irredentist claims or major territorial demands by foreign powers have also been contributing factors.

Sweden's foreign policy has both reflected and reinforced its tradition of noninterference in external affairs. Stockholm has eschewed alliances in peacetime and adopted a neutral stance in periods of war. Since the end of the Second World War, the bases of its foreign policy have been twofold: a strong defense designed to repulse attack and preserve the country's territorial integrity, and a diplomacy aimed at enhancing regional stability and reducing international tensions. These objectives have been pursued consistently in order to maintain the credibility of "armed neutrality." Military capabilities sufficient to safeguard national security have been developed, at the

same time that Sweden has asserted its nonaggressive intentions by following a policy of strict noninvolvement in military
alliances. Sweden's conduct has thus attempted to strike a
balance between creating a viable military capability in order to
avoid excessive vulnerability on the one hand, and not provoking serious concern among potential adversaries that vital regional interests will be put at risk on the other. Or, more simply,
Sweden has attempted to strike a balance between deterrence
and reassurance.

Sweden's position at the end of Second World War was
relatively weaker than during the interwar years. To be certain,
Sweden had not been invaded, and it was the only Western
country not to demobilize its armed forces. Also, it possessed
the second most effective air force in Europe, after Britain's
RAF. Nonetheless, Sweden's strategic position had deterior-
ated, due to the revolution in military technology, which rendered the country's peripheral location more accessible, and due
to the gains registered by the Soviet Union from the war. The
USSR had absorbed parts of Karelia, annexed the Baltic Re-
publics, and controlled the Baltic coast as far west as Lubeck.
Moscow had also effectively neutralized Finland. The worsen-
ing international climate, combined with Sweden's comparatively weak defense establishment, exacerbated Stockholm's fears that the country might be caught in the middle of a
military conflict between the United States and the Soviet
Union. Though deemed less likely, another scenario envisioned an isolated Soviet attack on Sweden; with a population
of seven million, it would have only been possible to provide
minimal resistance.

Sweden's anxieties grew with the communist coup in
Czechoslovakia in 1948. Stockholm authorized a substantial
increase in defense expenditures and entered into negotiations
with Norway and Denmark to form a Scandinavian Defense
Pact. This military alliance was to be based on the principle of
collective neutrality. Each country would abstain from involvement in a future war but would offer immediate military assistance if either of its alliance partners was attacked. However,

Norway desired greater reliance on the United States than a neutral defense union on Sweden's terms would have permitted. Moreover, both Norway and Denmark were dependent upon Washington for armaments, and in January 1949 the United States announced that no military aid would be forthcoming to those countries not members of the Atlantic Alliance. Norway and Denmark subsequently joined NATO in April 1949. Sweden declined, and continued its policy of unconditional neutrality.[1]

THE ORIGINS OF SWEDEN'S ATOMIC ENERGY PROGRAM

Sweden's self-reliance in matters of national security had as a corollary a desire for energy self-sufficiency. The country contained no oil or coal reserves, while the full exploitation of hydroelectric power was limited by environmental concerns. With an energy-intensive industrial sector, harsh climate, and steep energy requirements for long-distance transportation, Sweden became interested in the development of nuclear power. The primary concern was to reduce the country's energy dependence on overseas oil suppliers. A secondary reason was that nuclear energy was perceived as a technology of the future; it was hoped that scientific expertise in this new field would provide spinoff benefits to serve other sectors of Swedish industry.[2] The government established a study group in 1945 to examine the prospects of a Swedish nuclear energy program. The group presented its findings in 1947, recommending the creation of a semipublic corporation, AB Atomenergi, with a controlling interest to be retained by the government. AB Atomenergi was responsible for nuclear research and the technological development of research and power reactors.

Sweden decided at the start to base its civilian nuclear energy program on the development of heavy-water reactors.

SWEDEN: CHRONOLOGY OF SIGNIFICANT EVENTS

Nuclear Developments		*Political Developments*
AB Atomenergi established	1947	
	1949	Sweden declines to join NATO
	1952	Chief of the Swedish Air Force urges the government to acquire nuclear weapons
	1953	US "New Look" policy is presented, with heavy reliance on tactical nuclear weapons; (policy is adopted by NATO in December 1954)
R1 1-megawatt nuclear research reactor goes critical (July)	1954	ÖB 54 military planning statement requests Swedish nuclear weapons acquisition (October)
	1955	Conservative party leader Hjalmarson calls for Swedish nuclear weapons acquisition in the Riksdag (March)
		NATO's Carte Blanche exercise
	1956	SDP's Women's Organization annual conference takes firm stance against Swedish nuclear weapons acquisition (May)
	1957	FOA Director Hugo Larsson says Sweden can build nuclear weapons as soon as 1963 if given full government support (January)
		ÖB 57 military planning statement again argues for Swedish nuclear weapons acquisition (October)
	1958	Parliamentary Commission on Defense report recommends that FOA undertake

SWEDEN: CHRONOLOGY OF SIGNIFICANT EVENTS (*Continued*)

Nuclear Developments		*Political Developments*
		"research in the nuclear field" (April)
		SDP wins the special election on the pension issue, has a plurality in the Riksdag of one seat in association with the Communist Party (June)
	1958	1959/60 defense budget submission by the military requests nuclear weapons acquisition and nuclear weapons research program at FOA; the government turns down both requests, but leaves the issue open (October-November)
		Committee for the Study of the Atomic Weapons Question is formed consisting of 18 Social Democrats, with pro- and antibomb views both represented (November)
	1959	Committee for the Study of the Atomic Weapons Question issues its report; no decision is taken on nuclear weapons acquisition but approval is given for the expansion of "protective research" at FOA (November)
R 2 30-megawatt nuclear research reactor goes critical (May)	1960	France detonates its first nuclear research nuclear device (February)
		SDP wins the general election, has a full majority in the Riksdag

SWEDEN: CHRONOLOGY OF SIGNIFICANT EVENTS (*Continued*)

Nuclear Developments		*Political Developments*
	1961	Undén Plan proposed in the U.N. (December)
	1962	Sweden becomes a member of the newly formed ENDC (March)
		ÖB 62 military planning statement requests formation of special committee to examine the technical and economic problems facing a Swedish nuclear weapons program; the request is denied by the Defense Minister (October)
Ågesta small demonstration reactor goes critical	1963	Sweden signs PTBT in August and ratifies it in November
	1965	Military requests that Sweden obtain "the requisite knowledge and technical basis" for a nuclear weapons acquisition decision in order to realize the government's declared "freedom of action" policy; this request is denied
	1968	Parliamentary Commission of Defense report suggests that Sweden is under the U.S. nuclear umbrella in the same manner as the members of NATO (February)
		Sweden signs the NPT (August)
	1970	Sweden ratifies the NPT (January)

Note: This chronology omits the agreements on nuclear cooperation that Sweden signed with the U.S., and Sweden's agreements on safeguards application with the IAEA. For this information please consult the text.

The major reason for this decision was that it would allow Sweden to use its abundant supply of natural uranium as fuel, thereby avoiding dependence on foreign sources of enriched uranium and preserving the country's energy independence. The choice of heavy-water reactors could be justified on other grounds as well. Uranium enrichment services were not then generally available; the use of natural uranium was therefore a less expensive alternative to the development of domestic fuel enrichment facilities. Further, heavy-water reactors offered a flexible design that could utilize thorium and plutonium as fuels. They would also provide a source of plutonium for the expected next generation of fast-breeder reactors. Finally, it seemed the sensible choice at the time, since other countries (Canada, Britain, and France) had selected reactors using natural uranium as the basis for their nuclear energy problems.[3]

Sweden's first reactor was a one megawatt research facility which had been designed and constructed by AB Atomenergi. Labeled R1, it went critical on July 13, 1954.[4] The heavy water for the reactor came from Norway and the natural uranium fuel was obtained from France in exchange for Swedish uranium oxide.[5] Despite this foreign assistance, R1 was tangible evidence of Sweden's scientific and engineering prowess. By the end of 1955, AB Atomenergi already operated a uranium mine and fuel refinery at Kvarntorp, and had developed plans for five more reactors. In March the following year, a royal commission of inquiry on nuclear energy (1956 Års atomenergiutredning) predicted that Sweden would have an installed nuclear energy capacity of 100 megawatts by 1960, increasing to 6,000 to 12,000 megawatts by 1975.[6]

While Sweden's interest in heavy-water reactors was originally rationalized in terms of its expected benefits for civilian purposes, Swedish officials were not unaware of the potential military applications of this choice of technology. A nuclear fuel cycle based on heavy water and indigenously mined natural uranium would be independent of foreign controls, and weapons-grade plutonium would be easier to produce in heavy-water reactors than in the alternative light-water reactors. According to the official history of the Swedish nuclear energy program,

The decisive arguments for the nuclear energy program were based purely on civilian considerations. . . .

At the same time it is obvious that the freedom of action with regard to a later decision on the acquisition of nuclear weapons, which was then the policy of the Swedish government, presupposed a certain domestic industrial capacity. As a minimum, in order to preserve freedom of action that would have any real meaning it was required that we ourselves produced uranium, built reactors, and had expertise with regard to the technology of plutonium extraction. This activity was however part of the civilian program and the potential military application was rather seen as a byproduct.[7]

Furthermore, because Sweden lacked the funding to independently finance a civilian and a military program, it could save money if the two projects overlapped. Although a secondary consideration, a nuclear weapons option was thus deliberately preserved from the beginning of Sweden's civilian nuclear energy program.

THE NUCLEAR WEAPONS DEBATE, 1952 TO 1959

Public discussion of possible Swedish nuclear weapons did not arise until late 1952. In a speech in Göteborg in December, the Chief of the Air Force, Lt. Gen. Bengt Nordenskiöld, urged the government to acquire nuclear weapons. Nordenskiöld based his argument on military considerations. Due to the breakthrough in warhead miniaturization in 1951, it was now possible to construct low-yield, tactical nuclear weapons. Sweden's defense would be strengthened by the ability to deliver these weapons by aircraft against an invasion force. But because Sweden might not be able to build nuclear arms for ten to twelve years, Nordenskiöld recommended that Stockholm purchase them from Washington. Official and press commentary was largely negative. Minister of Defense Torsten Nilsson stated that the issue of Swedish nuclear weapons was not under consideration by either the government or the armed services. The Social Democratic, Conservative, and most of the Liberal newspapers were also critical.[8]

Events outside of Sweden during the next few years, however, caused the issue of nuclear weapons to resurface and the question of Swedish acquisition to be reexamined. This was due mainly to developments in nuclear weapons technology, which in turn produced changes in military doctrine. Since nuclear weapons could be constructed smaller in size and yield than previously, which made them more easily transportable, they could now be assigned to commanders in the field for battlefield missions. In 1953 George Reinhardt and William Kitner's *Atomic Weapons for Land Combat* was published. That same year the United States presented its New Look defense strategy, which placed heavy reliance on the use of tactical nuclear weapons. This policy was adopted by NATO in December 1954 as a means of bolstering Western Europe's ability to resist Soviet invasion. At this time SHAPE was authorized to base all its future military planning on the assumption that nuclear weapons would be used in a European conflict. In May 1955, 5,000 members of the Norwegian armed forces participated in joint maneuvers in northern Norway under simulated battle conditions of nuclear war. By mid-1956, "most influential German military men considered these weapons an integral, necessary component of the Western defense system."[9] Strategists such as Bernard Brodie, William Kaufman, Henry Kissinger, and Robert Osgood also emphasized the benefits of tactical nuclear weapons in waging limited war.[10] In addition, the 1957 British White Paper on Defense stressed the economic savings to be realized by the substitution of tactical nuclear weapons for trained military personnel.

Actions by the Soviet Union at this time paralleled the alterations in military doctrine in the West. In 1953, Moscow conducted maneuvers to test the military's defense plans against nuclear attack. In 1954 and 1955 the first articles on nuclear weapons appeared in Soviet military journals, and training for nuclear warfare was stepped up.[11] In August 1957 the Soviet Union announced the successful test-firing of an intercontinental ballistic missile. Five weeks later *sputnik* was launched. At the end of the year the United States tested an Atlas rocket of intercontinental range. During this period, both superpowers were investing heavily in nuclear weapons research, stockpiling nuclear armaments, and emphasizing that nuclear weapons were essential for deterring conflicts.

Against this background of rapid technological advance and doctrinal change, the Swedish Commander-in-Chief, General Svedlund, presented ÖB 54 in October 1954.[12] This planning statement, based on a study of the postwar strategic situation, outlined Sweden's military requirements over the next decade. Swedish defense planners at this time operated on the assumption that the greatest military threat to the country came from the Soviet Union.[13] An isolated attack on Sweden was deemed highly unlikely; if one occurred there was no level of military capability Sweden could attain adequate for defense. Judged more probable was a limited conflict where Sweden was viewed as a secondary objective. The two most likely avenues of approach were by land in the far north or by sea in the south-central region. An invasion from the north would have been the more difficult of the two. The Soviet Union would have encountered logistical problems in moving large numbers of its troops and equipment to the north. The Kola Peninsula had not yet been developed. There was only one railway linking Leningrad to Archangel on the White Sea, and there were no roads. If these hurdles could have been surmounted, the move from the Soviet Union into Sweden would have presented further difficulties. There were very few roads in either the Finnmark area, Lapland, or northeastern Sweden. In the temperate months (late April to early October), mechanized units and tracked vehicles would have had to ford numerous rivers and traverse marshy or swampy terrain. During the six winter months, the temperature could drop as low as $-35°$ centigrade, and northernmost Sweden would be dark twenty-four hours a day. Although the Gulf of Bothnia froze over at this time of year, the ice was not strong enough to support tank columns.

A more plausible scenario was an amphibious attack by the Soviet Union aimed at the southern end of Sweden. Such an attack would have required that the then relatively small Soviet Baltic fleet concentrate itself before debarkation, thereby presenting an attractive target for the Swedish air force. It was thought that only a few nuclear weapons would be required to deter either a ground or amphibious invasion. The level of destruction which even a small nuclear arsenal would have granted Sweden would be sufficient to escalate the potential cost of the conflict, and thus deter the Soviet Union.

Svedlund argued that Swedish nuclear weapons were necessary in order to prevent these types of attacks, and thus to enhance the country's security. "If a small state lacks nuclear weapons and it is not a member of an alliance having such weapons it might, under certain circumstances, be tempting for an aggressor to attack that state."[14] Consequently, "if we had nuclear weapons our possibilities for defense would increase considerably."[15] Svedlund declared that the military was only interested in tactical nuclear weapons, and that they would be made available to all three services. The target date for the production of nuclear weapons was placed at 1965.[16] Svedlund also stated that appropriations for defense should be increased and that the armed forces should be restructured to reflect the greater likelihood of an adversary employing nuclear weapons in battle.

ÖB 54 touched off a vociferous debate in Sweden over nuclear weapons acquisition which was to last five years, and which did not really end until the late 1960s. Arguments for and against development were based on considerations of national security, economics, radiation hazards, morality, the differences between tactical and strategic nuclear arms, and the impact on the Great Power test ban negotiations at Geneva. Members from across the political spectrum joined in the discussion. A domestic political crisis at a critical moment played an important role. Ultimately, Sweden's decision was not to decide at all.

One of the main criticisms leveled at General Svedlund's request for nuclear arms concerned the financial burden such arms would impose. Defense Minister Nilsson of the ruling Social Democratic Party presented the government's defense budget to the Riksdag in January 1955 without even mentioning nuclear weapons procurement. Among the major newspapers, only the conservative Svenska Dagbladet had maintained that nuclear weapons would not be too expensive.[17] Among the political parties, both the Conservative Party leader Jarl Hjalmarson and the Liberal Party head Bertil Ohlin in March 1955 raised the issue of nuclear weapons for the first time in the Riksdag, with Hjalmarson insisting that Sweden take active measures for their acquisition.[18] Prime Minister Tage Erlander was opposed, remarking that "We will leave that to those nations that are in a better position to evaluate the situation and where they have considerably more resources for experimentation than our little nation has."[19] In the defense debate that May, the Conservatives declared that nuclear weapons acquisition was necessary for a strong defense. The Liberals did not advocate immediate procurement, as the technical prerequisites for constructing nuclear armaments were not yet available; however, they favored military funding for weapons research. Defense Minister Nilsson rejected both demands. He stated that it would not "be good politics or good economics to commit our nation's limited resources in terms of qualified technicians and scientists to the production of tactical nuclear weapons." Further, it was not possible to purchase nuclear weapons abroad. And the government did not wish to underwrite a research program until a positive decision on acquisition had been made.[20]

The proceedings in the Riksdag provoked greater discussion of the nuclear issue, most of which took place in the press, public debates, and in pamphlets and books. The small Communist Party was against anything to do with nuclear weapons for Sweden. The Conservative Party was strongly in favor, along with many of the Liberals. The Agrarian Party,[21] which was a coalition partner with the Social Democrats, was also amenable to acquisition. The Social Democrats were split, with prominent members of the party on both sides of the issue.

Among those Social Democrats most ardently opposed to nuclear weapons was the party's Women's Organization (*Sveriges Socialdemokratiska Kvinnöforbund*), led by Inga Thorsson. The Women's Organization's May 1956 annual conference was particularly noteworthy for its focus on the nuclear weapons question.[22] The women emphasized the ethical dilemmas inherent in possessing nuclear arms, and the radiation hazards presented by testing. Nuclear weapons were seen as a threat to mankind's existence; they presented "the greatest moral challenge any generation has ever encountered."[23] NATO's Carte Blanche exercises in the Low Countries, northeastern France, and the Federal Republic a year earlier, which simulated the employment of more than 335 nuclear weapons, resulting in 1.7 million fatalities and 3.5 million wounded, with additional casualties from fallout, provided ammunition for their cause. In the spring of 1957, eighteen prominent West German physicists declared categorically their refusal to participate in any future German nuclear weapons program. Denmark announced in December 1957 that it would not accept nuclear weapons if they were offered, and it would not permit the use of its territory as launching sites for nuclear weapons during a war. In January 1958, a petition signed by 11,000 scientists from around the world calling for a ban on nuclear testing was presented to the United Nations Secretary-General. The following month the Campaign for Nuclear Disarmament was founded in Britain. In early November, Swedish newspapers reported that levels of radioactivity in the northern part of the country had increased drastically, due to Russia's nuclear tests in the Arctic region. All these events bolstered the position of the Women's Organization and other opponents of Swedish nuclear weapons development.

Nuclear weapons for Sweden were also resisted on financial grounds. Civilian reactors would have to be operated uneconomically to produce weapons-grade plutonium, which would detract from domestic energy requirements unless dedicated facilities were constructed. There was a general lack of personnel qualified for military research and there was no knowledge of weapons design. Domestic heavy-water production facilities would be needed if Norway no longer agreed to sell its heavy water for use in a Swedish nuclear weapons project. An expanded uranium mining capability and a uranium enrichment plant might also be necessary. These steps would be expensive, and their funding would impinge on the civilian nuclear energy program and defense spending on conventional munitions.[24]

In October 1957, General Svedlund presented ÖB 57, the clearest exposition yet of the military argument for nuclear weapons acquisition. Previously, it had been generally conceded that the next war would be waged with nuclear weapons. As early as 1954, Prime Minister Erlander had remarked: "If a Great Power war breaks out, it appears likely that nuclear weapons will be used. This means that, in a future war, we must be prepared to defend ourselves even against an enemy using nuclear weapons against us."[25] In October 1954 the Army had participated in maneuvers in Bergslagen in order to prepare it for combat in a nuclear war. From 1954 to 1958 the Swedish armed forces were restructured and tactics for combat were altered to create smaller, more dispersed, and more mobile forces to be able to continue to fight during a nuclear attack. In December 1955, the Army Chief of Staff had endorsed nuclear weapons acquisition for Sweden.[26] ÖB 57 provided the intellectual justification for these developments. It specifically explained how nuclear weapons would augment the country's defense capabilities.

General Svedlund based his presentation on the assumption that the aggressor would be armed with nuclear weapons. Against such an adversary, Sweden would be at a disadvantage even if nuclear weapons were not employed. The mere threat of their use would be sufficient to alter Sweden's tactics and pose problems for coordinating defenses.

We have to recognize that the aggressor has the possibility of using nuclear weapons. We would therefore have to limit our losses through dispersing our forces over wide areas. Despite this we have to count on great losses since we would have to use more weapons and also more personnel than we would need if we had nuclear weapons. It is going to be difficult to maintain command and control since our forces would be dispersed over wide areas, and it would also contribute to a less concentrated counterattack. These factors together contribute to the fact that our ability to repel an attack would be diminished.[27]

Svedlund was skeptical to the notion that Swedish nonpossession of nuclear weapons would induce nuclear restraint in an adversary.

It would be difficult to find an example where the aggressor refrains from using an effective weapon only because the defender does not have the same military capability. . . . There are also examples which can be produced where a warring state has used a weapon for the sole reason that the other side didn't possess that weapon or was not able to use it. Therefore, there are strong reasons to believe that if the Swedish armed forces did not have nuclear weapons it would increase rather than decrease the likelihood that an aggressor would use such a weapon against it.[28]

On the other hand, a Sweden armed with nuclear weapons would deter their use by other countries.

History provides ample examples where two adversaries that possess the same type of weapons effectively have refrained from using them because both parties were not certain about the consequences of what would happen if the other side used the same type of weapon.[29]

Furthermore, other military benefits would derive from Sweden's acquisition of nuclear weapons which would tend to equalize the battle.

However, if nuclear weapons are part of our arsenal, the aggressor must also disperse his units, thereby balancing the opportunities to use conventional weapons. Furthermore, it is a rule of thumb that it is more difficult for the aggressor than for the defender to protect himself against a nuclear attack. Nuclear weapons are also in many cases more cost effective if you compare the cost to conventional weapons. Only through a massive use of conventional weapons can one achieve the same effect as with nuclear weapons. However, one could never achieve the same type of instantaneous effect with a conventional weapon as with a nuclear weapon. Furthermore, one would need thorough and time-consuming preparations and a concentration of weapons and personnel that the aggressor could easily strike with his nuclear weapons. Thus the possession of nuclear weapons might be our only chance of making the battle even.[30]

ÖB 57 was noteworthy for a number of reasons. It was the most articulate and well-reasoned argument the armed services had offered on behalf of nuclear weapons acquisition. The proposition that an aggressor would be armed with nuclear weapons accorded with the general view at the time. In comparison with the 1954 military report (ÖB 54), its emphasis on the actual commitment of nuclear arms in battle reflected the view then prevalent in NATO that these weapons were traditional military instruments that were simply more powerful conventional munitions.

While Svedlund maintained that "All *military aspects* speak strongly for acquisition of nuclear weapons," he was also sensitive to the arguments against procurement. Specifically, the supreme commander felt compelled to answer those critics who alleged that there would be health hazards from testing Swedish nuclear weapons in the atmosphere. While he admitted that radiation effects were not fully understood, Sweden would only test warheads 1/1,000th the yield of the most recent large hydrogen bomb tests. Further, ÖB 57 dismissed the idea that Swedish tactical nuclear weapons would threaten other countries and provoke a preemptive strike.

The risk of an attack against us would increase only if we had nuclear weapons in our country that could be seen as a significant latent threat against an aggressor-to-be and his homeland. Swedish possession of nuclear weapons could be interpreted as such a threat only if we had nuclear warheads in significantly larger numbers or larger yields than would be required for our defense purposes, or if we had delivery vehicles that could reach targets of importance in the aggressor's homeland from bases in Sweden. However, we don't have the economic resources, neither at present nor in the future, to acquire such weapons and delivery vehicles. This fact is obvious both for us and for other countries.[31]

Thus a strategic nuclear weapons posture for Sweden would be precluded by its excessive cost. However, the development of tactical nuclear weapons could be accommodated within the defense budget. Tactical nuclear arms should therefore be added to the armed forces as soon as possible. As a step in that direction, Svedlund urged that nuclear weapons research begin immediately. With an investment of $60 million spread over seven years, plus the cost of research and testing, it was estimated that Sweden could produce nuclear weapons for approximately $2 million each. With full funding from the Riksdag, a tactical nuclear weapons force would be attainable by the end of the 1960s.[32]

In April 1958, the Parliamentary Commission on Defense submitted its report for inclusion in the annual defense budget. The Commission had been established in June 1955, and was composed of three members of each of the four largest parties, plus the chairman of the Social Democrats. A discussion of nuclear weapons research had not been included in the Commission's original mandate. That the panel had felt compelled to comment on the subject indicated the change in Swedish perceptions in three years' time, and the depth of feeling among supporters of acquisition.

It is obvious that the technological prerequisites are such that a certain prolongation of a final decision on [the nuclear weapons] question is possible. The Defense Research Institute [FOA] should receive funds to undertake research in the nuclear field and study different aspects that are of importance for nuclear weapons effects as well as developing necessary methods and equipment in order to increase protection against nuclear weapons. Research and testing within this field . . . should be given the highest priority when it comes to the distribution of money and personnel.[33]

Ostensibly, the Commission's report was a compromise between those advocating immediate measures to acquire nuclear weapons and those opposed. Yet, in one sense, it represented an encouraging sign to the probomb factions that their view had gained ascendancy and would ultimately triumph. Despite the opposition of many of the leading Social Democrats, they had succeeded in placing the issue on the Parliamentary Commission's agenda and in arriving at an interparty consensus on the preliminary stage of nuclear weapons research. Compared with the widespread criticism which had greeted the Supreme Commander's ÖB 54 report three and a half years earlier, it marked a clear trend toward greater acceptance of a national nuclear force.

However, in another sense, nothing of significance had actually changed. The National Defense Research Institute had been performing research for a number of years in the nuclear field with the object of studying weapons effects and protective measures. This type of nuclear research, while useful, was not directly applicable to the development and construction of nuclear bombs. Those most adamant in not allowing Sweden to develop nuclear weapons had been decidedly unconvinced by the military arguments forwarded by the supreme commander in ÖB 57. A decision to postpone research suggested that the entire nuclear weapons issue was too politically sensitive to be decided in the Riksdag. In presenting the national defense bill later that April, Minister of Defense Sven Andersson reasserted the government's prerogative on the issue. Andersson declared that research aiming at construction of nuclear weapons "will not be carried out without a decision given by the Parliament."[34] On July 31, 1958, the Riksdag agreed to delay any resolution of the question.

At the beginning of October 1958, General Svedlund submitted the 1959/60 defense budget to the government. The supreme commander again requested that the military be permitted to acquire nuclear weapons as soon as possible. Second, he asked that a program at FOA be specifically dedicated to nuclear weapons research. It would cost $5.5 million the first year, and $1.2 million for each following year.[35] The supreme commander drew a distinction between nuclear weapons acquisition and nuclear weapons research. For the first time the military indicated that although it would prefer immediate procurement of nuclear arms, it would be satisfied with a nuclear research program. The military was no more successful with this limited appeal than before. At the end of November, the government refused both requests, while officially leaving the issue open for the future.[36]

There were a number of reasons why the armed services decided to alter their tactics and press for nuclear weapons research rather than outright acquisition. In international affairs, the Great Power negotiations at Geneva offered some prospect of an agreement banning nuclear weapons tests. On March 31, 1958, the Soviet Union had unilaterally suspended its nuclear testing. Less than a month later, President Eisenhower suggested convening a conference of experts to discuss the technical characteristics of a control system in order to monitor a test ban in all environments. The conference met in Geneva in July and August, and was considered a success. On October 13, Foreign Minister Östen Undén, a staunch critic of nuclear weapons acquisition for Sweden, called in the United Nations General Assembly for an international treaty to prohibit nuclear testing.[37] After these developments, it would have been difficult for Sweden's military leaders to expect an affirmative reply to a request for nuclear weapons development. There was a chance, however, that the government might be more amenable to a program of nuclear weapons research. A research program might also appear innocuous enough to receive the backing of those in the Social Democratic, Liberal, and Conservative parties who favored a policy of delay on the larger issue of acquisition. The military could have hoped that nuclear weapons research might in turn have granted a momentum to the larger question and thus made easier a later decision in favor of production. In addition, by delaying a decision the supreme commander might have wanted to buy time to allay the Navy's opposition to acquisition, due to its fear that a nuclear arsenal would reduce its share of defense allocations and its role in the country's defense. Or the supreme com-

mander might simply have not wished to articulate the estimated expenditure for a nuclear weapons force at a time of
increasing costs for conventional munitions.

Furthermore, as the Parliamentary Commission's report
had noted, Sweden did not possess the technical requirements
for nuclear weapons development. In January 1957, the Director of the National Defense Research Institute, Hugo Larsson,
had announced that Sweden had the capability to produce its
own nuclear weapons, and that the first weapons could be
available as early as 1963 if given full government support.[38]
Whatever Larsson's intentions, his statement was misleading.
His estimate was based on the successful completion of a small
demonstration reactor, Ågesta, by 1960. Yet problems in construction had led to delays and rising expenditures. At the same
time, other developments in Sweden's nuclear energy program
had compromised its independence from foreign restrictions.
In the United States, the breakthrough in light-water reactor
design provided an attractive alternative to heavy-water reactors, especially when U.S. technology was offered at discount
rates. The American offer in 1956 of a research reactor under its
Atoms for Peace program presented Stockholm with the opportunity to acquire the facility earlier and at less cost than if it
were manufactured in Sweden. This facility, termed R2, was a
30-megawatt light-water reactor that required enriched uranium as fuel.[39] In addition, because Sweden had no domestic
production plants for heavy water and since its uranium production facilities were inadequate to fulfill its requirements, it
was compelled to rely on imported heavy water and uranium
fuel. The least expensive source of these materials was the
United States. On January 18, 1956, the U.S. and Sweden
signed an agreement for cooperation on the peaceful uses of
nuclear energy which leased six kilograms of enriched uranium
to Stockholm.[40] This was supplemented by three additional
agreements over the next six years which increased the amount
of uranium provided by the United States and the duration of
the original agreement.[41] Any facilities using American-supplied materials would be subject to controls and inspection to

ensure their use for peaceful purposes only. R2 went critical in May 1960; Ågesta not until 1963.[42] While the former was a light-water reactor and the latter a heavy-water reactor, both used nuclear materials provided by the United States and were therefore subject to bilateral safeguards. Even if Stockholm had desired to use its civilian nuclear power program for military purposes at this time, it was legally barred from doing so by Washington's nuclear export policy.

While technical conditions made possible a policy of postponement on nuclear weapons acquisition, the domestic situation in Sweden made it politically expedient. The ruling Social Democratic Party was divided over the issue of nuclear arms. This split became public in early 1957 with a series of articles in *Morgon Tidningen* by éminences grises of the party, Per Edvin Skiöld, the former defense and foreign minister, and a member of the Riksdag since 1918, in favor of nuclear weapons, and Ernst Wigforss, the former finance minister, opposed. The Social Democrats' position in the Riksdag could not withstand even a minimum number of defections from the party. The 1956 election had resulted in the Social Democratic-Agrarian Party coalition losing eleven seats to the Conservatives; by itself, the SDP had only a plurality, not a majority, of Parliamentary seats and was dependent upon Agrarian Party support in order to govern.[43] In October 1957, a disagreement over an expansion of the pension system (*Allmänn tilläggspension*) resulted in the dissolution of the government. The Social Democrats preferred a compulsory increase in the national old-age pension, while the Agrarian, Conservative, and Liberal parties favored instead voluntary agreements reached privately through collective bargaining. Without the support of the Agrarians, the Social Democrats could not remain in power and had to call for new elections. These were scheduled for June 1958. The 1958 special election was decided solely on the pension issue, and returned the Social Democrats to power, albeit with a plurality of a single seat in association with the Communist Party.[44] In this politically vulnerable condition, the Social Democrats could ill afford any division within the party. The overwhelming concern for the SDP leadership was to maintain party unity for the upcoming general election in 1960.

It was in this context that the government had to answer competing demands regarding nuclear weapons acquisition. A decision either way risked alienating some members of the party. In order to arrive at some form of intraparty consensus, on November 4, 1958, a special group of eighteen Social Democrats was formed to examine the entire issue of nuclear armaments. Advocates and opponents were both represented, and the committee was chaired by Prime Minister Erlander.[45] After a number of closed-door sessions, the Committee for the Study of the Atomic Weapons Question presented its report on November 11, 1959. The report was published as *Neutrality, Defense, Atomic Weapons* (*Neutralitet, Försvar, Atomvapen*) the following month.

Once again, the Social Democrats followed the path of least resistance and failed to decide either for or against acquisition. The Atomic Weapons Committee report stated that "A more definite decision should not be necessary until the mid-1960s because we will not, until then, have a real capability for manufacturing Swedish nuclear weapons."[46] However, as a partial concession to the nuclear weapons proponents on the committee, it was decided that "protective research" (*skyddforskningen*) should be expanded at the National Defense Research Institute: "With regard to the question of research, the committee says that only research on how to defend oneself against a nuclear attack should be pursued. The committee agrees, however, that the previous mandate for research should be expanded somewhat."[47] Freedom of action was formally preserved on the issue.

How did the Social Democrats arrive at this consensus? First, all members of the group recognized the party's precarious position in the Riksdag; defections over any issue would have been fatal to the Social Democrats remaining in power. The SDP's chances for the 1960 election would be jeopardized unless the antibomb (Undén-Thorsson) and probomb (Skiöld-Siegbahn) factions could be reconciled. A clear-cut decision either way would have divided the party. As chairman, the task of maintaining party discipline fell to Prime Minister Erlander. As Erlander recalled in his memoirs, "the party must not be split. That could be prevented if we accepted the policy of postponement and agreed to research with regard to nuclear bombs but had guarantees that the research would only deal with how to protect oneself from attack."[48]

A limited research program with the promise to reconsider the subject a few years hence mollified the advocates of nuclear weapons while not precipitating a rupture with those opposed. As insurance that the protective research program would not be subverted by FOA to its own ends, technical experts were assigned to monitor the research and to report back to the prime minister, the defense minister, and the foreign minister.[49] A further precaution was added in June 1960 when Defense Minister Andersson assumed personal responsibility for the nuclear research program. The National Defense Research Institute was also forced to submit all proposals to Andersson's office on an annual basis.[50]

A program of limited research, with freedom of action for the future, was also a means of preventing criticism from the nonsocialist parties that the Social Democrats were negligent on defense matters, and were thereby jeopardizing the country's security. It removed an argument from those who advocated tying Sweden's defense closer to the West, such as the Conservative leader Jarl Hjalmarson, who had suggested Swedish defense cooperation with Norway and Denmark, as well as those such as Herbert Tingsten, the influential editor of *Dagens Nyheter*, who had called for Sweden to become a full partner of NATO. The 1960/61 and 1961/62 defense budget increases submitted by the Social Democrats were also a means of deflecting criticism on this point.[51]

The Swedish debate has often been cited as an example of a country openly discussing the pros and cons of nuclear weapons acquisition. Yet public opinion exerted little influence on the Atomic Weapons Committee's deliberations and conclusions.[52] For those Swedish people interested in political affairs, the general supplementary pension scheme was of more immediate concern. For example, Östen Undén, one of the first to speak out strongly against nuclear weapons for Sweden, had formed his views prior to any public discussion of the issue. To be certain, the antibomb forces in the government were aided by the efforts of the Social Democrats' Women's Organization, but they used this support to buttress their own arguments within the bureaucracy. Notably, even after the Women's Organization's celebrated 1956 conference, Prime Minister Erlander was still disposed to acquiring nuclear weapons.[53] It was the handful of party leaders, editorial writers, and liberal activists who guided public opinion, not vice versa.

Even with the knowledge that party unity on the nuclear weapons issue was essential, it was still not predetermined that the Atomic Weapons Committee would arrive at some form of consensus, given the intensity of the debate and the gulf that separated the two factions. In fact, at first there was a clear majority *in favor* of nuclear weapons acquisition.[54] That the panel could unanimously agree on a common position opposed to nuclear weapons acquisition after a year's deliberation was due to the persuasiveness of economic, military, and foreign policy considerations.

According to one authority, constraints imposed by the defense budget convinced the military leadership, and in turn their advocates on the committee, that nuclear weapons could only be developed at the expense of the country's conventional defenses.[55] From 1956 to 1959, Swedish defense spending increased an average of 5.4 percent per year, and was greater than any other West European country save Italy, France, Britain, and the Federal Republic.[56] Expenditures on a Swedish nuclear force would erode conventional capabilities, with the result that the country would not be able to respond adequately to a conventional attack. Stockholm's only recourse would then be to escalate the conflict to the nuclear level. Given these alternatives, a strong conventional defense without nuclear weapons or a weak conventional defense with nuclear weapons, the supreme commander selected the former as the best method to safeguard the national security.

However, there are three objections to this interpretation. First, it attributes to the military leadership a view that is contrary to the position it had recently expressed in ÖB 57. The request for nuclear weapons development put forward in that document was made with a knowledge of the costs involved. It outlined a seven-year program for nuclear weapons construction at approximately $10 million per year, or less than 2 percent of the annual defense budget. Nothing had occurred in the intervening two years to raise the price of nuclear weapons procurement. To be sure, Sweden had signed a second atomic energy agreement with the United States in April 1958, which had the effect of placing the Ågesta reactor under bilateral safeguards. Yet, given ÖB 57's argument that a national nuclear force was possible by the end of the 1960s, it was clear that Svedlund was basing his forecast on the unsafeguarded, 200-megawatt heavy-water reactor at Marviken, due to be completed in 1968. Moreover, in his October 1958 defense budget request, General Svedlund had emphasized nuclear weapons research, which would have been much less expensive than acquisition. Finally, if nuclear weapons development would have sacrificed Sweden's conventional force readiness in 1959, why then did the supreme commander again stress the advantages to the country's defense of nuclear weapons acquisition three years later, in ÖB 62?

On the other hand, military considerations had occupied a central place in the debate since ÖB 54. The Conservative leader Hjalmarson often relied on military rationales for justifying the acquisition of nuclear arms.[57] In April 1959, the Social Democrats' Per Edvin Skiöld had edited a book of seven essays on the nuclear question, many of which emphasized the advantages nuclear weapons would grant to Sweden's defense.[58] Ironically, it was partly because of military considerations that the Atomic Weapons Committee unanimously decided to postpone acquisition.[59] During the year-long discussions, the armed services presented their case that nuclear weapons would enhance Sweden's ability to resist aggression, even going so far as to xerox a chapter of Kissinger's 1957 book advocating tactical nuclear weapons for defense, and distributing copies to all the members of the panel. However, the logic of the military's argument was not found persuasive. The deterrent ability of Swedish tactical nuclear weapons was thought to be negligible against an adversary armed not only with a greater number of tactical nuclear weapons, but also possessing hydrogen weapons with yields in the megaton range. Employment of nuclear arms by Stockholm against such an opponent would likely have resulted in national suicide by provoking overwhelming retaliation.

Moreover, the committee concluded that not only would nuclear weapons not deter aggression, they would in fact attract an attack, "like flypaper," in the words of one participant. While Sweden's military power would be increased with a stockpile of nuclear weapons, its overall security would be diminished because of the possibility that its nuclear arsenal would cause a Great Power (i.e., the Soviet Union), to intervene. As expressed by Erlander in November 1959 when he presented the Atomic Weapons Committee's report:

In general an increase in defense strength within certain limits means increased security, since the price of victory for an aggressor is raised. *But security does not necessarily increase in some direct relationship to military forces.* . . . Swedish foreign and defense policies can be said to be built on the assumption that an increase in military forces does not lead to greater security if it is carried out with such means that the risks of war are increased at the same time.[60]

Nuclear weapons would therefore decrease, not increase, the country's security, especially during a crisis, when a Great Power "could find it necessary to wipe out risks of that kind."[61] Conventional munitions could never provoke such a response. Sweden's "threshold defense" (tröskelförsvar) was better suited to its mission without nuclear arms. Security would be best assured if funding were directed toward conventional weapons.

If a postponement policy was required because of the Social Democrats' domestic political problems, the party made a virtue out of necessity. Outright renunciation of nuclear weapons might have been viewed as an incautious step which could compromise future security by unnecessarily limiting Sweden's defense options. It would have also encouraged those groups in Sweden who favored dismantling the country's conventional defense establishment. On the other hand, a decision to develop nuclear weapons might well have been perceived as aggressive and confrontational by the Soviet Union, and would have needlessly aggravated tensions in Scandinavia. A policy of delay which incorporated the possibility of future acquisition had the merit of avoiding both these extremes. Moreover, viewed in this manner, the Atomic Weapons Committee's decision was consistent with Sweden's previous behavior toward defense and foreign policy issues—in particular, the proposed Scandinavian Defense Pact and the question of membership in NATO. Actions which would have augmented Sweden's "purely military strength" were avoided, if it was thought that they would have provoked a reaction from the Soviet Union which might have upset the status quo in the Nordic region. Sweden's special interest in Finland's neutral status, based on its direct involvement in Finnish affairs from the thirteenth to the nineteenth century, and Finland's obvious geostrategic significance as a buffer state, was an important restraining influence on Sweden's freedom in foreign affairs.[62] Sweden's dilemma was how best to defend its own interests without threatening the interests of the Soviet Union. In all these instances—the neutral defense union, abstention from NATO coupled with a strong, independent military capability, and a postponement policy for nuclear weapons—Stockholm attempted to strike a balance between deterrence and reassurance.

NUCLEAR WEAPONS
AND INTERNATIONAL NEGOTIATIONS

The Atomic Weapons Committee's report marked a watershed in the Swedish debate. In the words of one Swedish scholar, this party document formed "the basis of Sweden's official nuclear policy."[63] The Swedish political characteristic of striving for consensus in foreign affairs reasserted itself after the November 1959 report. The Center and Liberal parties almost immediately supported the committee's conclusions and recommendations; only the Conservatives continued to insist on a nuclear weapons development program. France's detonation of a nuclear device in February 1960 was greeted with little enthusiasm in Sweden; most press commentary was critical.[64] In March, the Norwegian Storting rejected the authorization of funds for nuclear weapons development when it passed its defense bill. In the 1960 general election in Sweden, the Social Democrats returned to power, for the first time with an absolute majority over the nonsocialist parties, thereby granting them a more stable political foundation. That summer, the SDP's Congress endorsed the postponement policy. Support for nuclear weapons acquisition, as indicated by public opinion polls, weakened. By June 1961, only half as many people were in favor of Swedish nuclear arms as four years earlier.[65] That September, the Belgrade Conference of Nonaligned Countries excoriated the nuclear weapons states and called for "total disarmament." In an exercise similar to Carte Blanche, the National Defense Research Institute calculated the consequences to Sweden of an attack on cities and military installations with 200 nuclear weapons. The results from this study showed an estimated two to three million casualties, roughly 30 to 40 percent of the population.[66] Insofar as Swedish nuclear weapons were perceived to invite attack, this study illustrated the possible calamitous consequences of acquisition.

An important influence on the nuclear weapons debate in Sweden at this time was the international negotiations to control nuclear weapons. Sweden had long been active in international forums, which were viewed as important for reducing global tensions. Between the wars, under the guidance first of Hjalmar Branting and then of Östen Undén, Sweden played a leading role in the League of Nations and was a principal advocate of conventional disarmament. After the Second World

War, the United Nations offered a forum in which Stockholm could continue to promote its interests, especially with regard to the efforts to limit nuclear weapons. As Prime Minister Erlander remarked in 1954, "What should, then, be our attitude towards the fearful realities that face us in the shape of nuclear warfare? In the first place we naturally place our hopes on the possibilities of achieving an agreement within the framework of the United Nations."[67] For Sweden, a small country located between two nuclear-armed adversaries, the United Nations provided an opportunity to discuss issues of international security in order "to narrow the gap between divergent standpoints or to gain the understanding of one party for the other party's views."[68] By assuming a mediator's role, Sweden could hope to exert a positive influence on international disarmament negotiations.

This posture had immediate domestic political advantages. Given that the Social Democrats needed to preserve party unity for the 1960 general election, a policy of delay on the nuclear weapons issue would appease both pro- and anti-acquisition factions within the party. In addition, the retention of a nuclear weapons option could accord Sweden the ability to pressure the nuclear weapons states into some form of agreement at Geneva. Outright acquisition, on the other hand, would unduly complicate the negotiations. This argument exerted a powerful influence on the domestic debate, and was cited to justify the government's postponement policy. This reasoning was emphasized in the Atomic Weapons Committee's report.

Negotiations between the great powers about banning nuclear weapons tests are presently taking place. . . . It would be in accordance with Sweden's own national interest as well as in the interest of the international peace efforts . . . if these negotiations were to be successful. It might have a negative impact on the disarmament efforts if Sweden now decided to manufacture nuclear weapons.[69]

Similarly, total disavowal of interest in nuclear weapons development would eliminate Stockholm's bargaining leverage. Success in the international negotiations at Geneva was used to dissuade those who favored renunciation of nuclear arms as official policy. Defense Minister Sven Andersson in the Riksdag, Olof Palme before the SDP's Youth Organization's 1958 Congress, and Prime Minister Erlander argued that not the moral example of abstention but rather the prospect of Sweden producing nuclear weapons would prompt the Great Powers to reach an agreement.[70] The international negotiations furnished the ideal justification for the postponement policy.

Yet Sweden's behavior in the United Nations on the nuclear weapons issue was not consistent with its declared policy of pressuring the nuclear weapons states by using the threat to acquire nuclear arms. To be sure, Sweden attempted to stimulate agreement among the Great Powers. In September 1961, the Geneva Conference on the Discontinuance of Nuclear Weapons Tests adjourned *sine die*, followed by the Soviet Union's resumption of atmospheric nuclear testing. Three months later, Sweden's Foreign Minister Östen Undén introduced the so-called Undén Plan, which suggested the formation of a "non-nuclear club" in order to "facilitate agreement by the nuclear Powers to discontinue all nuclear tests and to prevent any increase in the number of nuclear Powers."[71]

Sweden's influence was increased by its elevation to the newly formed Eighteen Nation Disarmament Committee (ENDC) in March 1962. As one of eight countries outside the Great Power blocs, it could act as an arbiter between the United States and the Soviet Union, as well as promote its own views on nuclear disarmament. The Partial Test Ban Treaty in August 1963 was the culmination of years of negotiation, and was seen as a possible turning point in the nuclear arms race. Although stating that a final decision on Swedish nuclear weapons would await further arms limitation agreements, Sweden declared that it would sign the treaty "as soon as possible."[72] Despite the fact that in 1958 General Svedlund had maintained that Sweden could safely conduct underground nuclear tests, the alacrity with which Stockholm moved to sign and ratify the treaty suggested that it would not perform any actions contrary to the spirit of the agreement.[73]

In January 1965, Foreign Minister Torsten Nilsson submitted a "package" proposal before the U.N. General Assembly. Nilsson's plan aimed at achieving "a fair balance" of obligations between the nuclear and nonnuclear states. Further, he urged a production halt on all fissionable material for military purposes, and a nonproliferation agreement.[74] The appeal for equitable and nondiscriminatory measures on matters of arms control and disarmament was a recurring theme in Sweden's statements in the Eighteen Nation Disarmament Committee. In addition to advocating this package proposal, Sweden also urged ceasing production of chemical and biological weapons[75] and the application of IAEA safeguards to all nuclear activities of the nonnuclear weapons states and to all peaceful nuclear activities of the nuclear powers.[76] During the thirteenth session of the ENDC, Sweden was responsible for three alterations in the US-USSR joint Draft Treaty, which formed the basis for the eventual Nonproliferation Treaty. The two changes in Article VI, interjecting *at an early date* after "the cessation of the nuclear arms race" and *nuclear* before "disarmament," underscored the urgency with which Sweden viewed the control of nuclear weapons.[77] The Swedish delegation also recommended amending Article VIII to call for a review conference to be held every five years after the NPT's entry into force.[78] On August 19, 1968, Sweden signed the Nonproliferation Treaty. It was adopted for ratification by the Riksdag on December 16, 1968, and Sweden officially became a party to the agreement on January 9, 1970.[79]

Ultimately, the extent of Sweden's ability to pressure the nuclear weapons states because of its nuclear weapons option cannot be measured. Swedish observers themselves disagreed. Karl Birnbaum has written that Sweden's posture carried "definite weight" in the arms negotiations.[80] Nils Andrén's evaluation was more skeptical, maintaining that "It is doubtful if this attitude has in fact contributed to the very modest success" of the negotiations.[81] Östen Undén disputed any influence deriving from the country's nuclear option, arguing that Sweden's policy "is only a negotiating tactic and they [the Great Powers] know it."[82] Perhaps a more plausible explanation for Sweden's influence in the ENDC was simply the aggressive advocacy of its representative, Alva Myrdal, and the delegation's technical expertise, as evidenced by the ENDC accepting only Sweden's suggested alterations in the text of the joint draft nonproliferation treaty.

What can be demonstrated, however, is that Stockholm refused to take steps short of acquisition which would have made its threat to go nuclear more credible, and thereby would have generated greater bargaining leverage. In January 1962, the new commander-in-chief, Torsten Rapp, presented ÖB 62. General Rapp, like General Svedlund before him, stressed the benefits of nuclear weapons for defense. However, unlike before, Rapp did not ask for nuclear weapons or for an expanded research program. Instead, he requested the formation of a special committee to examine the technical and economic problems that a Swedish nuclear weapons project would face.[83] The defense minister denied this request.

The nuclear weapons question resurfaced in the 1965 military study, the year that the military had originally predicted for the production of the first Swedish nuclear arms. General Rapp again mentioned tactical nuclear weapons as a valuable addition to the Swedish armed forces. While there might exist valid military reasons for acquisition, it was recognized that "procurement is a question of a very political nature."[84] Yet the official policy of maintaining freedom of action implied having the option to acquire nuclear weapons, if the government so decided. General Rapp stated that under this definition, freedom of action did not exist because the technological basis for a nuclear weapons program was not present.

The civilian nuclear programs are presently, however, designed without any consideration for possible future requirements with regard to the production of Swedish nuclear weapons. . . . A Swedish nuclear weapons program would encompass so many uncertain factors and would take so long to complete that one must strongly question whether the present situation implies that we have real freedom of action.[85]

It was estimated at this time that it would take approximately seven years to manufacture nuclear weapons once a decision was taken.[86] Using the government's own argument, General Rapp maintained that in order to achieve true freedom of action, "it is necessary that we obtain the requisite knowledge and technical basis for an acquisition decision . . . in order to reduce the time to only a few years between a production decision and the delivery of the first nuclear device."[87] He suggested that $2 million per year be appropriated for exploratory research, with an additional $8 million a year authorized for stockpiling fissile materials for rapid assembly into weapons in the event that a positive decision be taken at a later date. These actions would not constitute a decision to build nuclear arms, Rapp contended.[88] Once again his request was denied.

In February 1968, the Parliamentary Commission of Defense presented its report after three years of deliberation. The report cited the previous reasons against acquisition, along with a more recent argument which suggested that Sweden's defense was tied to that of the Great Powers, although it was not a member of NATO or the Warsaw Pact.

The Party considering an attack on Sweden with or without the use of nuclear weapons must in this case also expect that nuclear weapons may be used against his operations even though Sweden does not have such weapons. . . .

The conclusion is that Sweden by and large is under the nuclear umbrella approximately in the same way that countries in our vicinity are, regardless which power bloc or great power sphere of interests they belong to.[89]

The defense study therefore concluded that "it is not in our country's national security interest to acquire nuclear weapons."[90] After almost a decade and a half of constant interest by the military in nuclear weapons acquisition, the government, acting upon this recommendation, submitted a bill to the Riksdag in which Sweden's renunciation of nuclear arms was enshrined as official policy.[91]

Sweden's behavior on the nuclear weapons issue both domestically and in the United Nations thus appeared to undermine its claim that it was preserving a nuclear option in order to increase the pressure on the nuclear weapons states. The government's refusal to accede to the minimal request in ÖB 62 for an investigatory committee, its speedy ratification of the Partial Test Ban Treaty, its refusal to narrow the time between a decision and nuclear weapons production, as requested in ÖB 65, and its official adoption of a policy of nuclear nonacquisition prior to the completion of the nonproliferation treaty negotiations, were all measures which arguably decreased Sweden's influence. As Alva Myrdal admitted in the First Committee of the U.N. General Assembly in June 1968, "It must have been evident for a considerable time that Sweden has had no intentions of becoming a nuclear weapons power."[92]

Prior to 1960, the government's reluctance to take actions to increase its diplomatic currency might have been a prudent means of not aggravating those members of the SDP opposed to acquisition. Yet after 1960, there was less need to placate this group. The SDP emerged from the general election with a full majority in the Riksdag, its leadership on the supplementary pension scheme and the nuclear weapons question recognized, and its prestige enhanced. Additionally, by the end of 1961, the antinuclear movement had lost much of its influence. Further, the following year Östen Undén retired as foreign minister, thereby removing a forceful opponent to nuclear weapons acquisition. Against this weakened opposition, it was unlikely that modest steps aimed only at increasing the threat to develop nuclear weapons would have provoked a split in the SDP. According to the government's own logic, these measures would have obtained greater respect for Sweden's voice in the Eighteen Nation Disarmament Committee.

CONCLUSION

Why did Sweden not acquire nuclear weapons? Domestic and international considerations both played a part. A positive decision would have split the SDP and doomed its chances for reelection in 1960. Also, by coincidence, the Atomic Weapons

Committee was established the day after the nuclear weapons testing moratorium went into effect. Moreover, the members of the committee discovered that many of the military justifications for a national nuclear force did not stand up to scrutiny. Nuclear weapons would have been an extra burden on the defense budget, and they also presented the danger of inviting a preemptive strike during a crisis. Their presence in Sweden would have increased Soviet demands on Finland, thereby risking the stability of the Nordic region. Questions of morality, concern over the radiation hazards from atmospheric testing, and the SDP's antimilitarist tradition and ideals of world disarmament also exerted some influence. The dramatic increase in the strategic nuclear stockpiles of the superpowers during the 1960s, and the corresponding view that nuclear weapons were useful primarily as political, not military, instruments, the American criticism of "relatively weak national nuclear forces" for deterrence,[93] and the Kennedy administration's emphasis on conventional defense and away from tactical nuclear weapons, further contributed to a decision against nuclear arms. In addition, Sweden's participation in the Eighteen Nation Disarmament Committee, and the achievement of the Partial Test Ban and Nonproliferation Treaties facilitated Stockholm's choice. Clearly, then, Sweden never had sufficient will to develop nuclear weapons.

If Stockholm did not want to acquire nuclear weapons, neither did it wish to unilaterally renounce its nuclear option. In October 1958, before the U.N. General Assembly, Foreign Minister Undén implied that Sweden might construct nuclear arms if there was not a nuclear test ban agreement. Eight years later, Alva Myrdal claimed that "We are playing upon our ability to become a nuclear power in order to goad the big ones into coming to terms."[94] During this period, the SDP leadership continuously explained to its constituency and to the country that the postponement policy was the optimum means of Sweden's exerting influence on the arms control and disarmament talks. Why, then, did Sweden not maximize its ability to develop nuclear weapons in order to increase its pressure on the nuclear weapons states?

To be sure, Sweden never had the technical means to acquire nuclear weapons. After 1958, proponents of acquisition had based their plans on obtaining weapons-grade material from the unsafeguarded Marviken plant. The 200-megawatt heavy-water reactor was originally designed to be fueled with natural uranium from Ranstad. However, as with Sweden's earlier reactors, problems emerged during its design and construction. It was discovered that it was necessary to use enriched uranium in order to achieve acceptable power economics.[95] As before, enriched uranium from the United States was available on concessionary terms. On July 28, 1966, Stockholm and Washington initialed an accord whereby the United States agreed to supply "all of Sweden's requirements for enriched uranium," up to 50,000 kilograms. In return, Sweden promised that the nuclear material would be used for peaceful purposes only. The IAEA was asked to assume the responsibility for safeguards application.[96] Thus by the mid-1960s, Sweden's entire nuclear power program was operating under bilateral or IAEA safeguards. Development for military purposes was only possible under these conditions by abrogating international treaty obligations.

Yet capability is in large measure a function of will. Aside from the Ågesta and Marviken reactors, there were other alternatives open to Sweden to enhance the credibility of its nuclear option, ranging from declarations in the United Nations to underwriting a substantial nuclear weapons research program. A reason for the Social Democrats' reluctance was hesitation at resurrecting a potentially controversial issue which had been laid to rest in 1959. Also, the SDP might have feared that those still in favor of acquisition would attempt to manipulate the issue to promote full-scale development. As evidenced by its defense studies, the military advocated nuclear weapons acquisition as late as 1965. The majority of the Conservative Party and prominent members of the Liberal party (at this time the largest opposition party) also favored nuclear weapons for Sweden.[97]

Sweden's unwillingness to make more credible its nuclear option can best be explained by placing it in the context of its defense and foreign policies. While domestic politics were central to the Atomic Weapons Committee's November 1959 report and to the SDP's desire to maintain party unity for the 1960 general election, these reasons declined in importance as the Social Democrats consolidated their political position during the 1960s. International security and diplomatic considerations, on the other hand, proved far more durable. Sweden's defense was designed to be strong enough to deter aggression, but in such a manner as not to be provocative. Nuclear weapons development was denied because it was felt that a national nuclear force would be perceived as overly aggressive; a territorial defense was better suited to the country's requirements.[98] Similarly, the postponement policy, without modifications, managed to signal neither vulnerability nor confrontation. Measures to increase the credibility of the nuclear option were avoided. Even though they might have increased Sweden's leverage in the ENDC, they might well have been threatening to the Soviet Union and, in the long run, disadvantageous to Nordic stability and Sweden's security.

Sweden's policy on the nuclear option was thus consistent with its stance in the United Nations, and with its earlier decisions on nuclear weapons acquisition, NATO membership, and the Scandinavian Defense Pact. On these occasions, Sweden sought a way of attaining a credible defense posture to safeguard its security, while at the same time trying not to provoke a counterproductive response. The achievement of this policy was aided by the Social Democratic Party remaining in power and consistently promoting the country's interests. Its success was due both to Sweden's understanding its position in world affairs, and to the limitations geography imposes even in the nuclear age.

ADDENDUM

In April 1985 an article published in a Swedish technical weekly newspaper, *Ny Teknik*, claimed that research designed to give Sweden nuclear weapons had been performed by the National Defense Research Institute (FOA) until 1975. It specifically alleged (1) that ten tests involving small amounts of weapons-grade plutonium had been carried out near Stockholm in 1972, two years after Sweden had ratified the Nonproliferation Treaty, and (2) that FOA had constructed a neutron pulse generator, which is a small accelerator unit that generates a very strong and intense pulse of neutrons that can be used to trigger a fission explosion.[99]

In fact, Stockholm carried out three different activities during the 1960s and early 1970s: implosion experiments, compressibility tests on plutonium, and neutron pulse generator experiments. These activities were theoretically within the "protective research" program which had been recommended by the Committee for the Study of the Atomic Weapons Question in November 1959. This research was not designed to give Sweden nuclear weapons, these tests were not nuclear weapons tests, and Sweden did not violate its obligations under the Nonproliferation Treaty or corresponding safeguards agreement with the International Atomic Energy Agency.

The implosion experiments were carried out in a steel-reinforced underground room of a laboratory at Grindsjön SE in Stockholm. They intended to analyze the compression of a metallic sphere caused by a conventional explosive, with the intention of simulating the process immediately prior to the triggering of a nuclear chain reaction in a nuclear explosive. (See the Technical Note in the Appendix, pp. 271–275.) No fissile material was used in these tests, for which X-ray measurement techniques were used. The experiments were concluded by the end of 1969, with the final set of tests relating to the special issue of the safety of implosion devices. A classified final report in early 1971 summarized the ten years of experiments.

The tests with one-gram pellets of plutonium took place in Ursvik, outside Stockholm. Sweden had received this plutonium from Britain and France. These tests aimed at analyzing the mechanical compressibility of plutonium, which is important for estimating the quantity of plutonium needed in a nu-clear device. There was no special requirement that the plu-tonium used be weapons-grade. One would have to increase the density of each one-gram pellet by a factor of approximately a hundred in order to make it go critical; such an increase in density cannot be achieved with conventional explosives. Moreover, it takes at least 4,000 grams (4 kilograms) of weap-ons-grade plutonium to make a sophisticated nuclear explo-sive. Any results derived from the test of a one-gram pellet would therefore have to be scaled up 4,000 times. This pro-cedure would not yield very accurate or useful information for building a bomb.

The neutron pulse generator experiments aimed at study-ing the principles involved in the initiation of nuclear war-heads. Such investigations helped FOA understand more about the effects of the electromagnetic pulse (EMP) generated by a nuclear explosion. A knowledge of EMP generation requires insight into the design of a nuclear device and the nuclear dynamics during the first microseconds of a nuclear explosion. These experiments were completed by October 1967, four months before the February 1968 Parliamentary Commission on Defense report and ten months before Sweden signed the NPT.

To be sure, the boundary between "protective research" and atomic weapons research was never explicitly drawn, and may well have been overstepped by FOA scientists eager to learn more about nuclear weapons. All the information from this research, along with the data from the compressibility tests and implosion experiments, improved Sweden's nuclear com-petence, and would have been helpful if ever Stockholm de-cided to develop nuclear weapons at some future date. How-ever, this research was intended to help FOA learn more about the nuclear capabilities of foreign powers and the possible countermeasures Sweden could take to strengthen its defenses. Specifically, FOA wished (1) to know to what extent nuclear devices could be miniaturized, in order to discover if an adver-sary's weapons system (for example, 152 mm. artillery) could be loaded with a nuclear explosive device, and (2) to protect, or harden, Sweden's command, control, and communications (C³) network to withstand an air-burst nuclear explosion designed to disrupt it.[100]

Much of the sensationalism surrounding the revelations about Sweden's nuclear program can be attributed to poor reporting. The *Times* (London) of April 26, 1985 and the *Observer* (London) of April 28, 1985 both reported that the *Ny Teknik* article had stated that the ten tests had been carried out underground, but without specifying that they had been performed in an underground room of a laboratory. The *Ny Teknik* article had stated that these ten tests were carried out in this underground room. If Sweden had detonated any nuclear devices, this would have been a violation of its obligations under the NPT. Also, it is difficult to see how any underground nuclear test could have gone undetected by the seismological institutes located in Norway, Britain, and in Sweden itself.

A CBS News reporter following up on the *Ny Teknik* article stated on April 26 that a FOA official had told him that Sweden had secretly stockpiled ten nuclear bombs since 1972. If correct, this too would have violated the NPT. Because the Treaty required Sweden to accept IAEA safeguards on all its nuclear material, any diversion of safeguarded material, or construction of clandestine facilities to produce unsafeguarded material, would have breached Sweden's Treaty obligations. Also, the reporter did not reveal from where Sweden might have obtained the weapons-grade material for these ten bombs. Given Sweden's open political system, a secret nuclear arsenal would have been extremely difficult to keep hidden from the public for well over a decade. A senior official at the Swedish Ministry of Defense denied the CBS News report.

Finally, it should be noted that there was an election in Sweden scheduled for September 1985. The *Ny Teknik* article stated that the Swedish prime minister, Olof Palme, was part of an "inner circle" of senior Social Democrats in the government who had permitted FOA to perform the research which would have allegedly given the country nuclear weapons. Such a charge five months before the election would be personally embarrassing to the prime minister, and politically damaging to him and his party. Palme denied that he was a member of any "inner circle," or that plans had been made to construct nuclear weapons. He ordered the defense minister, Anders Thunborg, to investigate the assertions contained in the article. It was originally promised that the report would be delivered in October 1985, but to date it has not appeared.

3.

South Korea

The strategic location of Korea, its comparatively small size, and its weak military strength have long made it an object of interest and interference by its more powerful neighbors. For years China and Japan vied for its control, while in this century Japan annexed Korea outright in 1910 and ruled the country until the end of the Second World War. At that time, Soviet forces moving down from the north and American troops coming up from the south occupied the peninsula, with the demarcation line between the two occupation zones resting roughly at the 38th parallel.

Over the next few years all attempts to peacefully unify the country proved unsuccessful.[1] After training a large army and installing a pro-Moscow communist government, the Soviet Union evacuated its forces from the north by the end of 1948. The American presence in the south was questioned in Washington in light of other priorities. In September 1947, a memorandum from the Joint Chiefs of Staff to President Truman had emphasized the relative unimportance of Korea to America's strategic interests, and cited a number of additional arguments in favor of troop withdrawal: a limited American presence was a military liability without reinforcements prior to hostilities, United States air power could neutralize the enemy in the event of a conflict, America's global commitments meant that there was a shortage of military manpower, and the stationing of 45,000 troops in Korea was a drain on limited funds.[2] In January 1949 the U.S. XXIV Corps left Korea; by the end of June all remaining American forces had been removed. In order not to relinquish all responsibility for South Korea's security, the United States offered to organize, equip, and train a native "scout force," and promised military and economic aid.[3] Yet American policy statements at this time left the impression that South Korea was not worth defending. Most notably, Secretary of State Dean Acheson's remarks before the National Press Club on January 12, 1950, traced an American defense perimeter in Asia that did not include South Korea.[4]

On the morning of June 25, 1950, 80,000 North Korean soldiers supported by 150 T-34 tanks crossed the 38th parallel and invaded the South. American forces were hastily reinserted to prevent the loss of South Korea to Pyongyang's aggression. After three years of fighting and the additional intervention of Chinese forces on the side of the North, an Armistice Agreement was initialed on July 27, 1953.[5] The war left a divided Korea, split approximately along the 38th parallel, with the communist Democratic People's Republic of Korea (DPRK) in the north and an American-supported Republic of Korea (ROK) in the south.[6] Chinese troops based in North Korea after the war were withdrawn in 1958. American forces remained in South Korea, signifying the U.S. commitment to its independence and providing the confidence necessary to help restore the country after the war.

Given its precarious position on the southern end of the Korean peninsula, its overwhelming dependence on a single ally, its disruption after invasion and three years of civil war, and an irredentist and implacable opponent on its northern border, the ROK's overriding concern became the preservation of its territorial integrity. All subsequent events were thus filtered through the prism of South Korea's national security interests.

From this perspective, changes in the strategic environment of East Asia during the 1970s were cause for unease; Seoul's inability to exercise influence over any of these developments only heightened its sense of insecurity. In February 1972, President Richard Nixon reversed years of American policy and traveled to the People's Republic of China. One result of this opening was Washington's severing of diplomatic ties with Taiwan. Despite possible benefits accruing to South Korea from a more normal Sino-American relationship, the 1972 Shanghai Communiqué's treatment of the Taiwan issue was seen as especially ominous by the Seoul regime; the Communiqué appeared to condition Washington's continued support for Taipei on Peking's acquiescence. The parallels between Taiwan and the ROK were easily discernible—both were products of civil wars, devotees of American interests since the end of the 1940s, outposts holding forth against communist adversaries, and allies of the United States for over two decades. Similarly, America's retreat from Indochina was also viewed with consternation. Among the lessons derived by South Korea from the American experience in Vietnam were that being anticommunist was alone insufficient to guarantee American support, that in any case there were limits to Washington's assistance to an ally, and that ultimately Seoul had to cultivate domestic support and increase self-reliance. In December 1978, Washington and Peking normalized relations, a move that was anticipated in Tokyo by the signing of the Japan-PRC Treaty of Friendship and Cooperation four months earlier. South Korea's fear over this development was that either the United States or Japan would recognize the DPRK without Seoul's knowledge and without demanding reciprocal ROK recognition by China and the Soviet Union.

In a larger sense, this period marked a clear trend of American disengagement from direct involvement in Asian affairs, a development not reassuring to South Korea. In 1969, after only six months in office, President Nixon indicated a shift in American foreign policy toward the region. On July 25, on Guam Island, he delivered some informal remarks to newsmen regarding his upcoming trip to Asia. Nixon reaffirmed the sanctity of American treaty commitments with Asian allies, but, reflecting the growing domestic disenchantment with the conduct of the war in Indochina, went on to state that

as far as the problems of internal security are concerned, as far as the problems of military defense, except for the threat of a major power involving nuclear weapons, that the United States is going to encourage and has a right to expect that this problem will be increasingly handled by, and the responsibility for it taken by, the Asian allies themselves [sic].[7]

Known as the Nixon or Guam Doctrine, this declaration in effect expressed America's desire to lower its profile in Asia in order to avoid situations which had the potential to develop into future Vietnams. The United States would refrain from direct military involvement while it would stress greater self-reliance by the Asian countries in meeting their defense requirements. Washington's handling of the Taiwan issue, the evacuation from Vietnam, President Ford's Pacific Doctrine speech,[8] and the withdrawal of American air bases from Thailand were viewed as further evidence of a continuing isolationist element in American foreign policy.

The implications of the Nixon Doctrine for South Korea were soon evidenced by a reduction in the number of American military personnel based in the country. In 1970 the Nixon administration entered into negotiations with the ROK for the partial withdrawal of American forces. By the end of 1971, one of the two American combat divisions had been removed. By the end of 1973, a total of 24,000 troops had been withdrawn. As compensation to Seoul, and in order to satisfy the part of the Nixon Doctrine which promised military assistance, the United States authorized $1.5 billion over five years to modernize the South Korean armed forces. Yet American reliability was questioned by the failure to fulfill the aid program on time. An additional two years were required.[9]

As insurance against the United States quitting its commitment to South Korea's security, the Seoul regime undertook a two-pronged strategy. First, to counteract American retrenchment after Vietnam, South Korea embarked on an aggressive lobbying campaign in the United States. Korean nationals acting on Seoul's behalf threw lavish parties and bribed American legislators to induce them to continue congressional funding and military assistance to the ROK. News coverage of the resulting scandal, revealed by the press in October 1976 and termed "Koreagate," caused the type of negative publicity that its lobbying efforts had intended to prevent. When combined with earlier criticisms of human rights abuses in the ROK, it plunged Korean-American relations to its lowest point in over two decades.

Second, and more successful, was South Korea's efforts at military self-reliance. In mid-1975, soon after the fall of South Vietnam, President Park Chung Hee initiated an ambitious and expensive ($4 to $5 billion) Force Improvement Plan (FIP). Financed primarily by a new income tax surcharge enacted by the National Assembly, the plan increased the percentage of South Korea's gross national product devoted to defense from 5 percent to approximately 7.5 percent per year. The FIP included substantial increases in modern fighter aircraft (F-4Es and F-5Es), air defense improvements, upgraded tank forces, acquisition of TOW (tube-launched, optically tracked, wire-guided) antitank missiles, domestic production of artillery and small arms, and reportedly, an enhancement of logistics and war reserve munitions.[10]

The object of this defense preparedness was North Korea, "the most xenophobic, extremist, and militaristic of all communist states."[11] The only power in the region actively seeking to alter the status quo on the peninsula, North Korea's military forces were "configured largely for offensive operations."[12] According to U.S. government estimates, during the 1970s Pyongyang spent approximately 15 percent of its total gross national product on its military forces;[13] by the end of the decade it had amassed the sixth largest armed force in the world.

The DPRK was not averse to using its power to foment tensions in the South. On January 21, 1968, thirty-one North Korean commandos reached within a few hundred yards of the Blue House in an attempt to assassinate President Park. Two days later, North Korean patrol boats and submarine chasers attacked and captured the United States Navy electronic surveillance ship *Pueblo* outside the twelve mile international limit off the North Korean port of Wonsan; the U.S. naval captain and his men were imprisoned by Pyongyang for almost a year. Less than four months after the *Pueblo* crew had been released, on April 15, 1969, North Korean aircraft shot down an unarmed EC-121 while the reconnaissance plane was ninety miles off the North Korean coast over the Sea of Japan. Tensions abated slightly in 1971 when direct negotiations took place between North and South Korean Red Cross Societies. These were followed by talks at the political level, which resulted in the July 4, 1972, joint communiqué on peaceful reunification. Further meetings over the next year, however, failed to register progress on any of the outstanding issues dividing the two sides; the dialogue was suspended indefinitely by North Korea in August 1973. Two months earlier, President Park had recommended that dual membership in the United Nations for the two countries be regarded as an interim measure pending reunification. This approach was vehemently rejected by the North. Another assassination attempt on President Park was mounted by Pyongyang in 1974, missing the South Korean leader but killing his wife. Immediately after the fall of South Vietnam, North Korea's Kim Il-sung visited China and other socialist states in what was viewed as an attempt to raise support for the military reunification of the peninsula at a time of supposed American weakness and retreat from world affairs. In August 1976, North Korean soldiers axed and clubbed to death two American army officers in the demilitarized zone. During this time, a number of North Korean underground infiltration and invasion tunnels under the demilitarized zone were also discovered.[14]

Against this background, on March 9, 1977, President

Jimmy Carter announced plans to withdraw all remaining American troops from South Korea over a period of four to five years.[15] Washington would remove 26,000 soldiers in three phases by July 1982, leaving behind air force and naval support units. Approximately 9,000 noncombat army support personnel would also remain to man communications and to facilitate reentry if necessary. The estimated 1,000 American nuclear weapons in the country would be removed, since they were entrusted to those units slated for withdrawal.[16] For the Carter administration, the withdrawal scheme was a logical continuation of the past policies of the Nixon and Ford periods.[17] Consistent with the intent of the Nixon Doctrine, Washington would encourage ROK self-reliance in place of American ground forces by providing a military assistance program to modernize and expand the South Korean armed forces, especially the air and naval units.[18]

The Carter withdrawal plan was viewed quite differently by Seoul. American forces had liberated the country in 1945 and had been permanently garrisoned there since 1950. They were the physical embodiment of Washington's commitment to South Korea's independence and, by extension, to the defense of Japan and the overall balance of power in the region. Their withdrawal in 1949 was widely perceived to have been a major reason why North Korea had attacked the South, while their presence since the war was cited as a leading disincentive to another invasion. American claims that the ROK could rely on air power from U.S. forces still stationed on the peninsula and from the Seventh Fleet in the Pacific Ocean were unconvincing after the recent inability of overwhelming American air superiority to decide the outcome of the Vietnam War. Those with still longer memories recalled the failure of General Claire Chennault's Fourteenth Air Force to stem the Japanese advance in mainland China in the absence of effective ground support during the Second World War.[19]

As long as American ground units were based in South Korea, Washington's continued interest in the ROK's defense seemed secure. But with the scheduled departure of United

States combat forces, the precise language of America's defense commitment now assumed greater importance. Article III of the 1953 Mutual Defense Treaty stipulated:

Each Party recognizes that an armed attack on either of the Parties in the territories now under their respective administrative control, or hereafter recognized by one of the Parties as lawfully brought under the administrative control of the other, would be dangerous to its own peace and safety and declares that it would act to meet the common danger in accordance with its constitutional processes.[20]

The caveat "in accordance with its constitutional processes" was a less than automatic commitment of American power in the event of hostilities, not as strong a pledge as the wording of NATO's Article 5. With the rise of congressional influence in foreign affairs in the early 1970s, culminating in the 1973 War Powers Act, Seoul's fear was that the United States might deliberate before deciding whether or not to defend South Korea. Augmenting Seoul's insecurity on this score was the fact that a widely attributed rationale for the Carter withdrawal policy was that it would create flexibility for the American president by avoiding instantaneous U.S. involvement in any future conflict on the peninsula.

Coming in the wake of continuous North Korean provocations and arms buildup, the Carter withdrawal policy was attacked by domestic opponents and foreign critics, most notably Japan, as potentially destabilizing the balance of power on the peninsula. As a reaction to the removal of American ground troops and nuclear weapons, it was argued that Seoul might seek its own nuclear arsenal. Contributing to this concern were statements by South Korean officials implying ROK nuclear weapons development if the American nuclear umbrella was removed, and South Korea's earlier interest in obtaining a reprocessing facility from France. A U.S. government study of the withdrawal plan concluded that "there seems little doubt that the withdrawal of the [Second] division could substantially increase South Korea's incentive to acquire nuclear weapons."[21] Given this possibility, the withdrawal scheme appeared to place America's policy of encouraging greater South Korean self-reliance in conflict with another objective high on the Carter administration's foreign policy agenda, namely, preventing the spread of nuclear weapons.

TECHNICAL AND ECONOMIC OBSTACLES TO NUCLEAR WEAPONS

From one perspective, the ROK seemed an unlikely candidate to arouse proliferation concern; its nonproliferation credentials were impeccable. Seoul had signed an agreement with the IAEA for the application of safeguards in 1968. This was updated in 1972.[22] As a reflection of confidence in the ROK's peaceful nuclear intentions, a 1973 study of potential proliferators did not bother to include any discussion of South Korea.[23] The ROK was a party to both the Partial Test Ban Treaty and the Nonproliferation Treaty. Under the terms of a November 1975 agreement with the IAEA, all of the country's present and future nuclear installations operated under Agency safeguards. Seoul did not have direct access to either plutonium or enriched uranium suitable for weapons manufacture. Further, its bilateral Agreement for Cooperation with the United States for the peaceful uses of atomic energy contained explicit language prohibiting any use of American-supplied material for military purposes.[24] Canada's conditions for nuclear cooperation with South Korea were equally rigorous.

During the 1970s, however, South Korea exhibited considerable interest in developing a civilian nuclear power program.[25] Given its enthusiasm for rapid industrial advance, its desire for prestige projects to highlight the difference between North and South, its status as a client of the world's leading exporter of nuclear technology, and its lack of indigenous energy resources, it was not surprising that the ROK became interested in nuclear energy. Most importantly, South Korea's

SOUTH KOREA: CHRONOLOGY OF SIGNIFICANT EVENTS

Nuclear Developments		*Political Developments*
	1945	The Second World War ends with Soviet forces in the northern part of the Korean peninsula and American forces in the southern part
	1949	Removal of all U.S. troops from South Korea
	1950	Outbreak of the Korean War (June)
	1953	Armistice Agreement is signed (July)
		U.S.-ROK Mutual Defense Treaty is signed (October)
	1958	Withdrawal of PRC troops from North Korea
	1964	ROK ratifies the PTBT (July)
	1968	USS Pueblo attacked and captured by North Korea (January)
		ROK signs the NPT (July)
	1969	President Nixon announces the "Guam Doctrine" (July)
Work on 564-megawatt Kori 1 nuclear power reactor begins (September)	1970	Start of partial withdrawal of U.S. forces from ROK; as compensation, the U.S. authorizes $1.5 billion in military assistance
	1972	U.S.-PRC Shanghai Communiqué (February)
It is revealed that the ROK is negotiating with France for a reprocessing facility (June)	1975	ROK ratifies the NPT (April)
		Last U.S. personnel leave South Vietnam (April)
		President Park Initiates FIP
		President Park declares that ROK might develop nuclear weapons if the U.S. nuclear umbrella is removed (June)

SOUTH KOREA: CHRONOLOGY OF SIGNIFICANT EVENTS (Continued)

Nuclear Developments		Political Developments
U.S. pressures ROK into canceling its order for the French reprocessing facility (January)	1976	Two U.S. soldiers killed by North Korea in the DMZ (August)
		"Koreagate" scandal (October)
	1977	President Carter announces plan to withdraw all remaining U.S. ground forces from ROK over a 4 to 5-year period (March)
		Reports from Seoul that it might develop nuclear weapons if the U.S. nuclear umbrella is removed (May)
		ROK announces successful test-firing of domestically manufactured SSM with range of greater than 100 kilometers (September)
Kori 1 goes critical	1978	Congress is informed that earlier in the decade the ROK had initiated a covert scheme to acquire all the equipment necessary to build nuclear weapons
	1979	Leaked CIA study on ROK-DPRK military balance states that previous analyses had greatly underestimated North Korea's military strength (January)
		President Carter's withdrawal policy is suspended (July)
	1980	Reagan is elected president (November)

Note: This chronology omits the agreements on nuclear cooperation that the ROK signed with the U.S., and the ROK's agreements on safeguards application with the IAEA. For this information please consult the text.

dependence on Middle East oil supplies made nuclear power appear all the more attractive, despite having to import the technology. In the aftermath of the 1973 OPEC price rise, the ROK had only two weeks worth of oil reserves in the country. The government instituted a strict rationing formula which curbed operations of all ground, sea, and air transportation systems. By 1975, oil imports accounted for 55 percent of the country's total energy consumption, a figure that continued to rise through the end of the decade.[26] Domestic nuclear power generation was seen as a means of reducing this dependence and increasing self-reliance, a policy consistent with and complementary to the country's efforts in military affairs.

Work on the first South Korean nuclear power reactor commenced in September 1970. Kori 1, a Westinghouse light-water reactor with a generating capacity of 564 megawatts, was successfully tested on August 20, 1977, and was commercially operational the following year. Another light-water reactor and a CANDU heavy-water reactor were commissioned in 1977. The next year construction began on two more light-water reactors. These were scheduled to be brought on line in the early and mid-1980s.[27] In addition, South Korea possessed two small research reactors, TRIGA Mark II (250 kilowatts) and TRIGA Mark III (2 megawatts), as well as a small fuel fabrication plant. All uranium used for producing nuclear energy was purchased from the U.S. and Canada, and enriched by the U.S. Department of Energy.[28]

To construct nuclear weapons on its own, South Korea would have had to develop a workable weapons design, acquire delivery vehicles, and obtain nuclear material suitable for weapons manufacture. The first two requirements posed little problem. By the beginning of 1976, South Korea's scientists were viewed as already possessing the theoretical knowledge and technical expertise to build nuclear explosives.[29] For political reasons, though, Seoul might have found it difficult to test a nuclear device. If operating under this constraint, its scientists would have had to select a relatively simple weapons design and rely on laboratory simulation techniques to gauge its feasibility.

The choice of delivery vehicle would have derived from the mission to be performed and the size and weight of the nuclear explosive. Atomic demolition munitions would have been the simplest, as a primitive device would have served just as well as a sophisticated one, and there would have been no size or weight limitations. These could have been placed along the likely invasion corridors leading to Seoul. The most readily available air delivery systems were the American-manufactured F-4D/Es, whose range, speed, and payload were sufficient to transport a first-generation nuclear weapon, weighing 2,000 to 4,000 pounds. Short-range surface-to-surface missiles could have been used against battlefield targets if the nuclear device could have been miniaturized. The Honest John rocket was capable of delivering a nuclear weapon over 20 to 30 kilometers, and a 155-millimeter field artillery piece could also deliver a nuclear explosive. Both systems were in the South Korean inventory.[30] In late September 1977, Seoul announced that it had successfully test-fired domestically developed medium- and long-range ground-to-ground missiles with a range of greater than 100 kilometers.[31] From the United States, South Korea had already come to possess the Nike-Hercules missile. To strike Pyongyang, however, it would have required a booster stage or a more powerful engine.[32] The nuclear warhead would also have had to be miniaturized to 500 to 1,000 pounds and packaged to fit within the Nike nose cone.[33]

The most difficult hurdle for South Korea to surmount would have been acquiring the fissile material appropriate for nuclear weapons manufacture, either enriched uranium or separated plutonium. The lightly enriched uranium (approximately 3 percent U-235) used for Kori 1 would have been inadequate for nuclear weapons unless its purity could have been increased. If South Korea decided to construct its own enrichment plant, a gas centrifuge facility would have presented the fewest difficulties. Still, the scientific and engineering competence would have been of a high order, and it would have taken at least five years and cost a minimum of $100 million.[34]

Plutonium, on the other hand, appeared to be a more accessible source of bomb material. Although the two TRIGA research reactors were much too small to make a substantial contribution to nuclear weapons production,[35] plutonium in the spent fuel from South Korea's civilian nuclear energy program could have been recovered. The spent fuel from Kori 1 was stored nearby. If reprocessed, the plutonium from this reactor could have been used to manufacture 20 to 28 bombs a year with a yield of twenty kilotons each.[36]

The one technical obstacle preventing Seoul from pursuing this approach was a lack of means to chemically separate plutonium from the spent fuel. Two options were available. South Korea could have built its own reprocessing plant. This would have been easier, quicker, and cheaper than constructing a uranium enrichment facility. At a minimum, it would have entailed an investment of $51 million and taken at least four years.[37] This outlay would not have been unduly burdensome to the South Korean defense budget. Spread over a period of four years, it would have constituted less than 1 percent of South Korea's annual defense expenditures.[38] Alternatively, Seoul could have sidestepped the problems involved in building its own facility and purchased a reprocessing plant on the open market.

Whether solely for its civilian nuclear energy program or also for possible future use in constructing nuclear weapons, the ROK decided to acquire a reprocessing facility. In June 1975, it was revealed that South Korea had entered into negotiations with France for a reprocessing plant.[39] South Korea maintained that the technology was necessary to ensure greater energy security. It was also impressed by the claims made at the time of the economic savings to be realized from reprocessing. Undoubtedly, a sense of competitiveness with Japan, which already owned a reprocessing capability with its Tokai Mura plant, played a part. Furthermore, South Korea argued that under Article IV of the NPT, nonnuclear parties were promised "the fullest possible exchange of equipment." The sale of the reprocessing facility was approved by the French Foreign Ministry, but was called into question at a meeting of the Nuclear Suppliers Group. In the autumn of 1975, France renegotiated the agreement with South Korea to include a clause on the nonreplication of equipment for a period of twenty years. Seoul accepted this condition; on September 22, 1975, a safeguards agreement among the IAEA, France, and the ROK entered into force.[40]

At this point, the United States belatedly raised its voice in opposition to the sale, on the basis that South Korea might use the reprocessing plant to produce weapons-grade plutonium. The proposed facility would have been capable of separating the plutonium from 50 to 100 metric tons of spent fuel per year, thereby providing approximately two hundred kilograms of bomb-grade material annually.[41] Although the ROK was a party to the NPT, the circumstances surrounding its ratification in April 1975 did not inspire confidence in South Korean good faith. For one, there was no indication of widespread support for the treaty among the government bureaucracy or populace at large. Also, a government statement at the time of ratification appeared to condition South Korea's membership on American support for its safety from nuclear threat and aggression.[42] Moreover, the timing of ROK ratification, almost seven years after signing the treaty, raised doubts about Seoul's sincerity and commitment to nonproliferation. Directly prior to ratification, South Korea was actively negotiating with France for a reprocessing plant. Considering that South Korea did not have a single working nuclear power reactor at the time, so advanced a technology seemed premature for the country's civilian nuclear energy needs. Ratification was viewed by skeptics as merely an opportune way to silence objections to the proposed sale. Moreover, ROK accession to the NPT was only taken after considerable pressure from the U.S. State Department and Congress. Ratification followed shortly after a joint congressional resolution was introduced requesting that the Export-Import Bank defer approval of financing the second South Korean nuclear power reactor.[43] In late 1975, the United States informed Seoul that fulfillment of the contract for the reprocessing facility would result in Washington withholding financial credits for the South Korean nuclear power industry and in Canada holding up its scheduled sale of a heavy-water reactor. Further, the U.S. told Seoul that the proposed deal would "jeopardize" the Korean-American security relationship.[44] Under this pressure, South Korea canceled the order.

Even without a reprocessing plant, speculation still centered on a possible nuclear weapons option for the ROK. National security was the incentive most often cited by observers for Seoul's acquiring nuclear arms. Given memories of the Korean War, an inferiority in the conventional balance of forces on the peninsula, and Pyongyang's perpetual hostility, nuclear weapons were thought to be attractive to South Korea in order to deter an attack by the North if U.S. nuclear weapons were no longer available.[45]

Fueling conjecture of a possible ROK nuclear weapons development program were official and semiofficial pronouncements emanating from South Korea. Lightly veiled hints that Seoul was seriously contemplating nuclear weapons acquisition were intermixed with statements pledging fidelity to the principle of nonproliferation. The overall message from these comments was that South Korea was capable of constructing nuclear devices but that it would not do so unless America's nuclear commitment to the country was removed. Implicitly, these statements acknowledged a belief that nuclear armaments were a deterrent to North Korean aggression and were therefore necessary for South Korea's defense.

Less than a month and a half after ratifying the Nonproliferation Treaty, on June 12, 1975, President Park was quoted as declaring that "If the U.S. nuclear umbrella were to be removed, we have to start developing our nuclear capability."[46] Three days later, a member of the opposition party who was visiting the United States commented that "we are capable of developing nuclear weapons whenever we want to," but admitted to there being no plans at the present time.[47] On June 27, President Park told an American journalist that South Korea would do everything in its power to defend its national security, including the development of nuclear weapons, if the United States nuclear umbrella was removed. He added, however, that "We have no plan or active research at this time for development of weapons in that field."[48] A few days earlier, Canada's external affairs secretary, in Seoul to finalize a bilateral agreement on the sale of civilian nuclear power equipment, had related at a press conference that President Park had assured him that nuclear weapons would not be in South Korea's interest because the Soviet Union and China were nuclear powers.[49] In November 1975, the ROK defense minister testified before the National Assembly that South Korea did not intend to build nuclear arms and that its nuclear energy program would be used only for peaceful purposes.[50] In January 1977, President Park unequivocally declared that South Korea would not seek a national nuclear force.[51]

After President Carter's March 1977 announcement of American troop withdrawals, South Korean statements on nuclear weapons acquisition again became threatening. In late May 1977, less than two weeks after the senior U.S. State Department official responsible for the region outlined the administration's plans to completely withdraw all nuclear weapons from the country, and coinciding with the first round of Korean-American consultations on the phase-out of American military forces, a senior South Korean government source stated that South Korea might develop its own nuclear armaments in order to safeguard its security if the United States removed its nuclear weapons. Another ROK government source was quoted at the same time as emphasizing the importance of nuclear weapons as a deterrent to North Korea, and asserting that South Korea would take whatever measures were necessary to ensure its survival.[52] The following month, Foreign Minister Tong-jin Park declared in the National Assembly that South Korea would reserve final judgment on nuclear weapons development "if it is necessary for national security interests and people's safety."[53] In April 1978, a report released by the National Unification Board expressed its support for South Korean nuclear weapons development. Nuclear weapons, the study maintained, were useful for political deterrence, military deterrence, and as compensation for the withdrawal of American forces.[54] Moreover, statements at this time concerning the country's civilian nuclear power program were also unsettling. In August 1977, the Ministry of Science and Technology announced plans to domestically produce nuclear fuel.[55] And in June the following year, the Ministry released a schedule for the construction of forty nuclear power plants by the year 2000,[56] a projection more ambitious than the country's future energy requirements would have seemed to warrant.

NUCLEAR WEAPONS AND POLICY OBJECTIVES

With a hostile and powerful adversary to its immediate north, the withdrawal of American troops beginning in the early 1970s and scheduled to accelerate under the Carter administration plan, American emphasis on tactical nuclear weapons for defense, most notably in the Schlesinger targeting doctrine in mid-decade, a proven scientific and technological competence, and a proclaimed interest in nuclear armaments for safeguarding its independence, South Korea certainly appeared to possess the capability and incentive to acquire nuclear weapons. Before taking this step, however, Seoul would have had to calculate how well a nuclear arsenal would have promoted its domestic and foreign policy objectives.

Broadly speaking, South Korea's domestic concerns during this period were twofold: to ensure political stability and to encourage economic growth. These goals were symbiotic; political tranquility would provide an environment attractive to investors, and a rising standard of living would help mollify internal discontent. It is uncertain whether or not nuclear weapons development would have aided South Korea in achieving either of these objectives, while it is possible that it would have been detrimental to these ends. Due to official censorship on all but the most mundane military matters, the South Korean public was generally unaware or uninformed regarding nuclear weapons. It would not have been difficult for the government to lead public opinion. By arguing that nuclear armaments were necessary to defend the country from North Korea, the regime could have even enhanced its prestige.[57] Yet nuclear weapons were hardly needed to rally national unity. South Korea was ethnically and linguistically homogeneous, and possessed a long tradition of obedience to a strong central authority.[58] The instruments of national control were already firmly in the hands of the government, especially after President Park's revision of the constitution in 1972. And, always, a sense of national solidarity was provided by the constant threat posed by North Korea.

Moreover, South Korea's rapid economic expansion during the 1960s and 1970s was due in large measure to attracting foreign capital and to a thriving export industry. The economic risk of developing nuclear weapons for the ROK would have been the possibility of antagonizing overseas investors, primarily Japan and the United States, or importers of South Korean goods. Japan and the U.S. might have reacted by curtailing, suspending, or withdrawing their investments in the country, or by boycotting South Korean products. Even a partial move in these directions would have been devastating to the South Korean economy. From 1972 to 1976, the ROK gross national product rose at an average annual rate of 10.2 percent.[59] During this period, Japan and the United States invested over $483 million in South Korea, or 85 percent of all direct foreign investment.[60] Further, by the end of 1979, Seoul had accumulated an external debt of $20 billion, the bulk of which was owed to American and Japanese banks.[61] Foreclosure on the loans or even the imposition of higher interest rates were two measures which would have hurt South Korea's international credit standing and placed a potentially crippling burden on the economy.

To be sure, there were actions open to Seoul to counteract the financial pressures that might have been brought to bear.

Historically, economic sanctions have not met with overwhelming success.[62] Unless ordered by their governments, American and Japanese banks would have been reluctant to interfere with traditional banking transactions. South Korea might have threatened to nationalize foreign investments in order to induce a continued money supply. In addition, Seoul might have sought alternative investors, perhaps by offering concessionary terms, in countries less concerned about nuclear proliferation. Or South Korea might simply have hoped that the international reaction to its developing nuclear weapons would have been as inconsequential as the response to India's 1974 test.

South Korean development of nuclear armaments, if aided by unauthorized use of fuel or facilities, would have entailed the abrogation of its treaty obligations to the United States, Canada, and the IAEA. The likely result would have been the cutoff of nuclear fuel and equipment, and the paralysis of South Korea's civilian nuclear energy program.[63] Yet this threat would have been most effective only after 1978, when Kori 1 began its commercial operation. To reduce the impact of the termination of nuclear cooperation, South Korea could have continued to rely on oil imports, diversifying its suppliers and improving relations with the Persian Gulf states, a diplomatic policy which Seoul in fact adopted after the 1973 oil price increase. To minimize adverse world opinion, the ROK could have cited Article X of the Nonproliferation Treaty as the basis for its withdrawal, arguing that the removal of U.S. troops had constituted an "extraordinary event" that "jeopardized the supreme interests" of the country.

The major economic consideration for Seoul would therefore have been gauging the willingness of Japan and the United States to use their financial leverage to disrupt the ROK economy. While South Korea could have adopted measures to insulate itself, or even have hoped that sanctions would not be implemented, the consequences of miscalculation would have been enormous. Not only would such a policy have jeopardized the impressive economic progress recorded during the previous two decades, it would have also risked creating economic hardship which would in turn have given rise to increased domestic unrest, thereby offering a more vulnerable target of opportunity for North Korea.

Even more compelling than these domestic considerations for a decision to acquire nuclear weapons would have been South Korea's foreign policy objectives, in particular those relating to national security, and the extent to which they would have been furthered or frustrated. The ROK's primary concern throughout its brief history was to defend itself from invasion from the North. The different means to achieve this end were (1) to preserve the military balance in order to deter conflict and (2) to stablize the partition of the country by diplomatic means in a manner that lowered tensions between North and South. The development of nuclear weapons by South Korea would have affected both these approaches. It would have caused a number of repercussions in South Korea's relations with the U.S., North Korea, the Soviet Union, and China, and possibly resulted in the adoption of countermeasures detrimental to the country's security.

Despite having almost as much territory and over twice as many people as the North, South Korea was the inferior military power. To rectify this imbalance and safeguard its security, Seoul's central foreign policy objective since the Korean War had been to tie America's military strength to the defense of the ROK. The acquisition of nuclear weapons by South Korea would have placed this commitment at risk. Much would have depended upon when the South Korean program was uncovered. If still in the development stage, Washington's reaction would likely have been to threaten to terminate its military support unless the ROK ceased its activities; in essence, this is what the U.S. conveyed to Seoul concerning the purchase of the French reprocessing plant. If South Korea had already advanced to the testing stage or accumulated a small inventory of nuclear devices, the U.S. would probably have withdrawn its forces immediately from the South, on the grounds that Seoul had violated a tacit understanding in their relationship and that the situation on the peninsula with a nuclear-armed South

Korea was too volatile for an American presence. Less likely, especially in the wake of expected congressional outrage, would have been a policy of increased reassurance to the ROK of the American defense commitment.[64] This would have entailed the continued basing of U.S. forces in the country, perhaps with an increase in military assistance, as a means of dissuading Seoul from proceeding from development to testing, or from testing to the deployment of an operational nuclear weapons system.

South Korea's calculations would have centered on the value it attached to the U.S. military commitment, as expressed concretely in the number and mission of American troops stationed in the country, and, more abstractly, in the credibility of Washington's promise to intervene in the event of a major conflict. This equation would have been reevaluated after the 1977 Carter withdrawal policy. Seoul might then have decided that if U.S. ground forces and nuclear weapons would be removed regardless of any action on its part, there would be less inhibition to acquisition. The remaining American air and naval units might not have been viewed as sufficient reason to forgo an independent nuclear arsenal.

Yet an ROK nuclear weapons program would have risked placing the country in a position where it had neither nuclear arms nor the American commitment. If Washington removed its support before Seoul possessed an adequate nuclear deterrent force, there would have been an increase in political tensions on the peninsula along with an erosion of the military balance. Under these circumstances, the result would have been a weakening of South Korea's overall conventional defense without the possibility of relying on nuclear weapons for deterrence. If the breach with the United States occurred early in the ROK development program it could have left South Korea vulnerable for a number of years. Despite impressive improvements in South Korea's conventional defenses under the Force Improvement Plan during the latter half of the 1970s, these were negated to a large extent by North Korea's upgrading of its military capabilities during this period.

However, it is possible that South Korea might have believed that its conventional strength was adequate to deter the North without American support until the actual deployment of an operational nuclear force. As early as 1975, one American analyst suggested that the ROK might be able to defend itself, without U.S. assistance, against a North Korean invasion.[65] In August 1975, President Park declared that the ROK, without American ground forces, was capable at that time of repelling a North Korean attack, if it was launched without Soviet or Chinese aid. In five years time, Park maintained, South Korea would not require U.S. ground, air, naval, or logistical support in order to defend itself from the North.[66] In January 1977, the South Korean leader remarked that "in terms of combat capabilities, the ROK is almost on a level with the North."[67]

The most likely scenario facing South Korean defense planners would have been a North Korean blitzkrieg across the demilitarized zone, through the Chorwon valley and Kaesung-Munsan corridors, toward Seoul, thirty-five kilometers distant. Such an attack could have taken place with little warning time, "at most 12 to 18 hours."[68] Because of Seoul's strategic importance, South Korea would not have had the option of trading space for stronger defensive positions. Nevertheless, the task of halting the North Korean invasion could have been performed by conventional armaments. One American study maintained that, "when adequately supplied, the 2,000 large ROK guns have a daily firing potential approximately equal to thirty 40 KT weapons and perhaps several times that number if cluster munitions are used." The study also argued that the three missions for the nuclear defense of South Korea—to cut off the advance of a division, to destroy parts of the enemy force in the invasion corridors, and to cut off forces for destruction by conventional weapons—could be accomplished by reliance solely on conventional munitions with no loss of effectiveness.[69]

Paradoxically, then, if South Korea believed that its conventional capabilities were sufficient to repel an attack by the North, nuclear weapons development was unnecessary. In this case, while the American presence provided an extra measure of firepower to the ROK's defense in the event of widespread hostilities, its primary function was political—to deter DPRK aggression in the first place. The U.S. military presence was a major factor contributing to the absence of full-scale hostilities since 1953. Although the ROK would have emerged victorious in a war with the North, an invasion would have been extremely costly in men and material, while the postwar recovery would have taken years. On the other hand, if Seoul in fact did not have adequate confidence in its military establishment, the retention of even limited numbers of U.S. forces was a military necessity, as of course would have been American reinforcements during a conflict. The American tactical fighter wing that would have remained in South Korea would have helped redress the ROK's inferiority in air power versus the DPRK. At the operational level, a rupture in relations with the United States would have meant that the ROK armed forces would have had to rely on their own limited stockpiles of replacements and spare parts during a war.[70] In either case, whether for deterrence or defense, an American presence would have been valuable for communicating a continued U.S. interest in South Korea's security, while symbolizing Washington's commitment to defending the country's sovereignty and territorial integrity. It is unlikely that Seoul would have been so sanguine about the prospects for stability on the peninsula that it was willing to completely discontinue its alliance with the U.S. in return for its own nuclear weapons program. Only if South Korea could have developed nuclear arms with American consent would its security have been enhanced and U.S.-ROK relations not jeopardized. Unfortunately for Seoul, this was one option that was not open to it.

The reaction of North Korea, like that of the United States, would have depended on how far the ROK nuclear weapons program had advanced. If nuclear weapons were not fully deployed, Pyongyang would have been tempted to eliminate the threat, possibly combining a preventive strike against the ROK nuclear facilities with a full-scale invasion. Some circles in the north would likely have pressed for a similar nuclear weapons program.[71] If a viable South Korean nuclear force was presented as a *fait accompli*, however, it ironically might have comprised a more credible deterrent than American nuclear weapons, because of the perception that Seoul would seemingly have operated under fewer inhibitions concerning nuclear weapons use than Washington. While it would have taken some years for South Korea to achieve the technical sophistication of U.S. nuclear arms, even a small inventory of relatively primitive, first-generation nuclear bombs might have been enough to deter the North.[72] The DPRK could not have been certain that an isolated South Korea would have exercised the same degree of self-restraint as the United States. Despite the possibility of having to carry out its threat against ostensible compatriots, the deterrent effect of South Korea's nuclear arsenal might thus have been stronger than that of the American tactical nuclear weapons stationed in the country.

In addition, the ROK would have had to consider the responses of China and the Soviet Union. The influence of Peking and Moscow over Pyongyang's behavior was thought to be one factor contributing to the lack of major conflict on the peninsula. For both China and the Soviet Union, the preservation of the status quo was tolerable; it was a preferred alternative to either a unified noncommunist Korea tied to the West, or a unified communist Korea allied to the other.[73] There was even some indication that some time in late 1978 China had provided information to the United States on the North Korean order of battle in order to persuade the Carter administration to cancel its plans for troop withdrawals. This information subsequently formed the basis of a top-secret CIA study which stated that the armed forces of the Pyongyang regime had been underestimated in previous analyses. In early January 1979, the results of this intelligence report were leaked to the press, provoking a new round of criticism of the American withdrawal scheme.[74]

It was also possible, though unlikely, that China and the Soviet Union would have viewed a South Korean nuclear arsenal as a form of compensation for the absence of American forces, and therefore as a means of restoring the military balance. Alternatively, Moscow or Peking could have decided to aid Pyongyang with its own nuclear development program.[75] Nuclear armaments in the North and South would then have risked an escalation in destruction on both sides of the demilitarized zone should war have erupted. Another option open to either China or the Soviet Union would have been to destroy in a preventive strike a nascent or modest ROK nuclear force, or to assist North Korea with this mission.[76] However, South Korea might have derived some comfort from the fact that Moscow had refrained from bombing China's fledgling nuclear force in the late 1960s.

From the perspective of South Korea, then, it is difficult to see how nuclear arms would have promoted domestic or foreign policy objectives. In domestic affairs, a nuclear weapons program might have jeopardized the substantial economic contribution of Japan and the United States to the ROK. More importantly, in foreign affairs, the development of nuclear weapons would have placed at risk the existing American military commitment. Depending on the timing, South Korea might have been left without America's conventional and nuclear strength, and without any nuclear weapons of its own. It would have chanced provoking a North Korean preventive response, and countermeasures by China and the Soviet Union. And it was not certain that nuclear weapons would have provided South Korea with a defensive capability superior to its reliance on purely conventional munitions. In sum, by the development and acquisition of nuclear arms, the ROK would have risked arresting its economic development, ending its military relationship with the U.S., and therefore reducing its security versus the North. It is far from clear that the benefits which would have accrued to South Korea would have been worth the gamble.

CONCLUSION

If there were few arguments compelling Seoul toward nuclear weapons acquisition, how can the South Korean statements expressing their appeal best be explained? To be fair, there probably was genuine interest in nuclear armaments from some quarters of the military. A nuclear weapons arsenal might superficially have appeared as the answer to the country's national security problems. It could have been argued that a national nuclear force would have enhanced Seoul's influence with Washington, in a manner similar to how Britain's nuclear force strengthened London's voice in Anglo-American relations. It is plausible that Seoul may have also wanted to keep open the option of acquiring nuclear weapons at some later date, as a hedge against unforeseen developments on the peninsula or a rupture in its relations with the United States. Policy pronouncements from Seoul could then be interpreted as veiled warnings to Pyongyang to moderate its revisionist tendencies, or as tests of American and world opinion on the prospect of a nuclear-armed South Korea.

With the absence of official statements from Seoul on the subject and without access to South Korean government documents, it is difficult to divine the precise intentions of the ROK leadership. An alternative source of information is the recollections of American officials. Curiously, the memoirs of President Carter and of his national security advisor, Zbigniew Brzezinski, contain no mention of the troop withdrawal affair.[77] Secretary of State Cyrus Vance's account mentions congressional opposition to the withdrawal scheme and the influence of the leaked CIA study, but provides little analysis of the administration's reasoning behind the policy reversal.[78]

Examination of Seoul's intentions and the full range of Washington's motivations must be based on inference and informed speculation. However, it is possible to look at the consequences of South Korea's behavior on its relations with the United States. A publicly proclaimed American policy to remove its ground forces and nuclear weapons from the ROK elicited a series of ambiguous statements from South Korea strongly hinting at nuclear weapons acquisition. The United States subsequently canceled its original plans and maintained its military presence. Viewed in this manner, South Korean pronouncements on possible nuclear weapons acquisition were directed squarely at Washington's sensitivity on the subject of nuclear proliferation. U.S. concern on this issue had been evidenced throughout the decade, as Washington had made clear its desire that South Korea not develop nuclear arms, nor be seen to be moving in that direction. For this reason, the U.S. told Seoul to cancel its deal with France, even though the reprocessing plant would have been subject to IAEA safeguards. Earlier in the decade there were some indications that the ROK had initiated a scheme to acquire covertly the equipment necessary for producing nuclear weapons. The United States reportedly intervened to prevent South Korea from proceeding.[79] By playing on this proliferation concern, South Korean statements were designed to provoke a strong American response, not only of criticism, but also, and more importantly from Seoul's vantage point, of a continued U.S. commitment to South Korea's security. In effect, the ROK was sending the simple message to Washington that the price of South Korea's nuclear abstention was the retention of the American military presence in the country.

The content and timing of South Korea's nuclear hints reinforces this reasoning. The specific objectives of a nuclear force were left ill-defined, suggesting the absence of a carefully conceived and predetermined nuclear strategy. These statements were also most prominent at times when Seoul perceived its security to be most imperiled, namely after the collapse of South Vietnam and after the announcement of President Carter's withdrawal plan. The attempt to purchase a reprocessing facility from France, even though unsuccessful, and the exaggerated claims made for South Korea's civilian nuclear energy program, can be viewed as alternative means of Seoul's "nuclear diplomacy." To be sure, other factors, such as congressional and other domestic opposition to the withdrawal scheme, the impact of the CIA intelligence estimate, strong criticism by Japan, and perhaps an independent change of heart by the administration, were also partly responsible for the policy reversal. Yet South Korea's actions increased the credibility of its threat to acquire nuclear weapons, and hence its leverage vis-à-vis the United States. In other words, at a time of American retreat from Asia, Seoul reminded Washington of the possible deleterious consequences of removing its military support from the South. Not surprisingly, after the suspension of the Carter withdrawal plan in July 1979, there were no more public statements by South Korea on possible nuclear armaments acquisition.[80]

In retrospect, it appears that the withdrawal of American nuclear weapons generated the greatest amount of concern among the Seoul leadership. The statements from 1975 to 1978 suggesting South Korea's development of an independent nuclear force conditioned this event on the removal of the American nuclear umbrella. American nuclear weapons, rather than U.S. combat troops, were viewed by Seoul as the ultimate guarantor of South Korea's security.

Yet there is evidence to suggest that this was not the case. Undoubtedly, Seoul's preference during this period was to retain both American ground troops and nuclear weapons in the country. But it is likely that it perceived U.S. conventional strength as more credible—as a symbol of American commitment, as a deterrent and defense against the North, and as reassurance for the South—than tactical nuclear weapons. Evidence for this rests in the fact that the withdrawal of nuclear weapons from South Korea was carried out after the July 1979 suspension. While the Second Division continued to be based in the South, by May 1983 there were only four American nuclear weapons left in the country.[81] Still, there were no outward signs of dissatisfaction from Seoul, nor were there any comments in the press which expressed South Korean interest in acquiring nuclear arms. Thus while Seoul's declaratory policy emphasized the importance of U.S. nuclear weapons, operational policy seemed more concerned with the retention of American ground forces.

To the question, "Why did South Korea not develop nuclear weapons?," a simple answer might be that it never had the fissile material required for nuclear weapons manufacture. Yet even if the ROK had possessed a sufficient amount of weapons-grade uranium or plutonium, it is not clear that Seoul would have produced nuclear explosives. The actual development of nuclear arms by South Korea would not have realized Seoul's primary goal of retaining American military forces in the country, and might have jeopardized any residual American links with South Korea if U.S. forces were removed. Rather, South Korea's preference would have been to use the *threat* of an ROK nuclear arsenal in order to persuade Washington to maintain its conventional and nuclear forces in the South. Failing that, Seoul would have been satisfied with an American conventional presence. If this too proved impossible to achieve, even American nuclear weapons positioned in South Korea with a token American presence would have been seen as preferable to an ROK nuclear force. Due to possible economic sanctions and adverse international ramifications, only after these other alternatives had been exhausted might Seoul have decided to develop its own nuclear arsenal.

President Carter's reelection defeat in November 1980 ensured that the withdrawal scheme would not be resurrected. President Reagan was personally opposed to the idea, and moved immediately to reassure the ROK that the United States was a trusted and faithful ally. Only a few weeks after the inauguration, Reagan hosted South Korean President Chun Doo Hwan, and told him that Washington had no plans to withdraw American ground forces from his country. To remove an incentive for South Korea to independently develop or acquire unsafeguarded nuclear technology for its nuclear power program that would also have military applications, Reagan stated that the United States would be "a reliable supplier of nuclear fuel, generation equipment, and power technology."[82]

By using the threat to develop nuclear weapons, the ROK was able to reverse America's troop withdrawal policy. Seoul realized this foreign policy success by escalating the stakes involved to encompass the vision of a nuclear-equipped South

Korea. At this level, Washington was unwilling to test Seoul's ultimate intentions, even if it appeared that nuclear weapons would have been detrimental to the ROK's own best interests. Forced to decide between enhancing its national security on the one hand, and having the power of independent choice over war and peace on the other, South Korea elected to bind itself to the United States and to reject national nuclear armaments.

4.

Japan

The end of the Second World War left Japan militarily defeated, economically devastated, and spiritually demoralized. Japan's policy of postwar recovery had three components: to regain its sovereignty from the American military occupation authorities, to ensure its security, and to rehabilitate itself as a leading member of the world community. The first objective was realized by a multilateral peace treaty, which entered into force on April 28, 1952. A security agreement with Washington at the same time satisfied Tokyo's second goal; it relieved Japan of assuming the burden of its external defense, and aligned the country's future security with the military strength of the United States.

Japan's relatively rapid attainment of the peace and security treaties released energy and talent which contributed to the accomplishment of its third objective: the steady accumulation of economic and diplomatic successes through the next four decades. By the mid-1960s, Japan had become an indispensible partner in international financial and commercial transactions; by the end of the decade it had the world's third largest gross national product. The growth of Japanese influence in world affairs was recognized by President Nixon, who suggested in 1973 that the U.N. Charter be modified to allow Japan a permanent seat on the Security Council. The Sino-Japanese relationship, which had been normalized in 1972, was consolidated in 1978 by a Peace and Friendship Treaty. By the end of the 1970s, Japan had surpassed the Soviet Union as the world's second ranking economic power. In September 1984, Prime Minister Nakasone delivered the International Institute for Strategic Studies annual lecture, on "Japan's Choice: A Strategy for World Peace and Prosperity." Its significance lay less with the substance of the speech than with the symbolism of a Japanese leader expounding a global vision for his country.

These economic and diplomatic accomplishments led numerous observers to examine the determinants supporting Japan's postwar resurgence. This, in turn, focused attention on the country's defense policy, and generated speculation concerning the prospect of a military posture commensurate with Japan's status in other fields. Some studies suggested that Tokyo was likely to develop nuclear weapons. This conclusion was based on the historical precedent of great military power deriving from great economic power,[1] or on Japan's desire to engage successfully in "competitive power politics in Asia" against a nuclear-armed China.[2] Other analysts maintained that Tokyo's acquisition of nuclear armaments was a possibility, due to "nationalism and self-respect, in addition to anxiety for its own security,"[3] or to deter attack by China.[4] The overwhelming body of opinion, however, argued that a Japanese nuclear weapons program was unlikely, and would be undertaken only as a last resort.[5] Japanese public opinion, domestic political considerations, legal constraints, and strategic concerns were all cited as factors inhibiting nuclear weapons acquisition.

JAPAN'S CIVILIAN NUCLEAR ENERGY PROGRAM

A major stimulus to speculation over Japan's nuclear intentions was the pace and sophistication of its nuclear power industry;

JAPAN: CHRONOLOGY OF SIGNIFICANT EVENTS

Nuclear Developments		*Political Developments*
	1945	U.S. drops nuclear bombs on Hiroshima and Nagasaki (August)
	1947	Japanese Constitution becomes law
	1952	Multilateral peace treaty, and U.S. and Japan security agreement, enter into force (April)
	1954	*Lucky Dragon* incident (March)
Japan Atomic Energy Commission is created	1955	*Gensuikyo* is formed (September)
Japan's Atomic Energy Basic Law is enacted (December)		
	1956	Japan and the USSR agree to a normalization of diplomatic relations (October)
	1960	Revised U.S.-Japan security treaty enters into force (June)
First Japanese-made nuclear research reactor goes critical	1962	
	1964	Japan ratifies the PTBT (June)
		PRC detonates its first nuclear device (October)
	1965	Japan normalizes relations with South Korea
Japan's first commercial nuclear power plant begins operations	1966	
	1967	Prime Minister Sato announces the policy of three nonnuclear principles
	1969	Japan has the world's third largest GNP
	1970	Japan signs the NPT (February)

JAPAN: CHRONOLOGY OF SIGNIFICANT EVENTS (*Continued*)

Nuclear Developments		*Political Developments*
		Japan launches its first satellite, using a solid-fuel propellant (February)
		U.S.-Japan security treaty is extended (June)
		First edition of *Defense of Japan* is published; it states that nuclear weapons acquisition is "permissable" under the Constitution but will not be attempted at the present time (October)
Work on the Tokai Mura pilot reprocessing plant is started (June)	1971	The Model Agreement on IAEA operating procedures (the "Blue Book") is produced (March)
		The three Nixon "shocks"
		The three nonnuclear principles are officially approved in a Diet resolution (November)
	1972	Nixon travels to the PRC (February)
		Okinawa reverts to Japanese control
		Japan and the PRC establish diplomatic relations (September)
Nuclear ship *Mutsu* becomes operational (August)	1974	USAEC suspends the signing of long-term uranium enrichment contracts (July)
		Rear Admiral LaRocque testifies before Congress that U.S. ships do not off-load their nuclear weapons before entering Japanese ports (September)
	1975	Japan reaches an agreement with the IAEA which as-

JAPAN: CHRONOLOGY OF SIGNIFICANT EVENTS (Continued)

Nuclear Developments		Political Developments
		sures Japan equality with Euratom's inspection procedures (February)
		Joint U.S.-Japan Subcommittee for Defense Cooperation is established (August)
	1976	Japan ratifies the NPT (June)
Tokai Mura reprocessing is plant ready to begin operations; difficulties with the U.S. over the recycling of nuclear fuel ends with an agreement that allows Japan to reprocess limited amounts of spent fuel	1977	
	1978	USSR places a division of ground forces equipped with tanks and artillery on Kunashiri, Etorofu, and Shikotan islands
Nongyo-Tohge pilot enrichment plant produces 300 kilograms of 3.2 percent U-235	1979	
	1980	Defense of Japan states that the USSR is "an increasing potential threat to the security of Japan"
U.S. and Japan agree that Japan can operate Tokai Mura at full capacity through 1984 (October)	1981	Former U.S. Ambassador to Japan Reischauer states in an interview with a Japanese newspaper that since 1960 U.S. ships with nuclear weapons on board have been permitted by Tokyo to transit and dock in Japan (May)

Note: This chronology omits agreements on nuclear cooperation that Japan signed with the U.S., and Japan's agreements on safeguards application with the IAEA. For this information please consult the text.

Tokyo has long had the scientific expertise and technological capability necessary to construct nuclear armaments. By the early 1980s, Japan's nuclear energy industry had become one of the most advanced and ambitious in the world.

Japan's civilian nuclear energy program[6] was initially encouraged by Washington's Atoms for Peace policy. It was also stimulated by Tokyo's belief at the time that the introduction of nuclear power would provide a reliable and inexpensive source of electricity, a necessary ingredient for the anticipated economic recovery, as well as diversification of energy supplies from the country's heavy dependence on imported oil, a point underscored by the 1956 Suez crisis. With the assistance of an Atoms for Peace program grant, the first Japanese nuclear reactor, a 10-megawatt research facility, went critical that same year. In 1958, the United States and Japan signed an Agreement for Cooperation for the supply of nuclear materials and technology.[7]

From 1956 to 1965 roughly $500 million was spent on nuclear power development in Japan. By March 1965, eight nuclear research reactors had gone critical, including the first Japanese-made research reactor in 1962.[8] At this time there existed almost 11,000 "technical experts" on nuclear power in the country. The first reactor to generate electrical power, the 12-megawatt Japan Power Demonstration Reactor, became operational in 1963. The first commercial nuclear power plant, a 166-megawatt British natural uranium gas-cooled reactor, started operations in July 1966.[9] Despite having only this one operational commercial reactor, Tokyo's optimism was reflected in the JAEC's revised 1967 *Long-Range Program for Development and Utilization of Atomic Energy*, which predicted an installed nuclear generating capacity of 30,000 to 40,000 megawatts by 1985.[10] However, due to difficulties in plant siting, construction, and operation, as well as substantial public opposition to nuclear power, the number of nuclear reactors in operation lagged behind schedule.[11] Still, by June 1984, over 18,000 megawatts of electricity was being generated by twenty-five nuclear power facilities, with a further twelve plants on order.[12]

Japan's desire to develop a complete nuclear fuel cycle to better ensure security was further spurred by two events in the early 1970s. The 1973 OPEC crisis caught Japan with less than five months' supply of oil, and exposed the fragile underpinnings of the country's impressive economic performance. Second, the United States Atomic Energy Commission in 1973 abruptly revised its criteria for ordering uranium enrichment services. This action was followed by its July 1974 decision to suspend the signing of long-term uranium enrichment contracts. Possessing only an estimated 8,000 metric tons of natural uranium,[13] Tokyo prudently moved to enhance its supply security by diversifying its sources.[14] In order to obtain the most efficient utilization of uranium, to facilitate the safe storage of radioactive waste, and to remain competitive in the nuclear industry, Japan also planned to acquire a domestic reprocessing capability in order to obtain separated fuel for recycle in nuclear power plants, to develop uranium enrichment technology in order to refine natural uranium as fuel for thermal reactors, and to construct fast breeder reactors (FRBs), which would produce more plutonium than they would consume.

Work on this "back-end" of the nuclear fuel cycle proceeded steadily during the 1970s. The construction of a pilot reprocessing plant at Tokai Mura in Ibaraki Prefecture was started in June 1971, completed in November 1974, and was ready to commence operations by the beginning of 1977. Since the only fuel available to be recycled was of American origin, Japan required the consent of the Carter administration, whose nuclear energy policy favored an indefinite delay on reprocessing. After several months of negotiations, in September 1977 it was agreed that Japan would be allowed to process up to 99 tons of spent fuel over a two-year period; this agreement was subsequently amended four times and extended until October 1981.[15] In May 1981, at a summit meeting between President Reagan and Prime Minister Suzuki, the president acknowledged the "particular importance to Japan" of reprocessing, and the two leaders agreed to arrive at a "permanent solution at an early date" for the Tokai Mura facility and the construction of an additional reprocessing plant.[16] Five months later the two countries negotiated an accord by which Japan could operate the Tokai Mura plant at full capacity (210 tons per year) through 1984.[17] In July 1984 it was announced that construction of a second reprocessing facility would commence in 1986, with a 1995 start-up date and an operating rate of 800 tons per year.[18]

Research on uranium enrichment in Japan originated in 1959. By the end of the 1960s, Japan had successfully enriched uranium in the laboratory by both the centrifuge and gaseous diffusion techniques. In December 1979, Tokyo announced that its pilot enrichment plant at Nongyo-Tohge had produced 300 kilograms of U-235 concentrated to 3.2 percent. Japan's optimism was reflected in the Atomic Energy Commission's June 1982 forecast, which called for a commercial enrichment plant to enter service by the end of the 1980s.[19] Japan also invested in the development of advanced type reactors (ATRs), whose ability to be fueled with plutonium was advantageous for acquiring the expertise needed for the expected transition to fast breeder reactors.

In short, Japan, exhibited remarkable progress in the development of its civilian nuclear energy program, moving from the importation of first-generation nuclear reactors to the indigenous manufacture of reprocessing and enrichment technologies within the space of twenty years. Further, it displayed a competency in handling advanced reactor techniques and fissile materials. While the amount of plutonium produced by a reactor is a function of a number of variables, including reactor design and average power level, since the completion of the Tokai Mura reprocessing facility it was evident that Japan possessed the technological infrastructure to construct a sizable inventory of nuclear weapons.[20] To understand why this option was not pursued, it is necessary to examine the dissuasive factors which confronted Japan.

CONSTRAINTS TO NUCLEAR
WEAPONS ACQUISITION

Domestic Political Considerations

Japanese opposition to nuclear weapons was founded on the country's special status as history's sole casualties of atomic attack. The bombing of Hiroshima and Nagasaki in August 1945 claimed 150,000 lives and left an estimated 100,000 suffering from burns and radiation sickness.[21] In March 1954, the Japanese tuna trawler *Lucky Dragon (Fukuryu Maru)* was accidentally showered with radioactive debris from the U.S. hydrogen bomb test at Bikini Island. The death of one of the crew, the general fear of contaminated fish, and the threat of radioactive fallout from continued testing in the Pacific Ocean stimulated widespread public opposition to nuclear weapons, which in turn led to the creation of the peace group *Gensuikyo* in September 1955, and in the signing of petitions by forty million Japanese urging the abolition of all atomic and hydrogen bombs.[22] Domestic sensitivity on the subject was sustained by extensive press coverage of nuclear testing and fallout reports, peace marches, and books and films. Japan's so-called "nuclear allergy," thus derived from its perception of victimization by both atomic and hydrogen bombs.

Public opinion in Japan exerted a potent influence on the country's politics, in particular those which related to national security. In 1960, public hostility to the revised U.S.-Japan security treaty was in some measure responsible for the cancellation of President Eisenhower's scheduled visit to Tokyo and the resignation of Prime Minister Kishi.[23] In February 1968, Cabinet Minister Tadao Kuraishi was forced to step down because of his remarks calling for Japanese rearmament, including nuclear weapons. Indeed, it was only toward the end of the 1960s that it became possible for elected officials to publicly articulate their views on national defense. Still, controversy over the word "alliance" (rather than "partners") in the May

1981 Reagan-Suzuki joint communiqué eventually led to the resignation of Foreign Minister Ito Masayoshi.

While public opinion poll results vary according to respondent sample, and the timing and phrasing of questions, it was clear that the Japanese people strongly opposed the acquisition of nuclear weapons. Japanese polls consistently revealed an aversion to nuclear armaments. A December 1967 nationwide survey by the *Kyodo News Agency* discovered that only 14 percent would have felt themselves safer if Japan possessed nuclear arms.[24] A *Yomiuri Shimbun* poll conducted in June 1969 registered only 16 percent who wanted nuclear weapons, while 72 percent did not. A *Sankei* survey in August 1971 showed 78 percent in agreement with the statement "the possession of nuclear weapons is undesirable." And a series of *Mainichi* polls carried out from 1969 to 1981 found on average that a mere 15 percent of all respondents favored Japanese nuclear weapons development "now" or "in the near future."

This antinuclear sentiment assumed political form in the shape of the policy prescriptions Prime Minister Sato presented to the Diet on January 30, 1968. Sato advocated (1) the use of atomic energy for peaceful purposes only; (2) the promotion of nuclear disarmament; (3) adherence to the three nonnuclear principles (*hikaku sangensoku*) which had been articulated the year before: not to possess, not to manufacture, and not to introduce nuclear weapons into Japan; and (4) reliance on the nuclear umbrella of the United States. Due to parliamentary maneuvering over ratification of the Okinawa reversion agreement, the three nonnuclear principles were subsequently incorporated in a Diet resolution and adopted as official government policy in November 1971. While not legally binding, they exercised a strong moral and political constraint on the behavior of the ruling Liberal Democratic Party (LDP). Furthermore, all four main opposition parties (the Democratic Socialist Party, the Japan Socialist Party, the Komeito, and the Japan Communist Party) were, if anything, more staunchly antinuclear than the Liberal Democrats, thereby adding another constraint on the LDP's freedom of maneuver.[25] Insofar as the representation of the Liberal Democrats declined in the Diet through the 1960s and 1970s, it was made more difficult for the government to retreat from its stance on nuclear weapons.

One area where theory and reality came into conflict was the interpretation of one of the three nonnuclear principles and its application to the American naval presence in the Far East. Specifically, it was alleged that U.S. vessels entered Japanese waters without first off-loading their stores of nuclear weapons. If true, this would have seemingly violated the Kishi-Herter note attached to the 1960 U.S.-Japan security treaty, which provided that any "major changes" in the deployment of equipment into Japan would be subject to bilateral "prior consultations."[26] Official Japanese acquiescence to such action would have also contravened its policy on the nonintroduction of nuclear weapons into the country.[27] Despite repeated denials by Japanese officials, public suspicion resulted in large-scale demonstrations, most notably in 1968 against the entry of the U.S.S. *Enterprise* and in 1973 against the U.S.S. *Midway*. It was sensitivity over this question that led the Sato government to seek explicit assurances from Washington that all nuclear weapons based on Okinawa would be removed before the island reverted to Japanese control in 1972. A new dimension to this issue was added in late 1974, after Rear Admiral Gene LaRocque testified to Congress that U.S. ships did not off-load their nuclear weapons before entering Japanese harbors.[28] A similar incident occurred in May 1981, after the former American ambassador to Japan, Edwin O. Reischauer, revealed to a *Mainichi* reporter during an interview that since 1960 nuclear-armed American ships had been allowed by Tokyo to transit and dock in Japan. As before, the Japanese government denied the allegation.[29]

Legal Constraints

More consistently contentious than the transit problem was the issue of Japanese rearmament, and the possibility of Tokyo's developing nuclear weapons. This, in turn, raised certain legal questions: could Japan develop nuclear armaments under its domestic laws and in accordance with its international treaty obligations?

The most formidable legal obstacle to Japanese nuclear weapons acquisition was Article IX of the Constitution, which stipulated:

Aspiring sincerely to an international peace based on justice and order, the Japanese people forever renounce war as a sovereign right of the nation and the threat or use of force as means of settling international disputes.

In order to accomplish the aims of the preceding paragraph, land, sea, and air forces, as well as other war potential, will never be maintained. The right of belligerency of the state will not be recognized.

The attempt to apply such a general and idealistic directive in effect meant that the limits, missions, and characteristics of the country's military forces became subject to interpretation. The legality of nuclear weapons was therefore a matter for legitimate debate. One juridical effort at explication was tendered by Japan's Commission on the Constitution. In 1964, after seven years of study, the commission delivered its verdict. Hesitant to intrude on the government's prerogative, it instead equivocated, stating that "Excluding the question of policy, in general, all nuclear weapons must be termed unconstitutional because of their nature."[30]

As a matter of government policy, the LDP maintained that nuclear weapons of a "defensive" nature were not banned by the Constitution. In 1955, the United States introduced to Japan dual-capable Honest John rockets. During the ensuing political furor, Prime Minister Hatoyama remarked that while nuclear weapons were not currently in Japan, their entry could be justified under certain conditions of national emergency.[31] Two years later, Prime Minister Kishi argued that defensive nuclear weapons were permissible under the Constitution.[32] China's testing of its first nuclear device in October 1964 increased Japanese attention on the subject. In December 1965, the director of the Cabinet Legislation Bureau testified before the House of Councillors that "when scientific knowledge advances, and it becomes possible to manufacture nuclear weapons which are in conformity with the purpose and within the limits of self-defense, then I don't believe it would be necessarily unconstitutional for us to own such weapons." This statement was subsequently endorsed by Prime Minister Sato.[33] In March 1969, in debate in the House of Councillors budget committee, Sato claimed that Japan could possess strategic nuclear weapons for the country's defense.[34] In October of the following year, the Defense Agency released its first white paper on defense, entitled *Defense of Japan* (*Nihon no Boei*). After declaring that "Japan cannot possess weapons which pose a threat of aggression to other nations, such as long-range bombers like B-52s, attack aircraft carriers, and ICBMs," and pledging fidelity to the three nonnuclear principles, the report maintained that nuclear weapons were not unconstitutional, if inappropriate for the time being for the country's defense.

Even though it would be possible to say that in legal and theoretical sense possession of small nuclear weapon [sic], falling within the minimum requirement for capacity necessary for self-defense and not posing a threat of aggression to other countries, would be permissible, the government, as its policy, adopts the principle of not attempting at nuclear armament which might be possible under the Constitution.[35]

This view was outlined in greater detail in March 1973 after Prime Minister Tanaka said that he would not rule out the possibility of Japan developing defensive nuclear weapons. Other officials explained that nuclear land mines for defense against enemy forces that had invaded Japan or nuclear air defense missiles would fall under this category.[36] This interpretation was repeated in a July 1973 policy paper written by the LDP's Security Research Council.[37] The significance of these statements was that they reflected the government's constant conviction, over a period of almost twenty years, that there was no need to undergo the arduous process of constitutional revision if Japan decided to acquire nuclear weapons. As one respected Japanese analyst observed as early as 1966, "although the Constitution remains as a considerable obstacle to the nuclear armament of Japan, it can no longer be considered an absolute barrier."[38]

One piece of domestic legislation which would have had to be amended was Article 2 of the Atomic Energy Basic Law of Japan. This law was promulgated in December 1955 in order to provide a framework for the country's peaceful nuclear energy program under civilian auspices. This provision stated that "The research, development, and utilization of atomic energy shall be limited to peaceful purposes." Nuclear weapons development would have certainly compromised the intent if not violated the letter of the law.

A number of international agreements also exercised a restraining influence on Japanese nuclear weapons acquisition. The 1958 Agreement for Cooperation with the United States concerning the civil uses of atomic energy expressly prohibited Japan from using American-supplied nuclear materials and equipment "for atomic weapons, or for research on or development of atomic weapons, or for any other military purpose." The task of safeguards application and inspection was transferred to the IAEA in 1963, extended in 1967, and expanded in 1968.[39] Any violation of this agreement would have risked crippling Japan's nuclear power industry, which during the 1970s was almost totally dependent on the United States for its supply of nuclear fuel. Additionally, under the terms of a 1969 accord on space cooperation between the United States and Japan, Tokyo was legally bound to use any American-supplied rocket technology or equipment "solely for peaceful purposes."[40]

Japan was also a party to multilateral arms control agreements, including the Partial Test Ban Treaty, the Outer Space Treaty, and the Seabed Arms Control Treaty. None of these barred absolutely Tokyo's development of nuclear armaments, or even a nuclear weapons test if performed underground. Japanese accession to these treaties, however, implied a commitment to the principle of nonproliferation. An explicit pledge of its nonnuclear intentions was obtained by Japan's ratification of the Nonproliferation Treaty in 1976, six years after signing it. Under its provisions, Tokyo agreed not to acquire nuclear weapons, and to accept IAEA safeguards on all of its nuclear energy activities. After becoming a party to this agreement, Japanese development of nuclear armaments would not only have violated the NPT but would also have contravened Article 96 of the Constitution, which required the nation to faithfully observe its international treaty obligations.

The Nuclear Nonproliferation Treaty

Due to memories of Japanese militarism, and to the dynamism of its civilian nuclear power program, particular attention was focused on Japan's behavior toward the Nonproliferation Treaty. Delay in first signing and then ratifying the agreement heightened speculation over Tokyo's intentions.

The first official Japanese comment on the nonproliferation negotiations in the ENDC was a speech delivered by then Foreign Minister Takeo Miki to the Diet on March 14, 1967.[41] After supporting the general need to limit the spread of nuclear weapons, Miki outlined three areas for greater consideration: nuclear disarmament by the nuclear powers so as to establish a balance of obligations, the security of those countries not possessing nuclear weapons, and the unhindered utilization of nuclear power for peaceful purposes, including equity between nuclear and nonnuclear states in realizing the benefits from peaceful nuclear explosions (PNEs). That September and the following May, Japan reiterated these concerns before the General Assembly.[42]

Over eighteen months elapsed after the completion of the NPT before Tokyo affixed its signature, on February 3, 1970, although not before issuing a government statement again urging progress on nuclear disarmament, on nondiscrimination in the peaceful uses of nuclear energy, and on the security of nonnuclear weapons states.[43] By this time several developments had occurred which at least partially addressed Japan's objections to the agreement's perceived deficiencies. In June

1968, the United States, the Soviet Union, and Britain sponsored U.N. Security Council resolution 255, which promised security guarantees to nonnuclear weapons states. The final text of the NPT itself stipulated in Article IV that every party had an "inalienable right" to develop nuclear energy for peaceful purposes, in Article V that any benefits from PNEs would be made available to nonnuclear weapons states "on a non-discriminatory basis," and in Article VI that NPT parties would undertake negotiations on arms control and disarmament. On this last pledge, the United States and the Soviet Union had announced on July 1, 1968 that they would begin strategic arms limitation talks. Also, in September 1968, the Conference of Non-Nuclear Weapons States recommended simplifying the IAEA safeguards procedures to permit the normal operation of civilian nuclear energy activities and to prevent industrial espionage by IAEA inspectors;[44] these two points had been especially stressed in Japan's speech the previous May. Further, the Federal Republic of Germany, whose attitude to the NPT was carefully monitored for many of the same reasons as Japan's, signed the treaty in November 1969, thereby shifting greater attention to Tokyo's recalcitrance.[45] It was possible that the U.S. agreement to return Okinawa implied some reciprocal gesture, that Japan wanted to further ensure the continued American supply of lightly enriched uranium for its nuclear power industry,[46] or that it simply wished to eliminate a potentially quarrelsome issue before the United States–Japan security treaty came up for renewal five months later. Finally, negotiations on a new formula for safeguards and their implementation were scheduled to start that spring in Vienna, and Japan would have greater influence as a signatory to the agreement.[47]

An additional six years elapsed before Japan ratified the NPT, on June 8, 1976. A government statement yet again stressed additional efforts toward nuclear disarmament, the security of nonnuclear weapons states, and nondiscrimination concerning nuclear energy programs.[48] Japanese ratification indicated that at least some of these concerns had been alleviated. In May 1972, the U.S. and USSR had signed the SALT I Interim Agreement and the ABM Treaty. On November 24, 1974, they agreed at Vladivostok to impose an aggregate ceiling of 2,400 strategic delivery vehicles for each country. Earlier, in June 1973, the two sides initialed an agreement on the prevention of nuclear war; each promised to "refrain from the threat or use of force against the other Party, against the allies of the other Party and against other countries." The need to ensure the security of nonnuclear countries was also recognized at the first NPT Review Conference in May 1975.[49] In addition, since 1973 the United States had refrained from conducting any peaceful nuclear explosions, thereby implying that PNEs conferred no special benefits. And in March 1975, Foreign Minister Miyazawa was dispatched by Tokyo to Washington, where he obtained a renewed pledge of American commitment to the defense and security of Japan.[50]

How these achievements were weighed by Tokyo is difficult to assess. However, the issue of safeguards application and IAEA inspection was subject to far greater attention by Japan, and was responsible for much of Japan's hesitation to sign and later ratify the NPT.[51] The meetings in Vienna ended in March 1971. From these discussions emerged a Model Agreement delineating IAEA operating procedures, the so-called Blue Book.[52] Japan's anxieties over IAEA inspection criteria were partly assuaged by the adoption of a system of material accountancy, containment, and surveillance that would be less intrusive, and therefore less disruptive to daily operations, than before.[53] The other point of contention was that this inspection system be equitably applied. Japan feared that it would suffer from a financial and commercial disadvantage when compared with the nuclear weapons states party to the treaty, who refused to submit all their nuclear facilities to international inspection,[54] and with the members of the European Atomic Energy Community (Euratom), which had a regional arrangement based on its own safeguards and inspection system.[55] On April 5, 1973, a protocol to the NPT was signed by Euratom which coordinated its safeguards activities with those of the IAEA.[56]

However, another obstacle was presented that same year, with the formation of Urenco, a consortium of German, Dutch, and British companies to enrich uranium. Tokyo was concerned that the close interaction of nonnuclear weapons states with a nuclear power might confer on Germany and the Netherlands a competitive advantage in a developing technology that was also of great interest to Japan. This problem too was resolved to Japan's satisfaction. One final difficulty was answered by France's decision to participate in the Nuclear Suppliers Group in late 1974. Although not a member of the Nonproliferation Treaty, France and the other major suppliers of nuclear materials and equipment would now be operating under similar export guidelines.

On February 26, 1975, the Japanese government reached a new safeguards agreement with the IAEA. Its basic demands were met. Japan received most favored nation status and was assured equality with Euratom's method of inspection. The Japan Atomic Industrial Forum, which had previously hesitated to support the NPT, now strongly advocated Diet ratification. In May the German Bundestag ratified the treaty, an action which once again concentrated relatively greater attention on Japan. After a period of consensus-building by the Miki government, Tokyo ratified the agreement in June 1976.[57]

Of the three general criticisms of the NPT voiced by Tokyo—nuclear disarmament, the security of the nonnuclear weapons states, and nondiscrimination in peaceful nuclear activities—Japan's behavior in ratifying the treaty suggested that the interests of its civilian nuclear energy program were paramount. The tangible results of Tokyo's diplomacy, the price of its accession in effect, were the Blue Book inspection system and the IAEA agreement awarding it equality with Euratom. Pressure from Canada and the United States to ratify the treaty after the May 1974 Indian nuclear detonation reinforced this point. Delays in the shipment of nuclear materials and equipment would have been detrimental to Japan's nuclear industry.[58]

If ratification guaranteed the future of Japan's nuclear

power program, it did not cancel possible nuclear weapons development, despite the claims of a small group of far-right Liberal Democrats who opposed the treaty because it infringed on national sovereignty, as well as on the grounds that in an uncertain world Japan's options should not be prematurely foreclosed. In fact the nuclear option remained open. Article X of the agreement stated that members could legally withdraw upon three month's notice, a provision Tokyo had emphasized when it originally signed the treaty. Moreover, because Article IV promised the "fullest possible exchange" of nuclear technology, it could be argued that the NPT actually enhanced Japan's nuclear option. In any event, Japan still retained the scientific and technological basis to build nuclear bombs, within two to twenty-four months, according to observers.[59]

Strategic Considerations

Japan's national security perspective has been shaped by its physical characteristics and immediate strategic environment. Japan consists of four main islands and over 3,300 smaller islands, roughly aligned in a long, thin, northeast to southwest configuration. These islands support a population of 120 million, a disproportionate share of which is concentrated, along with industrial development, in a narrow band on the east coast of Honshu. To the north, Hokkaido is only thirty-six miles across the Soya (La Perouse) Strait from Soviet Sakhalin. Korea is 130 miles across the Tsushima Strait, while mainland China is less than 500 miles across the East China Sea. The political, military, and economic interests of China, the Soviet Union, and the United States have all interacted in this area. International tensions have been maintained due to rivalries for regional influence, territorial disputes, irredentist claims, ideological and ethnic antagonisms, and the periodic outbreak of hostilities.

Due to its relatively small size and military weakness after the Second World War, Tokyo adopted a broad interpretation of national defense and how best to promote the country's security. Positive "peace diplomacy," the strengthening of the United Nations and respect for international law, and arms control and disarmament efforts, were all viewed as means which could effectively prevent conflict and promote regional and international stability. Further measures to enhance security were to ensure the country's economic vitality, social cohesion, and national consensus on defense. In sum, concentration on such essentially nonmilitary measures as economic growth and the attempt to reduce, or more accurately, to not aggravate, international tensions were seen by Tokyo as important contributions to its own security. Still, it was recognized that these were necessary but insufficient conditions; military means to defend the country against threats to its security were also required. Potential threats assumed many different forms: nuclear attack or blackmail by the Soviet Union, and later China; conventional aggression against Japanese territory; the unification of the Korean peninsula under a power hostile to Tokyo; and interference with Japanese merchant shipping, upon which Japan was dependent for its supplies of food, oil, and raw materials.

Japan endeavored to meet these threats by entering into an alliance with the United States to counter external aggression. The U.S.-Japan relationship was codified in 1952 by the Security Treaty. Under the terms of the agreement, Washington conditionally pledged its forces to contribute "to the security of Japan against armed attack from without." This relationship was strengthened in 1960 by the Treaty of Mutual Cooperation and Security, which eliminated some of the more onerous obligations of the 1952 agreement. Thus Japan, starting after the war from a position of military defeat, confronted by a Sino-Soviet pact directed against it, and provided with the example of communist aggression in Korea, resolved its postwar security dilemma by reliance on the military strength of the United States.

China's explosion of a nuclear device in October 1964 raised anxieties over Peking's use of nuclear weapons to blackmail or attack Japan.[60] As before, Japan's security was guaranteed by the United States. The American nuclear umbrella, which had previously protected Japan from the Soviet Union, was now extended to deter China. Two statements by President Johnson reaffirming U.S. support against nuclear intimidation were issued immediately after the Chinese test.[61] In addition, Prime Minister Sato visited Washington in January 1965. The joint Sato-Johnson communiqué pledged American determination "to defend Japan against any armed attack from the outside."[62]

Diplomatic events in the early 1970s lessened Japanese anxieties regarding the Chinese nuclear threat. Secretary of State Henry Kisinger's secret trip to China in July 1971 paved the way for President Nixon's official visit the following February, which in turn allowed Tokyo to seek its own rapprochement with Peking. In September 1972, Prime Minister Tanaka traveled to the PRC and established diplomatic relations.[63] While this development undoubtedly benefited Japanese security, two trends during the 1970s had a negative impact upon the country's specific defense concerns and the overall stability of the East Asian region. During this decade Soviet military strength in the Far East increased dramatically. This development was made all the more alarming for Tokyo because it coincided with a period of American disengagement from Asia.

Despite the signing of the 1956 agreement on normalization of diplomatic relations, the Soviet-Japanese relationship had been strained throughout the postwar period. Moscow's abrogation of its 1941 Neutrality Pact with Tokyo in August 1945, the death of over 200,000 Japanese POWs in Soviet camps after the war, the continuous harassment of Japanese fishing fleets, and Soviet intrusions of Japanese air space and territorial waters did nothing to foster friendship between the two countries. A more enduring source of animosity was the Soviet Union's annexation of a group of islands north of Hokkaido, and Moscow's subsequent refusal to acknowledge Japan's claim to these territories.[64]

While the 1970 edition of *Defense of Japan* did not refer to the Soviet Union as even a possible threat to Japan, subsequent volumes (beginning in 1976) devoted considerable attention to Soviet forces and activities. Indeed, during the 1970s the Soviet Union made significant quantitative and qualitative improvements in its military capabilities in the Far East. The Soviet Pacific Fleet and land units possessed an estimated 30 percent of the Soviet nuclear missile force, including mobile, intermediate-range SS-20s. One-quarter of Soviet ground forces and combat aircraft were deployed in the Far East, including Mig-23 and Mig-25 fighters, Mig-27 and Su-19 fighter-bombers, and Backfire bombers. One-third of Soviet naval strength was assigned to its Pacific Fleet; the Soviet Union added one new submarine and at least one major surface ship each year, including a Kiev-class aircraft carrier and an Ivan Rogov amphibious assault ship.[65] Their capabilities were impressively demonstrated in mid-decade by the OKEAN 75 naval maneuvers.[66] In addition, the Soviet fleet regularly traversed the Soya, Tsugaru, and Tsushima straits, and routinely operated in the seas around Japan. This ability to project power was aided by access to former U.S. facilities at Cam Ranh Bay and Da Nang in Vietnam. Particularly threatening to Japan was the Soviet decision in 1978 to reintroduce a division of ground forces, equipped with tanks and artillery, on the disputed Kunashiri, Etorofu, and Shikotan islands. The military build-up of the Soviet Far Eastern forces was viewed as "now affecting the military balance between the United States and the Soviet Union in the West Pacific," and was regarded as "an increasing potential threat to the security of Japan."[67]

During this period the United States gradually disengaged itself from direct involvement in Asian affairs, while urging that a greater share of the defense burden be assumed by the Asian allies. President Nixon first articulated this policy in July 1969. The American decision to transfer control over Okinawa four months later was a logical result. In return, Tokyo acknowledged the importance of Korea and Taiwan to its defense, thereby expanding the Japanese role in the security of the Far East.[68] The withdrawal of American forces stationed in Southeast Asia and the ROK, and reductions in the Seventh Fleet, raised questions over the U.S. commitment to its East Asian allies. The U.S. defeat in Vietnam, the Carter administration's plan to withdraw the remaining U.S. ground troops from South Korea, and the overthrow of the Shah, further undermined American credibility.

Against this background of increasing Soviet power, an eroding American commitment to the Far East, and an uncertain international environment, Japan decided that the best means of safeguarding its security was to reaffirm its ties to the United States. This task was facilitated by a reciprocal recognition in Washington that its position in the Far East was ultimately based on its maintaining a close relationship with Tokyo. In August 1975, Japan's Prime Minister Miki and President Ford recognized that "still closer consultations" on the implementation of the 1960 security treaty were required. Moreover, it was agreed that the two countries "conduct consultations within the framework of the Security Consultative Committee," which had been established in accordance with Article IV of the treaty to expedite cooperation on defense matters.[69] Later that month, Secretary of Defense James Schlesinger and Director-General of the Japan Defense Agency Michita Sakata decided to create a joint Subcommittee for Defense Cooperation. After two years of deliberations, in November 1978 "The Guidelines for Japan-United States Defense Cooperation" were completed.[70] This understanding outlined a plan for comprehensive military cooperation in order to realize more fully the objectives of the security agreement. It provided for coordination in advanced logistics planning and intelligence gathering, and delineated joint military actions in response to an armed attack against Japan. Joint naval exercises had already been conducted since the early 1970s, including antisubmarine and mine-sweeping operations. Further, in 1980 the Maritime Self-Defense Forces participated for the first time in the U.S. Navy's RIMPAC exercises, in conjunction with forces from Australia, Canada, and New Zealand. Joint U.S.-Japan air exercises were begun in 1978, while limited numbers of Ground Self-Defense Forces trained with U.S. personnel in

1981. Under Prime Minister Nakasone, the Japanese-American security relationship assumed an unprecedented degree of cooperation. In November 1983, the Japanese government agreed to sell or license military technology to the Pentagon and the U.S. private sector.[71] And in September 1984, a U.S.-Japan Advisory Commission, after surveying the Soviet military buildup in Northeast Asia, urged that the two countries begin joint development of advanced technology weapons.[72]

For Tokyo to have developed nuclear weapons during this period it would have had to evaluate whether a Japanese nuclear arsenal would have effectively countered threats to the country's security. Specifically, it would have had to examine how well nuclear armaments could have deterred other powers from nuclear or conventional aggression, averted a unified and hostile Korea, and prevented interference with its merchant marine, and whether these tasks could have been performed more ably by continued reliance on the United States.

Due to the size of Japan's economy, the financial cost of developing a nuclear inventory could have been absorbed "without seriously upsetting national priorities."[73] Still, Japan would have had to surmount numerous logistical and technological hurdles. First, it would have had to persuade members of its scientific and engineering communities, who formed "a nucleus of pacifists in Japan," to undertake such a project.[74] Yet even if a nuclear weapons team could have been assembled, this diversion of highly skilled personnel might have seriously disrupted important sectors of the Japanese economy.[75] Suitable locations for the program, those which had easy access for transportation of supplies and personnel, a sufficient water supply and power source, simply did not exist in Japan.[76] Indigenous sources of natural uranium were meager. Due to its highly concentrated population and its location in an earthquake zone, there would also have been severe constraints to underground nuclear testing within the country.[77]

In addition, Japan would have faced difficulties in constructing adequate delivery vehicles. In 1963 the Japan Nuclear Ship Development Agency was created, and entrusted with building a nuclear-powered surface ship. The nuclear ship *Mutsu* became operational in August 1974, but on its maiden voyage developed a radiation leak. For the next decade the status of the nuclear ship program was in doubt.[78] While the experience of the *Mutsu* might have been valuable for learning about nuclear ship propulsion, the *Mutsu's* reactor was not the type required for nuclear-powered submarines. Even if constructed, a Japanese nuclear-armed submarine fleet would have been faced with problems of command, control, and communications. For Japan to reach targets in the Soviet Union east of the Ural Mountains, where there was the greatest concentration of Soviet population and industry, it would have had to deploy its submarines in the Arabian Sea. This would have created problems of long transit times over an extended distance through uncertain waters. Moreover, a Japanese first-generation submarine force would have had to contend with advanced anti-submarine warfare technology.[79] Air-delivery of nuclear weapons would have also faced problems. Japan lacked the capability to produce its own jet engines.[80] The US-supplied F-4s in the Air Self-Defense Force inventory would have been constricted by range and payload limitations, as well as subject to air suppression measures.

A Japanese land-based nuclear force would have had to find available areas to house the missiles, a task made more difficult by the concentration of population and the likely opposition from surrounding communities. On the positive side, Japan did possess some experience related to missile technology. The Space Development Office was created in 1963 to promote the peaceful development of space research. Its mandate included the design and manufacture of satellites and rockets.[81] In February 1970, Japan launched its first satellite, using a solid-fuel propellant. It launched another thirteen during the decade. While Japan's advances in rocket technology were "useful in developing missiles to deliver nuclear weapons,"[82] there were still deficiencies in reentry vehicle technology and guidance systems. Transforming the rocket program to develop an IRBM capability would have taken an estimated

three years.[83] There would also have been technical difficulties
with an antiballistic missile (ABM) system. Due to the country's
lack of strategic depth, Japan would have needed a ballistic
missile early warning system effective in all directions to counter an adversary armed with submarine-launched nuclear
weapons. This was "almost a mission impossible."[84] Further,
any ABM system would have had to operate perfectly, because
the extreme concentration of population would have rendered
even the most limited penetration of nuclear missiles unacceptable.[85]

Even if all these obstacles could have been overcome, other
problems, no less formidable, would have remained. Serious
political, diplomatic, economic, and military risks would have
attended Japanese acquisition of nuclear weapons. Assuming
that domestic and international legal restrictions could have
been circumvented, the country's nuclear allergy would have
meant that a decision to build nuclear bombs would have split
the Japanese body politic as no other issue had done since the
termination of the war.[86] Some observers even questioned
whether anything recognizable as a democratic system of government would have been likely to survive the acquisition of
nuclear arms.[87] Diplomatically, nuclear weapons development
might have resulted in Washington severing its security links
with Tokyo. It could also have revived fears of Japanese militarism and might quickly have isolated Japan from the international community at large.[88] This, in turn, might have jeopardized access to overseas markets and resources, upon which
the country's commercial and financial success was founded.
Indeed, key economic activities could have been brought "almost to a standstill as a result of Japan's emergence as a nuclear
power."[89] Not least, Japan's entire civilian nuclear energy industry, upon which the country was dependent for one-sixth of
its electricity needs, could have been halted by an American
decision to stop all supplies of nuclear fuel.

To deter aggression by a nuclear weapons state, Japan
would have had to acquire a second-strike retaliatory capability. However, it would have taken "much more than ten years

before a plausible nuclear deterrent capability" could have been made operational.[90] During this time of "incipient vulnerability," Japan would have been exposed to a preemptive strike. Even if it managed to survive this period unscathed, it would have discovered it difficult to find suitable targets for possible retaliation in the Soviet Union or China; Soviet targets were too remote, while Chinese population and industrial concentrations were too dispersed.[91] Any use of nuclear weapons, whether strategic or tactical, against either of these countries would have risked the nuclear devastation of Japan's homeland because of the superior size and capability of their nuclear arsenals.[92] The overwhelming destruction of Japan could have been achieved by as few as four nuclear bombs.[93] Moreover, the mere possession of nuclear weapons by Japan would almost have certainly guaranteed that the country would have been a target in a nuclear war.[94]

Nor is it clear that nuclear weapons could have helped Japan with less than total threats. As vital as Korea was to Japanese security, it was unlikely that Japan would have forcibly intervened in the event of an armed conflict on the Korean peninsula.[95] Since there would have been no immediate threat to Japan, the use of nuclear weapons would have been difficult to justify in terms of self-defense. Nor would nuclear weapons have been either an appropriate or useful instrument to deal with interference with Japanese shipping.

While Japan might have garnered some marginal advantages from the development of nuclear weapons, such a policy would have been counterproductive on political, diplomatic, commercial, and military grounds, diminishing rather than enhancing the country's security. Furthermore, a viable alternative already existed. The American nuclear umbrella deterred Soviet and Chinese nuclear forces, while U.S. conventional strength addressed lesser threats to Japanese interests. The Japanese-American relationship, while perhaps not ideal in all respects when viewed from Tokyo, nonetheless provided Japan with an adequate—and when compared with a nuclear alternative—vastly superior, guarantee of its security.

CONCLUSION

A complex of overlapping and mutually reinforcing constraints was responsible for dissuading Japan from acquiring nuclear weapons, despite it having the scientific and technological foundation for such a project. Public opinion, government policy, domestic and international legal barriers, and strategic realities all influenced Tokyo's policy.

Of these factors, the security relationship with the United States was the most important. During periods of crisis and insecurity, Tokyo repeatedly sought to affirm its ties with Washington. For its part, the United States appreciated the importance of close relations with Japan. In 1952 with the original security treaty, eight years later with the amended version, in 1964 after the Chinese nuclear detonation, in 1970 with the extension of the security treaty, and during the latter half of the 1970s and into the 1980s in response to the Soviet military buildup in the Far East, Japan solicited and received an American commitment to its defense. Tokyo's ratification of the Nonproliferation Treaty underscored this point. The significance of Japan's accession to the NPT was less that it conclusively prevented the development of nuclear arms, which it did not, than that it implied that the foundation of the country's security would continue to rest on its ties with the United States. Tokyo's holding of defense expenditures below the 1 percent per annum level can be interpreted as further evidence of Japan's reliance on the U.S.

The durability of this entente undoubtedly benefited from the absence of a major disagreement which might have placed the American commitment in question and possibly sundered the security relationship. None of the potential threats to Japanese security materialized during this period. The three Nixon "shocks" of 1971—the American opening to China without first informing Japan, Washington's forced devaluation of the yen, and the imposition of a textile import quota—were nowhere near a magnitude sufficient to sever the relationship, even at a time of American retreat from Asia.

Still, it is not at all certain that Tokyo would have decided to acquire nuclear weapons even without the U.S. defense guarantee. Japan would have derived some measure of security from nuclear attack from the general international inhibition against the use of nuclear arms, but more particularly because the country's industrial base would have been an attractive prize for an aggressor if preserved intact. More concretely, Japan's geography and demographic characteristics argued against construction of a strategic nuclear arsenal, whose long development period would have left the country dangerously exposed. Also, tactical nuclear weapons would have been of dubious military value against the Soviet Union or China, and would have been vehemently opposed by Japanese and world opinion. Therefore, for reasons wholly removed from the U.S.-Japan security relationship, Tokyo would have been confronted with a number of pressures against nuclear weapons acquisition. It is difficult to imagine a set of circumstances where Japan could have enhanced its security by building a national nuclear force.

Since it was not clear that Japan's acquisition of nuclear arms was ever a serious possibility, Tokyo was unable to parlay its nuclear potential into a convincing "nuclear threat." It was effectively muzzled from publicly brandishing its nuclear option because of domestic sensitivity on nuclear matters. Japan's success during the NPT ratification process in obtaining concessions for its nuclear power program derived more from the symbolic importance of having one of the world's leading civilian nuclear energy programs bound by the terms of the treaty than from Japan threatening to go nuclear. Moreover, Tokyo never actually had to threaten to develop nuclear weapons because Washington never gave it sufficient cause to doubt its commitment to a free and independent Japan. Indeed, American recognition of the advantages for its own security of a democratic Japan tied to the West's economic and security systems was central not only for persuading Tokyo to refrain from nuclear weapons acquisition, but also for assuring Japan that it was unnecessary to communicate the threat to go nuclear in order to obtain its objectives.

5.

Israel

Few members of the international community have been confronted by such abiding animosity and pervasive threats to their security as Israel. The opposition of most of the Arab world to the country has been evidenced by its refusal to officially recognize Israel, by its propaganda and government statements, by its support of terrorist groups committed to the destruction of the Jewish state, and by the readiness of some of its members to resort to war. That Israel has been outnumbered in manpower, along with its small size and slender territorial configuration along the eastern Mediterranean littoral, have further intensified its sense of vulnerability. In addition, Israel has lacked a formal security guarantee with any other country. Situated in this Hobbesian environment, Israel's cardinal objective has been to preserve its viability. Methods for ensuring the country's continued survival have included the search for some form of Arab-Israeli *modus vivendi* predicated upon a cessation of hostilities and reciprocal diplomatic recognition, and the accumulation of superior military strength to deter aggression, and if necessary, to forcibly defend its sovereignty.

Since the passage of U.N. Security Council resolution 181

on November 29, 1947, outlining a plan to partition British-controlled Palestine, there has been an almost exclusive reliance on military means to settle disputes between the two sides. Initially, Arab resistance to the United Nations partition scheme compelled the Jewish inhabitants of Palestine to fight a civil war before achieving independence. After May 15, 1948, the date of Israel's establishment, forces from Transjordan, Egypt, Iraq, Syria, and Lebanon, loosely confederated under the banner of the Arab Liberation Army, attempted to destroy the fledgling state at birth. With little outside assistance, and at great loss of life, the Israelis managed to repulse the Arab forces. In January 1949, ceasefires between Israel and the other belligerents were arranged.[1]

Although sporadic skirmishing along its borders continued, Israel's next major conflict with its neighbors did not occur until 1956. Four years earlier, Egypt's King Farouk was toppled in a military coup, and in 1954 Colonel Abdul Nasser assumed the leadership of the country. Implacably opposed to the Jewish state, Nasser sponsored guerrilla activities and called for a unified Arab effort to eradicate Israel. In 1955 he appeared to obtain the means to unilaterally realize his ambition. That year the Soviet Union directed Czechoslovakia to provide an estimated $200 million worth of sophisticated weapons to Egypt. The Czech arms deal seemed to tip the military balance in Egypt's favor, while simultaneously "giving sudden and dramatic urgency to Israel's difficulties in securing matching armaments."[2] In addition, Nasser's nationalization of the Suez Canal Company the following August and his endorsement of the FLN rebels in Algeria incited the hostility of Britain and France. Due to these events, the interests of Tel Aviv, London, and Paris converged in forcibly removing Nasser from power. The initial Israeli military successes in late October 1956 in the Gaza Strip and the Sinai Desert were met, however, with British and French irresolution in the face of American opposition to the assault on Egypt. British, French, and Israeli forces were compelled to disengage, and Israel was forced to return the territory it had conquered.[3]

Following the Suez War, Israel enjoyed over a decade free from large-scale hostilities. This allowed it to concentrate on expanding its economy, establishing diplomatic relations with those countries willing to do so, and developing its military capabilities. In addition, a consequence of this war was that Israel and France were bound together in a "tacit alliance," of which nuclear cooperation comprised one important component. The contours of this relationship were first partially revealed in December 1960, when it was publicly admitted by the parties that Israel had constructed a nuclear research reactor, located at Dimona, with French assistance.[4] Still, Israel was unable to acquire a security guarantee or membership in a formal alliance, despite its repeated attempts.[5] That Arab-Israeli antagonism did not erupt into full-scale war during this period was aided by the refractory nature of the Arab states, whose secular interests, dissimilar interpretations of the pan-Arab ideal, and disparate views on political and social traditions retarded their ability to pose a united military challenge to Israel.

In May 1967, however, Egypt ordered the removal of the U.N. emergency force which had been inserted in the Sinai after 1956, announced that the Straits of Tiran were barred to Israeli shipping, and, in conjunction with Syria and Jordan, amassed its armies on Israel's borders. Placed once again in a position of "peril and solitude,"[6] Israel decided to launch a preemptive air strike against the Arab forces on June 5, 1967. Over the next five days, the performance of the Israel Defense Force (IDF) was stunningly successful. Israel's victory ended with its occupation of the Golan Heights, the West Bank of the Jordan River, and the entire Sinai Desert.[7]

Unfortunately for Israel, though, it was unable to translate this military ascendancy into some form of political rapprochement with its neighbors. In fact, Arab obloquy if anything became more extreme after the humiliation in the June 1967 war. At the Khartoum summit conference of Arab heads of state in late August that year, it was resolved that there should be "no peace with Israel, no recognition of Israel, no negotiations with it."[8] In order to salvage some measure of prestige and to reassert its leadership in the Arab community, Egypt engaged over the next few years in a "war of attrition" with Israel along the Suez Canal. Suspicion at this time over Israel's nuclear intentions was aroused by its failure to sign or ratify the Nonproliferation Treaty, and by a July 1970 article in the *New York Times* reporting that the CIA believed Israel capable of fabricating a nuclear bomb. While various initiatives aimed at an overall Middle East peace settlement were forwarded during the next few years by Israel, the United Nations, the United States, and the Soviet Union, none were successful in ending the conflict.

In October 1973, Egypt and Syria surprised Israel in a coordinated attack on its southern and northern fronts. Arab battlefield successes in the early stages of the war were only reversed by Israel at great cost in men and materiel. This was not accomplished until the United States was impelled to intervene by undertaking a massive airlift of equipment to replace Israeli losses.[9] Once again, the war illustrated Israel's inability to alleviate Arab enmity, its failure to deter aggression even after its overwhelming victory in June 1967, its dependence on potentially unreliable external sources of military assistance, and its almost total international isolation. The country's insecurity was exacerbated by Arab "oil diplomacy" after the October 1973 conflict. The fear of a cutoff of petroleum supplies was now an additional consideration for states when conducting their policies toward the Middle East. This reassessment was also reflected in the behavior of international organizations. In November 1974 Israel was expelled from UNESCO. Later that same month the United Nations granted observer status to the Palestine Liberation Organization (PLO), which personified national aspirations for a Palestinian homeland. World vituperation against Israel culminated in U.N. General Assembly resolution 3379 (XXX) of November 10, 1975, which described Zionism as "a form of racism and racial discrimination." Whether a concerted Israeli reaction to these developments or just coincidence, after the October 1973 war reports of Israel's nuclear activities and capabilities appeared more frequently in the press, along with statements by Israeli spokesmen alluding to the country's technical competence to build nuclear weapons.

In November 1977, Egypt's President Anwar Sadat took the wholly unexpected and unprecedented step of traveling to Israel. This set in motion a series of events which concluded with the March 1979 signing of a peace treaty establishing official diplomatic relations between the two former belligerents.[10] While Israel had to return the Sinai to Egypt, the accord's demilitarization provisions for this territory in effect meant that the country's southern flank was now protected from further hostilities. The opposition of the Arab world to Sadat's policy, however, indicated that Israel would have more difficulty in reaching a similar understanding with any of its other regional adversaries. The Israeli invasion of Lebanon in June 1982 further increased Arab anger and desire for revenge.

In its short but violent history, Israel had militarily defeated its opponents in four full-scale conflicts, as well as countered numerous smaller-scale threats to the country. Based on this performance, the capabilities of the Israel Defense Force were clearly superior to any foreseeable combination of Arab armies. Yet during the decade following the June 1967 war, Israel's military and political situation suffered a number of setbacks. Subsequent military conflicts did not mirror the rapid and decisive outcome achieved in this war. The war of attrition and the October 1973 war resulted in large numbers of casualties, to which Israel's social and demographic conditions were particularly ill-suited. The October 1973 war in addition demonstrated that Israel's dependence on the United States as an arms supplier constituted a potential source of vulnerability. When coupled with Israel's financial straits, caused in large measure by escalating military expenditures, it was feared that this might grant Washington sufficient leverage to impose conditions inimical to the country's own interests. The improved performance of the Arab armies, their growing proficiency with sophisticated battlefield technologies, and the ability of the oil-rich Arab states to underwrite the purchase of advanced armaments for the "confrontation" states, appeared to indicate that political, economic, and military trends favored the Arab countries against Israel. Moreover, during this period Israel had been unable to acquire a formal security guarantee or membership in an alliance, and had emerged from each military encounter relatively more isolated in the world community than before. And although Israel's security was greatly enhanced by Sadat's initiative in November 1977, Israel proved unable to arrive at a similar political understanding with any of its other Arab adversaries.

As a result of these adverse military and political developments, there was conjecture that Israel might acquire nuclear weapons. Only in this manner, it was suggested, would Israel be able to end the cycle of violence in the Middle East, win Arab acceptance and by extension regain international favor, reduce its dependence on foreign arms suppliers, and neutralize an arms race with the Arab countries it could otherwise only lose. Contributing to this speculation was the secrecy which surrounded Israel's nuclear activities, its close association in the nuclear field with France, Israel's refusal to sign or ratify the Nonproliferation Treaty, two incidents of suspected Israeli diversion of nuclear materials, rumors and reports of its possession of a nuclear arsenal, and its less than total public explanations of its nuclear status.

ISRAEL'S NUCLEAR PROGRAM

The origins of Israel's nuclear efforts dated from the first year of the country's independence, 1948, when large phosphate reserves containing uranium were discovered during a survey of mineral resources in the Negev Desert. By the following year, plans for a nuclear program had been formulated, a group of young scientists sent abroad for training, a Department of Isotope Research established at the Weizmann Institute, and ad-

ISRAEL: CHRONOLOGY OF SIGNIFICANT EVENTS

Nuclear Developments		*Political Developments*
	1948	State of Israel established (May)
	1949	End of the "War of Liberation" (January)
IAEC formed (June)	1952	
IAEC signs a nuclear cooperation agreement with CEA	1953	
	1954	Nasser assumes leadership in Egypt
	1956	The Suez War (October-November)
Nahal Soreq nuclear research reactor goes critical	1960	
24-megawatt heavy-water reactor at Dimona is revealed (December)		
	1964	Israel ratifies the PTBT (January)
	1965	Allon announces that Israel will not be the first to have nuclear weapons in the Middle East, but will not be the second either (December)
	1967	The "Six Day War" ends with Israel occupying the Golan Heights, the West Bank, and the Sinai Desert (June)
		Arab heads of state at the Khartoum summit conference agree to refuse to make peace with, negotiate with, or recognize Israel (August)
	1968–1970	The "war of attrition" along the Suez Canal

ISRAEL: CHRONOLOGY OF SIGNIFICANT EVENTS (Continued)

Nuclear Developments		Political Developments
	1970	New York Times reports that the CIA believed Israel could construct nuclear weapons for the Jericho SSM, 11 of which were said to have been shipped from France to Israel in 1968, with 14 more by 1970 (July)
	1973	Yom Kippur War (October)
	1974	President Katzir admits Israel has the potential to build nuclear weapons (December)
	1975	Boston Globe reports that U.S. analysts believe that Israel has more than 10 nuclear weapons (July)
		UNGA resolution declares Zionism a form of racism (November)
	1976	Washington Post reports that Israel is thought to have 10-20 nuclear weapons (March)
Time magazine reports that Israel constructed a pilot reprocessing plant after the Six Day War, which was completed in 1969; also that Israel contemplated using nuclear weapons during the early stages of the Yom Kippur War		
The "Plumbat affair" is revealed, alleging that Israel had hijacked app. 200 tons of uranium oxide in 1968.	1977	President Sadat travels to Jerusalem (November)

ISRAEL: CHRONOLOGY OF SIGNIFICANT EVENTS (*Continued*)

Nuclear Developments		*Political Developments*
It is disclosed that during the mid-1960s over 200 lbs. of highly-enriched uranium was missing from NUMEC; Israel is suspected of being the final destination of the material but the case is not proven (August)		
	1978	Leaked CIA memo reveals that the Agency concluded in 1974 that Israel already had nuclear weapons (January)
	1979	The peace treaty between Israel and Egypt is signed (March)
Reports that a 1957 agreement between Israel and France committed France to lend assistance to Israel to build a pilot reprocessing plant, to share results of French nuclear tests during the 1960s, and to agree to reprocess Dimona's spent fuel and then return the material to Israel	1981	Israel destroys Iraq's Osiraq reactor (June)
	1986	*Sunday Times*, on information supplied by a former technician at Dimona, reports that Israel has 100 to 200 nuclear weapons (October)

Note: This chronology omits the agreements on nuclear cooperation that Israel signed with the U.S., and Israel's agreement with the IAEA on safeguards application. For this information please consult the text.

vanced research in heavy-water production undertaken at the same institution. In order to coordinate and supervise the country's growing nuclear activities, on June 13, 1952, the Israel Atomic Energy Commission (IAEC) was formed, and placed under the auspices of the Ministry of Defense.[11]

In 1953 Israel entered into an agreement for nuclear cooperation with France's Commissariat à l'Energie Atomique (CEA), which was interested in the IAEC's development of a less expensive process of producing heavy water than the electrolytic method used by Norway.[12] This collaboration was not made public until November 1954, when it was also revealed that a pilot plant for heavy-water production was already in operation in Israel.[13] This French-Israeli relationship enabled Israel to gain access to technical data and information, to train its scientists and technicians at advanced nuclear installations, and to profit from the experience of France's early work in the nuclear field.[14]

Israel also received nuclear assistance from the United States. In July 1955, in connection with Washington's Atoms for Peace program, the two countries signed an agreement for cooperation on the civil uses of atomic energy.[15] Under its terms, a research reactor using 90 percent highly enriched uranium as fuel with heavy water as its moderator was offered under license to Israel. Washington contributed $300,000 toward the installation's total cost of approximately $3,000,000.[16] Located at the Nahal Soreq Research Establishment south of Tel Aviv, the new facility went critical in 1960. Until 1965, the reactor remained under American inspection. At that time, safeguards responsibility was transferred to the IAEA.[17] This agreement was amended in April 1975.[18] Two years later, a protocol was initialed which extended IAEA safeguards beyond the 1977 termination date of the U.S. agreement.[19]

Israel's nuclear cooperation with France increased after the 1956 Suez debacle. Negotiations led to a decision the next year to build a 24-megawatt natural uranium/heavy-water reactor at Dimona, situated near Beersheba in the Negev.[20] Construction on the facility remained secret until December 1960.[21] The

Dimona reactor became operational three years later. Estimates of its cost ranged from $75 to $130 million.[22] France supplied the initial load of heavy water, while it was assumed that Israel could fulfill the smaller additional make-up requirements.[23] Uranium for the reactor was reportedly obtained from Israel's indigenous phosphate deposits, as well as from Argentina, South Africa, France, Belgium, Gabon, Niger, and the Central African Empire.[24] It was estimated that Dimona's production rate of fissile plutonium was eight to ten kilograms per year, which would be sufficient for the manufacture of one 20 kiloton nuclear bomb if it could be separated from the spent fuel.[25] In August 1980 it was reported that Dimona's capacity had been increased to 70 megawatts.[26] If correct, this could mean an annual plutonium production rate of 20 kilograms, or enough for three nuclear bombs if the material could be separated from the spent fuel.[27] Since France had dropped its demand in 1960 that Dimona be placed under international supervision,[28] the nuclear facility was unsafeguarded. Nonetheless, the Kennedy administration's strong nonproliferation stance pressured Israel into allowing annual, unofficial examinations of the Dimona facility by U.S. experts.[29] In 1969, the American inspection unit complained that limitations had been imposed at the site so that they could not guarantee that weapons-related work was not being conducted.[30] After this visit, further inspections were canceled; in 1976, thirteen U.S. senators were barred from visiting the Dimona plant.[31]

By itself, the Dimona reactor did not present Israel with a nuclear weapons capability. Still required was some means of obtaining either highly enriched uranium or separated plutonium for a nuclear bomb. The Nahal Soreq facility was too small to produce sufficient amounts of weapons-grade plutonium. If operated at peak efficiency, it would take approximately 2,000 years to produce enough plutonium for one sophisticated nuclear device.[32] Also, in addition to the IAEA safeguards on Nahal Soreq's operations, Israel was explicitly prohibited by a 1975 agreement with the United States from using any American-supplied materials or equipment "for any nuclear explosive device, or for nuclear research on or development of any such device, regardless of how the device itself is intended to be used."[33] With respect to uranium enrichment capabilities, it was reported in 1974 that Tel Aviv had developed a process based on laser technology which promised a very quick, relatively inexpensive, and virtually undetectable route to obtaining weapons-grade material.[34] Expectations for this method's success appear to have been excessive, and it is believed that work on this process is still in its research and development phase in Israel.

Separating plutonium from spent fuel was an alternative method of securing material for nuclear weapons. While some form of reprocessing capability by Israel had long been suspected, only in the 1974 edition of *Strategic Survey* was it first stated that Israel possessed a reprocessing plant. Its capacity (in tons per year) was not known.[35] Three years later, a 1977 U.S. Senate investigation into American nonproliferation interests in the Middle East reported that Israeli Prime Minister Yitzhak Rabin had remarked to the American delegation that "Israel was not now reprocessing spent fuel." Further discussions at the technical level yielded no response as to whether Israel had ever previously reprocessed spent fuel.[36] That same year, the October issue of the *International Atomic Energy Agency Bulletin* cited Israel as owning an unsafeguarded "pilot reprocessing facility," but gave no indication how it had acquired this information.[37] The 1979 *SIPRI Yearbook* also reported that Israel had this capability.[38] In 1981, it was revealed that assistance with building a pilot reprocessing plant had been a second element of France's 1957 deal with Israel to construct the Dimona reactor. According to Francis Perrin, the scientific chief of France's CEA from 1951 to 1970, while Paris refused to directly provide Tel Aviv with a chemical separation plant, it did not interfere with an Israeli request for assistance from a French firm, Saint Gobain Techniques Nouvelles (SGN), which built reprocessing facilities for the French nuclear program. This company provided the blueprints to Israel, whose own scientists and engineers were responsible for the installation's construction.[39] A 1962 study estimated that a separation facility would take Israel "at least two years to build."[40] Given this time schedule, and assuming that Perrin's remarks were accurate, it is possible that Israel could have possessed the capability to obtain material for nuclear weapons as early as 1959.

In addition to these reports concerning Israel's reprocessing capability, a number of other factors gave rise to proliferation concern. Given the level of Israel's interest in nuclear activities, the absence of any official statements or reports by the IAEC, or of a visible civilian nuclear energy component, rendered suspect the direction and purpose of its nuclear program. To be sure, Israel had been interested in purchasing commercial nuclear facilities. In 1964, the United States had first proposed a dual-purpose installation which would have generated electrical power and desalted seawater simultaneously.[41] Discussions between the two countries foundered first over political differences (i.e., safeguards on the entire Israeli nuclear program), and later over doubts in Israel regarding the economic justification for desalted water.[42] During President Nixon's June 1974 Middle East tour, he announced American willingness to negotiate nuclear cooperation agreements with both Egypt and Israel, including the sale of nuclear power reactors. Six months afterwards Israel indicated that it was not interested, due to Washington's insistence on a number of preconditions, including NPT ratification.[43] Through the end of the decade Israel conducted preliminary surveys for a possible nuclear reactor site, but made no final decision.[44] In January 1984, however, the government announced that it had commissioned a study to select a site for the country's first nuclear power plant. According to reports, the planned facility was a 250-megawatt heavy-water reactor, with an estimated cost of $1 to $2 billion. Israel encountered difficulties in finding nuclear exporters who did not insist on Israel's ratification of the Nonproliferation Treaty as a precondition to the sale. Since the obstacles of domestically manufacturing the reactor have been viewed as insuperable,[45] and in light of the country's recent financial problems, the future status of this reactor is uncertain.

Israel's reluctance to sign or ratify the Nonproliferation Treaty was another source of concern. Although it endorsed

U.N. General Assembly resolution 2373 (XXII) supporting the treaty, Israel had misgivings, especially in light of its particular security situation. Earlier, in May 1968, the Israeli representative to the General Assembly's First Committee had reiterated some of the qualms which had been expressed by other countries. He then went on to state:

For obvious reasons, my country has a special sensitivity to the security aspect. We are involved in an unresolved conflict in which our security is being threatened, and which has thrice in two decades erupted into armed hostilities. That conflict is marked by a massive and unchecked arms race of conventional weapons which, by our standards, have a vast capacity to kill and destroy. We cannot know what dangers and threats may confront us in the future.[46]

This view reflected Israel's belief that its security was indivisible. In other words, since the level of conventional munitions in the Middle East was more than adequate to endanger the country's survival, Israel could not afford to foreclose any available option to defend itself. Implicitly, it also suggested Israel's skepticism over the international community's willingness to come to its aid in a crisis, and therefore the country's preference to rely on its own capabilities. In addition, it was unclear what advantages would accrue to Israel in return for its signature. While there were reports that Israel demanded the reestablishment of diplomatic relations with the Soviet Union or a bilateral U.S.-Israeli defense agreement as a quid pro quo for ratification, these remained unsubstantiated, and in any case, if offered, never fulfilled.[47] Moreover, Israel had cause to doubt the impartiality of the IAEA. Due to the regional structure of the Agency's election process, Israel could not have hoped to obtain a seat on its Board of Governors; in 1976 the PLO was accorded observer status at the Agency's annual General Conferences.[48] Israeli accession to the treaty would have opened its nuclear program to inspections and subjected it to full-scope safeguards. In return, it was unlikely that it would have won any plaudits from its Arab adversaries.

As an alternative to NPT accession, since 1974 Israel had recommended the establishment of a Middle Eastern nuclear-

weapons-free-zone, based along the lines of the Treaty of Tlatelolco. The original Israeli proposal was actually in response to
a U.N. resolution calling for a regional nuclear-free zone, which
had been sponsored by Iran and Egypt in November 1974. The
operative provisions of the Iranian and Egyptian plan requested
that all Middle Eastern countries proclaim their intention to
refrain from producing, testing, obtaining, acquiring, or in any
other way possessing nuclear weapons, that they all ratify the
NPT, and that the United Nations Secretary-General act as
an intermediary by soliciting the views of all the relevant
parties.[49] Israel, on the other hand, supported the concept but
insisted that "the holding of direct consultations between the
States of the region and ultimately the convening of a regional
conference on this matter" was a superior approach.[50] In this
manner, Israel could hope to obtain the best of both worlds:
Arab recognition conferred by direct negotiations, without any
obligation to renounce its nuclear weapons option. For this
reason, the Israeli proposal remained stillborn.

Concern over the Israeli nuclear program was also aroused
by the country's development and purchase of delivery vehicles suitable for nuclear warheads. In July 1961, Israel launched
a two-stage, solid-fuel rocket, *Shavit-II*, which attained a height
of eighty miles. Three months later it tested a three-stage rocket
of greater range, *Shavit-III*.[51] Although ostensibly carried out
for monitoring atmospheric conditions, these experiments had
obvious applications for ballistic missile research. Israel reportedly also obtained surface-to-surface missiles from France
in the mid-1960s. In 1963, Israel contracted with the French
company Marcel Dassault Aviation for twenty-five MD-660
missiles. The MD-660, or "Jericho" as it was termed later by
American analysts, was capable of carrying warheads weighing
1,000 to 1,500 pounds up to 260 miles. Israel paid more than
$100 million for this weapons system. Eleven were supposedly
shipped to Israel in 1968, and another fourteen were transferred
two years later.[52] In 1974 there was one report which specu-
lated that Israel was itself manufacturing the Jericho at the rate
of three to six per month.[53] Whether imported or produced
domestically, the missile's expense and lack of accuracy raised

doubts about its military value unless it was fitted with nuclear warheads. For similar reasons, the possibility that the United States might provide Israel with Pershing ground-to-ground missiles in 1975 was viewed with alarm.[54] Israel later dropped this request. Nonetheless, in addition to the Jericho, Israel after 1976 had nuclear-capable Lance surface-to-surface missiles, which had a seventy-mile range. If modified, the Kfirs, Skyhawks, Phantoms, Mirages, and the F-15 and F-16 fighters in the Israeli Air Force's inventory could also deliver nuclear bombs.[55]

Lending support to the presumption that Israel's nuclear program was dedicated to nuclear weapons development were press reports which accused Israel of covertly acquiring weapons-grade material and/or owning a secret nuclear arsenal. All such accounts, however, have to be viewed through the prism of Middle Eastern events at the time they appeared. At any specific point, Arab, Israeli, American, or Soviet sources might have had reason for exaggerating, or inventing, stories on the scope and nature of Israel's nuclear activities.

In July 1970, the New York Times reported that as early as 1968 the White House had been informed by the CIA that Israel possessed the relevant technical competence to manufacture a nuclear warhead for the Jericho missile. The CIA did not have any concrete proof of an Israeli nuclear arsenal or even of a reprocessing capability, but based its judgment on a wealth of circumstantial evidence. The secrecy initially surrounding the Dimona reactor, reports that Israel was surreptitiously purchasing uranium from foreign suppliers, hints from Israeli officials that Israel would soon have nuclear weapons, the contract with Dassault for the MD-660 missiles, and reports that factories had been established for manufacturing solid propellants, engines, and mobile erector platforms for such missiles, all contributed to Washington's suspicion that Israel was developing nuclear arms. Further, in December 1968, during negotiations with the Johnson administration for the purchase of fifty Phantom F-4 jets, Israeli officials had reportedly asked the Defense Department if some of the aircraft could be equipped with racks for nuclear explosives. This request was denied.[56] In addition, in

October 1970, a British newspaper reported that Israeli pilots flying Skyhawk A-4 aircraft had been spotted practicing the distinctive flight profile for delivering nuclear weapons.[57]

In July 1975, the *Boston Globe* reported that senior U.S. analysts believed that Israel had more than ten nuclear weapons. These bombs, each with a yield of ten to fifteen kilotons, were built after the October 1973 war.[58] In March 1976, the *Washington Post* reported that Israel owned ten to twenty nuclear weapons, "ready and available for use."[59] The next month, *Time* magazine devoted a special report to "How Israel Got the Bomb." According to *Time*, Israel decided to construct a pilot separation plant after the June 1967 war. This was completed in 1969. After suffering battlefield reverses during the early stages of the October 1973 war, Israel ordered its nuclear inventory of thirteen bombs assembled and deployed to the assigned air force units. Before the nuclear triggers were activated, though, the battle on the Egyptian and Syrian fronts turned in Israel's favor, and the bombs were returned to their desert arsenals.[60]

In April 1977, the first details of what became known as the "Plumbat affair" were revealed. Almost ten years earlier, in 1968, approximately 200 tons of uranium oxide had disappeared while under Euratom's supervision. It was determined that through an elaborate mixture of front men, dummy corporations, guile, and resourcefulness, Israel had escaped with a shipload of yellowcake, supposedly to use as fuel in its Dimona reactor.[61] In addition, in August 1977, it was disclosed that during the 1960s over 200 pounds of highly enriched uranium was unaccountably missing from the Nuclear Materials and Equipment Corporation (NUMEC) of Apollo, Pennsylvania. Unlike yellowcake, this material could be directly used to fashion thirteen to twenty nuclear bombs. Although it was widely suspected that the weapons-grade material had ended up in Israel, U.S. government investigations failed to find any conclusive evidence that Israel was the final destination of the missing uranium.[62]

In January 1978, a CIA memorandum supposedly released by mistake revealed that American analysts had concluded in

1974 that Israel had already produced nuclear weapons. The Agency study, entitled "Prospects for Further Proliferation of Nuclear Weapons," declared that

We believe that Israel already has produced nuclear weapons. Our judgment is based on Israeli acquisition of large quantities of uranium, partly by clandestine means; the ambiguous nature of Israeli efforts in the field of uranium enrichment; and Israel's large investment in a costly missile system designed to accommodate nuclear warheads. We do not expect the Israelis to provide confirmation of widespread suspicions of their capability, either by nuclear testing or by threats of use, short of a grave threat to the nation's existence. Future emphasis is likely to be on improving weapon designs, manufacturing missiles more capable in terms of distance and accuracy than the existing 260-mile Jericho, and acquiring, or perfecting weapons for aircraft delivery.[63]

Interestingly, the report did not mention whether or not Israel had a reprocessing capability.

In June 1981 it was reported that CIA analysts testifying before Congress had disclosed that Israel was now believed to possess ten to twenty nuclear warheads that could be delivered by fighter-bombers or Jericho missiles.[64] Also in 1981, it was reported that a third element of the original 1957 French-Israeli agreement on nuclear cooperation was that in return for Israel's assistance with France's nuclear program, Israel had received scientific data on the French nuclear testing program. If true, there would have been less need for Israel to test a nuclear device of its own. This same source reported that a fourth element to the deal was that Paris had agreed to reprocess spent fuel from the Dimona facility and then ship the separated plutonium back to Israel. Under this arrangement Israel could have obtained weapons-grade material sufficient for fifteen to twenty nuclear weapons without having to construct its own chemical separation plant.[65] Two years later, in 1983, it was alleged that American intelligence services had reported as early as 1966 that Israel owned a nuclear weapon; by the end of 1969, the Nixon Administration had estimated that Israel had between twelve and sixteen deployable nuclear warheads.[66]

In early October 1986, the Insight Team of the London

Sunday Times published a detailed report of Israel's nuclear program. On the basis of testimony from Mordechai Vanunu, formerly a nuclear technician at Dimona, and using photographs taken by Vanunu and sketches of an underground reprocessing facility and nuclear bomb factory, the Insight Team reported that Israel possessed "at least 100 and as many as 200 nuclear weapons," and could increase this arsenal by five to ten nuclear weapons per year. Moreover, it declared that Israel had "almost certainly begun manufacturing thermonuclear weapons." The Insight Team concluded that "Israel now ranks as the world's sixth most powerful nuclear power." Israel confirmed that Vanunu had worked for the Israeli Atomic Energy Commission at Dimona, but otherwise refused to comment on the *Sunday Times* article.[67]

The Israeli response to these reports was invariably to deny their authenticity. Yet at the same time, Israel's statements on the subject were not as categorical a rejection of nuclear weapons acquisition as was possible. The result of these ambiguous remarks was greater uncertainty over Israel's precise nuclear status.

One of the first official Israeli replies to foreign reports of Israel's work on nuclear weapons was delivered by the then Minister of Labor, Yigal Allon, in December 1965. Allon announced that "Israel will not be the first to introduce nuclear weapons into the Middle East, but it will not be the second either."[68] Five months later, Prime Minister Eshkol, speaking before the Knesset, declared that "I have said before and I repeat that Israel has no atomic arms and will not be the first to introduce them into our region."[69] In December 1974, President Efraim Katzir exceeded the position adopted by previous government spokesmen when he revealed that "It has always been our intention to provide the potential for nuclear weapons development. We now have that potential. We will defend this country with all possible means at hand. We have to develop more powerful and new arms to protect ourselves."[70]

Retreating from the boldness of this statement, Prime Minister Rabin stressed over the next few weeks that Israel would not be the first to use nuclear weapons in the Middle East.[71] In March 1976, former Defense Minister Moshe Dayan remarked that Israel was now capable of producing nuclear bombs, and that it must have nuclear weapons before the Arab countries.[72] That September, Allon, now Israel's foreign minister, declared that his country would not be the first nuclear power in the Middle East, but that it would not tolerate the Arabs having a monopoly on nuclear weapons either.[73] After it was reported in February 1980 that an Israeli nuclear detonation was responsible for the unidentified "flash" in the South Atlantic the previous September, Israeli officials termed the story "complete nonsense" and revoked the journalist's press credentials.[74] And in June 1981, Dayan was again quoted as saying, "We are not going to be the first ones to introduce nuclear weapons into the Middle East, but we do have the capacity to produce nuclear weapons, and if the Arabs are willing to introduce nuclear weapons into the Middle East, then Israel should not be too late in having nuclear weapons too."[75] The impression gained from these statements was that Israel did not possess nuclear armaments in the sense of having fully fabricated bombs, but that it had all the components for nuclear weapons ready to be assembled in a relatively brief period if necessary.

From this overview, what can be concluded about Israel's nuclear program? If Israel's nuclear cooperation with France, the secrecy regarding the Dimona installation, its refusal to join the Nonproliferation Treaty, various rumors and reports in newspapers, and ambiguous public statements regarding its nuclear capabilities were insufficient to constitute conclusive proof, they certainly amounted to a mass of circumstantial evidence which suggested that Israel had acquired a nuclear option and possibly had constructed a secret nuclear arsenal. Still, any final judgment on the question of Israeli nuclear weapons must be the Scottish verdict of "not proven."

Yet if Israel did not have nuclear weapons, then why did it not ratify the NPT and open its nuclear program to inspection? Conversely, if Israel had covertly stockpiled nuclear bombs, why did it not publicly articulate its nuclear status or conduct a nuclear test? In other words, why did Israel neither admit nor irrefutably deny that it possessed nuclear armaments? In order to understand why Israel maintained this policy of uncertainty, it is necessary to examine the possible inhibitions to and motivations for Israeli nuclear weapons acquisition.

ISRAELI NUCLEAR WEAPONS: INHIBITIONS, MOTIVATIONS, CONSEQUENCES

Nonacquisition and Full Disclosure

For Israel to have adopted a credible policy of no nuclear weapons, it would have been necessary to ratify the Nonproliferation Treaty and open its nuclear facilities to inspection. Domestic, regional, and international considerations might all have persuaded Israel to select this course.

Domestically, in the early 1960s there were voices in Israel which argued that the country should renounce nuclear armaments on moral grounds. The Jewish people, as victims throughout history, had a special obligation not to develop weapons of mass extermination; having suffered one holocaust, they should seek to prevent a war of atomic destruction.[76] More prosaically, expenditures on a nuclear weapons program would have been a constant drain on the budget for conventional munitions. If funding levels for conventional weapons were left unaffected, nuclear armaments would have then imposed an extra burden upon Israeli taxpayers.[77] In addition, Israel's plans for commercial nuclear power would have been assisted by NPT accession. Nuclear suppliers would have been willing to sell nuclear technology once Israel was a party to the treaty.

Within the Middle East, an Israeli nonnuclear policy might have aided diplomatic efforts for a peace settlement. By reducing the threat to the Arab regimes, a trend toward moderation and restraint might have been encouraged, which in turn could have fostered an atmosphere more conducive to direct negotiations between the belligerents.[78] In international affairs, Israel could have also hoped to curry favorable world opinion by forswearing nuclear weapons. It would have assuaged U.S. proliferation fears, and won support from the American and European Jewish communities. Moreover, ratification of the Nonproliferation Treaty would not have seriously diminished Tel Aviv's option of acquiring nuclear arms at a later date. If necessary, it could have always legally withdrawn from the agreement. Also, under the terms of the NPT, Israel would not have been prohibited from obtaining all the elements required for fabricating nuclear bombs upon short notice.

These reasons for a public nonacquisition policy appeared more persuasive because of the level of Israel's conventional military strength. Israel could have afforded to forgo nuclear weapons because after June 1967, with the possible exception of the first days of the Yom Kippur War, its security was never severely threatened. In fact, Israel emerged at the end of the 1970s in a stronger position militarily and politically than at any time in the country's history.

At the nuclear level, Israel had little to fear from its neighbors in the Middle East. Nuclear programs in the region were either nonexistent or negligible. Egypt, for example, had only the 2-megawatt research reactor it had received from the Soviet Union, and which had become operational in 1961. While perhaps valuable for training scientists and technicians, it was not capable of producing weapons-grade material.[79] The exceptions to this general rule were Iran and Iraq, both of whom had ambitious nuclear programs. Tehran's plans in the nuclear field, however, were derailed by the overthrow of the Shah in 1979 and its war with Iraq the following year. Baghdad's nuclear activities were first impeded in April 1979 when a reactor core due to be shipped to Iraq was sabotaged while in storage in the French town of La Seyne-sur-Mer, later by Iran's bombing of the Osiraq research facility in September 1980, and most thoroughly by Israel's destruction of the 40-megawatt reactor on June 7, 1981.[80] It was likely that Israel's raid also inhibited prospective nuclear exporters from furnishing technology and assistance to countries in the region.[81]

At the conventional level, the IDF was clearly the Middle East's dominant military actor. Israel's occupation of the territories seized during the June 1967 war more than doubled its size, and provided a buffer between its adversaries and the country's heartland. Washington's greater involvement in Middle Eastern affairs following the Six Day War resulted in the United States becoming Israel's primary arms supplier; after October 1973, the transfer of advanced American weaponry accelerated, thereby cementing Israel's qualitative advantage over its opponents. In addition, Egypt's military forces were weakened after July 1972, when Cairo ordered the departure of the estimated 20,000 Soviet military advisers and experts from the country and Moscow retaliated by imposing an arms embargo. Further, Syria's attention after April 1976 was primarily concentrated on its direct military intervention in the Lebanese civil war. As a consequence of these events, by 1977 Israel was stronger in main battle tanks, armored personnel carriers, artillery, and high-performance combat aircraft relative to its own position, and versus its main Arab adversaries, than four years previous. (See Table 5.1.)

TABLE 5.1
Changes in Weapons Inventories, 1973–1977:
Israel, Egypt, Syria, Iraq*

Ratios	1973 Arabs:Israel	1977 Arabs:Israel
Main battle tanks	2.21:1.00	1.90:1.00
Armored personnel carriers	3.30:1.00	1.47:1.00
Artillery	6.41:1.00	2.90:1.00
Fighter-bombers	3.16:1.00	2.03:1.00

*The addition of Jordan would not have appreciably altered these figures.
SOURCE: Geoffrey Kemp and Michael Vlahos, "The Arab-Israel Military Balance in 1977," in Colin Legum and Haim Shaked, eds., *Middle East Contemporary Survey*, vol. 1, 1976–77 (London: Holmes and Meier, 1978), p. 76.

Moreover, the introduction of new conventional weapons technologies, in particular the development of precision-guided munitions (PGMs), was generally judged to favor the defense, thereby aiding Israel's task of defending its borders.[82] Toward the end of the decade, internal turmoil in Iran and the outbreak of the Iran-Iraq war removed two potential actors from participating in hostilities against Israel. Due to Israel's improvement in the material indices of military power, its traditional supremacy in tactics and strategy, and internecine struggles among competing Middle Eastern states, most observers believed that the result of another Arab-Israeli war would be a decisive Israeli victory within only a few days.[83]

The largest increment of security was provided not by armaments, however, but by diplomatic initiative, namely by President Sadat's November 1977 journey to Jerusalem, and the political process this set in motion. With the United States serving as intermediary, on March 26, 1979, President Sadat and Prime Minister Menahem Begin signed the Treaty of Peace between the Arab Republic of Egypt and the State of Israel. According to the agreement's provisions, Cairo was barred from stationing more than one mechanized infantry division and four lightly armed battalions in the Sinai Desert. This accord not only demilitarized Israel's southern flank, and allowed it to turn its attention to possible encroachment on its northern border, it also removed the country's most powerful opponent in the Middle East from future military encounters. This diplomatic success, coupled with Israel's enlarged weapons stockpiles, immeasurably enhanced the country's security. In part as a reflection of this, Israel's 1981 military expenditures were lower than at any time since 1972.[84] For all these reasons, then, Israel could have publicly rejected nuclear weapons acquisition.

On the other hand, the certainty of a nonnuclear Israel might have removed an incentive for the Arab regimes to arrive at some negotiated solution to the dispute. Further, it might have emboldened them to once again try to overrun the Jewish state by conventional means. And it might also have stimulated

Arab interest in developing or purchasing nuclear bombs by offering the prospect of an "ultimate" weapon with which it could finally destroy Israel.

Acquisition and Full Disclosure

For Israel to have become the world's sixth nuclear weapons state, it would have had to publicly articulate its nuclear status or test a nuclear device. That such a policy might have furthered the country's diplomatic objectives in the Middle East and in international affairs, enhanced Israeli deterrence, and if necessary, defended the country against military aggression, were all sufficient inducements for Israel to construct nuclear weapons.

Neither domestic opinion nor cost would have been an impediment to Israel's acquisition of nuclear weapons. By the 1970s the earlier appeals for nuclear abstention were less frequent. In a March 1976 opinion poll conducted by the Tel Aviv newspaper Ha-Aretz, 77 percent of those questioned thought Israel should have nuclear arms.[85] Concerning the expense of building and maintaining a nuclear force, it was believed even by opponents of Israeli nuclear armament that the country's ample military budget could absorb this added cost without too great a dislocation.[86] Further, economic savings could have been realized by having nuclear weapons serve as a substitute for conventional munitions.[87]

According to some observers, Israel could have used nuclear weapons as a means of procuring Arab recognition and acceptance as a permanent figure on the Middle East landscape. A nuclear-armed Israel would have disabused Arab leaders of the notion that the Jewish state could be militarily defeated. The ensuing immobilism would have countered economic and military trends in the Arab countries adverse to Israel's interests. More important, Tel Aviv's possession of nuclear weapons would in time have produced a psychological reorientation throughout the region which would first persuade the Arab regimes of the futility of continued hostilities, and then pressure them to seek a negotiated solution to the conflict. In this manner, an Israeli nuclear arsenal would have been employed as an instrument of political intimidation in order to impose a peace settlement which would permit Israel to retain control of the occupied territories.[88] Other analysts shared the belief that nuclear weapons could succeed in arranging a cease-fire in the Arab-Israeli dispute, but argued that real peace could only be attained if an overt Israeli nuclear posture were coupled with territorial concessions, namely Israeli withdrawal to lines approximating its pre-1967 borders.[89] Yet a third possible outcome of Israeli nuclear weapons acquisition would have been a joint Soviet-American diktat to all the parties to the conflict, prior to the extension of superpower guarantees in order to prevent future hostilities.[90] Whether by compellence, conciliation, or coercion, common to all three scenarios was the view that Israeli nuclear arms would have heralded some form of diplomatic settlement to the Arab-Israeli dispute.

In international affairs, it was claimed that nuclear weapons were necessary for Israel in order for it to escape a potentially dangerous dependency on the United States. Given America's manifold interests in the Middle East, there was a natural divergence between Washington's objectives in the region and how Israel interpreted its security needs. If unrelieved, this tension might have impelled the United States to use its influence as Israel's major external source of armaments and financial support to force its client to tailor its policies to coincide with U.S. strategy for the area. Israel's acquisition of nuclear weapons would have guaranteed its freedom of maneuver by reducing its reliance on the U.S., thereby eliminating the possibility that Israel might be pressured into making political concessions injurious to the country's welfare.[91] In addition, a nuclear arsenal would have served as a form of insurance against possible American desertion of the country.[92]

Even if such policy transformations could not be imputed to an overt nuclear posture, tradition held that nuclear weapons were useful for deterrence. With the Yom Kippur War seen as a victory by the Arab world, with Israel's political credibility impaired by its failure to obtain the Pershing missile system it requested from Washington in 1975, and with an escalating and economically debilitating arms race with the Arab states, Israel might have sought to bolster its conventional deterrent by the acquisition of nuclear arms.

Israeli nuclear weapons might have been valuable to deter a range of threats that otherwise could have jeopardized the country's security. Given past Arab interest in developing or purchasing nuclear bombs,[93] eventual Arab acquisition of nuclear armaments seemed certain. Israel's nuclear arsenal would have acted as a deterrent to nuclear attack once this situation obtained.[94] This nuclearization of the Middle East would have gradually evolved into a stable nuclear balance, not too unlike the US-USSR nuclear deterrent relationship.[95] Prior to Arab acquisition, Israel's nuclear weapons would have countered the threat to the country's existence posed by the Arab preponderance in manpower and conventional munitions by raising the prospect of inflicting unacceptable damage to Arab military units, infrastructure, and population groups.[96] The injection of a nuclear component in the Arab-Israeli struggle would also have deterred less than total threats to Israel. Uncertainty over what interests Israel would have deemed peripheral or essential, along with a general sense of caution induced by the presence of nuclear weapons, would have moved Arab countries to deny the use of their territory as sanctuary for terrorists, for fear of provoking an Israeli nuclear response.[97] Further, the Soviet Union might have been dissuaded by an Israeli nuclear force from assuming a greater role in Middle Eastern affairs, either indirectly through arms transfers to Arab regimes or by direct military intervention. Restraint would have been engendered by the possibility that a nuclear Israel might deliver a punitive strike against cities in the southwestern Soviet Union, or alternatively, target Arab capitals in the event of Soviet aggrandizement.[98]

Finally, if deterrence failed, Israeli nuclear weapons could have also been employed for defensive purposes under a number of scenarios. If a situation arose similar to May 1967, Israel might have been tempted once again to launch a preemptive strike, only this time with nuclear warheads.[99] If a conventional war broke out, tactical nuclear weapons might have been preferable to conventional weapons in opposing Arab tank columns, especially in light of Israeli sensitivity to casualties.[100] And if the battle was going against Israel, Israel would have had little hesitation in using nuclear weapons in a "last resort" attempt to save the country from imminent destruction.[101]

On the other hand, it was maintained that an Israeli policy of open acquisition of nuclear weapons would have been detrimental to diplomatic efforts toward peace in the region, harmful to U.S.-Israeli relations, unnecessary and possibly counterproductive as a deterrent, and inappropriate to defend the country.

A nuclear Israel would not have been able to convert its exalted military strength into diplomatic currency. Past Israeli conventional superiority and its possession of the occupied territories as potential bargaining chips had been unable to bring Jordan and Syria to officially recognize and negotiate with Israel. Moreover, by implying the collective scientific and military backwardness of the Arab world, Israel's nuclear monopoly would have humiliated its opponents; no other single action could have better served as a catalyst for Arab unity. In such circumstances, the result would have been greater Arab intransigence rather than flexibility on the question of a Middle East peace.[102] In addition, Israel's behavior would have outraged world opinion and increased the country's isolation. More important, its association with the United States might have ended. Although domestic and strategic considerations might have tempered the American reaction, an overt Israeli nuclear posture would nonetheless have violated a tacit understanding between the two countries, contravened Washington's nonproliferation policy, and alienated the American Jewish community upon which Israel depended for support. Confronted by an unruly client, and facing a nuclear Middle East and the risk of escalation to the superpower level, the United

States might have decided that the wisest course would be to abandon Israel and minimize its involvement in the region.[103]

As long as Israel's conventional capabilities were maintained at adequate strength, nuclear weapons were unnecessary for either deterrence or defense. With the series of disengagement agreements in the Sinai between Israel and Egypt after the Yom Kippur War, a process which culminated in the March 1979 peace treaty, the threat of another full-scale conflict gradually diminished. With the removal of the major Arab actor from the contest, deterrence and defense requirements were considerably reduced. Further, analysts had declared that Israeli nuclear weapons would not in any case have necessarily deterred the outbreak of a war waged by the Arabs for limited objectives.[104] Lesser threats, the ones in fact Israel was most likely to face, would likewise not have been deterred. In these situations, Israeli tactics specifically designed to handle guerrilla transborder incursions would have been more discriminating and hence more suitable than nuclear weapons employment.[105]

In addition, while certain Arab countries had been interested in nuclear weapons, none had made a concerted commitment to actual development. An overt Israeli nuclear posture, however, could have provoked Arab determination to match its acquisition.[106] Given Israel's concentration of population and industry in a narrow band along the Mediterranean, its relative vulnerability in a nuclear Middle East would have been decidedly unfavorable when compared with the greater number and dispersion of targets in the Arab world. Also, nuclear weapons in the Middle East would have constantly been subject to the alleged irrational impulses of Arab despots.[107] Nor need one subscribe to such an uncharitable portrayal of the Arab character to realize that the delicate balance of nuclear deterrence in the region would have been contingent upon a number of variables: the possession of stable, second-strike capabilities, clear lines of communication among all parties, the security of nuclear weapons from nongovernmental seizure, and a shared sense of mutual vulnerability. That such a system could have been established and operated without error was, at best, questionable.[108] Somewhat contradictorily, it was also argued that even if an Arab country acquired nuclear armaments before Israel, it would have been self-deterred because any nuclear strike would have risked killing Israel's one million plus Arab inhabitants as well as destroyed the very property that had been the object of Arab discontent since 1948.[109]

Further, open possession of nuclear arms by Israel could have augmented, not lessened, the Soviet role in the Middle East. Faced with a loss of influence after years of investment in an area of strategic importance, and entreated by its Arab client states, Moscow might have felt compelled to increase the amount and type of conventional arms supplies, extend formal security guarantees, station nuclear weapons under its control on Arab territory, or even transfer nuclear armaments to Arab countries.[110] In sum, according to this view, Israel's acquisition of nuclear weapons would have been harmful for obtaining the country's diplomatic, deterrent, and defense objectives.

A Policy of Uncertainty

Given the ambiguity of Israel's nuclear status, cultivated by the secrecy of its nuclear program, its development and purchase of nuclear-capable delivery vehicles, its stance on the Nonproliferation Treaty, and its semantic contortions on the question of an Israeli nuclear force, it appeared that Israel hoped to derive the advantages of both overt nuclear acquisition and nonacquisition, without any of their attendant liabilities, by adopting a deliberate policy of nuclear uncertainty. Whether Israel had only a nuclear option or actually owned a "bomb in the basement" was immaterial for the success of this policy. As long as secrecy was preserved, this was merely a distinction without a difference. By exploiting its indeterminate nuclear status, Israel attempted to maximize its position vis-à-vis its Arab adversaries and in international affairs.

Within the Middle East, the threat to go nuclear might have deterred conventional aggression, or limited an opponent's military objectives, equally as well as an overt Israeli nuclear posture. The possibility that Israel had secretly stockpiled nuclear bombs would have deterred a conventional attack due to the fear of provoking nuclear retaliation.[111] Or, if full-scale hostilities did occur, the Arab countries would have been deterred from progressing beyond a certain threshold to strike at Israel's vital interests. According to some observers, Egypt's limited aims and Syria's reluctance to cross Israel's pre-1967 borders in the Yom Kippur War were attributed to their belief that more vigorous prosecution of the battle might have triggered a nuclear response.[112] In addition, the assumption of a secret Israeli nuclear arsenal could have persuaded Arab leaders that Israel could not be militarily defeated and therefore the most intelligent course was to end the prevailing state of war. This motive was frequently mentioned to explain President Sadat's change of policy toward Israel during the 1970s.[113] Moreover, in view of several factors—the country's history of isolation and insecurity, the number of actors and interests in the Middle East, and the region's volatility—prudent statesmanship would dictate an Israeli nuclear option, or even secret acquisition. Israel's policy of uncertainty in fact placed no constraints upon the country's nuclear program nor compromised future employment of nuclear weapons in the event of a national emergency.

In international affairs, if Israel refrained from publicly revealing that it had developed nuclear weapons, it would have conferred greater legitimacy and persuasiveness upon its requests that a Middle East nuclear-weapons-free zone be established. Politically, this would have given the impression that the nuclearization of the region could be avoided if the Arabs denied themselves nuclear weapons, while at the same time removing, or at least reducing, the main rationale for an Arab nuclear development program. For Israel, this position would also have presented a positive public image before the world.[114]

It was further claimed that Israel's nuclear ambiguity was

especially productive in regard to its relations with the United States. While the U.S. might have continued to assist Israel militarily and financially because of moral, domestic, or strategic considerations even if Israel publicly renounced any nuclear aspirations and opened all its nuclear facilities to inspection, the possibility of a secret nuclear arsenal invested Washington's policy toward Israel and the region with a nuclear component that made it more receptive to Israeli concerns. As a result, Washington's sensitivity to the spread of nuclear weapons in effect precluded both excessive American pressure on Israel to alter its policies and American indifference to the country's fate. In order to ensure that Israel did not move to an overt nuclear posture, the U.S. was willing to lend substantial financial and diplomatic support, and, in particular, transfer advanced conventional armaments. As an early example, it had been reported that during the 1960s Israel had agreed to curtail its nuclear activities at the Dimona installation in return for American supplies of Skyhawk light bombers and other conventional weapons.[115] Fear that Israel might have resorted to nuclear arms during the early days of the Yom Kippur War was also supposed to have been a factor in U.S. willingness to resupply Israel at the cost of entertaining substantial Arab criticism.[116]

In addition to influencing its relationship with Washington, Israel could have used this same logic to dissuade the United States from selling certain amounts and types of conventional munitions to the Arab states by arguing that an insecure Israel would be compelled to publicly disclose its possession of a nuclear arsenal.[117] Nor would the Soviet Union have been immune from this reasoning. An Israeli policy of nuclear ambiguity might thus have forced Moscow to reconsider its Middle East arms transfer policy, while at the same time also have deterred it from greater direct involvement in the dispute.[118]

This policy of uncertainty seemed the best possible strategy for Israel to pursue. It offered many of the benefits with few of the liabilities of its other alternatives. It provided a measure of compellence to assist the search for a diplomatic solution to the Arab-Israeli conflict, deterrence against conventional attack, and, if required, defense by using nuclear weapons in extremis.

Yet there were limits to the advantages this policy could bestow. It was not an unalloyed success. It could not force the Arab states to officially recognize and accept the Jewish state; the correlation between Egypt's diplomatic volte-face and its suspicion of Israeli nuclear weapons was questionable. Further, it might have even obstructed a peaceful solution to the dispute by infusing a psychological dimension of deep distrust and fear that reduced the prospects for reconciliation.[119] Nor did this Israeli policy of ambiguity deter conventional attack or lesser threats to the country—witness the Yom Kippur War and continued terrorist incidents. According to some observers, rather than discouraging an arms race, the nuclear factor helped stimulate and intensify the qualitative and quantitative competition in conventional armaments.[120] And because Israel's policy combined uncertainty over capability with uncertainty over intentions, there was the risk that miscalculation by adversaries, or allies, might result in a nuclear catastrophe.

Finally, while Israel appeared able to exercise its indeterminate nuclear status to acquire sophisticated conventional weapons from the United States, and was one factor which at times appeared to transform the relationship into one approaching that of formal allies, Israel was unable to obtain from Washington a security guarantee or bilateral defense agreement.[121] Fearful of being dragged into a costly political and military involvement, of provoking a Soviet response, of alienating Arab countries and jeopardizing its overall strategy for the region, and of compromising its position as honest broker between the two rival sides, Washington found it preferable simply to supply conventional arms and financial assistance. Therefore, while Israel derived important benefits from its uncertain nuclear posture, it was unable to use this instrument to fully realize its policy objectives.

CONCLUSION

Given the magnitude of the diplomatic and military problems that confronted Israel, it is perhaps surprising that a policy of nuclear uncertainty could alleviate any of them. That it was able to do so was due in part to the skill with which Israel maintained its ambiguous nuclear status. The secrecy which enveloped Israel's nuclear activities, its refusal to sign or ratify the NPT, reports of its covert acquisition of a nuclear arsenal, and its less than total public explanations of the country's nuclear capabilities, all contributed to creating the impression that Israel either possessed or could quickly acquire nuclear weapons. Its intention to use nuclear arms to defend its sovereignty if required was made more credible by the memory of the six million Jews killed during the Second World War; the preservation of the state of Israel was necessary in order to prevent a similar tragedy from ever again overwhelming the Jewish people.[122]

Interestingly, however, the policies of the other major parties to the conflict—Arab, Soviet, and American—were also served by Israel retaining its uncertain nuclear posture rather than announcing that it possessed a nuclear arsenal. For the Arab countries, a recognition of Israel's nuclear capabilities would have been an admission of impotence that could have demoralized the Arab world. By placing the hope of eliminating Israel from the Middle East beyond its grasp, it would have removed a prime force in the Arab states for maintaining domestic cohesion. Such an admission might also have been seen as a betrayal of the pan-Arab cause and thereby jeopardize the already precarious stability of some Arab regimes. Moreover, it would have focused world attention on nuclear weapons proliferation, and thus displaced the main source of Arab grievance—the belief that all of historic Palestine should be occupied by the Arabs. Given these calculations, it was far better to remain silent on the issue.

For the Soviet Union, a continuation of a state of tension

short of war in the region presented it with the optimal environment for increasing its influence. It was not forced either to commit itself directly or to disengage from the region. Between the extremes of a full-scale conventional war, in which Israel was certain to triumph, and a general Arab reconciliation with Israel, which was highly unlikely, Moscow's policy could best operate. Open acknowledgment by the USSR of an Israeli nuclear arsenal would have jeopardized its policy by chancing that Arab countries might move closer to either extreme, by waging a preventive war or by signing a comprehensive Middle East peace settlement. The state of no-war, no-peace maintained the Arab countries in the role of supplicants for conventional munitions and enhanced Moscow's value as a diplomatic counter to American support for Israel. Based on this assessment, the Soviet Union would not have wanted to draw public attention to Israel's nuclear capabilities.[123]

Finally, since at least the 1974 CIA report, and probably earlier, the United States had been aware of Israeli nuclear weapons development. Were a country with which it maintained such intimate relations to adopt an overt nuclear posture, Washington would not only have experienced considerable embarrassment, but would also have been held responsible for Israel's action by the Arab states and, as a result, would have suffered a loss of prestige and influence throughout the Middle East. Further, it would have introduced a new and more dangerous factor into any American efforts to manage a crisis in the region. In return for Israeli nuclear "restraint," the United States was willing to dispense military and economic assistance, and lend diplomatic support. Thus, because Israel could use its nuclear option to realize some if not all of its policy objectives, it preserved its uncertain nuclear status. And since an overt Israeli nuclear posture was not in the interests of any of the other major actors involved in the Arab-Israeli dispute, Israel was able to conduct this policy unchallenged.

6.

South Africa

Contrary to the idea of racial equality, which was elevated to a universal principle after the Second World War, were the racial practices of South Africa. Alone among the countries of the world, South Africa determined legal and political rights on the basis of racial characteristics, and sought to preserve the privileged position of whites in society through a legislatively mandated and comprehensively institutionalized system of separate development, or apartheid. With the 1948 election of the Nationalist Party, it was the maintenance of the distinctive Afrikaner *volk* that commanded not only the country's internal policies, but also dominated its foreign affairs.

During the 1950s South Africa was able to pursue its internal racial program unhindered by outside interference. Its value as a source of critical minerals, its strategic location astride the South Atlantic and Indian Oceans, and its devotion to opposing the spread of Soviet influence in Africa were viewed as important assets for the West. South Africa proved its worth as an anticommunist ally by dispatching a fighter squadron to Korea, and by contracting with the United States and Britain to supply uranium for their expanding nuclear weapons projects. Pretoria further consolidated its ties with London by signing the Simonstown naval base agreement in 1955.[1] Although the apartheid issue was first formally placed on the agenda of the U.N. General Assembly in September 1952, international attention at the time was far more occupied with East-West tensions and areas of superpower competition. Pretoria's relations with much of Africa during this period were amicable. As a result of these developments, South Africa was largely successful at attracting overseas investment and at muting international criticism of apartheid.[2]

South Africa's relative tranquility was broken by a number of events in the early 1960s. Most important was the March 1960 Sharpeville tragedy, in which sixty-seven blacks were killed during a demonstration to protest the pass laws. For the white community, this incident raised the spectre of black urban violence, and was a forceful reminder of their minority status. Further, it undermined the government's previous claims of political stability; in the following twelve months there was an outflow of over half the country's gold and foreign exchange reserves.[3] In November 1960, Ethiopia and Liberia mounted a legal challenge before the International Court of Justice over South Africa's right to administer the former League of Nations mandate territory of South West Africa.[4] Five months later Pretoria was forced to withdraw from the British Commonwealth. In June 1963, the Organization of African Unity (OAU) was formed, with one of its express goals the achievement of independence for those countries still under minority rule. In the United Nations, a special committee on apartheid was established and a host of resolutions condemning the Republic were passed.

South Africa was able to withstand these pressures and emerge in mid-decade with renewed confidence. Incidents of black violence were virtually eliminated after the outlawing of black resistance organizations and the Rivonia raid in July 1963. Domestic order, economic growth, and increased military expenditures reversed earlier forecasts of the Republic's imminent collapse. The economic and military weakness of the new

African states made any threat of direct action against South Africa all but inconceivable. And the International Court's unexpected dismissal of the South West Africa case in July 1966 illustrated the essential impotence of the United Nations and removed any possibility of international intervention.[5]

From this position of strength, Pretoria attempted to extend its influence beyond the Limpopo River and throughout Africa. This "outward movement" (uitwaardse beweging) sought to use the country's superior economic power to overcome political inhibitions to dealing with the Republic. For South Africa, it provided the opportunity to satisfy its traditional aspiration of assuming a leading role in Africa, to develop new markets for South African products, and to enhance its security by creating a network of cooperative commercial, cultural, and scientific relations. Through this "dialogue" with other African states, it hoped also to persuade the Western powers that they would not risk international opprobrium by joining with the Republic in some form of military association, either in an enlarged NATO or in a South Atlantic Treaty Organization designed to protect the Cape Route.[6] The policy's broad goal was to moderate external hostility to the regime's racial practices. After receptive responses to its policy from Botswana, Lesotho, and Swaziland, which had in fact already been linked to South Africa through a joint customs union and common currency, Pretoria achieved uneven success, only appealing to the few African countries more anxious about the spread of communism than about the adoption of a publicly defiant stance against apartheid. Prime Minister Vorster's September 1970 offer to sign a "nonagression pact" with any African state seemed to presume that the cause of African enmity was suspicion over South Africa's territorial ambitions rather than its racial policies. In any case, it did little to enhance the attractiveness of Pretoria's overtures.

South Africa's position in world affairs endured a series of setbacks during the 1970s. In June 1971, the International Court delivered an Advisory Opinion on South West Africa that effectively rescinded its 1966 decision. It ruled that the Republic's mandate for the territory had been lawfully terminated by General Assembly resolution 2145 (XXI) of October 27, 1966, which declared that since South Africa had failed to fulfill its obligations under the mandate the territory was now "the direct responsibility" of the U.N. This was followed in 1974 by an attempt to expel South Africa from the United Nations, a move which was only blocked by the vetoes of the U.S., Britain, and France. The Republic was nevertheless barred from the General Assembly's XXIXth session. Far more damaging to Pretoria's interests was the overthrow of the Caetano regime in Lisbon in April 1974 and the subsequent devolution of Portugal's holdings in Africa. The breakdown of the January 1975 Alvor accord for the peaceful transference of power in Angola led to civil war among the three rival liberation movements, and tempted South Africa into an ill-conceived military intervention in late October 1975. The mission's failure ended not only with the imposition of a hostile government in Luanda, but also with the introduction of substantial arms transfers from the Soviet Union and 20,000 Cubans to support the new regime.[7] This, in turn, increased the Republic's exposure in neighboring Namibia to guerrilla raids by the South West Africa People's Organization (SWAPO). These developments, together with the emergence of an avowedly Marxist regime in Mozambique, made it apparent that the situation of the white settler regime in Rhodesia was no longer tenable. Despite a record of assistance to Salisbury since its 1965 unilateral declaration of independence, Pretoria's priority was to avoid a protracted guerrilla war on its northern border and instead to help install a government well-disposed to South Africa. The inability of Ian Smith and Joshua Nkomo to arrive at an understanding during their April 1975 meeting at Victoria Falls, however, ruined any immediate chance of a nonviolent transfer to black rule.

South Africa received few accolades for its diplomatic efforts to achieve a peaceful resolution of the Rhodesian hostilities, and actually became further estranged from the international community during this period. In 1975 the Simonstown naval base agreement expired and was not renewed. In April

1976, the United States reversed its previous policy of "selective relaxation" toward the white minority regimes in southern Africa and strongly endorsed majority rule.[8] The Soweto riots two months later, in which 176 blacks were killed, elicited worldwide censure of the Republic's racial policies. This reaction, coupled with the general hostility toward South Africa, moved Pretoria to inform the country that in the event of a military conflict it would not be supported by the West. The Republic's absence of allies, and the fear of possible aggression from neighboring states simultaneous with internal turmoil, led the government to outline a "total national strategy" to mobilize the country's resources for defense.[9] International criticism of South Africa increased in late 1977 with the death of black consciousness leader Steven Biko while in police detention and with the banning of domestic critics of apartheid. The Carter administration's emphasis on human rights ensured a continued American commitment to the cause of black independence; further, its professed absence of "an inordinate fear of communism"[10] signaled to Pretoria that it could no longer hope to win sympathy in Washington by portraying itself as the last anticommunist bastion in southern Africa. In the United Nations, SWAPO was extended observer status in 1976, and the following year Security Council resolution 418 made mandatory the voluntary arms embargo which had existed since 1963. In addition, five Western states (the U.S., Britain, France, West Germany, and Canada) created a "Contact Group" in order to take a more active role in settling the Namibia dispute. Their efforts led to a September 1978 Security Council resolution calling for U.N.-supervised elections, thereby placing additional pressure on South Africa to relinquish its control over the territory.

South Africa's standing was further damaged by a number of developments toward the end of the decade. In domestic affairs, the government's authority was harmed by revelations in late 1978 of high-level corruption and misuse of funds by officials. A rise in black unemployment in the late 1970s and the exodus of blacks from the Republic to join militant opposition organizations fueled an upsurge in violence against the regime. As a response to Prime Minister's Botha's "constellation of states" scheme for economic cooperation in the region, black African leaders assembled in 1979 and 1980 and established a Southern African Development Coordination Conference (SADCC) to promote greater trade among themselves. Once they could escape South Africa's economic orbit, they would then have the freedom to pursue active measures against Pretoria.[11] The Lancaster House accords in October 1979, which outlined a peaceful transition from white to black rule in Rhodesia, were negotiated without Pretoria's participation. This inability to shape the political destiny of the region was confirmed when South Africa's hopes for a moderate government in Rhodesia led by Bishop Abel Muzorewa were thwarted by the election of the more ideological Robert Mugabe in April 1980. The continued presence of Cuban and East German personnel in southern Africa was a constant source of concern for Pretoria. When weighed cumulatively, these setbacks spurred talk of a "Fortress South Africa," with that country a solitary actor against the outside world. And although the Republic believed that it had won a dispensation as a result of the 1980 American presidential election, there was little actual indication that the Reagan administration's policy of "constructive engagement" envisioned any relaxation of U.S. commitment to a nonviolent evolution toward a stable, nonracial South Africa.[12]

By the latter half of the 1970s, it appeared that South Africa's search for security and a measure of international legitimacy had failed. At home, the continued disenfranchisement of seventeen million blacks by four and a half million whites fed black discontent and violence. In southern Africa, the fall of the Portuguese African empire and the white Rhodesian government removed a cordon sanitaire from around the Republic, while Pretoria's intervention in the Angolan civil war had been a serious miscalculation. If on the basis of its economic vitality South Africa was able to court African countries, it was absolutely incapable of translating these ties into more durable bonds of friendship and mutual interest. The hostility of the countries in the region, their political commitment to majority rule, and their financial support—and in some cases offers of sanctuary—to guerrilla movements pursuing a military solution, all contributed to South Africa's growing insecurity. In international affairs, Pretoria's inability to forge military links with the West, the change in U.S. policy toward the region, and the level of abuse South Africa was constantly subjected to in the United Nations, further contributed to the regime's isolation. Above all, South Africa failed to stem domestic and international condemnation of apartheid. By 1981 the Republic had formal diplomatic relations with only fifteen states.[13]

Responsibility for South Africa's deteriorating security situation ultimately pointed to the country's domestic affairs, and the government's reluctance to fundamentally alter its doctrine of apartheid. The historical inability of the white regime to entertain substantial power-sharing with the black majority appeared to foreclose any chance of a peaceful transfer of political power. This pessimistic appraisal, in turn, stimulated some foreign observers to speculate that Pretoria might therefore develop nuclear weapons in order to alleviate the country's insecurity and to guarantee the preservation of its peculiar racial policies. The technical sophistication of Pretoria's nuclear development, statements by South African officials alluding to potential military applications of the country's nuclear program, two enigmatic events in the latter half of the 1970s, and the Republic's refusal to sign the Nonproliferation Treaty, all contributed to supposition that South Africa possessed both the capability and intention to acquire nuclear weapons.

SOUTH AFRICA'S NUCLEAR PROGRAM

South Africa's nuclear program was initially based on the country's abundant uranium reserves. The presence of uranium in

SOUTH AFRICA: CHRONOLOGY OF SIGNIFICANT EVENTS

Nuclear Developments		*Political Developments*
	1948	Election of the Nationalist Party
South Africa contracts with the Combined Development Trust to supply uranium and receives technical assistance for its nuclear industry in return	1950	
	1955	South Africa and Britain sign the Simonstown naval base agreement
	1960	Sharpeville killings (March)
	1961	South Africa is forced to leave the Commonwealth
	1963	South Africa accedes to the PTBT (October)
The 20 megawatt Safari-1 nuclear research reactor goes critical (March)	1965	
	1966	ICJ dismisses the South West Africa Case (July)
		UNGA declares that South West Africa is "the direct responsibility" of the U.N. (October)
Prime Minister Vorster announces the development of a "unique" uranium enrichment process (July)	1970	
Chairman of AEB states that South Africa's uranium enrichment capability now allows it to make nuclear weapons (April)	1971	ICJ Advisory Opinion says South West Africa is lawfully the responsibility of the U.N. (June)
AEB's Vice President says that South Africa's nuclear program is more advanced	1974	Overthrow of the Caetano government in Lisbon (April)

SOUTH AFRICA: CHRONOLOGY OF SIGNIFICANT EVENTS (Continued)

Nuclear Developments		Political Developments
than India's, and that South Africa can make a nuclear bomb if it wants to (July)		Attempt to expel South Africa from the U.N. is vetoed by the U.S., Britain, and France
Valindaba pilot enrichment plant begins operations (April)	1975	Simonstown naval base agreement expires and is not renewed
	1975–1976	Civil war in Angola; South Africa intervenes
South Africa contracts with a French consortium for the Koeberg facility (May)	1976	U.S. reverses its policy toward southern Africa (April)
		Soweto riots end with 176 blacks killed (June)
Discovery of the Kalahari site (August)	1977	Carter administration is installed, emphasizes human rights
		UNSC resolution makes mandatory the arms embargo against South Africa (November)
U.S. cancels its nuclear fuel supply contract with South Africa (November)	1978	UNSC resolution calls for U.N.-supervised elections in South West Africa (September)
Vela satellite detects a "flash" over the South Atlantic (September)	1979	
	1980	Election of Robert Mugabe in Zimbabwe (April)
South Africa announces that it has manufactured 45 percent HEU for its Safari-1 reactor (April)	1981	

Note: This chronology omits the agreements on nuclear cooperation that South Africa signed with the U.S., and South Africa's agreements with the IAEA on safeguards application. For this information please consult the text.

South Africa's gold mining operations was first suspected in 1923, and was later seized upon by U.S. geologists working for the Manhattan Project. Early predictions stated that South Africa would be "the largest potential foreign source" of uranium after the war.[14] Pursuant to its mandate to control and develop uranium production, the Combined Development Agency of the U.S., Britain, and Canada in 1950 contracted with South Africa to secure uranium supplies for their nuclear programs. The American and British governments invested £50 million toward the creation of a uranium extraction industry, and the first processing plant began operation in 1952.[15] By the 1960s, South Africa was responsible for approximately 16 percent of the world's total uranium production. According to a 1983 OECD/IAEA estimate, there were 313,000 tons of reasonably assured recoverable uranium resources in the country at less than $130/kg.U.[16]

South Africa's nuclear development was aided by the United States and Britain. During the negotiations for its uranium, Pretoria requested technical assistance in starting its own nuclear industry. Washington and London agreed to help place South African students in American and British universities for advanced nuclear studies, to provide access on a priority basis to American and British declassified information, to lend assistance in obtaining scientific equipment and materials for research purposes, to supply information necessary for the design and development of research reactors, and to arrange visits of South African scientists and engineers to observe unclassified atomic energy work.[17] By virtue of its importance as a uranium supplier, South Africa was one of four countries initially enlisted by the U.S., Britain, and Canada to help formulate plans for the creation of the International Atomic Energy Agency; Pretoria was awarded a seat on its Board of Governors. Under the U.S. Atoms for Peace program, Washington signed an atomic energy agreement with South Africa in 1957. According to its terms, the United States offered to transfer up to 500 kilograms of 20 percent enriched uranium and 6 kilograms of 90 percent enriched uranium. A clause in the agreement obligated South Africa to use all American-supplied materials and equipment "solely for civil purposes."[18] In 1961 the U.S. issued under license to South Africa a light-water reactor for nuclear research. Named Safari-1, it went critical in March 1965 with a capacity of 20 megawatts.[19] The United States supplied the necessary fuel loads, which consisted of approximately 14 kilograms of highly enriched uranium per year, with the spent fuel being reprocessed in the U.S.[20] This reactor was subject to IAEA safeguards under a 1965 agreement with the Agency.[21]

South Africa's independent nuclear expertise was indicated by its design and construction in 1967 of a critical assembly, Pelinduna-Zero, located at the South Africa Atomic Energy Board (AEB) nuclear research center at Pelindaba. It was a heavy-water reactor fueled with 2 percent enriched uranium, and used to investigate reactor physics and associated technical aspects for Pretoria's possible development of a commercial heavy-water facility. Due to financial constraints, however, work was discontinued in 1971, the critical assembly decommissioned, and the enriched uranium reprocessed in Britain and returned to the United States.[22]

Competing for AEB funds at this time was work on uranium enrichment, which had started in 1961. On July 20, 1970, Prime Minister Vorster declared in the House of Assembly that South Africa had developed a "unique" uranium enrichment process.[23] Emphasizing South Africa's sole intention to use its discovery "to promote the peaceful application of nuclear energy," the Prime Minister explained that an indigenous uranium enrichment capability would allow the country to profitably market enriched uranium in order to meet the rising worldwide demand for nuclear-generated electricity and, in addition, to supply the future fuel requirements of the country's own nuclear industry.[24] In April 1975, it was announced that a pilot enrichment plant at Valindaba had begun partial operation.[25] Aside from the Urenco facility at Almelo in the Netherlands, South Africa became the first nonnuclear weapons state to possess this capability.[26] It was also expected that a separate commercial-scale uranium enrichment facility would be completed by the mid-1980s, with a capacity of 5,000 tons SWU per year.[27] By selling enriched uranium rather than natural uranium oxide (yellowcake), the Republic would receive an additional revenue of $375 million per year from foreign transactions.[28]

Domestic and international developments over the next few years, however, forced Pretoria to alter its plans. A drop of almost 50 percent in the price of gold in the mid-1970s contributed to a devaluation of the rand and a recession in the South African economy. Previous calculations that a commercial enrichment plant could be constructed at 65 percent of the cost of a gaseous diffusion facility of comparable size had to be abandoned as the price estimate doubled. South Africa's difficulty in securing overseas financial assistance had been predicted from the project's inception.[29] This obstacle, together with the country's extensive coal reserves (about 10 percent of the world total), raised doubts over Pretoria's alleged commercial justification for uranium enrichment. Anxieties in Washington over possible military applications, caused by the Republic's disinclination to accede to the Nonproliferation Treaty, compelled the Ford administration to express its displeasure by suspending fuel deliveries to the Safari-1 reactor, refusing to sell components needed for the enrichment facility, and convincing other potential suppliers to do the same.[30] The recession in the international nuclear industry at this time robbed South Africa of much of its traditional influence based on its uranium market share, and thus made it more vulnerable to such outside pressure. In February 1978, Pretoria declared that it had canceled its plans for a large-scale commercial enrichment facility for uranium export.[31] It would instead expand its prototype enrichment plant to sustain its domestic requirements. By 1985, it was expected to have a total enrichment capacity of 200 to 300 tons SWU per year.[32]

The Republic had meanwhile decided to purchase civil nuclear power plants. Due to its indigenous supply of coal, as well as skepticism regarding the economic feasibility of nuclear power for the country's electricity requirements, South Africa had been relatively slow to move to commercial development of nuclear energy. By 1968, however, an AEB study favored building nuclear power facilities in Cape Province. After rejecting heavy-water (CANDU) reactors because of financial considerations, it was decided in 1974 to acquire two light-water reactors with a combined output of 1,850 megawatts, to be situated outside of Cape Town at Koeberg.[33] In May 1976 the French consortium of Framatone, Alsthom, and Spie-Batignolles was awarded the $1 billion contract to build the Koeberg facility.[34] Eight months later, on January 5, 1977, a safeguards agreement between the IAEA, France, and South Africa was signed for the Koeberg power plant.[35] Although South Africa did not possess a reprocessing capability, nor had any plans to develop one,[36] this agreement ensured that the spent fuel from the Koeberg reactors would be reprocessed and stored outside the country.[37] In addition, in an exchange of notes attached to a 1974 agreement with the United States for the export of nuclear fuel for the Koeberg reactors, South Africa had pledged that it would not employ this material "for any nuclear explosive device, regardless of how the device itself is intended to be used."[38] A "peaceful" nuclear explosion by South Africa using this material would have violated this accord. The first Koeberg reactor was expected to become operational in 1981, and the second the following year.

In part due to these restrictions, it was not the possibility that South Africa might derive weapons-grade plutonium from its Koeberg facility, but rather its ability to manufacture enriched uranium at its Valindaba plant that aroused the most unease. Proliferation concern was heightened in August 1977, when the Soviet Union disclosed to the U.S. that South Africa was finalizing preparations to explode a nuclear device.[39] Photographic reconnaissance satellites overpassing the Republic had detected what appeared to be a nuclear test site in the Kalahari Desert. Washington independently confirmed Moscow's information, and then notified Pretoria that a nuclear test would have severe repercussions.[40] Similar diplomatic warnings were transmitted by Paris, London, and Bonn.[41] Prime

Minister Vorster adamantly denied that South Africa possessed nuclear weapons, and stated that Pretoria did not plan to detonate a nuclear device "now or in the future."[42]

The reaction to the Kalahari incident was significant not only for illustrating global fears of nuclear weapons proliferation, but also because it confirmed that South Africa was officially believed capable of constructing a nuclear explosive. Earlier predictions had not assumed that Pretoria had nuclear arms, but agreed that it owned the scientific manpower and technological prowess required to fabricate a device. During congressional testimony in 1976, a U.S. State Department official commented that South Africa was still "a small number of years" away from producing a nuclear weapon.[43] In February 1977, a U.S. government source remarked that the Republic could explode a nuclear device within two to four years; this period could be reduced to a matter of months if South Africa allocated sufficient funds and personnel to the project.[44] Two months later, an independent study commissioned by the U.S. government estimated that it would likely take Pretoria one to two years to produce enough highly-enriched uranium for a weapons program.[45] The Kalahari incident stimulated further speculation. Immediately after details of the event were revealed, American analysts were reported to estimate that South Africa could develop a nuclear weapon within a year, or possibly sooner.[46] Others submitted that Pretoria was still somewhere between one and four years off from constructing a bomb.[47] Despite the varying lengths of time in these estimates, common to them all was the conviction that the lack of scientific competence was not an obstacle. The major short-term constraint was rather the small size of the Valindaba pilot enrichment plant (originally six tons SWU per year), while longer-term developments depended upon the political calculations of the white regime.

Contributing to the discomfort over Pretoria's nuclear weapons potential were a number of previous statements by South African officials. In February 1965, one of the members of the AEB, Dr. Andries Visser, endorsed the idea of South African nuclear weapons development.[48] Six months later at the inauguration ceremony for the Safari-1 reactor, Prime Minister Verwoerd declared that "it is the duty of South Africa not only to consider the military uses of the material but also to do all in its power to direct its uses to peaceful purposes,"[49] thereby seeming to assign a military priority to the country's nuclear program. In December 1968, the army chief of staff was reported to state that the Republic was prepared to build nuclear weapons, and implied that a missile development program then in progress was designed to provide delivery vehicles.[50] The AEB's 1969 annual report revealed that research was being performed on possible applications of peaceful nuclear explosions.[51] The chairman of the AEB, Dr. A.J.A. Roux, remarked in April 1971 that although the government's policy was to use enriched uranium for peaceful purposes, the new process placed South Africa "in a position to make its own nuclear weapons."[52] The following year the AEB released a study analyzing the seismic damage which would result from an underground nuclear explosion. The study concluded that while yields of between 10 and 100 kilotons could be detonated safely anywhere in large areas of the country, nuclear devices above 1 megaton could only be exploded in the Northern and Northwestern Cape.[53] After the May 1974 Indian nuclear detonation, the vice-president of the Atomic Energy Board, Dr. Louw Alberts, claimed that South Africa's nuclear program was more advanced than India's, and that it could manufacture a nuclear bomb if it wished.[54] The following year, Minister of Defense P.W. Botha also asserted that the country could produce nuclear weapons.[55] In February 1977, Minister of Information Connie Mulder alluded to this capability when he maintained, "Let me just say that if we are attacked, no rules apply at all if it comes to a question of our existence. We will use all means at our disposal, whatever they may be."[56] And in August 1977, after substantial diplomatic pressure was exerted on the Republic by the U.S., Britain, France and the FRG upon the discovery of the Kalahari site, the South African Foreign Minister, Owen Horwood, remonstrated that, "I, for one, reject absolutely and entirely that anyone should tell us what we should do" with the country's nuclear program.[57]

Aggravating international anxiety on this issue further was Pretoria's refusal to sign or ratify the Nonproliferation Treaty. In May 1968, while the treaty was still in draft form, the South African representative to the U.N. listed a number of criticisms, which included the agreement's lack of "positive and effective provisions" for superpower nuclear disarmament, its general discrimination against nonnuclear weapons states, the broad scope of the safeguard provisions in Article III, and the absence of guarantees for the sharing of benefits from peaceful nuclear explosions and for the unhampered commercial and techno- logical development of nuclear energy.[58] After 1970, South Africa's uranium enrichment capability created a dual source of proliferation concern; Pretoria could build its own nuclear arsenal and it could sell unsafeguarded enriched uranium to other countries.[59] After the Kalahari incident, the United States undertook a major effort to obtain either South African ad- herence to the NPT or its acceptance of full-scope safeguards. In exchange for its agreement Pretoria requested that Washington lift its suspension of nuclear fuel for the Koeberg reactors, resume deliveries of highly enriched uranium for the Safari-1 facility, and affirm that transfers of nonsensitive technology for the Valindaba enrichment plant would not be impeded. In addition, South Africa asked for Washington's assistance in obtaining the Republic's reinstatement on the IAEA's Board of Governors, from which it had been removed in June 1977.[60] Intensive negotiations between the two countries failed to reach an understanding, however. As a result, in November 1978 the U.S. canceled its contract to supply the fuel for Sa- fari-1.[61]

In October 1979 it was first reported that a month earlier, on September 22, an American Vela satellite over the South Atlan- tic Ocean had recorded two light flashes yielding a double- peaked signature characteristic of a nuclear explosion.[62] Inter- national suspicion soon concentrated on South Africa, which stated that it had "no knowledge of any nuclear explosion having occurred in or in the vicinity of southern Africa recently."[63] The Carter administration assembled a panel of distinguished scientists to aid the investigation. The panel's final report, issued in July 1980, offered that the light signal on the Vela's two bhangmeters was "possibly a consequence of the impact of a small meteoroid on the satellite" and "probably not from a nuclear explosion."[64] While other studies, including those conducted by the Defense Intelligence Agency and the Naval Research Laboratory, argued that a nuclear explosion had in fact occurred,[65] it was not possible to conclusively assign responsibility. In December 1980, another light flash was detected by a U.S. early-warning satellite, again in the South Atlantic region. This time U.S. government experts unanimously agreed that the signals had resulted from a meteor entering the earth's atmosphere.[66]

Definitive evidence of South Africa's capability to produce weapons-grade material was provided in April 1981, when Pretoria announced that it had manufactured 45 percent highly-enriched uranium to keep Safari-1 in operation.[67] The research reactor had been running at one-eighth its capacity because of the U.S. fuel supply termination. It was declared that the AEB had deliberately enriched the uranium to only 45 percent, the lowest grade on which the Safari facility could operate, instead of the 93 percent normally supplied by the United States, because of the government's sensitivity to international concern over using such fuel for nuclear weapons. South Africa stated that this lower-grade enriched uranium could only be used for a crude nuclear device unsuitable for military purposes.[68] Although the pilot enrichment plant could fulfill Safari-1's small-scale needs, it did not have the capability to supply the quantities of enriched uranium fuel for the Koeberg facility, which required 100 tons of 3 percent lightly enriched uranium to start up.[69] Without its fuel supply from the U.S., or any alternative source, the Republic risked losing $1.3 million every day the facility lay idle. In November 1981, however, South Africa announced that it had obtained the necessary fuel from an unidentified supplier.[70] It was later discovered that a Swiss-French-West German company, using American brokers, had sold Pretoria the lightly enriched uranium, which was being made into fuel rods at the Eurodif center in France.[71] Construction delays, and sabotage by African National Congress (ANC) guerrillas in December 1982, postponed the start of operations of the first Koeberg reactor until March 1984. Koeberg II began operating in the fall of 1985, shut down soon thereafter due to technical problems, and then resumed operations in 1986.

From an examination of South Africa's nuclear development, it seems clear that Pretoria decided to maintain a degree of independence from external control. In particular, it refused to allow inspections of or to apply safeguards to its pilot enrichment plant. Its 1976 decision to purchase the Koeberg reactors from France was determined less on financial grounds than on political considerations. The competing bids tendered by American and Dutch firms were generally considered to offer more favorable financing terms, but were strongly opposed in the U.S. and the Netherlands by elected officials and anti-apartheid groups.[72] France, on the other hand, was recognized as a reliable partner who was willing to divorce political matters from economic transactions. The South African-French relationship paid dividends five years later when Paris declined to prevent the Eurodif facility from exporting the fuel for the Koeberg reactors. This incident again illustrated Pretoria's resolve to avoid any restrictions on its nuclear program. South African statements periodically asserting the country's freedom to determine its own nuclear affairs provided rhetorical emphasis to these actions.

The most obvious example of South Africa's commitment to retain its nuclear autonomy was its refusal to accede to the NPT. In his 1968 statement to the United Nations, the South African representative contended that the treaty's provisions were too intrusive and could restrict the development of nuclear energy for research and commercial purposes. Prime Minister Vorster reiterated this view in his July 1970 announcement of the country's uranium enrichment breakthrough. The Prime Minister offered "to collaborate in the exploitation of this process with any non-communist countries willing to do so, but subject to the conclusion of an agreement safeguarding our interests." The claim that IAEA inspection of the Valindaba pilot enrichment plant could be used as subterfuge for industrial espionage in order to compromise commercial secrets was repeated by South Africa throughout the 1970s as a major reason for its reluctance to sign the NPT. In addition, South Africa must have had serious doubts as to whether it would be treated fairly by the IAEA on the safeguards issue, and whether international opposition to apartheid would prevent it from receiving the "fullest possible exchange of equipment, materials and scientific and technological information for the peaceful uses of nuclear energy" and the "potential benefits from any peaceful applications of nuclear explosions" if it indeed became an NPT party. Although South Africa was reportedly close to agreeing to NPT ratification during its negotiations with the United States in 1977 and 1978, it decided to decline and instead operate its Safari-1 reactor below capacity with its own limited fuel supplies. South Africa subsequently exhibited similar resolve during its attempt to secure nuclear fuel for the Koeberg facility. While its last-minute procurement of highly enriched uranium rendered the issue moot, Pretoria appeared willing to let the plant sit idle rather than ratify the NPT or submit its nuclear program to full-scope safeguards as a condition for obtaining the necessary nuclear fuel. In sum, Pretoria preserved a measure of autonomy and hence flexibility in its nuclear program. Whether originally intended or not, this granted South Africa a nuclear weapons option.

SOUTH AFRICAN NUCLEAR WEAPONS: INCENTIVES AND DISINCENTIVES

On the basis of its enrichment technology, Pretoria possessed the ability to fabricate nuclear bombs. Yet if it was undisputed by the latter half of the 1970s that the Republic could become a nuclear weapons state, it was less evident what purpose would be served by a nuclear arsenal. South Africa would have had to balance the possible strategic, political, economic, and psychological benefits of openly acquiring nuclear armaments against the potential liabilities.

The Republic's deteriorating security position, and its lack of viable options, were responsible for its sense of vulnerability. South Africa did not have any security guarantees or treaties, and after the termination of the Simonstown agreement, had no formal defense ties with any country.[73] Its apartheid policy made it impossible to garner any support in the international community. Pretoria's development of a nuclear stockpile would have been in line with the greater emphasis placed on defense after the demise of the Portuguese African empire. Conversely, nuclear armaments could have been viewed as a means of economizing on rapidly escalating military expenditures on conventional munitions during a time of fiscal austerity. In either case, it would have been consistent with South Africa's conception of a "total national strategy" to utilize all available means to defend the country from the "total onslaught" of communist forces.

Nuclear weapons development would have been dramatic evidence of South Africa's technological expertise. It would have demoralized the black population inside South Africa and reminded other African countries of their scientific and military inferiority; in short, it would have conveyed the impression of military impregnability.[74] In addition to whatever accoutrements nuclear status would have accorded, it would have embodied white defiance against world opinion. The psychic satisfaction derived from this gesture would have boosted the government's popularity, invigorated national resolve, and retrieved the prestige that had been dissipated in the 1975–1976 Angolan intervention.[75] Alternatively, nuclear weapons might have been perceived by reform-minded (verligte) officials in the government as a means of strengthening their position, internally versus more conservative (verkrampte) colleagues and externally versus regional and international adversaries, prior to dismantling apartheid. Under this optimistic and somewhat far-fetched scenario, nuclear weapons would have been used not to forestall change, but to grant Pretoria immunity from political pressures in order for it to determine the pace at which divestiture should proceed.[76]

Nuclear weapons might also have been useful instruments for intimidation, in order to extract economic and political concessions from other states, for deterrence, in order to discourage actions inimical to South African interests, and for battlefield employment, in order to compensate for the white regime's numerical inferiority. In military affairs, a tactical nuclear weapons capability could have been used to strike at sizable transborder incursions, or at guerrilla bases in neighboring countries.[77] Likewise, nuclear bombs would have been an effective means of repelling attack by conventional forces, especially in light of Pretoria's sensitivity to white casualties. The mere possession of nuclear armaments would have forced enemy commanders to alter their tactics and strategy.[78] At a moment of extreme crisis, South Africa could have targeted the capital cities of neighboring African states.[79]

Undoubtedly, however, South Africa would have preferred to use its nuclear strength to reduce its international isolation, if not to obtain a degree of international consent for its racial program. Nuclear arms could have been viewed not only as necessary to shield the Republic from the "wind of change," but also as useful to modify the regional and international climate of opinion towards the country. Nuclear weapons would have invested Pretoria's "outward movement" with a military component which might have altered African calculations regarding the wisdom of continued ostracism of South Africa. This nuclear threat might have compelled them to engage in greater economic interaction with the Republic or even to extend diplomatic recognition.[80] A national nuclear force might well have dissuaded neighboring African states from harboring insurgents, or the OAU from undertaking preparations for a unified military offensive. A nuclear "warning shot" over a remote area would have demonstrated Pretoria's resolve as well as the potential cost in black lives if an invasion was attempted.[81] More severe threats were possible. Aircraft in the South African Defense Force (SADF) inventory could have delivered nuclear weapons up to 625 miles.[82] In this manner, Pretoria could have hoped to restrain African states on its northern border from adopting military measures, or further economic and political sanctions, against it.

This logic would have applied in part to South Africa's relations with the West. Pretoria's nuclear capability would likely have been viewed as a source of regional and international instability.[83] The threat of potential nuclear catastrophe resulting from continued isolation might then well have outweighed opposition to apartheid. Greater political interaction with the Republic might have been viewed as preferable to further restrictive policies. Previous measures, such as the 1977 U.N. arms embargo, might have been overturned.[84] Moreover, Pretoria could have attempted to pressure the United States into guaranteeing white rule, extending its nuclear umbrella to cover South Africa, or inviting the Republic to join a formal military alliance.[85] Even if not coerced into a military relationship with the Republic, the West would have had to reevaluate its advantages, given Pretoria's new military might and regional influence.[86] By threatening to employ nuclear weapons, by promising to refrain from their use, or in exchange for dismantling its nuclear arsenal, South Africa could have hoped to secure these and other benefits.[87] The world community would have been forced to revise its estimates of the white regime's long-term survivability, and perhaps admit a measure of international legitimacy.[88]

In the event of a military conflict in southern Africa, the threat to use its nuclear weapons could have been invoked if the war was turning against Pretoria in order to prompt Western intervention and mediation efforts.[89] Alternatively, this threat could have been employed to deter joint Soviet-American pressure, however unlikely, to impose a solution to racial discord in the region.[90] More probable could have been the use of nuclear arms to deter the Soviet Union's direct military intervention in southern Africa. The Soviet navy's presence in the Indian Ocean since 1968, Moscow's activities in the Horn of Africa, its traditional support of national liberation movements, the infusion of considerable numbers of Cuban and East German personnel in southern Africa, and the signing of Peace and Friendship Treaties with Angola and Mozambique, all contributed to the Soviet Union's growing influence in the region. This Soviet threat furnished the principal external cause of the Republic's insecurity. In 1972, the SADF's commandant-general had suggested that nuclear weapons were a "prerequisite" for deterrence and defense against communist threats in the southern hemisphere.[91] Despite the meager capabilities of any South African nuclear inventory as compared to that of the Soviet Union, Pretoria could nonetheless have hoped to deter direct Soviet military intervention, conventional or nuclear, by threatening to destroy a number of African capitals in response. In effect, South Africa would have held the black population in southern Africa hostage in order to secure Soviet restraint.[92] And supplementing all these incentives for nuclear acquisition would have been the fact that South Africa's general insecurity and isolation, of which a nuclear arsenal would have been the most obvious manifestation, would have made more credible any threat to actually use nuclear weapons. This, in turn, would have enhanced its bargaining leverage in seeking its objectives.

On the other hand, it is far from certain that nuclear weapons acquisition would have been either militarily necessary or politically beneficial for South Africa. By marrying the fear of nuclear proliferation with the extant international hostility to apartheid, Pretoria would have risked escalating what had hitherto been only a partially successful economic and diplomatic campaign against the country to an international crusade certain to increase the white regime's isolation. Moreover, it would have chanced shifting this confrontation from the political realm, where the Republic retained at least some influence, to the military realm, where any South African nuclear capability would have been completely outclassed by the nuclear arsenals of the superpowers.

To be certain, nuclear weapons development would have presented few financial difficulties for South Africa. With a defense budget of almost $3 billion in 1979,[93] additional expenditures of $100 million per year would not have constituted an intolerable burden. Still, in light of the problems Pretoria encountered in producing a sufficient amount of highly enriched uranium for its Safari-1 reactor, a bomb project would have had to compete with the country's civilian nuclear requirements.

Nuclear arms would have been ill-suited to the most likely military challenge to the regime—internal violence and disorder. Protests, demonstrations, and industrial unrest could have all been handled better by other means. The sporadic, low-level violence caused by guerrilla infiltration was a nuisance but no real threat to Pretoria. If these attacks were launched from outside the country, the Republic commanded a range of economic and paramilitary means to punish those neighboring African states which provided sanctuary for insurgents. If they were initiated from urban areas or the black "homelands" scattered throughout the country, there were a variety of police and administrative measures which South Africa had developed over the years to suppress internal resistance. If required, a security force of over 400,000 could have been mobilized.[94] The indiscriminate characteristics of nuclear weapons would have made them wholly inappropriate for this task.[95]

A nuclear arsenal would also have been unnecessary for repelling a conventional attack on South Africa. In the first place, the threat of a combined African assault on the Republic was "negligible."[96] Although the black African states had over twice as many men under arms as South Africa,[97] it was doubtful that this could have been translated into military advantage. At this time, attention was focused more on the transition in Rhodesia/Zimbabwe and the struggle in Namibia, where there was a more immediate chance of a favorable outcome, than on military adventures against Pretoria. Indeed, military and diplomatic support was directed to these areas and not toward an invasion of South Africa. In addition, the central government in Angola was still trying to assert its authority over its territory. Even without these diversions, an African offensive would have encountered numerous obstacles. Often resting on shaky political foundations, or governing in unstable regions, black leaders would have been hesitant to send their military forces outside the country for fear of a coup d'état, tribal revolt, or attack by a neighboring state. If a multinational force could have been assembled, political divisions within the OAU would have complicated the task of establishing a unified command structure. Ethnic antagonisms and linguistic differences would have presented other impediments. The logistic difficulties would have been enormous. No African country owned the sea- or air-lift capability to project military forces on this scale into southern Africa. Black African states were not joined by railway, nor was there an all-weather road system to connect the countries.[98] Even if these hurdles could have been surmounted, African armies had previously revealed little talent for waging modern warfare.[99]

Not least, compounding the difficulties of a successful conventional invasion would have been South Africa's military capabilities. Beginning in 1975, the Republic had embarked on a substantial modernization program of its forces. The length of compulsory national service was doubled, pay was upgraded to attract and retain skilled personnel, and advanced weaponry was acquired for all branches.[100] Although the mandatory U.N. arms embargo prevented purchasing equipment from overseas, South Africa was able to fulfill much of its own defense needs; by 1977 it claimed to be 75 percent self-sufficient in arms production.[101] In the event of a conflict, the Republic would have outnumbered any pan-African force in tanks, armored personnel carriers, and sophisticated aircraft.[102] According to knowledgeable observers, South Africa would have faced little difficulty in defeating any African military force.[103]

Nuclear weapons might also have been counterproductive

to Pretoria's policies and interests in Africa. A South African nuclear arsenal could have irrevocably damaged relations with black African states, and jeopardized any chance of future success for the country's "outward movement." Previous economic and commercial arrangements could have been terminated in retaliation.[104] In addition, African states could have requested security guarantees or military assistance from the Soviet Union; Moscow's influence on the continent as a defender of black interests would then have increased.[105] Or black African countries might have attempted to counter the threat themselves by developing a similar nuclear capability.[106] Nigeria was the candidate most frequently mentioned for this task.[107]

Although less directly threatened by Pretoria's development of nuclear weapons, it was likely that the West would also have reacted negatively. The vigorous diplomatic response to the discovery of the Kalahari site testified to international concern over nuclear proliferation. A nuclear South Africa would have further complicated an already awkward relationship with the West, and would have mocked the rationale that dealing with the Republic was the best way to moderate its policies and assist the peaceful transition to majority rule. A South African nuclear arsenal could have also precipitated the type of collective global outrage that its foreign policy had long endeavored to prevent.[108] A boycott of South African products would have been crippling to the local economy. The Republic's self-reliance was not so great that it could have afforded to jettison its financial, technological, and commercial relations with the outside world, in particular, with Britain and the United States.[109]

Moreover, there was even some possibility that South Africa enjoyed a measure of safety because of the West, due to the Republic's strategic location and its value as a source of critical minerals.[110] In other words, the arguments with which Pretoria had traditionally appealed to the West in order to obtain a formal military relationship, while unpersuasive in peacetime, might have been convincing in the event of a conflict that white South Africa appeared to be losing. In addition, the general desire to maintain regional stability and to preempt any direct Soviet attempt to use its military power to forcibly alter the status quo would have compelled the United States to intervene. In this manner, it was maintained that the Republic could have refrained from nuclear weapons acquisition because it was already under a de facto Western security umbrella.[111]

Finally, the chance of a more direct Soviet role in the region at this time was remote.[112] Historically, African affairs had been low on the list of Moscow's priorities. Its policies in Africa had tended to be reactive and opportunistic, as it had generally preferred to lend diplomatic and low-level military support to liberation movements.[113] The conflict in Afghanistan, where its military efforts were concentrated after its December 1979 invasion, was a more urgent requirement for Soviet defense planners. Even if it had wanted, the Soviet Union would have been hard-pressed to project conventional forces sufficient to defeat the Republic as far as southern Africa. Nuclear threats against Pretoria would not have been credible, because any use would have killed more blacks than whites.[114] If either policy was attempted, it would have risked provoking a crisis with the West. On ideological grounds alone, the situation in southern Africa would have warranted a cautious approach and militated against "adventurism." It would have been preferable to wait until the "correlation of forces" had shifted in Moscow's favor.[115]

In sum, South African acquisition of nuclear weapons at this time would have been inappropriate to defend the country against internal challenges and unnecessary to meet external threats. Politically, it could have been counterproductive, further alienating other African countries and possibly causing a rupture in the associations the country still maintained with the West. Nuclear weapons development would likely have incited calls for more restrictive measures against the Republic and would have further ostracized the government. For Pretoria, then, the open construction of a nuclear arsenal would have brought few benefits at the risk of corroding the country's security and international standing.

CONCLUSION

If overtly acquiring nuclear weapons would have been detrimental to South Africa's interests, and if complete nuclear abstention seemed imprudent in light of possible future threats to the regime, a middle path might have appeared to offer the best of both alternatives with none of their liabilities. A covert nuclear stockpile could have been viewed as a precautionary measure reserved for a moment of extreme national emergency. Prior to this point, there would not have been the risk of exciting a reaction which would have exaggerated the country's isolation. Moreover, this posture could have been exploited to realize more immediate policy objectives. The belief, without the certainty, that South Africa owned nuclear armaments could have been used to force the international community to choose between its fear of nuclear proliferation and its opposition to apartheid. On the one hand, continued pressure on the white regime might have triggered a decision to publicly reveal its nuclear status. On the other hand, a more conciliatory stance towards the Republic, despite its racial policies, might have reduced Pretoria's insecurity and removed a major proliferation incentive. By manipulating the variable in this equation—its nuclear intentions—South Africa could have hoped to attain the international acceptance which had always eluded it.

Whether or not the Republic actually possessed a covert inventory of nuclear arms, there was evidence that it deliberately tried to foster ambiguity over its nuclear intentions. Pretoria's equivocal behavior was demonstrated by the 1977 Kalahari event. This incident was significant perhaps more for how South Africa attempted to mold international perceptions than if a nuclear test was actually scheduled. In response to Western pressure after the discovery, Prime Minister Vorster warned that if "these things continue, the time will arrive when South Africa will have no option, small as it is, to say to the world, so far and no further; do your damndest if you wish."[116] After President Carter stated at a press conference in late August 1977 that the United States had been informed by South Africa that a nuclear test had not been intended and would not be performed in the future, Vorster denied ever having made such a promise. The White House thereupon made public the letter with the prime minister's pledge.[117] Indeed, there was some speculation that the entire affair had been engineered by South Africa as a hoax.[118] The fact that South Africa had extensive experience with deep-level mining also raised questions over why it chose to make its activities at the Kalahari site so conspicuous, rather than simply testing a nuclear device at greater depth, where it would be less easily detected. Further, that South Africa needed four years after the Kalahari incident to obtain 45 percent highly enriched uranium for its Safari-1 reactor suggested that it might not have had sufficient time from the start-up of its pilot enrichment plant in April 1975 to August 1977 to produce enough highly enriched uranium for a nuclear explosion.[119] As the site was discovered during the preparations in the U.N. for a mandatory arms embargo against the Republic, Pretoria might have wanted to illustrate its disdain for international opinion, or to signal that a cutoff of conventional munitions might compel it to go nuclear in order to defend itself. Suspicion over South Africa's motives was exacerbated when work on the Kalahari site continued until December, and the site itself was not dismantled until June 1978.[120] In a December 1981 interview, the South African ambassador to the U.S., Donald Sole, divulged that "we were going to test something—but not a weapon," suggesting a possible peaceful nuclear explosion.[121] At no point was any official explanation for the site offered.

If the September 1979 flash registered by the Vela satellite had been caused by a nuclear detonation, it suggested that tremendous care had been taken to conceal the matter; the abundance of suspicion and lack of conclusive evidence might have been precisely the objective. Regardless if it was a nuclear explosion, Pretoria's disingenuous explanations for the event— it was caused by an accident aboard a Soviet submarine or by a Soviet missile which had laid dormant on the ocean floor— indicated a contempt for international proliferation concerns that raised doubts over its nuclear intentions. This uncertainty was maintained by Pretoria's refusal to sign the Nonproliferation Treaty. Furthermore, elliptical or conditional statements by South African officials regarding nuclear weapons development had been issued since the mid-1960s. While these became less frequent after the Kalahari incident, in October 1980 naval Commodore H.F. Nel asserted that South Africa reserved the right to build nuclear arms if the need arose.[122] And in the February 1982 issue of *Paratus*, the official monthly of the South African Defense Force, an article from a British journal entitled "Military aspects of Enhanced Radiation Weapons" was reprinted. This was all the more unusual when contrasted with the general morale-boosting and primitive anticommunist content of the magazine.[123]

South Africa's policy of deliberately promoting uncertainty regarding its nuclear intentions was important in three respects. First, it was clear by the late 1970s that the Republic possessed the capability to construct nuclear weapons. If a decision was taken not to acquire them, or if it was determined to build them in secret, this was a tacit admission that according to Pretoria's own calculations an openly declared nuclear posture was unnecessary and perhaps counterproductive. Although the parameters within which South Africa could maneuver gradually narrowed during this period, the country's position never became so desperate that there was ever a mortal danger to the white regime's survival. That this time may have been perceived by South Africa to have been imminent or steadily approaching would have justified covert assembly of nuclear arms. That this time never in fact arrived was reason enough not to reveal its actual nuclear posture.

Second, if the Republic thought it best not to overtly develop nuclear weapons, it also decided not to publicly renounce all nuclear ambitions. South Africa refused to join the NPT or to allow any inspection of its pilot enrichment plant. Whether to strike a posture of independence and defiance as a means of reassuring its white constituency, in order to deter its regional adversaries from seeking to impose a final military solution, to win economic and political concessions from proliferation-sensitive governments in the West, or simply as a hedge against an uncertain future, Pretoria deemed it prudent not to assume any obligations which might restrict its exercising its nuclear option at some later date.

Finally, the fear of South African nuclear weapons acquisition was never so great as to cancel, or even moderate, international opposition to apartheid. The 1977 U.N. arms embargo, Western pressure over Namibian independence, and the formation of SADCC, along with U.N. resolutions and worldwide protests, were examples of the unceasing attempt to impel the Republic to alter its racial policies. In this respect, the dilemma for South Africa's nuclear policy was that the primacy the international community placed on ending apartheid made it difficult, if not impossible, for the country to realize any advantages from either acquiring nuclear weapons, maintaining an ambiguous nuclear posture, or convincingly renouncing all nuclear ambitions.

7.

India

Emerging from years of colonial subservience, India achieved its independence on August 15, 1947. From what was formerly British India, decolonization yielded two countries, a secular India and a theocratic Pakistan, which was itself comprised of eastern and western entities flanking its larger neighbor. Economic deprivation, already prevalent on the subcontinent, was further aggravated by the communal bloodshed and human misery which preceded and attended partition as millions of Hindus and Muslims relocated. To meet its pressing economic, societal, and political problems, India adopted a policy of nonalignment. This stance had three interconnected strands. First, nonalignment reflected India's desire to resist alliance with either the United States or the Soviet Union in order to preserve its newly acquired freedom. Second, once removed politically as well as geographically from the center of Great Power tension, New Delhi would be well situated to receive assistance from both Washington and Moscow to help realize its domestic goals of economic development and "nation-building." Third, as an independent actor seen overcoming industrial backwardness, centrifugal social forces, and economic underdevelopment, India could promote itself as a leader of its fellow Third World countries as well as of those oppressed peoples still subjugated by colonialism. Moreover, the idea of nonalignment itself, with its suggestion of a moral component to Indian diplomacy which rejected traditional notions of power politics, enhanced the attractiveness of India's example. The nonalignment policy was thus intended to prevent any outside interference or intervention in South Asia so that India would be able to achieve internal unity and prosperity, to become the dominant regional power, and to gain international stature as a voice for decolonization, equality, and world peace.

Developments on the subcontinent during the next few decades prevented New Delhi from fully realizing its objectives. Animosities between India and Pakistan, deriving from partition and the manner in which New Delhi coerced the princely states of Hyderabad and Junagadh to join the Indian union, erupted into open conflict in late October 1947. Four days after Pathan tribesmen infiltrated Kashmir from Pakistan in order to instigate a rebellion by the Muslim majority, the Hindu Maharajah pledged his allegiance to India. New Delhi rushed troops to Srinigar to confront the Pakistani forces which had meanwhile been deployed. After a brief period of fighting the two sides agreed to a ceasefire, supervised by a United Nations peacekeeping force.[1]

India's attention was also drawn to its northern border, as the People's Republic of China seized the Himalayan mountain kingdom of Tibet in October 1950. New Delhi, which in the hope of fostering friendly relations had immediately recognized the new regime in Peking when it had come to power the previous year, failed to muster any military response. It instead attempted to counter Chinese aggrandizement by diplomatic means. This approach culminated in the Sino-Indian agreement of April 29, 1954, in which New Delhi relinquished its legal claims to Tibet. More important from the perspective of Indian Prime Minister Jawaharlal Nehru, however, was the preamble, which set out the five principles of peaceful coexistence, or *panch sheel*, that would guide relations between the two countries.[2] Notwithstanding this agreement, Chinese pronouncements during the latter part of the decade indicated that China still harbored irredentist ambitions along its 2,000 mile border with India. Correspondence between Nehru and PRC Foreign Minister Chou En-lai in January 1959 confirmed that China claimed over 40,000 square miles of territory India regarded as its own in the Aksai Chin area of Ladakh, in the middle sector of the Himalayas, and in the North East Frontier Area (NEFA). Nehru's response to this demise of the *panch sheel* era was to increase defense spending and to demand the withdrawal of Chinese troops from Indian soil, while simultaneously seeking to settle the issue by conference. Nehru's strategy failed, as the People's Republic on October 20, 1962, launched major attacks in Ladakh and the North East Frontier Area, overrunning the inadequately prepared Indian forces. With a Chinese armistice proposal rejected by India, China launched a second successful offensive three weeks later. On November 21, Peking announced that it was withdrawing its forces 20 kilometers, subject to an armistice, noninterference with the withdrawal, New Delhi's acceptance of a 20 kilometer demilitarized zone, and no attempt to reestablish any of the Indian posts captured by the Chinese in Ladakh.[3]

India's humiliation at its defeat was acute. The country's military weakness was exposed, and the Himalayas no longer were viewed as an impregnable barrier to invasion. Nehru's diplomacy had proved inept, and it was reported that China's "betrayal" had personally shocked the prime minister. Disillusion with India's stress on morality in world affairs, coupled with a questioning of the country's claim to international leadership, now characterized much of the debate over India's future. The result was a modification of India's policy, with relatively less emphasis on proselytizing on behalf of world peace and more on tending to its own defense and security needs. Further, it was decided that nonalignment, in order to be effective, must be founded on credible military might. Consequently, the year after the border war the Ministry of Defense reviewed India's security requirements. In early 1964 the Indian government released a five-year defense program; defense spending would double to $2 billion by 1969, consuming 5 percent of the national income, and India would develop its own defense industry.[4]

China's nuclear test two years later, on October 16, 1964, administered a second shock to India. Up to this time, India's security requirements had been defined exclusively in terms of conventional weaponry. In addition, Nehru had been in the forefront of the movement for nuclear disarmament; his April 1954 statement on the hazards of radioactive fallout from nuclear tests had contributed to concentrating global attention on the subject. Yet the prospect of a neighboring Asian power acquiring nuclear weapons, coming so soon after that country's decisive military victory over India, sparked renewed discussion of India's security. Unlike the aftermath of the 1962 war, however, the public debate this time heard widespread calls for India's development of nuclear weapons.[5]

INDIA'S SECURITY CONCERNS
AND CAPABILITIES, 1964 TO 1974

The Chinese nuclear detonation introduced a new dimension into India's security environment. Until 1962, New Delhi's main external concern was Pakistan, which was militarily weaker than India and beset by even graver domestic difficulties; in short, Rawalpindi was a potential irritant but not a major threat. After 1962, India had to plan for a two-front war against both Pakistan and China. Admittedly, the Chinese threat was mitigated somewhat by Peking's self-restraint during the border war and its apparent satisfaction with its outcome. Nonetheless, this dual contingency underscored the geographic advantages Pakistan could exploit in Kashmir should New Delhi's attention be diverted elsewhere, and quickened India's need to rebuild, reorganize, and reequip its armed

INDIA: CHRONOLOGY OF SIGNIFICANT EVENTS

Nuclear Developments		Political Developments
	1946	India achieves independence (August)
		Hostilities in Kashmir
	1954	India and China sign the *panch sheel* agreement (April)
India and Canada sign a nuclear cooperation agreement for the CIRUS heavy water reactor; the U.S. provides the heavy water	1956	
The decision is taken to build the Trombay reprocessing facility	1958	
CIRUS goes critical	1960	
	1962	China overwhelmingly defeats Indian forces in a border dispute (October-November)
	1964	China detonates its first nuclear device (October)
		In response, Bhabha declares that India can match China's feat within 18 months (October)
		Prime Minister Shastri shifts India's nuclear policy to allow nuclear explosions for peaceful purposes (November)
Trombay reprocessing facility is commissioned	1965	
The decision is taken to build the Purnima reactor	1968	India announces that it will not sign the Nonproliferation Treaty (May)
	1971	The United States, using Pakistan as an intermediary,

INDIA: CHRONOLOGY OF SIGNIFICANT EVENTS (Continued)

Nuclear Developments		Political Developments
		seeks a rapprochement with China (July)
		India and the Soviet Union sign a 20-year Treaty of Peace, Friendship and Cooperation (August)
		India sends troops into East Pakistan, defeating the central government's forces and helping to establish the independent state of Bangladesh
Purnima goes critical (May)	1972	India decides to test a nuclear device (January-March?)
	1974	On May 18 India detonates a "peaceful nuclear explosion" (May)
		Canada suspends its nuclear cooperation with India (May)
	1975	Indira Gandhi calls an Emergency; civil liberties are suspended
India buys Soviet heavy water, accepting strict safeguard provisions (November)	1977	Morarji Desai becomes prime minister; vehemently opposed to nuclear weapons (March)
	1977–1980	Nuclear fuel shipments for Tarapur dominate U.S.-Indian relations
		Evidence mounts of Pakistan's covert acquisition of a uranium enrichment capability; the United States invokes the Symington Amendment in June 1979,

INDIA: CHRONOLOGY OF SIGNIFICANT EVENTS (*Continued*)

Nuclear Developments		*Political Developments*
		which terminates all American assistance to Pakistan
It is reported that Pakistan's New Labs reprocessing plant is nearing completion (September)	1980	
IAEA announces that it cannot guarantee that nuclear fuel had not been diverted from the KANUPP heavy-water reactor (October)	1981	U.S. reverses its policy toward Pakistan after the Soviet invasion of Afghanistan and agrees to a six year $3.2 billion assistance package for Pakistan (June)
Director of Pakistan's uranium enrichment program announces that Pakistan can now "efficiently enrich uranium" (February)	1984	
Reports that reprocessing has already occurred at Pakistan's New Labs facility is denied by U.S. officials (June)		
Reports that China provided technical assistance to Pakistan, including a proven weapons design (June)		
The Kahuta facility is reported to have produced uranium enriched to 30 percent (March)	1986	
Abdul Qadir Khan discloses that Pakistan has built a nuclear bomb; he later denies the statement (February)	1987	

Note: This chronology omits the agreements on nuclear cooperation that India signed with the U.S., Canada, and the Soviet Union, and India's agreements on safeguards with the IAEA. For this information please consult the text.

forces. To these concerns, the PRC's test in October 1964 added the possibility of China employing nuclear weapons militarily against Indian targets or utilizing them politically to extract concessions from New Delhi.

The nuclear debate in India triggered by China's detonation revolved around four main issues: (1) the morality of India possessing nuclear weapons; (2) whether the Chinese nuclear test constituted an essentially political or military threat to India; (3) the financial cost of an Indian nuclear weapons program; and (4) whether Indian security was in effect assured by implied Soviet and American guarantees against Chinese aggression. Not surprisingly, proponents and opponents of nuclear weapons acquisition each justified its approach by claiming that it would best strengthen the country's policy of nonalignment.

Moral concerns constituted an important objection to nuclear weapons. An Indian nuclear arsenal was thought to be contrary to Mahatma Gandhi's legacy of nonviolence, as well as inconsistent with Prime Minister Nehru's previous efforts in the United Nations and other international forums to portray nuclear arms as evil weapons of mass destruction. Concerning India's own nuclear energy program, Nehru and other government officials had always emphasized that the country's nuclear development was devoted solely to peaceful purposes.[6] Were India now to manufacture nuclear weapons it would appear hypocritical. In addition, India's infusion of an ethical dimension into international affairs, due primarily to its criticism of the nuclear arms race and the emphasis on military force to resolve disputes, had won the country a measure of respect. Continued abstention from nuclear weapons would solidify India's claim to a special place in the world, and would further the cause of general and complete disarmament. In the words of one Indian analyst,

A country [which], when it is exposed to a threat, refuses in the interests of the world community to develop nuclear weapons, has the right to demand that some progress should be made in the direction of arms control or disarmament. Therefore, India is in a stronger position now, as a result of the reaffirmation of her basic policies.[7]

Advocates of nuclear weapons attacked this position as being self-righteous and unrealistic in a world which already had five nuclear weapons states. While morality might have some role to play in world affairs, the imperatives of national security took precedence. India, like other countries, must do whatever was necessary to defend itself. And since India wanted nuclear weapons for deterrent purposes only, acquisition could be reconciled with Gandhi's teachings.[8]

Nuclear weapons opponents also argued that China's nuclear detonation was animated primarily by political factors of status and prestige, and was directed more toward the Soviet Union and the United States than India. A corresponding Indian nuclear capability would thus be militarily irrelevant, a point underscored by the logistical difficulties of India's reaching high-value targets in the PRC. The more tangible Chinese threat was conventional, which New Delhi was striving to meet through its defense reorganization. And even if this analysis proved incorrect, the PRC still did not pose an immediate nuclear threat; since it would take the better part of a decade for China to develop the missile technology needed to strike India, New Delhi need not overreact by prematurely developing nuclear arms. Nuclear weapons proponents, on the other hand, stressed that Chinese nuclear aggression could not be dismissed so casually, especially in light of the recent history between the two countries. In addition, nuclear weapons would earn China important political benefits in South Asia, by undermining the confidence of the countries in the region of India's support against external threat, by encouraging Pakistan to renew its probings in Kashmir, and by forcing New Delhi in general to tread more cautiously than it might otherwise. Only an Indian nuclear arsenal could elevate India to a position of equality with China where it would not be subject to nuclear coercion.[9]

Given India's economic situation, the discussion over the costs of a nuclear arsenal was especially heated. Those opposed to nuclear weapons stressed the domestic ramifications of a development program. India could ill-afford any further drain on the country's limited finances. Because nuclear weapons were not intended to substitute for India's conventional defenses, they would be an added burden on a defense budget that had already been recently increased. According to a former Secretary General of the Ministry of External Affairs,

India will be playing straight into the hands of China if because of fear or emotional reaction or prestige considerations, it enters into a nuclear race with China. The enormous diversion of resources . . . will retard India's economic and social development programs indefinitely and . . . not only weaken India internally but eliminate it as a political factor in Asia and Africa.[10]

Placing this sentiment in more concrete terms, one member of Parliament estimated that a bomb program would consume three-fourths of the entire outlay of the proposed Fourth Five-Year Plan.[11]

Those favoring nuclear weapons argued that the country should accept whatever financial sacrifices were necessary to defend itself, and that in any case a modest nuclear weapons program could be accommodated within the government's present level of expenditures. The most influential support for the economic feasibility of nuclear weapons came from Homi Bhabha, the Chairman of the Indian Atomic Energy Commission. Bhabha's initial reaction to the Chinese nuclear test was to announce that India could duplicate Peking's feat within eighteen months.[12] Speaking on national radio eight days after the Chinese detonation, Bhabha used a talk ostensibly devoted to nuclear disarmament in commemoration of United Nations Day to suggest that nuclear weapons were both useful and affordable for India. In the context of proposing that a U.N. security force be established and armed with nuclear arms to enforce adherence to international law, Bhabha commented that

atomic weapons give a state possessing them in adequate numbers a deterrent power against attack from a much stronger state. Indeed, the importance of nuclear weapons is that they enable a country possessing them in adequate measure to deter another country also possessing them from using them against it.

Bhabha went on to remark that plutonium sufficient for the annual production of between 20 to 35 atomic bombs could be generated by a single 300-megawatt electrical power station. Moreover, Bhabha declared that the expense of producing nuclear weapons would not be prohibitive.

A 10 kiloton explosion, i.e. one equivalent to 10,000 tons of TNT, would cost $350,000 or Rs. 17.5 lakhs—that is an explosion of the same order of magnitude as the Hiroshima bomb—while a 2 megaton explosion, i.e. one equivalent to 2 million tons of TNT, would cost $600,000 or Rs. 30 lakhs . . . a stockpile of some 50 atomic bombs would cost under 10 crores [$20,000,000] and a stockpile of 50 two megaton hydrogen bombs something on the order of Rs. 15 crores [$30,000,000]. These expenditures are small when compared with the military budgets of many countries.[13]

Regardless of the inaccuracy of these figures,[14] Bhabha's cost estimates would now be repeated to justify the economic feasibility of acquiring nuclear weapons.

The final issue that characterized the nuclear debate was whether India's nonaligned position in a bipolar international system conferred a measure of protection from the Chinese nuclear threat. In other words, the nuclear arsenals of the Soviet Union and the United States would deter Peking from using, or threatening to use, its nuclear force against India. Opponents of India's nuclear weapons development thought this informal nuclear guarantee sufficient; proponents, while not completely conceding that the superpowers would in fact come to India's defense in a crisis with China, argued that India would enjoy greater security if it codified this tacit arrangement in some form of official understanding with Washington and Moscow.

Despite this division of opinion on the nuclear weapons issue, the preponderant view opposed nuclear arms. Few of the influential government bureaucrats, including the secretaries to the defense and foreign affairs ministers, the prime minister's personal private secretary, the cabinet secretary, and the chief of civilian intelligence, favored nuclear weapons. The media, which generally followed the government's lead in foreign policy matters, was duly against acquisition. The military also did not want nuclear armaments, because of the diversion of conventional weapons funding and of the fear that a nuclear arsenal might diminish, if not eliminate, the need for an army, air force, and navy.[15]

More significantly, the majority of the ruling Congress Party, including Lal Bahadur Shastri, who had become prime minister upon Nehru's death in May 1964, opposed India's developing nuclear weapons. New Delhi's initial reaction to China's nuclear test was to reiterate the country's commitment not to build nuclear arms. On October 24, 1964, Defense Minister Chavan articulated this view by declaring that the country would not alter its nuclear policy because of Peking's explosion.[16] Two weeks later, on November 8, Shastri prevailed upon his colleagues at the All India Congress Committee to formally endorse the policy of developing nuclear energy for peaceful purposes only.[17] The following day Shastri publicly remarked that India ought to refrain from making nuclear weapons and instead concentrate its efforts on nuclear disarmament.[18] And on November 23, the prime minister pledged in Parliament that the government would use nuclear energy solely for peaceful purposes.[19]

Yet the intensity and persistence of calls for nuclear weapons, coupled with Shastri's own political vulnerability, gradually forced the government to alter its policy. Shastri owed his position largely to the efforts of senior Congress Party officials, which in turn made him less able to pursue a policy that did not enjoy broad party support. A substantial minority of Congressmen favored nuclear weapons acquisition. Many did so primarily for domestic political reasons. The Congress Party bore full responsibility for the country's defeat in 1962, and did not want to be perceived as being perpetually incapable of meeting the country's defense requirements; continuing economic woes and political setbacks in the intervening two years also argued for a dramatic gesture to reverse the party's declining fortunes.[20] Dating from Peking's test in mid-October, numerous members of Parliament and of the state legislative assemblies had petitioned Shastri to develop nuclear weapons. Despite the resolution of the All India Congress Committee in early November, over 100 party members at the session had endorsed a memorandum requesting that a secret meeting to consider further the nuclear weapons issue be convened in January at the Congress Party's annual conference.[21]

Despite his own misgivings, Shastri was consequently compelled by this pro-bomb coalition to modify official policy. In the Lok Sabha on November 27, the prime minister explained that although he opposed nuclear weapons development, he supported the development of nuclear energy for such peaceful purposes as the manufacture of nuclear explosives for tunneling, excavating, and other peaceful uses.[22] This marked the first time that an Indian prime minister had publicly supported the possibility of developing nuclear explosives, if only for peaceful purposes.[23] At the annual conference in January 1965 Shastri went one step further. After announcing that "our present policy is not to manufacture the atom bomb, but to develop nuclear energy for constructive purposes," the prime minister cautioned that "I cannot say anything about the future."[24] This open-ended policy contrasted even more sharply with Shastri's earlier categorical refusals to develop nuclear weapons and with the nuclear energy policy articulated during Nehru's tenure. It suggested the government might shift further, to sanction nuclear weapons manufacture at some future point, while in the short-term it indicated that India's scientists and engineers could work on "peaceful nuclear explosives" (PNEs). And since the technology involved with PNEs was virtually indistinguishable from that of nuclear weapons, this research would provide valuable information and training if New Delhi ever decided to build nuclear bombs.

Curiously absent from all these discussions was any thorough examination of India's nuclear energy program and the country's ability to manufacture nuclear arms. This was mostly due to Bhabha's boast that India could test a nuclear device within eighteen months, which was accepted uncritically, but also due to a general lack of appreciation of the technological and engineering processes involved in nuclear weapons acquisition and of the time-frame their mastery would entail.[25]

India's nuclear program at this time was not as advanced as many of the advocates of nuclear weapons assumed. By 1964 India had only imperfectly realized the three goals of its nuclear program, namely, economic development, self-reliance in building all stages of the nuclear fuel cycle, and the option to manufacture nuclear weapons.[26]

Responsibility for the country's nuclear development can be traced to one individual, Homi Bhabha. Bhabha's academic training at Cambridge University before the Second World War had convinced him that nuclear power could serve as the engine to propel India forward by providing an inexpensive source of energy for industrial and agricultural development. A letter in March 1944 to the Indian philanthropist J.D.R. Tata succeeded in obtaining funds for a center for physics research; Bhabha served as its first director. Discussions during this period between India and the United States and Britain over access to India's deposits of thorium, which was thought at the time to be useful for atomic energy,[27] further encouraged New Delhi to develop its own nuclear industry. Within a year after independence, India promulgated an Atomic Energy Act, which had the two-fold purpose of requiring that all research and development be conducted in secret and of placing all uranium and thorium reserves under state control. The Act also authorized the creation of an Atomic Energy Commission, which with Bhabha as its first chairman set out to train Indian scientists and to survey the country for uranium and thorium deposits.[28] India's ambitions in the nuclear field were noted even at this early date by the U.S. State Department, which observed that "the aspirations of Indian officials in atomic energy development appears illimitable."[29]

These aspirations evidenced themselves in the three-stage, long-term nuclear program that Bhabha outlined at the Conference on the Development of Atomic Energy for Peaceful

Purposes held in New Delhi in November 1954. Bhabha envisioned three types of reactors that would generate electricity as well as produce fuel for other reactors. The country's vast reserves of thorium would act as the basis for the program. The first stage would consist of a natural uranium fuel cycle with heavy water reactors which would produce plutonium and electric power. The second stage would use the plutonium which had been obtained by reprocessing the reactors' spent fuel, and combine it with thorium-232 to produce uranium-233 and electric power. The third stage would have breeder reactors using thorium-232 and uranium-233; because more uranium-233 would be produced from this method than would be consumed, India would have an inexhaustible supply of electricity available for the country's economic development.[30] No one at the time voiced any doubts over whether India required such an ambitious nuclear program for its modest energy needs or whether a largely unindustrialized country could afford to devote its limited human and financial resources to the research, development, and production of a highly complex and sophisticated technology.[31] Bhabha and other Indian officials would from now on justify their opposition to all forms of international safeguards, as well as their desire for a plutonium separation capability, by maintaining that it was demanded for the country to fulfill its three-stage plan for nuclear development.

India's eagerness to develop its nuclear energy program coincided with Canada's interest during the 1950s to promote its CANDU heavy-water technology as an alternative to American light-water reactors. Negotiations between Ottawa and New Delhi began in 1954 for a research reactor based on the NRX design at Chalk River. Canada's offer to finance the reactor under the Colombo Plan meant that India would pay less than half of the $14 million total, and Canada would underwrite the costs of training visits to the Chalk River plant by Indian scientists and engineers.[32] Canada and India signed a nuclear cooperation agreement in April 1956. A month earlier, the United States had sold India 21 tons of heavy water for the Canadian reactor, which was named CIRUS. Significantly, in neither instance were the nuclear equipment and materials comprehensively safeguarded. India had agreed to use the reactor and any products resulting from its use for "peaceful purposes only," but what constituted "peaceful" was no where defined. The absence of rigorous safeguard provisions can be partly explained by the reputation Nehru enjoyed as a man dedicated to international peace, and by Ottawa's eagerness to market its CANDU design.[33]

By far the most important explanation, however, was India's steadfast refusal to accept more stringent safeguards on the CIRUS facility. Led by Bhabha, India fiercely resisted safeguards on the twin grounds that they would infringe upon the country's sovereignty and would inhibit the eventual transition to fast breeder technology. This attitude also manifested itself during the negotiations in the mid-1950s on the statute of the International Atomic Energy Agency. Looking toward the anticipated second stage of India's nuclear plan when it would require a reprocessing capability, Bhabha told the international audience that "we consider it to be the inalienable right of states to produce and hold fissionable material required for their peaceful power programs."[34] Bhabha further stated that safeguard provisions must be "objective and nondiscriminatory." The agency should not make distinctions between "atomic 'haves' and 'have-nots,' " which would be tantamount to a "new form of economic colonialism."[35] Bhabha's themes of equality, independence, and self-sufficiency reflected the country's nonaligned policy and, not coincidentally, provided India with a logic for accommodating a nuclear weapons option in its nuclear program.

Necessary at some point for India's three-stage nuclear plan was a reprocessing plant to separate the spent fuel from the natural uranium/heavy-water reactors. Yet in July 1958, despite not having any reactors of this type save for the 40-megawatt CIRUS research facility, which was still under construction, India decided to build a chemical separation plant near Trombay, outside of Bombay. This decision aroused suspicion, given the state of India's nuclear development and the country's need to study other, equally important, technologies, such as the separation processes for irradiated thorium.[36] Nehru stated in the Lok Sabha the reasons for constructing the facility.

Plutonium is of the greatest importance as it is not available from outside as a commercial commodity. Its production is essential in order to enable the country to set up breeder power stations using thorium which we have in ample measure.[37]

Nehru's justification did little to explain why the country needed separated plutonium so urgently. The true reason was India's realization in May 1958 that China was developing nuclear weapons, which the prime minister was understandably hesitant to disclose.[38] Ground was broken at Trombay in April 1961, and the reprocessing facility was officially inaugurated on January 22, 1965. Six months later, a British reporter related after a tour of Trombay that it "has not yet separated the ten kilograms of plutonium generally said to be desirable for a single atom bomb, but it soon will."[39] Since India had designed and constructed the plant itself, there were no safeguards. In conjunction with the CIRUS reactor, which was capable of producing ten kilograms of plutonium annually, the reprocessing facility at Trombay theoretically could provide India with the material needed for one to two nuclear devices per year.

Yet difficulties at these two plants prevented Bhabha from realizing his claim that India could detonate a nuclear explosive by May 1966, eighteen months after China's nuclear test. Although CIRUS had been operating since 1960, it had been marked by technical problems and was operating far below capacity. By 1964, the amount of plutonium produced by CIRUS was negligible. Even if CIRUS had been operating smoothly, the reprocessing plant was also experiencing operational difficulties. Bhabha's claim therefore had no basis in the technological realities of India's nuclear program in 1964. For the next two years as well, Indian scientists had access to only "very small quantities of plutonium; they had very little experience in handling this dangerous, fissionable material; they had done no work at all in the physics of nuclear explosions."[40] Despite Bhabha's intentions, then, the country's limited capabilities foreclosed its nuclear weapons option.

Notwithstanding these limitations, or in anticipation of overcoming them in the near future, Bhabha in November 1965 requested permission from Prime Minister Shastri to initiate work on a subterranean nuclear explosion project (SNEP). The following month Shastri approved the proposal. This allowed Bhabha to conduct research on bomb design and its nonnuclear components up to a point where India would be three months away from detonating a nuclear device once the political decision was taken.[41] However, Bhabha's death in a plane crash in January 1966 interrupted this project. Vikram Sarabhai, who had headed India's space program, became Chairman of the Atomic Energy Commission. Sarabhai, along with two directors on the Commission, Homi Sethna and Raja Ramanna, opposed SNEP, at least in part because they did not believe India capable of conducting a nuclear explosion successfully at this time. With Shastri's death following soon after Bhabha's, any residual political momentum was also curtailed. Indira Gandhi, who succeeded Shastri as prime minister, was untutored in atomic affairs, and faced the immediate task of consolidating her position within the Congress Party. In addition, India at this time was building the Rajasthan Atomic Power Station (RAPS-I) with Canadian assistance, and was negotiating for a second identical CANDU reactor; if word of the subterranean nuclear explosion project became public, Canada would terminate its nuclear cooperation. Due to these factors, Sarabhai canceled the project.[42]

The technological constraints on India's nuclear program blocked, at least in the near term, one avenue for redressing the country's security dilemma. Other possibilities included seeking bilateral security guarantees from the nuclear weapons states or pursuing multilateral initiatives in the United Nations aimed at guaranteeing the security of all nonnuclear states. In neither instance did Indian diplomacy meet with success.

The desire for external security guarantees stemmed from

the little comfort New Delhi derived from Peking's denial of aggressive intent which had accompanied the announcement of its nuclear explosion, and from President Lyndon Johnson's subsequent pledge of American support for those Asian countries threatend by the PRC. The decision to seek guarantees rested solely with Prime Minister Shastri, who first broached the subject to British Prime Minister Harold Wilson in December 1964 without his having previously informed his cabinet or foreign office.[43] An inherent tension in this policy became immediately apparent: a security guarantee of any real value to India risked compromising the country's commitment to nonalignment. Wilson spared Shastri the problem of reconciling this contradiction by only listening to the Indian prime minister's hope for a nuclear guarantee for India and all other nonnuclear countries.[44] Upon his return to India, Shastri emphasized in the Lok Sabha that the initiative for such a step must come from the two superpowers; implicit in this statement was the belief that a *joint* guarantee would allow the country to preserve its nonaligned posture. To seek out Washington's and Moscow's thoughts, New Delhi dispatched a senior civil servant, L.K. Jha. India's skepticism over the sincerity of any American security guarantee, due to Washington's ties to Pakistan since the mid-1950s and to its cutoff of military aid during India's September 1965 war with Pakistan, made Jha's task more difficult. According to one report, the U.S. refused to give India an official guarantee codified in treaty form, but would agree to a nuclear guarantee under United Nations auspices with provision to go to the General Assembly should the Security Council become paralyzed by the veto.[45] India similarly found the Soviet Union's response lacking.[46]

Simultaneous with India's attempts to extract superpower guarantees were India's efforts in the U.N. for nuclear disarmament. Since the mid-1950s India had been one of the leaders in opposing nuclear testing; it had been among the first signatories of the Partial Test Ban Treaty and had called for its extension to all environments. On the subject of nonproliferation, India supported U.N. General Assembly resolution 2028, which was adopted on November 19, 1965. The resolution outlined the principles an acceptable nonproliferation treaty would embody: (1) the treaty should not have any loopholes through which nuclear or nonnuclear weapons states could proliferate directly or indirectly; (2) there must be an equal balance of mutual responsibilities and obligations between the nuclear and nonnuclear weapons states; (3) the treaty should be viewed as a first step toward general and complete disarmament, with special reference to nuclear disarmament; and (4) the provisions should be designed to ensure the treaty's effectiveness.[47] This resolution was noteworthy for its emphasis on equity and reciprocity between the nuclear and nonnuclear weapons states. In negotiations in the United Nations during the next few years, India's three main criticisms of subsequent draft proposals centered on how far they departed from this model. Specifically, India objected that the nuclear weapons states were not required to disarm, while the nonnuclear weapons states promised never to acquire nuclear arms—in other words, that only horizontal, not vertical, proliferation was constrained. Second, safeguards were applied to the facilities of the nonnuclear weapons states, but not to those of the nuclear weapons states. And third, the nonproliferation treaty prohibited the nonnuclear states from experimenting with certain peaceful uses of nuclear energy, such as nuclear explosions.[48]

Despite this perceived imbalance, Indian officials gave serious consideration to signing the Nonproliferation Treaty. Senior members of the Ministry of External Affairs, led by L.K. Jha, generally favored signing, in part because of British pressure and the fear of American threats to terminate aid. Sarabhai initially did not oppose India joining the NPT, but subsequently developed reservations. As of November 1967, however, India supposedly was prepared to sign the treaty.[49]

India's ultimate decision to reject the treaty was based on a combination of substantive objections and Prime Minister Indira Gandhi's domestic considerations. New Delhi's diplomacy by the beginning of 1968 had failed to obtain a superpower nuclear guarantee or a nonproliferation agreement that promised to reduce the distance between the nuclear and nonnuclear states. In addition, the prime minister's entire cabinet opposed joining the treaty. Supporting those officials against the NPT were public opinion polls which purportedly indicated that a majority of the Indian people wanted nuclear bombs and did not want the country to sign the NPT.[50] India announced its decision before the United Nations in May 1968.[51]

By mid-1968, India almost in spite of itself had remained both nonnuclear and nonaligned. Although it had not signed the NPT, it had canceled the subterranean nuclear explosion project and had refrained from entering into any agreements with nuclear weapons states guaranteeing its security. It is not clear if the failure to bring about an acceptable nonproliferation agreement or to elicit superpower protection spurred New Delhi's decision in 1968 to build its 10-megawatt Purnima research reactor, or if India would have gone ahead in any case. By this time India had accumulated sufficient stockpiles of plutonium to begin the theoretical calculations for nuclear explosions. The Purnima plant was essential for this work. Still, while the two-year hiatus between the 1966 termination of SNEP and the decision to build Purnima may have been due to Mrs. Gandhi's preoccupation with domestic problems, it also suggests that there existed no overriding, urgent desire at this time to test a nuclear device or build nuclear weapons. This in turn implies that the 1968 decision on Purnima indicated that India wanted to possess the option for the future to detonate a nuclear explosive, but that it had not yet committed itself to doing so. The cost of this research reactor was buried in the budget of the Kalpakkam fast breeder reactor which was under construction near Madras.[52] Interestingly, Purnima did not receive mention in the ten-year plan Vikram Sarabhai published in May 1970 on India's atomic energy and space research.[53] The Sarabhai plan also omitted any reference to nuclear weapons or peaceful nuclear explosions in its list of objectives for the country.

While India gradually moved closer toward possessing the

technological foundation for manufacturing nuclear devices, the entire diplomatic landscape of South Asia underwent dramatic change. In July 1971, U.S. Secretary of State Henry Kissinger traveled to Peking, ushering in a new era in Sino-American relations. That the United States had used Pakistan as the key intermediary through which it conducted its rapprochement with China incited New Delhi's fear that the balance of power on the subcontinent might become unfavorable. To counter the advantage Pakistan would derive from its close ties to Washington, India the following month felt compelled to sign a twenty-year Treaty of Peace, Friendship and Cooperation with the Soviet Union. The treaty provided for immediate "mutual consultations" should either party be subject to attack or threat.[54] Meanwhile, Pakistan's President Yahya Khan had been faced with increasing unrest in East Pakistan after the Awami League, which sought greater autonomy from the central government in West Pakistan, had won a majority of seats in the National Assembly in the December 1970 elections. Khan had ordered the army to suppress dissident Awami League members and their followers; the resulting carnage drove millions of East Pakistanis into the neighboring Indian state of West Bengal. Faced with a mounting refugee problem, as well as presented with what one Indian strategist termed the "opportunity of the century," India in December 1971 sent its troops into East Pakistan. The United States in response sailed a task force led by the aircraft carrier U.S.S. *Enterprise* into the Bay of Bengal. Despite Washington's show of support for its client, India within a few days routed the Pakistani forces.[55] India's subsequent promotion of an independent Bangladesh succeeded in severing politically Pakistan's two halves. Although largely reacting to external developments beyond its immediate control, India had nonetheless outmaneuvered Pakistan, China, and the United States.

By the beginning of 1972, India was more powerful than at any point since independence. In domestic affairs, the popularity of Mrs. Gandhi and the Congress Party was evidenced by sweeping electoral successes in the parliamentary and state-level elections of 1971 and 1972. Pakistan's dismemberment had assured India's dominance in the region for some time to come. Further, the Simla Agreement which the two countries signed in July 1972 offered some hope for "a friendly and harmonious relationship" between the two traditional adversaries. The August 1971 agreement with Moscow benefitted India in two ways, by providing it with a superpower patron to counter American support of Pakistan and by supplying a deterrent to both conventional and nuclear threats by China.

Yet despite this position of strength, the preceding twelve months had conferred on India a mixed blessing. America's ordering the U.S.S. *Enterprise*, widely believed to be carrying nuclear weapons, to the Bay of Bengal had angered and offended Indian officials. More importantly, Washington's diplomacy seemed to foreshadow the unwelcome prospect of greater superpower involvement in the subcontinent and Indian Ocean. India's Peace, Friendship and Cooperation Treaty with the Soviet Union had already seriously compromised the country's policy of nonalignment. Washington's opening to Peking, and its collaboration with Pakistan, suggested that India would have need to rely on further Soviet assistance in the future. Paradoxically, then, the events of 1971 instilled confidence in New Delhi because the Soviet Union ensured a measure of protection against the PRC and the U.S., while at the same time created unease that India's independence might be jeopardized.

Searching for a manner in which it could reassert its autonomy without risking the gains realized in 1971, India decided to reactivate its nuclear explosion project. Better than any other single event, a nuclear detonation would express symbolically India's freedom from external pressures. It would act as a rebuke to the Nonproliferation Treaty regime, which had been crafted by the United States and the Soviet Union, would illustrate the limits of Moscow's influence with New Delhi, and would remind China that India could develop nuclear weapons if it wished. A single test only would not invite a punitive response, and had greater likelihood of being viewed as the political signal New Delhi intended. In India's eyes, then, a nuclear explosion would be an expression of its nonalignment policy.

In addition, however, the financial, security, and ethical arguments against nuclear weapons acquisition that had been espoused during the mid-1960s in response to China's nuclear test retained continuing validity, and thus militated against proceeding beyond one test. The cost of a nuclear weapons program would divert enormous resources from the country's industrial and agricultural development. Real hardship would result should donor countries cut off economic assistance in retaliation for India's investing its scarce resources in a nuclear bomb project. Further, India's nuclear program in 1974 could not support a sustained bomb program, as the country lacked the means to produce the necessary quantities of unsafe-guarded weapons-grade plutonium. Moreover, India lagged ten years behind China in the development of a nuclear arsenal; to catch up with Peking at a time when tens of millions of Indians hovered at or below the poverty line would demand enormous sacrifice and political willpower. India already enjoyed by vir-tue of its treaty with the Soviet Union a form of insurance against Chinese aggression. And by labeling its test a "peaceful nuclear explosion," combined with subsequent abstention from additional nuclear explosions or nuclear weapons de-velopment, India could hope to preserve its image of ethical behavior. By irrefutably proving that it could develop nuclear weapons, and then choosing not to do so, India could even claim a moral superiority over the nuclear weapons states. A single PNE thus offered India the best of all possible worlds—a political signal of singular forcefulness without the negative consequences involved in manufacturing nuclear weapons. The technological foundation for this political imperative was provided in May 1972, when the Purnima reactor went critical. For the first time in its history, India had an authentic capability to detonate a nuclear device.

In early 1972, Prime Minister Indira Gandhi instructed the atomic energy establishment to perform all the necessary scien-tific and engineering tasks. A test supervising committee, which included Homi Sethna, the Chairman of the Atomic Energy Commission, and Raja Ramanna, the Director of the Bhabha Atomic Research Center, was formed to oversee the project. The theoretical calculations for the nuclear device were finished by December.[56] The committee selected a site in Andhra Pradesh, south India, where in March 1973 it conducted a small number of chemical explosions in order to test the implosion mechanism and to calibrate the measuring instruments for the nuclear test.[57] These explosions were responsible for the erroneous reports which circulated after May 1974 that India had tried and failed in an earlier attempt to detonate a nuclear device. In February 1974, Mrs. Gandhi was informed that the preparations were complete. By this time the prime minister's political fortunes had declined. Increasing factionalism within the Congress Party, the deteriorating economy, and an ongoing railway strike, all contributed to Mrs. Gandhi's unpopularity. While the prime minister had already committed herself in early 1972 to detonating a nuclear device as soon as technologically possible, it is probably fair to say that her domestic difficulties made a nuclear explosion more attractive, as it would divert people's attention from more prosaic concerns, unify the country in a display of nationalistic pride, and, not incidentally, boost the standing of the prime minister and her party. After consulting with only a few of her closest advisors, and without informing the Ministry of External Affairs, Gandhi gave final permission for the test.[58]

At 8:05 A.M. on May 18, 1974, India detonated what it termed a "peaceful nuclear explosion." The device had been placed in an L-shaped trench 107 meters below the surface at Pokharan, in the sparsely inhabited Rajasthan Desert in western India. The estimated 10 to 12 kilograms of plutonium for the device had come from the CIRUS heavy-water reactor, and had been separated at Trombay. The yield was 12 to 13 kilotons, as the unfamiliar geological conditions prevented a more precise reading. Since the spheric device was designed to be tested underground, it "wasn't optimized for size."[59] Nonetheless, it still measured a compact three feet in diameter, including the surrounding monitoring equipment and safety locks.[60] The test cost Rs. 30 lakhs, or approximately $370,000.[61] It had taken ten years, but India had finally realized Bhabha's 1964 claim that it could explode a nuclear device.

INDIA'S POLICY POST-POKHARAN: REPERCUSSIONS AND RESTRAINT

India's motivation for its 1974 test indicated that the country never intended to proceed to a second test or to the more arduous launching of a nuclear weapons program. The PNE had been designed to fulfill certain policy objectives which derived from the events on the subcontinent within the previous three years. While Bhabha personally had wanted to test PNEs and perhaps even acquire a nuclear arsenal since the 1950s, and though a latent desire to demonstrate India's expertise in the nuclear field in this manner had existed since October 1964 and had acquired momentum with the 1968 decision to construct Purnima, the events of 1971 resulting in the realignment of power relationships in South Asia were the precipitating cause. The critical international reaction that followed India's PNE, the setbacks encountered by the country's nuclear program, which stemmed in large part from this adverse reaction, and changes in India's domestic political scene all reinforced New Delhi's prior decision not to exceed a single peaceful nuclear explosion.

For its part, India had taken steps with regard to the May 18 event in order to minimize the criticism which it anticipated might result from its explosion. The device was tested underground so that India would comply with its obligations under the Partial Test Ban Treaty. In addition, the official government announcement stated that India had no intention of producing nuclear weapons and reiterated India's strong opposition to all military applications of nuclear energy.[62] India claimed that the device was "a hundred percent Indian effort" that did not violate any of its nuclear cooperation agreements. Moreover, in an attempt to defuse criticism, India labeled its nuclear explosion "peaceful." The concept of peaceful nuclear explosions originated in 1957 with the U.S. Project Plowshares, which was designed to investigate possible applications of nuclear energy for excavation, tunneling, oil extrusion, and mining.[63] In the years immediately preceding India's test, the International Atomic Energy Agency sponsored three technical conferences to discuss the peaceful applications of nuclear explosions. By May 1974, the United States had detonated forty-one PNEs, and the Soviet Union thirty-one.[64] India protested that it had a similar legitimate scientific interest in exploring all possible peaceful uses of this technology. Viewed against this background of widespread research with PNEs, India maintained that its test was not so extraordinary an event that its motives should be impugned and its behavior vilified.

The reactions of the international community varied. While a few countries openly hailed India's achievement, many expressed deep concern over whether the spread of nuclear weapons could now be stopped. Most countries did not publicly comment on India's explosion.[65] India had hoped that its nuclear explosion would demonstrate the country's self-sufficiency and independence. In this it succeeded, though in a manner not originally intended. India's detonation provoked a level of censure and retaliatory measures which greatly exceeded India's expectations. Ironically, it was in India's ability to endure these actions during the next decade that best allowed it to prove its autonomy.

Critics of India's action assumed that it signaled an official commitment to become the world's sixth nuclear weapons state. India's explanation that its test was for peaceful purposes seemed mere pretext. The results of the earlier PNE experiments performed by the United States had proved disappointing, and Washington had ended funding for the program in 1970. Although India's officials had referred publicly to PNEs, there was little Indian contribution to the literature, thereby suggesting a lack of any sincere scientific interest. Moreover, when interviewed immediately after the PNE, Homi Sethna appeared at a loss when asked to what constructive endeavors these types of experiments might lead. The Chairman of India's Atomic Energy Commission replied, "It is too early to give a definite indication . . . I would like to impress upon you that we are looking into it."[66] This uncertainty over India's use of PNEs only confirmed the suspicions of those who interpreted the May 18 event as the beginning of an Indian bomb program.

Of those countries which condemned India's action, Canada was the most vehement. Ottawa was not mollified by New Delhi's explanation of peaceful intent. Even before it had confirmed that the plutonium for Pokharan had come from the CIRUS reactor, Canada believed that India had violated a mutual understanding that nuclear cooperation between the two countries should be devoted exclusively to peaceful purposes, of which testing a nuclear device was not one. Indeed, since 1966 Canada had repeatedly warned India that it considered the provisions of its nuclear cooperation agreements as preventing the use of Canadian-supplied nuclear equipment and materials for nuclear explosives.[67] Four days after the test, on May 22, the Canadian Secretary of State for External Affairs, Mitchell Sharp, announced that Canada was suspending shipments of all nuclear equipment and materials, and suspending all cooperation with India on reactor projects and technological exchanges between its contractor, Atomic Energy of Canada, Limited, and the Indian Atomic Energy Commission.[68] This meant the suspension of Canadian assistance on the Rajasthan-II power reactor and the Kota heavy-water plant, both of which were still under construction. As the price for resuming cooperation, Canada insisted that India accept IAEA safeguards on all its nuclear activities, including the CIRUS reactor and the Trombay reprocessing facility. After two years of unsuccessful discussions, Canada terminated all cooperation with India in the nuclear field.

Unlike Canada, the Soviet Union remained noticeably restrained in its public pronouncements concerning India's peaceful nuclear explosion. But Moscow made its displeasure known to New Delhi in private.[69] The Soviet Union also conditioned its future sales of nuclear materials on India's acceptance of safeguards. Indian engineers had managed to complete in 1978 the Rajasthan-II reactor, but it and Rajasthan-I required amounts of heavy water that India was incapable of producing indigenously. New Delhi, foreseeing this shortfall, had approached Moscow in late 1976, and the Soviet Union had promptly supplied 25 percent of the total Indian order of 240 tons of heavy water without attaching any bilateral or international safeguards. This raised concern within the Nuclear Suppliers Group, of which the Soviet Union was a member, that Moscow was not committed to placing safeguards on its nuclear exports as a means of retarding nuclear proliferation. However, when India the following year requested the remaining heavy water, the Soviet Union this time insisted on safeguards on all India's reactors as a condition of sale, not just those which would use the heavy water. The Indians balked at these terms, preferring instead safeguards on Rajasthan-I and II and only for the period of time the Soviet heavy water was physically present in the reactors. The compromise arrived at in November 1977 provided that safeguards would apply to the two Rajasthan power reactors once the Soviet heavy water was introduced, to any plutonium produced in these reactors, and to any nuclear material produced if this plutonium were later used in other Indian reactors. Further, safeguards would apply to these nuclear materials and reactors indefinitely.[70]

The reaction of the U.S. government to India's PNE was almost tolerant. The State Department issued a perfunctory statement that "the United States had always been against nuclear proliferation for the adverse impact it will have on world stability. That remains our position."[71] The following month the U.S. agreed to reschedule Indian debts under forty-seven loan agreements amounting to over $29 million, and in conjunction with other Western industrialized countries to increase economic assistance to India by $200 million.[72] In addition, the United States approved the shipment of previously authorized nuclear fuel for the two nuclear power reactors at Tarapur, which the U.S. had helped finance and construct under the terms of a December 1963 agreement with India.[73] The administration also initially failed to inform Congress that American-supplied heavy water had been used to fuel the CIRUS reactor from which the plutonium for the PNE was produced.[74]

Angered at India's use of American heavy water and frustrated by the administration's earlier lenient response to India's PNE, Congress decided to assume the initiative in reformulating U.S. nonproliferation policy. During 1976 and 1977 Congress enacted legislation which sought to use American military and economic assistance as a lever to persuade countries to accept full-scope safeguards and to pledge themselves not to detonate nuclear explosions. Congressional involvement peaked with the passage of the 1978 Nuclear Nonproliferation Act (NNPA), which tightened the criteria under which American nuclear equipment and materials could be exported. The NNPA had two immediate consequences for India. First, to engage in nuclear cooperation with the United States India had to agree to safeguards on all its nuclear activities. Second, it had to pledge not to manufacture or acquire nuclear explosives. The immediate focus of contention between the two countries concerned American supplies of nuclear fuel for the Tarapur power reactors. Because the NNPA mandated that all preexisting bilateral agreements and supply contracts must be in accordance with these new requirements or else be renegotiated, India was asked to alter the terms of its 1963 agreement with the U.S., under which Washington consented to provide regular shipments of lightly enriched uranium fuel. New Delhi responded that the American legislative requirement was both retroactive and unilateral, and refused. If the United States terminated its obligations, India threatened that it would in turn consider the Tarapur reactors and the plutonium contained in their spent fuel no longer under IAEA safeguards, and American permission no longer required before reprocessing this spent fuel to obtain weapons-grade plutonium.[75] Fearing this contingency, the Carter administration, despite some delays, approved nuclear fuel shipments for Tarapur before March 1980, the date when the NNPA became law; after this date, in mid-1980, the president had to invoke his authority in order to waive the Act's insistence on full-scope safeguards to overcome congressional opposition to supplying India with the Tarapur fuel. In 1981 India informed the newly installed Reagan administration that it intended to terminate the 1963 agreement because of the repeated delays in receiving fuel supplies. By July 1982, the U.S. and India had come to an understanding, where France would be responsible for supplying the Tarapur fuel. The United States would be able to comply with the NNPA provisions ending nuclear assistance, while India would continue to apply IAEA safeguards to the facility but would not be compelled to accept full-scope safeguards.[76]

All these measures taken by Canada, the Soviet Union, and the United States had the cumulative effect of retarding the Indian nuclear program by two to three years according to some estimates[77] and by six to eight years according to others.[78] Yet by the beginning of the 1980s, India had for the most part weathered this adverse reaction and had emerged more independent and self-sufficient in its nuclear development than it would have otherwise. Still, India chose not to conduct any further nuclear tests or develop nuclear arms. Indeed, New Delhi actually took steps which prevented it from obtaining weapons-grade plutonium that could have been used for nuclear weapons. Despite Canada's termination of nuclear assistance with the Rajasthan-II power reactor, India decided against using the plutonium contained in the reactor's nuclear fuel. As with the Tarapur plant, India selected to leave the nuclear fuel in the reactor instead of reprocessing it to gain bomb material. In addition, it devoted considerable effort and expense in bringing on line its fast breeder reactor at Kalpakkam. This reactor required 50 kilograms of unsafeguarded plutonium in order to start up, which would deplete most of India's stock of unsafeguarded plutonium.[79] If India were intent on a nuclear weapons project, it would not have undertaken these steps.

To be sure, domestic developments since May 1974 might have tempered any residual desire for another PNE or a bomb project. The euphoria within India from its PNE was shortlived; by 1975 Indira Gandhi felt compelled to call an Emergency in order to retain her hold on power. If India's May 1974 nuclear explosion had been motivated primarily by domestic consider-ations, internal developments up to and after the prime minis-ter's suspension of civil liberties argued for a second peaceful nuclear explosion, yet none took place. Further, with the end of Emergency rule and the elevation of Morarji Desai to prime minister in March 1977, the country had a leader irrevocably committed to not developing nuclear weapons, or to further testing of nuclear devices. Upon entering office, the new prime minister declared that India would not acquire nuclear arms. Desai repeated this policy before the Special Session of the U.N. Conference on Disarmament in April 1978, stating that

We are the only country which has pledged not to manufacture or acquire nuclear weapons even if the rest of the world did so. I sol-emnly reiterate that pledge before this august Assembly. In fact, we have gone further and abjured nuclear explosions even for peaceful purposes.[80]

While the prime minister's speech to the Lok Sabha upon his return to India appeared to hint that the country might still consider testing a peaceful nuclear explosion, Desai subse-quently clarified his opposition to nuclear testing and weapons development. Any member of his cabinet who dissented from the prime minister's stance would have been censured.[81]

If ever India needed a reason or excuse to test a second nuclear device or develop nuclear weapons, Pakistan's reaction to its May 1974 PNE provided one. Pakistan's Prime Minister Bhutto expressed his apprehension at India's action, writing to Prime Minister Gandhi that "the testing of a nuclear device is no different from the detonation of a nuclear weapon."[82] Al-though Pakistan had earlier expressed interest in acquiring a nuclear weapons capability, in particular after its defeat by India in 1971,[83] the Indian explosion now infused this desire with renewed purpose. Bhutto's negotiations with France for a reprocessing plant culminated in October 1974, when the French firm Saint Gobain Techniques Nouvelles (SGN) formally agreed to construct the $60 million facility at Chasma. Pakistan's interest in this technology was suspect, as the country's nuclear energy program had no real need for the estimated 100 to 200 kilograms of plutonium the Chasma reprocessing plant could produce annually. U.S. pressure on France to break off its deal with Pakistan on the grounds that it intended to build nuclear weapons, along with the adoption of a new French nonproliferation policy in 1976 under President Giscard, resulted in Paris terminating its contract in August 1978. Although Pakistan attempted to complete the Chasma facility on its own, it quickly encountered insurmountable obstacles.[84]

Pakistan nonetheless retained two alternative paths to acquiring weapons-grade material for nuclear bombs. First, at the same time as the Chasma negotiations with France had been initiated, Pakistan had begun secret construction of a small reprocessing plant, named New Labs, next to the Pakistan Institute of Nuclear Science and Technology near Rawalpindi. This facility reportedly could produce 10 to 20 kilograms of plutonium per year.[85] Second, shortly after India's PNE, Pakistan set out to obtain a uranium enrichment capability. Abdul Qadir Khan, a Pakistani scientist working for a Dutch company in the Netherlands, gained access to the Urenco uranium enrichment facility at Almelo, where he pilfered and transferred back to Pakistan highly classified documents on the uranium enrichment process. In addition, Khan stole the lists of those firms manufacturing the highly sophisticated components needed for ultracentrifuges. With this information, Pakistani agents using a number of front organizations and false identities began purchasing the necessary items.[86] As evidence mounted during the late 1970s of Pakistan's designs for a uranium enrichment facility located at Kahuta, outside Islamabad, and after Washington's inability to persuade Pakistan to cancel the uranium enrichment project, the United States in April 1979 ended all bilateral military and economic assistance, as required by the terms of the Symington amendment.[87]

The Soviet Union's invasion of Afghanistan in December 1979 reversed U.S. policy toward Pakistan, which was now viewed as a valuable strategic bulwark to contain further Soviet expansion. During 1980 the Carter administration negotiated unsuccessfully with Pakistan over the size and content of a new American aid package. In June 1981, the Reagan administration and Pakistan's President Zia were able to agree on a six-year, $3.2 billion assistance plan, which included forty F-16 aircraft. Congress, as a condition of approval, insisted on including a provision in the aid plan that stipulated that U.S. assistance would terminate if Pakistan detonated a nuclear device.[88]

Despite these warnings from the United States, Pakistan obtained a nuclear weapons capability during the 1980s. In October 1981, the Director General of the International Atomic Energy Agency revealed that the Agency could not guarantee that nuclear fuel had not been diverted from Pakistan's IAEA-safeguarded KANUPP heavy water power reactor.[89] This disclosure attained greater significance because it had earlier been reported, in September 1980, that work on the New Labs reprocessing plant was nearing completion, and the KANUPP reactor constituted the sole indigenous source of plutonium that could be separated.[90] In June 1984, U.S. Senator Alan Cranston declared that reprocessing had already occurred at the New Labs facility; American government officials denied this allegation.[91]

Pakistan also continued its pursuit of a uranium enrichment capability. In February 1984 the director of Pakistan's uranium enrichment project announced that Pakistan could now "efficiently enrich uranium."[92] News reports five months later stated that the Kahuta uranium enrichment facility had produced weapons-grade uranium; while some U.S. officials doubted that Islamabad had progressed this far, they admitted that Kahuta was at least partially operational.[93] If Pakistan decided to use enriched uranium as the material for a nuclear explosive, it could enjoy a high degree of confidence in the device's reliability, and therefore would not have to conduct a test. Pakistan nonetheless received assistance in this area from China, according to press reports. China allegedly aided Pakistan's development of its uranium enrichment capability, provided weapons design information, and gave Pakistan the design of the fourth nuclear device, a low-yield uranium-based explosive, that China had tested in 1966. Peking denied all these charges.[94] In March 1986 it was reported that the Kahuta facility had produced uranium enriched to a purity of 30 percent; eight months later, the United States apparently obtained information that Pakistan had produced weapons-grade uranium.[95] And in February 1987, Abdul Qadir Khan in an interview with an Indian journalist disclosed that Pakistan had developed a nuclear bomb; he later denied having made this remark.[96]

Reflecting on the decade following India's May 1974 peaceful nuclear explosion, two conclusions emerge. First, the confluence of incentives which prompted India's test did not arise again. Since the May 1974 event was the ultimate assertion of nonalignment, this by itself precluded repetition. The PNE had demonstrated India's skill in the nuclear field and independence from external forces. After its test New Delhi had less reason to fear excessive Soviet influence or Chinese blandishments. And because New Delhi had underestimated the harshness of the reactions to its nuclear explosion, it was presented with the additional opportunity to display its self-sufficiency as a response to the international measures instituted against it.

Second, factors constraining India's detonating a second PNE or developing a nuclear weapons program followed the May 1974 test. While it is unlikely that India would have proceeded beyond a single nuclear explosion, the resultant domestic and international constraints reinforced New Delhi's policy of nuclear abstention. In domestic affairs, the Emergency invoked by Indira Gandhi in 1975 turned the country's attention to the deteriorating internal situation, while Morarji Desai's tenure as prime minister effectively stilled all talk of an Indian nuclear bomb. In international affairs, while the Canadian, Soviet, and American measures concerning nuclear assistance caused difficulties for India's nuclear program, the country avoided any significant reduction in economic assistance.

India was on notice that a second nuclear test or any other indication that it was manufacturing nuclear weapons would risk terminating essential financial aid for India's development. In addition, India's claim to the moral high ground because of the peaceful intent of its May 1974 explosion and its subsequent refusal to build nuclear arms would have quickly faded if it had tested a second time.

Moreover, even without these constraints, the arguments against an Indian nuclear arsenal were no less persuasive than after the first Chinese nuclear test in October 1964. Conducting only a single peaceful nuclear explosion would preserve India's desire to be viewed as a moral actor in world affairs. China had not threatened India with its nuclear weapons, nor had conventional hostilities again erupted between the two countries along India's northern border. The treaty with the Soviet Union provided India with a measure of insurance against Chinese aggression in any case. And perhaps most importantly, by not developing nuclear weapons India avoided the diversion of its scarce human, scientific, and economic resources from problems of industrial and agricultural development, which constituted the country's most urgent requirement. Even without any international criticism or punitive measures, compelling reasons existed for India not to test a second peaceful nuclear explosion or to build a nuclear arsenal.

CONCLUSION

Although the traditional reasons against India's building nuclear weapons remained strong after its May 1974 PNE, Pakistan's nuclear development during the 1970s and 1980s constituted the greatest change in India's strategic environment and the most persuasive, if indeed not compelling, reason for New Delhi to acquire nuclear arms. Yet despite the April 1979 invocation by the United States of the Symington amendment, the revelation of the secret New Labs reprocessing facility, the IAEA's inability to certify the KANUPP reactor, Pakistan's surreptitious acquisition of uranium enrichment technology for its Kahuta plant, allegations of Chinese nuclear cooperation with Islamabad, and alarming reports of Pakistan's advances with uranium enrichment, India evidenced a not unremarkable degree of nuclear restraint.

One indication of India's nuclear restraint was the lack of any coherent nuclear policy, despite the seeming immediacy of the Pakistani nuclear threat. To be sure, for a number of years the so-called bomb lobby in India had advanced a variety of nuclear doctrines for the country, but its influence upon the Indian government was negligible.[97] More significantly, since Rajiv Gandhi assumed office in October 1984 upon the assassination of his mother, his public pronouncements on India's possible acquisition of nuclear weapons were confused and contradictory. While much of this could be attributed to the prime minister's political inexperience, it also suggested a more profound unwillingness on the part of the government to articulate clear policy options in response to developments in Pakistan.

Reflecting this lack of direction was an inattention to minimizing the impediments and reducing the time delays that India would encounter should it decide to build nuclear arms. Until recently, there was no evidence or reports that India had stockpiled any weapons-grade plutonium or covertly assembled any nuclear devices.[98] This lack of advance preparation translated into a delay of up to six months in assembling nuclear weapons.

While New Delhi undoubtedly had the competence to build nuclear arms, more problematic was finding the means of delivering any nuclear weapons it might have constructed. Since India had no means of enriching uranium, the only nuclear material India's nuclear program could produce was weapons-grade plutonium. India's nuclear explosives would therefore have had to use the implosion technique and been spherical in shape. The plutonium-based device India had detonated in May 1974 measured three feet in diameter. Yet a nuclear device of this size could only have been transported with great difficulty by any of the aircraft in the Indian Air Force inventory. The Canberra bomber was an extremely slow aircraft with which to deliver nuclear weapons; it would have been vulnerable to Pakistani interceptors and anti-aircraft weapons. More importantly, the Canberra had only about two feet of ground clearance under the fuselage, with the bomb-doors closed. The nuclear device would have had to be loaded into the aircraft from a pit, and even then the bomb-doors would probably have been unable to shut. The Canberra did not carry major armament under its wings.

The Jaguar jet fighter did have the ground clearance to load such a device under its wing (its underwing clearance was just over six feet). Rather, the problem was the aerodynamic drag associated with carrying the weapon. For aerodynamic reasons, the weapon would have had to be streamlined. Conventional designs tend to have a length to diameter ratio of 10:1. A device three feet in diameter would thus have had to be encased in a tube thirty feet long, which is more than half the length of the aircraft. A device encased in this manner would have been dangerous to fly, as it would have made precarious the handling and maneuvering of the aircraft. If such a payload could have been carried, it would have had to be placed under the fuselage, because carrying it underwing would require that one be placed under *each* wing, for reasons of in-flight stability, and that the two devices be released simultaneously in order to avoid losing control of the aircraft. In any case, the fuselage ground clearance of the Jaguar was approximately 38.5 inches, not enough to allow a 36 inch payload to be attached and carried.

For carriage under the fuselage, the Mirage-2000 was a better delivery vehicle, as it had a ground clearance of 4 feet, 3 inches. However, the requirement for streamlining the payload still existed, and the size of the casing would have presented enormous control problems in flying the aircraft.

Finally, the Mig-29, which the Soviet Union agreed to sell to India in 1986, was essentially an air interceptor. It was equipped with a sophisticated radar system to give it an excellent look-down, shoot-down capability, and it operated best when placed up high in the battle area to increase its radar horizon. As a low-level, high-speed delivery vehicle, it was not extraordinary. It, too, would have been confronted with the problem of aerodynamically streamlining its payload.

Of course, India could have always attempted to miniaturize any plutonium bombs it may have manufactured in order to achieve a warhead diameter of 13 to 15 inches, the approximate size of the U.S. B-57 and B-61 aircraft deliverable bombs. Yet to have a high degree of confidence that the new design would be reliable, New Delhi would have wanted to conduct a series of nuclear tests. This option was not implemented. A testing program would have entailed numerous domestic, regional, and international difficulties for New Delhi. And if India could not have miniaturized its May 1974 device without testing, it could not have delivered nuclear weapons.

Adding to India's concerns was the fact that Pakistan's nuclear program did not present Islamabad with the same impediments. The emphasis of Pakistan's nuclear program aimed at possessing a uranium enrichment capability. Unlike a plutonium-based bomb, one using enriched uranium would not need to be tested for Islamabad to have had great confidence that it would work. Pakistan could thus have avoided conducting any nuclear tests, the one undeniable signal that would have provoked India to launch a preventive conventional attack upon Pakistan's nuclear facilities, a threat which Prime Minister Desai on at least one occasion personally conveyed to President Zia.[99] A uranium-based weapon would also not have presented the size constraints under which India had to operate, and could have been delivered by any of the more advanced fighter jets in Pakistan's inventory (e.g., F-16s). Worse, from India's perspective, would have been if Pakistan had covertly accumulated an arsenal of uranium bombs and then confronted New Delhi with a fait accompli, accompanied by a list of political demands. Due to the time constraints involved with altering India's policy of nuclear restraint and acquiring operational nuclear weapons, Islamabad would have been assured of strategic surprise.

Whether intentional or inadvertent, the question remained whether this nuclear restraint exhibited by India constituted the best or worst of all possible worlds. On the one hand, India had demonstrated its technical and scientific competence, avoided the economic sacrifice attendant to full-scale nuclear weapons development, preserved the financial benevolence of the Western donor countries, and retained the option to acquire nuclear armaments in the future. On the other hand, India's PNE had garnered little additional influence for the country in international affairs, stimulated the nuclear supplier countries to adopt restrictive measures for nuclear exports, and, most importantly, provoked Pakistan to undertake a determined and ultimately alarming nuclear program.

Much uncertainty currently surrounds India's nuclear policy, an uncertainty that must await future developments on the Indian subcontinent. However, events during the 1970s and 1980s have shown that New Delhi preferred not to develop a nuclear arsenal. If it does decide to go nuclear in the future, India's reasons will be vastly different from those which animated its 1974 nuclear explosion.

PART III: EVALUATION

Part Three of this study will summarize the findings from the previous section in order to determine where the responsibility for the degree of nuclear restraint demonstrated by each country resided. In this manner, the impact of domestic pressures and bilateral disincentives, and the effectiveness of the international nonproliferation regime discussed in Part One, will be evaluated. It will be possible from this analysis not only to come to a fuller understanding of the decisions on nuclear weapons acquisition taken by these six countries, but also to derive some general conclusions on the subject of nuclear nonproliferation.

8.

Sources of Nuclear Restraint

Nuclear proliferation is a function of two variables: technological capability and political motivation. Both must be present for a country to acquire nuclear weapons. The capability without the motivation is innocuous. The motivation without the capability is futile.

Pessimistic predictions concerning nuclear proliferation have tended to concentrate on only one of these variables: technological capability. Fears that the spread of nuclear weapons among states was both inevitable and imminent stemmed from the wide dissemination of scientific expertise, engineering skills, and sophisticated nuclear technologies. These capabilities were thought to be a fairly accurate barometer of future nuclear weapons acquisition. The rate of nuclear proliferation could be extrapolated from the number of countries with these capabilities, and the different distances they still had to travel to develop nuclear armaments. According to this view, nuclear proliferation could be prevented or forestalled only by erecting technical barriers and restricting the dissemination of sensitive technologies.

These predictions have operated within the parameters set

by two assumptions concerning the importance of political motivations for nuclear weapons acquisition. At one extreme, political motivations were assumed to be irrelevant. What impelled a country toward acquisition was instead the momentum generated by its nuclear program. In other words, nuclear weapons development was ascribed solely to technological determinism. All countries which possessed nuclear programs would eventually end up with nuclear arsenals. At the other extreme, political motivations for nuclear weapons acquisition were presumed to be present in every country. Since each country wished to augment its security and enhance its prestige, and since nuclear weapons were generally purported to confer these benefits, each country would try to develop nuclear arms. Analyzing political motivations in order to determine future nuclear weapons spread was unprofitable, because on the basis of these criteria it was impossible to differentiate among countries. A far better indicator of potential proliferators was provided by an assessment of a country's technological capabilities.

This study, on the other hand, has tended not to concentrate on an evaluation of technological capabilities. It has not assumed that the pace of a country's nuclear development automatically transforms it into a nuclear weapons power, nor has it assumed that the desire to acquire nuclear weapons is both intense and universal. It has rather been primarily concerned with the political motivations which inspire, or discourage, nuclear weapons acquisition. It has attempted to show that for those countries which already possess the technical capability conferred by their advanced nuclear programs, only an analysis of the persuasive and dissuasive political pressures can reveal why they might, or might not, develop nuclear weapons. The decision over whether or not to acquire nuclear armaments in turn can best be understood when placed in the larger framework of a country's domestic and foreign policy objectives. Will nuclear weapons facilitate or frustrate the achievement of policy objectives? Will a nuclear arsenal augment a country's security and enhance its prestige? Or will nuclear weapons acquisition in fact diminish its security and reduce its prestige? Only by addressing these questions is it possible to discover the extent to which technically competent countries have refrained from acquiring nuclear weapons, and the reasons for their behavior.

This study has investigated the political motivations of six of these technically competent countries. Sweden, South Korea, Japan, Israel, South Africa, and India have all displayed varying degrees of restraint on the issue of nuclear weapons acquisition. Sweden, South Korea, and Japan demonstrated nuclear restraint by not developing nuclear weapons, by submitting their nuclear programs to full-scope safeguards, and by becoming parties to the Nonproliferation Treaty. Israel and South Africa, even though reported to be interested or involved in developing nuclear weapons, repeatedly denied that they possessed secret nuclear arsenals. In addition, there was no evidence to prove that they had tested nuclear devices. India decided not to reproduce its 1974 peaceful nuclear explosion or to develop nuclear arms. This chapter will discuss the sources of nuclear restraint for these six countries.

DOMESTIC PRESSURES

Domestic disincentives to nuclear weapons acquisition were significant in three countries—Sweden, Japan, and India. They were largely absent from the considerations of South Korea, Israel, and South Africa.

In Sweden, the domestic political situation in the late 1950s was responsible for the delicacy with which the government handled the nuclear weapons issue. As a result of the June 1958 special election on the pension issue, the Social Democratic Party (SDP) was returned to office. However, it governed, in association with the Communist Party, with a plurality of only a single seat in the Riksdag. Any disaffection within the

SDP, over any issue, would have jeopardized party unity and prejudiced the Social Democrats' chances in the 1960 general election. The party was in fact already divided over the subject of a Swedish nuclear force. The task for the SDP leadership was therefore to arrive at some form of intraparty consensus. In November 1959 the Committee for the Study of the Atomic Weapons Question, which was comprised of eighteen prominent Social Democrats, presented its report. It recommended that nuclear weapons development be deferred, but approved a limited and carefully monitored nuclear research program. This political compromise, which remained Sweden's official nuclear policy for almost a decade, satisfied both pro- and antibomb factions of the party and allowed a united Social Democratic Party to win reelection and remain in office.

Japan possessed a broad range of domestic disincentives to nuclear weapons acquisition. Stemming originally from its experiences at Hiroshima and Nagasaki, as well as from fears over radioactivity and food contamination which surrounded the *Lucky Dragon* incident, the Japanese people evinced an overwhelming opposition to all things nuclear. Public opinion polls consistently substantiated this so-called nuclear allergy. This sentiment assumed political form in the shape of the three nonnuclear principles: not to possess, not to manufacture, and not to introduce nuclear weapons into Japan. Further, legal obstacles to nuclear weapons acquisition were imposed by Article IX of the Constitution and by Article 2 of the 1955 Atomic Energy Basic Law. If a decision to acquire nuclear arms had been taken, the country's political stability might well have been undermined.

India's key domestic constraint to progressing beyond a single peaceful nuclear explosion was economic. The expense involved in nuclear weapons manufacture would absorb much of the country's small scientific base and limited financial resources, and prevent New Delhi from redressing more immediate problems of economic development. To produce weapons-grade plutonium in addition to or in place of generating electrical energy would have increased the inefficiencies and cost of India's already-plagued nuclear program. As the May 1974 nuclear device was not small enough to be effectively transported as a bomb, New Delhi would have had to invest time and money to miniaturize the device, as well as conduct a series of nuclear tests to ensure the design's reliability. Training of pilots and the modification of aircraft to become nuclear-capable would have been one more expense. A secure system of command, control, and communications to prevent the un-authorized use of nuclear weapons would have also cost money. As nuclear weapons would have complemented, and not replaced, its conventional forces, India would have had to allocate additional funds to its defense budget. The overall effect of a nuclear weapons program, then, would have been greater distribution of government expenditure toward the military and away from much-needed industrial and agricultural development schemes.

For South Korea, Israel, and South Africa, on the other hand, domestic pressures were not strong enough to restrain them from acquiring nuclear weapons. For these countries, their domestic political situations did not mirror Sweden's; the social, political, and legal barriers to nuclear weapons acquisition which were present in Japan exercised far less influence on their decisions; and the internal constraints which handi-capped India either did not exist or were less binding for them. The reasons for their nuclear restraint was due to other factors.

BILATERAL DISINCENTIVES

For all six countries, there were significant, and often multiple, bilateral disincentives to nuclear weapons acquisition.

Sweden's security position vis-à-vis the Soviet Union was a major factor in its nuclear weapons decision. Debate centered on whether a national nuclear force would enhance Sweden's policy of "armed neutrality." Beginning with the appeal by the Chief of the Air Force in 1952, and as a formal request two years later with the submission of ÖB 54, the military argued that the addition of nuclear arms to the country's inventory would help deter conflict by raising the potential costs to an aggressor. According to this reasoning, articulated most forcefully in ÖB 57, a Swedish nuclear arsenal would counter the Soviet superiority in manpower and conventional munitions, as well as deter the employment of Moscow's nuclear stockpile. Yet closer examination of this argument raised serious questions over the wisdom of nuclear weapons acquisition. During the year-long deliberations in the Atomic Weapons Committee, the military's contention that nuclear armaments would increase the country's security was discredited. More convincing to the committee was the view that nuclear weapons acquisition would be counterproductive by provoking an attack by the Soviet Union, especially during times of international tension. A nuclear-equipped Sweden, in addition, would have compelled the Soviet Union to assign a higher priority to Scandinavian affairs, which in turn would have placed Finland's neutral status at risk, upset regional stability, and possibly compromised Stockholm's policy of noninvolvement in foreign affairs. Even if Sweden managed to avoid this fate, its possession of a small nuclear force would have been little use against an adversary not only armed with a far greater number of atomic weapons, but also possessing hydrogen weapons with yields in the megaton range. Any employment of a Swedish nuclear force, no matter how limited, would have invited overwhelming retaliation. Due to all these considerations, the Atomic Weapons Committee and subsequent Swedish governments agreed that although nuclear weapons would increase the country's "purely military strength," its overall security would be reduced.

Moreover, U.S. policies indirectly and directly inhibited Swedish nuclear weapons development. Despite Sweden's refusal to join NATO, its strategic value and geographical proximity to the NATO countries ensured that the American nuclear guarantee extended to Sweden in much the same manner as it did to Washington's European allies. This was formally acknowledged by Stockholm in February 1968, in a report by the

Parliamentary Commission on Defense. American nuclear export policy also constituted a source of influence on Sweden's nuclear weapons decision. Starting in 1956, the bilateral nuclear cooperation agreements negotiated between the United States and Sweden prohibited the use of American-supplied nuclear materials and equipment for nuclear explosives, or for research on nuclear explosives. Due to these agreements, Stockholm could not have legally used its R 2, Ågesta, and (if it had ever become operational) Marviken facilities in order to produce weapons-grade material for nuclear bombs. It would have had to build additional, unsafeguarded nuclear facilities, a policy which would have been prohibitively expensive.

For South Korea, its primary disincentive to constructing a national nuclear force was that this action might have precipitated a rupture with the United States. Following the Korean War, Seoul's primary objective was to retain the American military presence, which was viewed as a leading disincentive to another North Korean invasion. The 1953 Mutual Defense Treaty had codified the U.S. commitment. A South Korean nuclear weapons program would have jeopardized this American military support. After the March 1977 announcement of President Carter's withdrawal plan, Seoul might have had less reason not to develop nuclear armaments, as all U.S. ground forces and nuclear weapons were scheduled to be removed from the country. Still, American army and navy support personnel, along with one fighter squadron, would have remained. The risks of forfeiting this contribution, along with American reinforcements in the event of full-scale hostilities on the peninsula and U.S. diplomatic support during peacetime, were strong dissuasive pressures to a South Korean nuclear weapons project. If Washington had discovered Seoul's intentions prior to the development of any operational nuclear bombs, the ROK could have been placed in the highly vulnerable position of having neither an American military presence nor a South Korean nuclear force. Without the protection afforded by the U.S. commitment to the country's security, South Korea could have been exposed to threats from North Korea, China, and the

Soviet Union. Domestic support for the Seoul regime might have eroded, with adverse consequences for the country's economic growth and for stability on the peninsula.

If by virtue of its political and military support the United States could influence South Korea's nuclear policy, Seoul could also use this relationship to influence Washington's troop withdrawal policy. Due to American sensitivity to nuclear proliferation, the statements from ROK officials conditioning the country's nonnuclear status on the retention of the U.S. nuclear umbrella and the exaggerated claims for the projected scope and sophistication of the South Korean nuclear power program aroused concern that South Korea would develop nuclear weapons unless Washington reversed its troop withdrawal decision. Whether or not Seoul would have actually developed nuclear armaments if the U.S. Second Division had been removed, the United States was unwilling to test its ultimate intentions. By using this "reverse leverage," South Korea was able to introduce another factor for Washington to consider in order to help persuade the United States to suspend the withdrawal policy. In July 1979 the withdrawal plan was suspended, and American ground forces remained in the country.

For Japan, the country's relationship with the United States checked any inclinations for nuclear weapons which might have existed. In 1952 with the original security treaty, in 1960 with an amended version, and in 1970 with the treaty's extension, the U.S. formally committed itself to Japan's defense. With the protection offered by the American nuclear umbrella, Tokyo saw little need to develop its own nuclear armaments. In the unlikely event that a Japanese nuclear weapons program had been initiated, the United States might have distanced itself from Japan. With a deterioration in the Japanese-American relationship, and before Tokyo had an operational nuclear arsenal, Japan would have been vulnerable to threats from Peking and Moscow. In addition, under a series of nuclear cooperation agreements between the U.S. and Japan, Tokyo was legally prohibited from using American-supplied nuclear materials and equipment for a Japanese nuclear weapons program. If Tokyo contravened any of these agreements, it would have risked an American cutoff of nuclear fuel supplies, upon which Japan was heavily dependent. Unless alternative suppliers could have been found, this would have resulted in the collapse of Japan's entire commercial nuclear industry, which was responsible for one-sixth of the country's electricity needs.

Although Israel appeared to have the greatest motivation to acquire nuclear weapons of all the countries under consideration, its bilateral relations with its Arab adversaries, and its relations with each superpower, presented significant disincentives to an overt nuclear posture. It was far from certain that a declared or demonstrated nuclear weapons capability would have furthered Israel's diplomatic, deterrent, and defense objectives.

It was in Israel's interest to prevent any Arab-Israeli conflict from escalating to the nuclear level. As long as the Israel Defense Force's conventional capabilities were maintained at adequate strength, and it retained its traditional air superiority, nuclear weapons were unnecessary for the country's security. If Israel had adopted a nuclear posture, this would have been an affront to the Arab world. The humiliation and anger it would have engendered could have spurred a united Arab military response to the Jewish state. Further, it would have stimulated a greater determination by the Arab countries to purchase or develop nuclear armaments. Nuclear proliferation in the Middle East would have been to Israel's disadvantage. Given the country's high concentration of population and industry along its Mediterranean coastline, it would have been more vulnerable to nuclear attack than the Arab world, which had a greater number and dispersion of targets. An overt Israeli nuclear posture would also have increased the insecurity of Israel's regional adversaries. Arab countries might then have looked to Moscow to obtain increased levels of conventional arms and formal security guarantees. As a result, the Soviet Union's influence in the region would have been enhanced. Most importantly, U.S. distress at Israel's behavior might have led to a termination of American military and financial assistance to the Jewish state.

The Israeli-American relationship also provided Israel

with the means of assuring that an overt nuclear posture need not be adopted. Due to Washington's general opposition to nuclear proliferation, and because an overt Israeli nuclear posture would have undermined American credibility and severely handicapped its policies throughout the Middle East, the United States endeavored to ensure that Israel had sufficient confidence that it could counter the range of potential threats to its security. To this end, the U.S. provided substantial military, economic, and diplomatic support to the country. There was therefore little reason for Israel to adopt an overt nuclear posture. In short, Israel's nuclear option was one factor which helped ensure continued American support for the country, which in turn made an overt nuclear posture unnecessary.

For South Africa, nuclear weapons were also militarily unnecessary. The country faced virtually no external threat to its security. Its armed services were in any case the best-equipped in Africa, and were easily a match for any black African force that could have been assembled; Pretoria also possessed an impressive security apparatus to preserve internal order. If a nuclear test had been conducted or an overt nuclear posture adopted, this would have risked the limited success of South Africa's "outward movement," as well as previous financial and commercial links with African countries. In addition, the African countries, due to a heightened sense of insecurity, might have requested security guarantees and greater military assistance from the Soviet Union. The expansion of Moscow's influence in the region was a development which was contrary to Pretoria's interests. Most importantly, South African nuclear weapons development would have complicated further its relations with the West, and in particular with the United States. This was evidenced by the diplomatic furor in August 1977 which surrounded the discovery of the Kalahari site. By combining criticism of apartheid with opposition to nuclear proliferation, sufficient domestic pressure in Western countries could have been generated to force them to sever their ties to a nuclear-armed South Africa.

India, too, did not require nuclear weapons for defense, deterrence, or prestige reasons. New Delhi's military buildup during the 1960s provided it with a clear conventional advantage over Pakistan in naval, air, and armed forces. This Indian superiority was evidenced in the 1965 engagement between the two countries and in the 1971 East Pakistan crisis, which led to the creation of an independent Bangladesh and further consolidated India's military position on the subcontinent. The territorial dispute on its northern border with China persisted, but neither country attempted to settle the issue by armed force. To deter the possibility of Chinese nuclear threats or aggression, India retained a Peace, Friendship, and Cooperation Treaty with the Soviet Union. While the May 1974 peaceful nuclear explosion had arguably clothed India with some international prestige, especially among Third World countries, a move to develop nuclear weapons would not have been greeted with anywhere near the same modest level of enthusiasm. Moreover, India's ability to weather the adverse international ramifications of its 1974 PNE demonstrated its independence and self-sufficiency, and hence provided it with an alternative source of status.

In addition, India's relations with Western donor countries and Japan would have suffered, perhaps terminally, if it had tested a second nuclear device or developed a nuclear arsenal. In financial terms, India had been fortunate that the reaction to its May 1974 event was so mild; although a few countries reduced developmental assistance, this was shortlived. New Delhi could not be certain that a second nuclear event would produce the same tolerant response. Nor could India afford to assume this risk, as the country's dire economic condition perpetually required as much economic assistance as could be provided.

From this summary of bilateral disincentives, it emerges that only some of the countries were able to use the threat to go nuclear to help realize their policy objectives. Success depended upon two factors, both of which had to be present: whether a country was perceived to have sufficient motivation to acquire nuclear weapons, and whether it had strong links to the United States. Only South Korea and Israel fulfilled both these requirements. Although Japan had longstanding ties to the U.S., it lacked a persuasive motivation to develop nuclear weapons. While the Soviet threat to Scandinavia provided Sweden with an incentive to construct a nuclear arsenal, Stockholm's policy of strict neutrality prevented it from having close relations with Washington. South Africa had neither a convincing reason to adopt an overt nuclear posture nor strong bonds to the United States. India's nonaligned policy required a certain distance between New Delhi and Washington, while its 1971 treaty with the Soviet Union made a closer relationship with the United States less necessary. Thus every country will not be able to profit from threatening to go nuclear. Only those with both a persuasive motivation and strong ties to the U.S. will be able to affect American policy to their advantage.

These findings also reveal that the motivations to acquire the technological capability which would allow a country to build nuclear weapons, the motivations to test a peaceful nuclear explosion, and the motivations to actually acquire nuclear weapons, are very different. A country's nuclear development may be motivated by many factors: the desire for nuclear-generated electricity due to a lack of alternative energy resources, the hope that sophisticated nuclear technologies will have spin-off benefits for other sectors of the economy, a desire for high-prestige projects to demonstrate modernity, or a combination of these factors. It might also be motivated by the desire to retain a nuclear option against an uncertain future in a dangerous world, or to detonate a single PNE as an assertion of national independence and self-sufficiency. And it might be motivated by the belief that the threat to acquire nuclear weapons will extract rewards from proliferation-sensitive countries, i.e., the United States, in exchange for not going nuclear. All these motivations, however, are distinct from those which will impel a country to test and deploy nuclear weapons. These two sets of motivations are too frequently confused with one another. Each must be analyzed separately.

The role the United States played in the decisions taken by the six countries is best understood within this framework. On the one hand, the U.S. used the various instruments at its command—its nuclear umbrella, military, economic, and diplomatic support, and bilateral agreements for nuclear cooperation—to help prevent proliferation in all six countries. On the other hand, due to Washington's sensitivity to nuclear weapons spread, some countries with which it was closely allied had an added incentive to acquire the technological capability to build nuclear weapons, in the hope of affecting U.S. policy to their benefit in return for not going nuclear. In other words, while the United States actively, and successfully, discouraged nuclear proliferation, it unwittingly encouraged a few countries to threaten to acquire nuclear weapons.

Nor did this threat have to be supported by the country having the immediate technological capability to construct nuclear weapons. Though important, the level of technological capability was secondary to political motivations. Anxiety over nuclear weapons spread was not caused by Japan's owning one of the world's most advanced nuclear programs, but it was excited in the case of South Korea, which did not even possess the necessary facilities for obtaining weapons-grade material for nuclear bombs. Political motivation, not technological capability, was the key to arousing proliferation concern. This in turn underscores the importance of examining the political motivations to nuclear weapons acquisition.

Finally, despite the different pressures which confronted Sweden, South Korea, Japan, Israel, South Africa, and India, two elements existed common to all their decisions on nuclear weapons acquisition: alternatives to nuclear weapons were available, and acquisition would have actually damaged the interests of each country. As an alternative to acquiring nuclear weapons, Sweden increased its defense spending on conventional weapons and redoubled its efforts to achieve international arms control and disarmament agreements. South Korea likewise increased its defense expenditures, and used the threat to go nuclear to help persuade the U.S. to maintain

American ground forces in the country. Japan relied on the United States for its defense. Israel increased its spending on conventional munitions, and used the threat to go nuclear to help ensure continued American military, economic, and diplomatic support. South Africa depended upon its own defense resources. India maintained its conventional superiority over Pakistan, countered China by signing a treaty with the Soviet Union after having unsuccessfully sought a joint superpower or multilateral nuclear guarantee, and was satisfied with the international recognition it had won from detonating a peaceful nuclear explosion. Furthermore, if any of these countries had openly constructed a nuclear arsenal, there would have been adverse reactions from neighboring states, allies, and adversaries. To the extent that nuclear weapons were counterproductive, nonacquisition was its own reward.

INTERNATIONAL NONPROLIFERATION ARRANGEMENTS

The international nonproliferation arrangements discussed in Part One of this study included the IAEA's safeguards system, the Partial Test Ban Treaty, the Treaty of Tlatelolco, the Nonproliferation Treaty, the Nuclear Suppliers Group guidelines, and the International Nuclear Fuel Cycle Evaluation. For the six countries examined in Part Two, these arrangements appeared to have little restraining influence on their decisions concerning nuclear weapons acquisition.

Sweden's debate on the nuclear issue during the 1950s predated the implementation of all these arrangements. The Atomic Weapons Committee delivered its report in November 1959. Its recommendation not to develop nuclear weapons remained the country's nuclear policy until February 1968, when the Parliamentary Commission on Defense advised that Stockholm should officially declare that it would not acquire nuclear armaments. Although Sweden ratified the Partial Test Ban Treaty in 1963, agreed to IAEA safeguards in 1966, and signed the Nonproliferation Treaty in 1968, these measures were only further confirmation of an earlier decision not to develop nuclear weapons.

South Korea's application of IAEA safeguards to all its nuclear activities and its ratification of the NPT were barriers to nuclear weapons development. Still, there was considerable doubt that these measures constituted effective restraints on South Korea's nuclear ambitions, or even indicated Seoul's intention to refrain from constructing nuclear armaments. These formal nonnuclear assurances did not prevent South Korea from threatening to acquire nuclear weapons, and indicated that IAEA safeguards and NPT membership were not viewed by Seoul as impediments should it decide to develop a nuclear arsenal. The concern expressed by the United States over these threats, and over the ROK's deal with France for a reprocessing facility, implied that Washington too did not believe that South Korea would necessarily abide by its nonproliferation agreements.

Japan's decision in 1976 to ratify the Nonproliferation Treaty was a confirmation of a policy that had been previously formulated. This nonnuclear pledge was simply a formal acknowledgement that the country did not wish to become a nuclear weapons state; it was a consequence, not a cause, of a decision on nuclear weapons acquisition that had depended on other factors.

Israel had neither signed nor ratified the NPT, and so was under no legal obligation to refrain from acquiring nuclear weapons. To be sure, IAEA safeguards were applied to its Nahal Soreq research reactor, but the more worrisome Dimona facility (and a possible reprocessing plant) remained unsafeguarded. That Israel did not publicly reveal its nuclear status was not due to this limited application of international nonproliferation arrangements. The maintenance of Israel's ambiguous nuclear posture was in fact aided by its refusal to accept full-scope safeguards or ratify the Nonproliferation Treaty.

Similarly, South Africa had refused to become a party to the NPT, and was therefore not legally prohibited from acquiring nuclear armaments. While its Safari-1 nuclear research reactor and its Koeberg facility operated under IAEA safeguards, there were no safeguards on the country's Valindaba uranium enrichment plant, which provided South Africa with the capability to obtain highly enriched uranium for nuclear bombs. If South Africa decided not to conduct a nuclear test or not to adopt an overt nuclear posture, this was due to other factors.

India did not sign the Nonproliferation Treaty and had successfully resisted the imposition of full-scope safeguards. In particular, it refused to allow safeguards on the Trombay reprocessing facility used for the 1974 test, on its Madras and Narora power reactors, and on all its heavy water plants. Despite the termination of Canadian nuclear assistance on the Rajasthan-II reactor and the Kota heavy-water plant, the Soviet insistence on IAEA safeguards incorporating "pursuit" and "perpetuity" provisions for its heavy water (and upon the heavy water's introduction, for Rajasthan-I and II), and the measures adopted by the Nuclear Suppliers Group, India retained the capability to produce weapons-grade plutonium. Although these steps by the nuclear suppliers inflicted considerable hardship upon India's nuclear program, New Delhi's decision not to test a second peaceful nuclear explosive or manufacture nuclear weapons rested on different calculations.

It seems clear that the international nonproliferation arrangements did not determine the decisions on nuclear weapons acquisition taken by these six countries. Yet this is too harsh a verdict, and misunderstands the influence they did exert. The acceptance of full-scope safeguards and ratification of the Nonproliferation Treaty were earnests of the intent not to develop nuclear weapons. And although the durability of these pledges was questioned in the case of South Korea, still the ROK did not abrogate its legal commitments. Moreover, they were accurate indicators of the nuclear intentions of Sweden and Japan. In general, this was the major value of international nonproliferation arrangements. These arrangements, in particular the IAEA safeguards system, the Partial Test Ban Treaty, and the NPT, provided mechanisms with which countries could advertise their nonnuclear intentions, both to those countries which were parties to these arrangements and those countries which were not. They specified and codified under international law a political commitment not to develop nuclear armaments, and projected this commitment into the future. This provided evidence of nuclear restraint and reduced the perception of an unbridled competition among states. The result was increased international security due to greater predictability and stability in world affairs. To the extent that the international nonproliferation arrangements achieved this objective, they had a restraining influence on the decisions to acquire nuclear weapons taken by Sweden, South Korea, Japan, Israel, South Africa, and India.

GENERAL CONSENSUS
AGAINST NUCLEAR WEAPONS

In addition to domestic pressures, bilateral disincentives, and international nonproliferation arrangements, there was another source of nuclear restraint: a general consensus against nuclear weapons. This general consensus, or world public opinion, contained both an ethical and strategic dimension. Nuclear weapons were perceived to be immoral, and their actual use in war, even if only in retaliation, could never be justified. Nuclear weapons were also seen as being dangerous to national and international security, and their dissemination should therefore be curbed. Any actions or measures which questioned, discounted, or discredited the utility of nuclear weapons contributed to this general consensus.

One evidence of this source of nuclear restraint was the international nonproliferation arrangements themselves. That these arrangements had been established attested to a view shared by most of the world community that nuclear proliferation should be prevented. All the international arrangements which were proposed and those which were established were manifestations of this concern. These arrangements in effect legitimized and universalized a consensus against nuclear proliferation. The Nonproliferation Treaty, in particular, was a major contribution to this general consensus because it was the clearest and most cogent example of international political concern over nuclear weapons spread. The degree of participation in all the international nonproliferation arrangements furnished additional confirmation of this general consensus. This source of nuclear restraint was also strengthened by the language contained in various arms control agreements calling for general and complete disarmament, by the declared intentions of the two superpowers for nuclear arms reductions, by the vociferous criticism leveled at the two superpowers for not making good on this claim and for in fact continuing to stockpile nuclear weapons, by United Nations resolutions and special sessions on disarmament, by the pastoral letter of the U.S. bishops on war and peace, and even by books advocating nuclear disarmament and by public protests against nuclear weapons.

While it is possible to find evidence of this general consensus, it remains something more than an intuition but less than a theory. Its actual impact on the nuclear weapons decisions taken by our six countries is difficult to assess. In general, its influence would be related to how sensitive to world opinion and reluctant to invite widespread criticism each country was. It is doubtful that world public opinion would have much effect on any country that possessed strong motivations for nuclear weapons acquisition. For those countries in which pressures in favor were balanced by those against, however, it was possible that this general consensus might have swayed a final decision. In the majority of cases where countries did not acquire nuclear weapons, this source of nuclear restraint would simply have reinforced the other sources of restraint that were present. It is likely that the general consensus against nuclear weapons performed this role in the decisions taken by Sweden, South Korea, Japan, Israel, South Africa, and India on nuclear weapons acquisition.

CONCLUSION

The identification of four distinct sources of nuclear restraint argues for expanding the previous conception of the international nonproliferation regime. This regime is more complex and more extensive than is generally understood. It does not consist solely, or even primarily, of the international nonproliferation arrangements with which it is most commonly associated. Domestic pressures, bilateral incentives, and the general consensus against nuclear weapons and nuclear proliferation are also integral parts of this regime. Any examination of the international nonproliferation regime which overlooks any of these four sources of nuclear restraint is both inadequate and incomplete.

This criticism of the previous conception of the nonproliferation regime raises the question of whether the problem of nuclear proliferation has been viewed correctly in the past. Originating with the proposals forwarded during and immediately after the Second World War, the problem of nuclear weapons spread has been seen in global terms. The key assumption of all these proposals was that many countries would want to acquire nuclear arms. Consequently, only institutions and arrangements international in scope could hope to halt nuclear weapons spread. This in turn led to an emphasis on establishing international nonproliferation arrangements. As a result, success in halting the spread of nuclear weapons came to be measured primarily in terms of the number of participants in these international institutions. Much of the pessimism which has surrounded the issue of nuclear proliferation has derived from observing the number of countries that have refused to become bound by these international arrangements, and concluding that this behavior could only mean that they have wanted to acquire nuclear weapons. While not denying that there might be some correlation between those countries that remain outside the purview of the international institutions and the likelihood of nuclear weapons acquisition by additional countries, participation in these institutions is not necessarily the best indicator of a country's nuclear intentions. Countries may decide not to join for any number of reasons, e.g., that they discriminate between the rights and obligations of the nuclear and nonnuclear weapons states, and yet still elect not to acquire nuclear arms. Of the six countries considered in this study, Israel and South Africa are examples of countries which fit into this category. They have refused to accept full-scope safeguards and to sign the NPT, and yet they have not conducted nuclear tests nor deployed nuclear weapons. India, too, did not accept IAEA safeguards on all its nuclear activities, sign the NPT, or conduct a second nuclear test or manufacture nuclear weapons.

This is not to say that international legal and technical barriers do not provide a worthwhile contribution to efforts to control nuclear proliferation. They have a useful, and indeed vital, role to play. Nonetheless, too great an emphasis on any one source of nuclear restraint will tend to distort the problem, and lead to faulty prescriptions for retarding nuclear proliferation. When this approach meets with less than total success the result is unwarranted pessimism.

The most effective nonproliferation strategy will be one based on a recognition of the multiple sources of nuclear restraint. Ideally, a nonproliferation strategy should encompass ways of strengthening all four sources: domestic pressures, bilateral disincentives, international nonproliferation arrangements, and the general consensus against nuclear weapons. Yet it is possible that certain policies which strengthen one source will at the same time undermine another source of nuclear restraint. An example is the nuclear arms buildup by the United

States and the Soviet Union, and the implications this has for nuclear weapons acquisition by additional countries; or expressed differently, the link between vertical and horizontal proliferation. On the one hand, continued U.S. strategic force modernization is necessary to maintain an effective nuclear umbrella over America's nonnuclear allies. This makes nuclear weapons development by these countries less necessary and therefore less likely. From this perspective, vertical proliferation inhibits horizontal proliferation. On the other hand, the superpower nuclear competition may make some countries not protected by either the Soviet or American nuclear arsenals feel less secure; it also appears to contravene the obligations assumed in Article VI of the Nonproliferation Treaty, while it associates power and prestige with nuclear weapons development. Viewed in this manner, the superpower arms race provides an incentive to countries to alleviate their insecurity by acquiring nuclear arms, weakens international nonproliferation arrangements, and subtracts from the general consensus against nuclear weapons. From this perspective, vertical proliferation tends to encourage horizontal proliferation. The debate over the link between vertical and horizontal proliferation is thus a dispute over which source of nuclear restraint is more salient, and for which country. Any intelligent discussion of this issue must recognize these complexities.

Since nonproliferation will be just one of a country's policy objectives, it is also possible that the task of preventing nuclear weapons spread will conflict with other, more pressing, priorities. Yet even assuming that it will not always be possible to incorporate all four sources of nuclear restraint into a coherent and comprehensive nonproliferation strategy, omitting a single source of nuclear restraint will not necessarily prove fatal to the chances of checking nuclear weapons spread. Any one source may by itself be sufficient to restrain a country from going nuclear. Japanese domestic pressures alone, for example, would likely have prevented Tokyo from developing nuclear weapons even if other disincentives had not existed. Still, the nonproliferation strategy which offers the greatest chance for success will be the one which attempts to harmonize all four sources of nuclear restraint.

Chances for success will improve further if a nonproliferation strategy recognizes that the problem of nuclear weapons spread is not a global one, but in fact only involves a few specific countries. Motivations for and against nuclear weapons acquisition in these countries will vary, and each case must be individually analyzed. The most effective nonproliferation strategy will be the one which calibrates specific policies to the particular circumstances and concerns of each country. To be sure, components of a nonproliferation strategy should be global in their approach, such as measures to reinforce the international nonproliferation arrangements and efforts to support the general consensus against nuclear weapons. But a strategy which combines these with an understanding of the idiosyncrasies of potential nuclear weapons states will be more successful.

Finally, in addition to the four sources of nuclear restraint that have been identified, there is another factor which is more subtle but no less significant. This is not a specific pressure from any source, but is rather a gradual realization, among government leaders and military planners in nonnuclear weapons states, that nuclear arms are simply not very useful instruments for achieving policy objectives. Nuclear weapons are not ends in themselves, and are increasingly viewed as largely unsuitable, and sometimes even counterproductive, means to the ends countries wish to pursue. The belief that the Soviet-American nuclear arms race has resulted not in greater safety for either participant, but only in greater burdens imposed by the constant development and maintenance of costly weapons systems, is perhaps the single most influential force shaping this perspective. Moreover, the observation that the nuclear weapons states have obtained a monopoly of a certain type of force that they are generally incapable of using has also supported this view. These "negative examples" have contributed to a perception that nuclear weapons will not necessarily enhance a country's prestige, nor automatically increase its security.

When viewed in this manner, the international nonproliferation regime assumes a strength and resiliency that is almost always underestimated when predictions of nuclear weapons spread are made. The benefits which derive from nuclear weapons acquisition are fewer, and the liabilities greater, than has generally been perceived. Previous forecasts of widespread proliferation have erred not only by exaggerating the potential advantages to be realized by a nuclear arsenal, but also by insufficiently appreciating the numerous, and formidable, restraints to nuclear weapons acquisition. While many countries may acquire the technological capability to build nuclear bombs, and some even threaten to construct nuclear weapons, few countries will actually test nuclear devices and develop nuclear arsenals.

Appendix:
Technical Note

This book concentrates on the political motivations involved in national decisions on nuclear weapons acquisition. Nonetheless, it is desirable to have some knowledge of the physics of fission and fusion weapons, and the sources of materials which can be used to fabricate nuclear explosives, in order to appreciate the significance of the various stages involved in the development of nuclear weapons.

In a nuclear explosion, the nuclei of atoms are transformed. In this process some mass is converted into energy, which is distributed by the explosion as heat, blast, and nuclear radiation. This nuclear transformation, with its accompanying large energy release, and the emission of nuclear radiation, differentiate nuclear explosions from all other physical and chemical processes.

FISSION WEAPONS

Nuclear fission is a process in which nuclei of certain heavy elements, i.e., uranium and plutonium, are split, or fissioned, into two lighter nuclei after being bombarded by neutrons. During this splitting process, more neutrons are "released," or emitted. A chain reaction is sustained in a mass of fissile material when at least one of the neutrons released during each fission process initiates a subsequent fissioning. When more than one neutron released by a fissioning produces additional fissionings, then the intensity of the chain reaction increases with time. In a nuclear explosion, many of the emitted neutrons cause increasingly large numbers of subsequent fissionings, thereby producing a rapidly growing fissioning rate. As a result, an enormous amount of energy is produced very quickly. For a fission explosion to take place, it is necessary to have a mass of fissile material large enough to sustain a chain reaction. This mass is known as the "critical mass."

Although different elements, and combinations of elements, can sustain a fission chain reaction, uranium-235 and plutonium-239 are the fissile materials most commonly used in fission weapons. The nuclear properties of both these elements make them especially likely to fission when bombarded by neutrons in a nuclear explosion. The main obstacle to constructing a workable fission device is the difficulty of acquiring sufficient quantities of fissile material, rather than the technical problems of designing and building the device.

FUSION WEAPONS

When isotopes of hydrogen, a very light element, are combined, or fused together, into heavier nuclei, a great amount of energy is produced, an amount of energy that is even larger as a percentage of the mass involved than that released by fission weapons. The isotopes of hydrogen used for fusion weapons are deuterium and tritium. The initiation of fusion reactions requires very high temperatures in order to overcome the electrical repulsion between hydrogen nuclei. Such high temperatures are generated by the energy produced by a fission explosion. Fusion weapons thus use a fission device as a "trigger," or detonator. Even if all the materials necessary for a fusion explosion can be obtained, however, it takes technical expertise of a very high order to construct a workable fusion weapon.

SOURCES OF MATERIALS
FOR NUCLEAR WEAPONS

The basic material from which uranium-235 and plutonium-239 are eventually derived is natural uranium ore, which contains 99.3 percent uranium-238 and approximately 0.7 percent uranium-235. Uranium-238 is incapable by itself of sustaining a fission chain reaction in a nuclear explosion. To obtain material for a nuclear explosive, uranium ore must therefore either be processed to obtain a higher concentration of uranium-235, or irradiated in a nuclear reactor to produce plutonium-239.

To obtain *uranium-235*, it is necessary to carry out the process known as uranium enrichment, whereby the concentration of uranium-235 is artificially increased by separating out some fraction of the uranium-238. At least four general techniques of enriching uranium have either been used or are under development: gas-centrifuge, gaseous-diffusion, aerodynamic, and laser methods. Uranium enrichment is inherently difficult because of the identical chemical composition of uranium-235 and uranium-238, and it must therefore rely on the small difference in their atomic masses. All four enrichment techniques consume a great amount of energy. To be suitable as fuel for some nuclear reactors, the uranium must be enriched to about 3 percent uranium-235. Material of this grade is sometimes referred to as lightly enriched uranium (LEU). For nuclear explosives, enrichment to at least 90 percent uranium-235 is preferable. Material of this degree of enrichment is sometimes referred to as highly enriched uranium (HEU), or more generally as weapons-grade material. Only about fifteen kilograms of 100 percent uranium-235 are required for a nuclear explosive device. A nuclear detonation can be achieved, however, with lower levels of enrichment (down to about 10 percent uranium-235), although the critical mass must then be greater.

To obtain *plutonium-239*, uranium must first be irradiated in a nuclear reactor. In order to keep the fission chain reaction under control, nuclear reactors use a "moderator" to absorb the neutrons which have been emitted. Although there are a number of different types of nuclear reactors, the two that dominate the commercial nuclear power market are light-water reactors (LWRs) and heavy-water reactors (HWRs). LWRs use lightly enriched uranium as fuel. HWRs, on the other hand, are able to be fueled by natural (i.e., unenriched) uranium. HWRs use heavy water (D_2O) as a moderator, because heavy water absorbs fewer neutrons than light water (H_2O), thereby allowing the small concentration of uranium-235 nuclei in natural uranium to sustain a chain reaction. HWRs can have individual fuel elements replaced while operating at full power. This operating characteristic makes HWRs more suitable for possible diversion of used nuclear fuel for military purposes.

Once the natural uranium has been processed into uranium oxide and fabricated into fuel elements, it is then loaded into a reactor for a controlled fission chain reaction. Some of the neutrons released in this process are "captured," or absorbed, by uranium-238 without its being fissioned. The resulting uranium-239 decays within about twenty minutes into neptunium-239, which in turn decays into plutonium-239 after about three days. Unlike uranium, plutonium does not occur in nature; it can only be created in this manner in nuclear reactors. This plutonium is present in the used, or spent, fuel from a nuclear reactor, and can be extracted, or separated, by chemical means from the other fission waste products in order to be suitable as nuclear fuel or as material for nuclear explosives.

This procedure is known as reprocessing. A nuclear explosive can be constructed with as little as four kilograms of plutonium-239.

The isotopes of hydrogen used for fusion weapons are deuterium and tritium. Deuterium is derived in the electrolysis of water. When an electric current is passed through water, hydrogen is separated from oxygen, and deuterium, or heavy hydrogen, is separated more readily. This electrolysis process can be repeated in order to obtain greater concentrations of deuterium. Tritium does not occur in nature in significant amounts. It can be artificially manufactured by bombarding lithium with neutrons in a nuclear reactor or in a hydrogen bomb during a nuclear explosion.[1]

Notes

Introduction

1. On this point, see Farooq Hussain, *The Future of Arms Control: The Impact of Weapons Test Restrictions*, Adelphi Paper 165 (London: IISS, 1981), pp. 15–17. This has been true since the inception of the nuclear age. The bomb dropped on Hiroshima, with a highly enriched uranium core, had not been previously tested. For a plutonium-based device, however, it is still necessary to have a series of tests to obtain a high degree of confidence in its reliability.

2. Raymond Aron, *Peace and War: A Theory of International Relations* (New York: Praeger, 1968), p. 60.

1. Changing Perspectives on Nuclear Proliferation

1. See Richard G. Hewlett and Oscar E. Anderson, *The New World, 1939–1946: A History of the United States Atomic Energy Commission*, vol. 1 (University Park, Pa.: Pennsylvania State University Press, 1962); Margaret Gowing, *Britain and Atomic Energy, 1939–1945* (London: St. Martin's Press, 1964). See also Bertrand Goldschmidt, *The Atomic Adventure* (New York: Pergamon Press, 1964); Wilfred Eggleston, *Canada's Nuclear Story* (London: Harrap Research Publications, 1966), pp. 40–206.

2. At the beginning of the war American officials thought that Germany had an eighteen-month headstart on atomic energy research. Hewlett and Anderson, *The New World*, p. 119; see also Henry L. Stimson and McGeorge Bundy, *On Active Service in Peace and War* (New York: Harper, 1947), pp. 612–613. How successful the Allies were in preventing any information on atomic energy from reaching Germany is revealed in Samuel A. Goudsmit, *Alsos* (New York: Henry Schuman, 1947); Leslie R. Groves, *Now It Can Be Told* (London: Andre Deutsch, 1963), pp. 230–249.

3. See Hewlett and Anderson, *The New World, passim*; Gowing, *Britain and Atomic Energy, passim*; Alice Kimball Smith, *A Peril and a Hope* (Chicago: University of Chicago Press, 1965).

4. The resulting text of the Three-Nation Agreed Declaration can be found in *Public Papers of the Presidents of the United States: Harry S. Truman, 1945*, (Washington, D.C.: USGPO, 1961), pp. 472–475. For background information on the Conference, see Harry S Truman, *Memoirs, Vol. One: Year of Decision* (Suffolk: Hodder and Stoughton, 1955), pp. 473–484; Joseph I. Lieberman, *The Scorpion and the Tarantula* (Boston: Houghton-Mifflin, 1970), pp. 168–175; Hewlett and Anderson, *The New World*, pp. 461–469; Gowing, *Britain and Atomic Energy*, pp. 73–74.

5. On January 24, 1946, the U.N. General Assembly unanimously passed a resolution creating an Atomic Energy Commission. UNGA/Res/1(1), January 26, 1946.

6. U.S. Department of State, *A Report on the International Control of Atomic Energy* (Washington, D.C.: USGPO, 1946). For a discussion of the preparation of this report, see *The Journals of David E. Lilienthal*, vol. 2 (New York: Harper and Row, 1964), pp. 10–33; Dean Acheson, *Present at the Creation* (New York: W.W. Norton, 1969), pp. 151–156. Forty years later, a modified version of the Acheson-Lilienthal Report was

suggested as a means of abolishing nuclear weapons. See Jonathan Schell, *The Aboli-tion* (New York: Knopf, 1984).

7. The text of the Baruch Plan is reprinted in Atomic Energy Commission, *Official Records*, First Meeting, June 14, 1946 (New York: United Nations, 1946), pp. 4–14. An account of how the Acheson-Lilienthal Report was modified by Baruch and his aides can be found in Lilienthal, *Journals*, pp. 33–59; Bernard G. Bechhoefer, *Postwar Nego-tiations for Arms Control* (Washington, D.C.: Brookings, 1961), pp. 35–40; Gregg Herken, *The Winning Weapon* (New York, Knopf, 1980), pp. 151–170.

8. The Soviet Union's proposal of June 19, 1946 is reproduced in Atomic Energy Commission, *Official Records*, Second Meeting, June 19, 1946 (New York: United Nations, 1946), pp. 23–30.

9. The text of the second Gromyko Plan can be found in Atomic Energy Commis-sion, *Official Records*, June 11, 1947 (New York: United Nations, 1947), pp. 20–24. For a discussion of the negotiations in the UNAEC from June 1946 to June 1947, see Atomic Energy Commission, *Official Records*, Special Supplement, Report to the Security Council (New York: United Nations, 1947); Joseph L. Nogee, *Soviet Policy towards International Control of Atomic Energy* (Notre Dame, Ind.: University of Notre Dame Press, 1961), pp. 33–98; U.S. Department of State, *The International Control of Atomic Energy: Policy at the Crossroads* (Washington, D.C.: USGPO, 1948), pp. 43–104.

10. One indication of this change in attitude is provided by comparing the titles of the two-volume official history of the United States Atomic Energy Commission. Volume 1 is entitled *The New World, 1939/46*, while volume 2 is *Atomic Shield, 1947/52*. "This central idea [to organizing volume 2] was the inexorable shift in the Commission's aims from the idealistic, hopeful anticipation of the peaceful atom to the grim realization that for reasons of national security atomic energy would have to continue to bear the image of war." p. xiv.

11. See *FRUS*, 1947, vol. 1, pp. 459–464, 577–583, 602–614. Frustrated by the snail's pace and then deadlock in the negotiations, some observers suggested employ-ing coercive measures to ensure agreement. Two early examples along these lines were offered by Bertrand Russell and Senator Brien McMahon. Writing in 1946, Russell recommended that the U.S. launch a preventive atomic strike against the then-nascent atomic weapons facilities of the Soviet Union if Moscow refused to join in forming an international government. Bertrand Russell, "The Atomic Bomb and the Prevention of War," *Bulletin of the Atomic Scientists*, vol. 2, nos. 7 and 8 (October 1, 1946), p. 21. In a speech before the Senate in May 1947, Senator McMahon stated: "I assert that for the first time in human history, the failure to agree to a sane, effective and righteous control of weapons of war constitutes in and of itself an act of aggression." *Congressional Record*, 80th Cong., 1st sess., May 21, 1947, p. 5740. After the Soviet Union acquired atomic weapons, Senator McMahon adopted a more conciliatory approach. Again speaking before his colleagues, this time in 1950, he suggested that the U.S. offer $10 billion a year for five years to all countries, including the Soviet Union, for economic aid and for developing atomic energy, in return for "general acceptance of an effective program for international control." *Congressional Record*, 81st Cong., 2d sess., Febru-ary 2, 1950, p. 1340.

12. Atomic Energy Commission, *Official Records*, Special Supplement, Second Meeting, September 11, 1947 (New York: United Nations, 1947).

13. This phrase was the title of a popular book of the period, *One World or None*,

Dexter Masters and Katherine Way, eds. (New York: McGraw-Hill, 1946). It is a compendium of essays, predominantly by atomic scientists, advocating international control of atomic energy. For an examination of the Soviet atomic weapons project, see Arnold Kramish, *Atomic Energy in the Soviet Union* (Stanford: Stanford University Press, 1959), especially pp. 3–123; George A. Modelski, *Atomic Energy in the Communist Bloc* (Melbourne: Melbourne University Press, 1959), especially pp. 21–42; David Holloway, "Entering the Nuclear Arms Race: The Soviet Decision to Build the Atomic Bomb, 1939–45," *Social Studies of Science*, vol. 2 (1981), pp. 159–197.

14. Public Law 79–585, 60 Stat. 755. This piece of legislation is also referred to as the McMahon Act, after Senator Brien McMahon, its chief sponsor.

15. For a discussion of the British program, see Margaret Gowing, *Independence and Deterrence, Britain and Atomic Energy, 1945–1952*, vols. 1 and 2 (New York: St. Martin's, 1974). See also, Andrew J. Pierre, *Nuclear Politics, The British Experience with an Independent Strategic Force, 1939–1970* (London: Oxford University Press, 1972), pp. 9–85; Richard N. Rosecrance, "British Incentives to Become a Nuclear Power," in R.N. Rosecrance, ed., *The Dispersion of Nuclear Weapons, Strategy, and Politics* (New York: Columbia University Press, 1964), pp. 48–65.

16. The bomb the Soviet Union tested in August 1953 was transportable while the earlier American device was not. See *New York Times*, February 8, 1960; Herbert York, *The Advisors, Oppenheimer, Teller, and the Superbomb* (San Francisco: W.H. Freeman, 1976), p. 92; David Holloway, "Soviet Thermonuclear Development," *International Security*, vol. 4, no. 3, (Winter 1979/80), pp. 192–197. On this general subject, see Holloway, *The Soviet Union and the Arms Race* (London: Yale University Press, 1983).

17. As one indication of this, in the 1953 Godkin Lecture at Harvard University, John J. McCloy's talk on "The Challenge to American Foreign Policy" did not once mention the subject of international control.

18. Harold L. Nieburg, *Nuclear Secrecy and Foreign Policy* (Washington, D.C.: Public Affairs Press, 1964), p. 75.

19. See the testimony of Secretary of State John Foster Dulles, U.S., Joint, *S. 3322 and H.R. 8862, To Amend the Atomic Energy Act of 1946*, Hearings. Part II. Committee on Atomic Energy, 83rd Cong., 2d sess. (Washington, D.C.: USGPO 1954), pp. 685–702.

20. The text of President Eisenhower's speech is in *Public Papers of the Presidents of the United States: Dwight D. Eisenhower*, 1953 (Washington, D.C.: USGPO, 1960), pp. 813–822. For Eisenhower's thinking on the Atoms for Peace proposal, see Robert H. Ferrell, ed., *The Eisenhower Diaries* (New York: W.W. Norton, 1981), pp. 261–262.

21. John Foster Dulles, "Challenge and Response in United States Policy," *Foreign Affairs*, vol. 36, no. 1 (October 1957), p. 33.

22. See the testimony of Secretary of State Dulles, in U.S., Senate, *Statute of the International Atomic Energy Agency*, Hearings. Committee on Foreign Relations. 85th Cong., 1st sess. (Washington, USGPO, 1957), pp. 3–83.

23. For an account of these deliberations, see Bernard G. Bechhoefer, "Negotiating the Statute of the International Atomic Energy Agency," *International Organization*, vol. 13, no. 1 (Winter 1959), pp. 38–59; see also, Bechhoefer, "The International Atomic Energy Agency," *Bulletin of the Atomic Scientists*, vol. 14, no. 4 (April 1958), pp. 147–150.

24. *Statute of the International Atomic Energy Agency*, 8 UST 1093; TIAS 3873; 276 UNTS 3.

25. For a history of France's path to nuclear status, see Lawrence Schienman, *Atomic Energy Policy in France Under The Fourth Republic* (Princeton, N.J.: Princeton University Press, 1965); Goldschmidt, *The Atomic Adventure*; Wolf Mendl, *Deterrence and Persuasion; French Nuclear Armament in the Context of National Policy, 1945–1969* (London: Faber and Faber, 1970); Wilfred L. Kohl, *French Nuclear Diplomacy* (Princeton, N.J.: Princeton University Press, 1971).

26. *The Times* (London), February 24, 1947.

27. "The physics of the pure fission bomb is so widely understood today that a nation determined to manufacture a bomb would not have to hesitate for lack of basic scientific information." Howard Simons, "World-Wide Capabilities for Production and Control of Nuclear Weapons." *Daedalus*, vol. 88, no. 3 (Summer 1959), p. 400. On this same point, see Hedley Bull, *The Control of the Arms Race* (London: Weidenfeld and Nicolson, 1961), p. 150.

28. The term "proliferation" was first used in this context by Secretary of State Dulles, in the submission of a disarmament proposal at the London meeting with the Soviet Union in 1957. It did not achieve widespread usage until the mid-1960s, however.

29. *New York Times*, December 28, 1960.

30. National Planning Association, *1970 Without Arms Control*, Planning Pamphlet 104 (Washington, D.C.: NPA, 1958), p. 42.

31. The countries placed in Group I were France, China, India, Belgium, Canada, West Germany, Italy, Sweden, Czechoslovakia, Japan, East Germany, and Switzerland. Those in Group II were the Netherlands, Australia, Austria, Denmark, Finland, Hungary, Poland, and Yugoslavia. Group III consisted of South Africa, Argentina, Brazil, Norway, Spain, and Mexico. See National Planning Association, *The Nth Country Problem and Arms Control*, Planning Pamphlet 108 (Washington, D.C.: NPA, 1960), p. 27. One notable study to take issue with these pessimistic predictions was by Beaton and Maddox: "there is no justification for the fatalism which has surrounded the problem of the nuclear spread and which has given it the ironic name of the Nth power problem. N at present appears to be a surprisingly small number." Leonard Beaton and John Maddox, *The Spread of Nuclear Weapons* (London: Chatto and Windus, 1962), p. x.

32. *Public Papers of the Presidents of the United States: John F. Kennedy, 1963* (Washington, D.C.: USGPO, 1964), p. 280.

33. For a history of the negotiations leading to the Partial Test Ban Treaty, see Anthony Nutting, *Disarmament: An Outline of the Negotiations* (London: Oxford University Press, 1959); Robert Gilpin, *American Scientists and Nuclear Weapons Policy* (Princeton, N.J.: Princeton University Press, 1962), pp. 162–298; Bechhoefer, *Postwar Negotiations for Arms Control*, pp. 258ff.; Harold Karan Jacobson and Eric Stein, *Diplomats, Scientists and Politicians* (Ann Arbor: University of Michigan Press, 1966); Arthur H. Dean, *Test Ban and Disarmament* (New York: Harper and Row, 1966); Glenn T. Seaborg, *Kennedy, Khrushchev, and the Test Ban* (Berkeley: University of California Press, 1981).

34. *Treaty banning nuclear weapon tests in the atmosphere, in outer space, and under water.* 14 UST 1313; TIAS 5433; 480 UNTS 43.

35. See testimony of Secretary of Defense Robert McNamara, in U.S., Senate, *Nuclear Test Ban Treaty*, Hearings. Committee on Foreign Relations. 88th Cong., 1st sess. (Washington: USGPO, 1963), p. 189.

36. *DOSB*, vol. 49, no. 1259 (August 12, 1963), p. 237. One author has argued that President Kennedy exaggerated this aspect of the treaty in order to win Senate consent to ratification. See William B. Bader, *The United States and the Spread of Nuclear Weapons* (New York: Pegasus, 1968), p. 55. On Moscow's desire to use the PTBT to score diplomatic points at Peking's expense, see William E. Griffith, *The Sino-Soviet Rift* (Cambridge: MIT Press, 1964), *passim*; Walter C. Clemens, "The Nuclear Test Ban and Sino-Soviet Relations," *Orbis*, vol. 10, no. 1 (Spring 1966), pp. 152–183.

37. See McNamara testimony, in *Nuclear Test Ban Treaty*, p. 108.

38. See testimony of Edward Teller, in *Nuclear Test Ban Treaty*, p. 421.

39. *Nuclear Test Ban Treaty*, pp. 275, 325, and 371.

40. See testimony of William C. Foster, in U.S., Senate, *Military Aspects and Implications of Nuclear Test Ban Proposals and Related Matters*, Hearings. Committee on Armed Services. 88th Cong., 1st sess. (Washington, D.C.: USGPO, 1963), p. 9; and *Nuclear Test Ban Treaty*, p. 150.

41. For a discussion of the multilateral nuclear force (MLF), see Philip Geyelin, *Lyndon B. Johnson and the World* (New York: Praeger, 1966), pp. 159–180; John D. Steinbruner, *The Cybernetic Theory of Decision* (Princeton, N.J.: Princeton University Press, 1974).

42. For a discussion of China's development of nuclear weapons, see Morton H. Halperin, *China and the Bomb* (New York: Praeger, 1965); Alice Langley Hsieh, "The Sino-Soviet Nuclear Dialogue: 1963," *Journal of Conflict Resolution*, vol. 8, no. 2 (June 1964), pp. 157–185; Jonathan D. Pollack, "China as a Nuclear Power," in William H. Overholt, ed., *Asia's Nuclear Future* (Boulder, Co.: Westview Press, 1977), pp. 35–65; *Beijing Review*, vol. 28, no. 17 (April 29, 1985), pp. 15–18.

43. For a history of the Tlatelolco negotiations, see Alfonso Garcia Robles, *The Denuclearization of Latin America* (Washington: Carnegie Endowment for International Peace, 1967). See also, Robles, "The Treaty for the Prohibition of Nuclear Weapons in Latin America (Treaty of Tlatelolco)," in *SIPRI Yearbook*, 1969/70 (Stockholm: Almqvist and Wiksell, 1970), pp. 218–236; John R. Redick, "The Tlatelolco Regime and Nonproliferation in Latin America," in George H. Quester, ed., *Nuclear Proliferation, Breaking the Chain* (Madison: University of Wisconsin Press, 1981), pp. 103–134; Felix Caldéron, "Nuclear-weapons-free Zones: The Latin American Experiment," in David Carlton and Carlo Schaerf, eds., *The Arms Race in the 1980s* (New York: St. Martin's, 1982), pp. 252–272.

44. *Treaty on the nonproliferation of nuclear weapons*. 21 UST 483; TIAS 6839; 729 UNTS 161. For an examination of the deliberations leading to the NPT, see Mohamed I. Shaker, *The Nuclear Nonproliferation Treaty, Origin and Implementation, 1959–1979*, vol. 1–2 (New York: Oceana, 1980); U.S., ACDA, *International Negotiations on the Treaty on the Nonproliferation of Nuclear Weapons* (Washington, D.C.: USGPO, 1969); William Epstein, *The Last Chance* (New York: The Free Press, 1976), pp. 61–86. A detailed analysis of the NPT can be found in Mason Willrich, *Nonproliferation Treaty: Framework for Nuclear Arms Control* (Charlottesville, Va.: Michie, 1969).

45. For a technical discussion of the possible applications for PNEs, see David B. Brooks and Henry R. Myers, "Plowshares Evaluation," in Bennet Boskey and Mason Willrich, eds., *Nuclear Proliferation: Prospects for Control* (New York: Dunellen, 1970), pp. 87–101; Frank Barnaby, *The Nuclear Age* (Cambridge, Ma.: MIT Press, 1974), pp. 102–111. An advocacy position on the PNE issue is Edward Teller, et al., *The Constructive Uses of Nuclear Explosions* (New York: McGraw-Hill, 1968). A critical view

can be found in Alva Myrdal, " 'Peaceful' Nuclear Explosions," *Bulletin of the Atomic Scientists*, vol. 31, no. 5 (May 1975), pp. 29–33; and F.A. Long, "Peaceful Nuclear Explosions," *Bulletin of the Atomic Scientists*, vol. 32, no. 8 (October 1976), pp. 18–28.

During the 1970s most countries became skeptical of the value of PNEs. Since 1973 the United States has conducted no peaceful nuclear explosions. The Soviet Union has conducted sixty-two. *SIPRI Yearbook*, 1984, p. 51. For Soviet views of PNEs, see V.S. Emelyanov, "On the Peaceful Use of Nuclear Explosions," in Bhupendra Jasani, ed., *Nuclear Proliferation Problems* (Cambridge: MIT Press, 1974), pp. 215–224; Igor Dmitriyev, "Nuclear Blasting for Peaceful Purposes," *New Times* (February 1975), pp. 1–20; A.K. Kruglov, "Atomic Science and Technology in the National Economy of the USSR," *Atomnaya energiya* (February 1976), pp. 113–116; I.D. Morokhov et al., "Peaceful Uses of Nuclear Energy and the Problem of Nonproliferation of Nuclear Weapons," *Atomnaya energiya* (February 1976), pp. 90–102.

46. The Interim Agreement did not reduce the nuclear arsenals of either country and even allowed for increases in certain categories of weapons. The ABM Treaty restricted the number of defensive ballistic missile systems that could be deployed by each side to one for defending the nation's capital and one for protecting an ICBM field. A 1974 protocol to the treaty further limited each side to one site of its own choosing. The text of the SALT I agreement can be found in *DOSB*, vol. 66, no. 1722 (June 26, 1972), pp. 918–921. For a history of the SALT I negotiations, see John Newhouse, *Cold Dawn: The Story of SALT* (New York: Holt, Rinehart, and Winston, 1973); Thomas W. Wolfe, *The SALT Experience* (Cambridge, Ma.: Ballinger, 1979); Gerard Smith, *Doubletalk: The Story of the First Strategic Arms Limitation Talks* (Garden City, N.Y.: Doubleday, 1980).

47. While SALT II left certain areas of weapons development unconstrained, it did impose an aggregate ceiling of 2,250 delivery systems and placed MIRV (multiple, independently targetable reentry vehicle) limitations on each party. It also obligated the Soviet Union to dismantle 250 of its land-based missiles. The text of the SALT II Treaty can be found in *DOSB*, vol. 79, no. 2028 (July 1979). For a history of the SALT II negotiations, see Strobe Talbott, *Endgame: The Inside Story of SALT II* (New York: Harper and Row, 1979). See also, Roger P. Labrie, ed., *SALT Handbook: Key Documents and Issues, 1972–1979* (Washington: AEI for Public Policy Research, 1979).

48. See, for example, *Documents on Disarmament, 1968* (Washington: USGPO, 1969), pp. 278–336, 378–387, 397–404, 425–427; see also K. Subrahmanyam, *The Indian Nuclear Test in a Global Perspective* (New Delhi: India International Centre, 1974); Anne W. Marks, ed., *NPT: Paradoxes and Problems* (Washington: Arms Control Association, 1975).

49. See O.B. Falls, Jr., "A Survey of Nuclear Power in Developing Countries," *IAEA Bulletin*, vol. 15, no. 5 (October 1973), pp. 27–38; James A. Lane, "The Impact of Oil Price Increases on the Market for Nuclear Power in Developing Countries," *IAEA Bulletin*, vol. 16, no. 1/2 (February-April 1974), pp. 66–71.

50. IAEA Board of Governors *Annual Report for 1980*, GC (XXV)/642 (Vienna: IAEA, 1981).

51. See, for example, Mason Willrich and Theodore B. Taylor, *Nuclear Theft: Risks and Safeguards* (Cambridge, Ma.: Ballinger, 1974). A more recent study on this subject is Paul Levanthal and Yonah Alexander, eds., *Nuclear Terrorism: Defining the Threat* (London: Pergamon-Brassey's, 1986).

52. See, for example, Albert Wohlstetter et al., *Moving Toward Life in a Nuclear*

Armed Crowd? (Los Angeles: Pan Heuristics, 1976); Wohlstetter, "Spreading The Bomb Without Quite Breaking The Rules," *Foreign Policy*, no. 25 (Winter 1976–77), pp. 88–96, 145–179.

53. Concern over technology transfer had been expressed earlier. In 1971 the IAEA had formed a committee chaired by Claude Zangger, the Swiss representative to the Agency, to interpret the safeguards provisions of the NPT. Due to the inability of this committee to reach a consensus and to the urgency of the problem, a second round of negotiations was called in late 1974. The original seven members were the United States, the Soviet Union, West Germany, France, Britain, Canada, and Japan; this group was later expanded to fifteen with the addition of Belgium, Czechoslovakia, East Germany, Italy, the Netherlands, Poland, Sweden, and Switzerland.

54. See testimony of George Vest, Director of Politico-Military Affairs, Department of State, in U.S., Senate, *Nonproliferation Issues*, Hearings. Committee on Foreign Relations. Subcommittee on Arms Control, International Organizations and Security Agreements. 94th Cong., 1st and 2d sess. (Washington: USGPO, 1976), pp. 308–314; Joseph A. Yager, *International Cooperation in Nuclear Energy* (Washington: Brookings, 1981), *passim*; William Walker and Måns Lönnroth, *Nuclear Power Struggles* (London: Allen and Unwin, 1983), pp. 145–148. Over two decades earlier, the U.S. had organized a secret association of uranium suppliers whose members regularly exchanged information on uranium sales and worked out a common safeguards policy. See Peter Pringle and James Spigelman, *The Nuclear Barons* (New York: Avon, 1981), p. 203. At the beginning of the 1960s this Western Suppliers Group disbanded.

55. The "Guidelines for the Export of Nuclear Material, Equipment or Technology," labeled INFCIRC 254 by the IAEA, is reproduced in Report of the Atlantic Council's Nuclear Fuels Policy Working Group, *Nuclear Power and Nuclear Weapons Proliferation*, vol. 2 (Boulder, Co.: Westview Press, 1978), pp. 63–75. The NSG was also referred to as the London Suppliers Group. In April 1987, seven members of the NSG—the U.S., Japan, Canada, Britain, France, West Germany, and Italy—agreed to restrict exports of large missiles and related technology. See *New York Times*, April 17 and 19, 1987.

56. One particularly influential study at this time was Report of the Nuclear Energy Policy Study Group, *Nuclear Power Issues and Choices* (Cambridge, Ma.: Ballinger, 1977). See also, Thomas L. Neff and Henry D. Jacoby, "Nonproliferation Strategy in a Changing Nuclear Fuel Market," *Foreign Affairs*, vol. 57, no. 5 (Summer 1979), pp. 1123–1143.

57. See Public Law 94–329 (the Symington amendment), June 30, 1976; Public Law 95–92 (the Glenn amendment), August 4, 1977; and Public Law 95–242 (referred to as the Nuclear Nonproliferation Act, or NNPA), March 10, 1978. Both the Glenn amendment and the NNPA had provisions permitting the U.S. president to continue economic and military assistance under certain conditions. On U.S. nonproliferation policy during this period, see Michael J. Brenner, *Nuclear Power and Nonproliferation: The Remaking of U.S. Policy* (New York: Cambridge University Press, 1981).

58. *International Nuclear Fuel Cycle Evaluation*, Report of Working Group 1, "Fuel and Heavy Water Availability"; Report of Working Group 2, "Enrichment Availability"; Report of Working Group 3, "Assurances of Long-Term Supply of Technology, Fuel and Heavy Water and Services in the Interest of National Needs Consistent with Nonproliferation"; Report of Working Group 4, "Reprocessing, Plutonium Handling, Recycle"; Report of Working Group 5, "Fast Breeders"; Report of Working Group 6, "Spent Fuel Management"; Report of Working Group 7, "Waste Management and Disposal";

Report of Working Group 8, "Advanced Fuel Cycle and Reactor Concepts"; "Summary Volume" (Vienna: IAEA, 1980).

59. The findings of INFCE were more diverse and open to interpretation than can be summarized here. For various viewpoints, see U.S., House, Progress in U.S. and International Nonproliferation Efforts, Hearings. Committee on Foreign Affairs. Subcommittee on International Security and Scientific Affairs, Subcommittee on International Economic Policy and Trade. 96th Cong., 1st sess. (Washington, D.C.: USGPO, 1979); Pierre Lellouche, "International Nuclear Politics," Foreign Affairs, vol. 58, no. 2 (Winter 1979–80), pp. 336–350; Joseph S. Nye, "Maintaining a Nonproliferation Regime," International Organization, vol. 35, no. 1 (Winter 1981), pp. 15–38; U.S., Senate, European Reactions to the International Nuclear Fuel Cycle Evaluation, Print. Committee on Governmental Affairs. Subcommittee on Energy, Nuclear Proliferation, and Government Processes, 97th Cong., 2d sess. (Washington, D.C.: USGPO, 1982). One result of INFCE was the creation by the IAEA of the Committee on Assurances of Supply (CAS). Its purpose was to ensure that nuclear fuel supplies would be insulated from political pressures in supplier states. For a discussion of the CAS, see Charles Van Doren, Nuclear Supply and Nonproliferation: The IAEA Committee on Assurances of Supply, CRS Report No. 83–202S (Washington, D.C.: Library of Congress, 1983).

60. The other seven countries were Argentina, Brazil, Israel, Iran, Pakistan, Taiwan, and South Korea. OTA, Nuclear Proliferation and Safeguards (New York: Praeger, 1977), p. 93.

61. Bertrand Goldschmidt has commented that had this information been available to French scientists, it would have saved France five years in constructing its fusion bombs. Goldschmidt, The Atomic Complex: A Worldwide Political History of Nuclear Energy (La Grange Park, Ill.: American Nuclear Society, 1982), p. 212.

62. See Ted Greenwood, George W. Rathjens, and Jack Ruina, Nuclear Power and Weapons Proliferation, Adelphi Paper 130 (London: IISS, 1976), p. 32. One expert, seeing how widespread the technology had become by the 1980s, declared that "Technical barriers clearly are a 'wasting asset' for nonproliferation." Lewis A. Dunn, Controlling the Bomb: Nuclear Proliferation in the 1980s (New Haven: Yale University Press, 1982), p. 43.

63. Effects of Possible Use of Nuclear Weapons and the Security and Economic Implications for States of the Acquisition and Further Development of These Weapons. United Nations Doc. A/6858 (New York: United Nations, 1968), p. 24.

64. Albert Wohlstetter et al., Moving Toward Life in a Nuclear Armed Crowd?, p. 41.

65. Jan Prawitz, "Arguments for extended NPT safeguards," in Bhupendra Jasani, ed., Nuclear Proliferation Problems (Cambridge: MIT Press, 1974), pp. 164–165; see especially the corroborating footnote by Carson Mark, p. 164. See also Wohlstetter, "Spreading the Bomb," Foreign Policy, pp. 93–96, 145–164; Office of Technology Assessment, Nuclear Proliferation and Safeguards, pp. 16, 201.

66. The IAEA's advisory group on safeguards, meeting in Vienna in January 1978, looked at the issue of "critical time." Assuming that a country already possessed a weapons design, "The group agreed it would take only ten days to convert the fissile plutonium in reprocessing plants into metal and as little as two days to make the separated plutonium metal into a weapon." Pringle and Spigelman, The Nuclear Barons, p. 385.

67. For a fuller discussion of this concept, see Harold A. Feiveson and Theodore B.

Taylor, "Alternative Strategies for International Control of Nuclear Power," in Greenwood, Feiveson, and Taylor, *Nuclear Proliferation: Motivations, Capabilities, and Strategies for Control* (New York: McGraw-Hill, 1977), pp. 125, 148–154.

68. Wohlstetter et al., *Moving Toward Life in a Nuclear Armed Crowd?*, p. 44.

69. For a brief discussion of possible "triggering events," see Lewis A. Dunn and Herman Kahn, *Trends in Nuclear Proliferation, 1975–1995: Projections, Problems, and Policy Options* (Croton-on-Hudson, N.Y.: Hudson Institute, 1976), pp. 6–9.

70. Dunn and Overholt have posited fourteen "rungs" on a "ladder of capabilities" indicating degrees of development. See Lewis A. Dunn and William H. Overholt, "The Next Phase in Nuclear Proliferation Research," *Orbis*, vol. 20, no. 2 (Summer 1976), pp. 497–524. See also Thomas C. Schelling, "Who Will Have The Bomb?" *International Security*, vol. 1 no. 1 (Summer 1976), pp. 77–91.

71. Kenneth N. Waltz, *The Spread of Nuclear Weapons: More May Be Better*, Adelphi Paper 171 (London: IISS, 1981), p. 28. See also Waltz, "What Will The Spread of Nuclear Weapons Do to the World," in John Kerry King, ed., *International Political Effects of the Spread of Nuclear Weapons* (Washington, D.C.: USGPO, 1979), pp. 165–196; R. Robert Sandoval, "Consider the Porcupine: Another View of Nuclear Proliferation," *Bulletin of the Atomic Scientists*, vol. 32, no. 5 (May 1976), pp. 17–19. The classic exposition of this argument remains Pierre Gallois, *The Balance of Terror: Strategy for the Nuclear Age* (Boston: Houghton-Mifflin, 1961), especially pp. 95–166.

72. For an analysis of the possible dangers of a proliferated world, see Dunn, *Controlling the Bomb*, pp. 69–94. See also Louis Rene Beres, *Apocalypse: Nuclear Catastrophe in World Politics* (Chicago: University of Chicago Press, 1980), pp. 74–98; Wohlstetter et al., *Moving Toward Life in a Nuclear Armed Crowd?*, pp. 145–154; Dunn and Kahn, *Trends in Nuclear Proliferation*, pp. 114–136. Some earlier warnings can be found in Richard A. Brody, "Some Systemic Effects of the Spread of Nuclear Weapons Technology: A Study Through Simulation of a Multinuclear Future," *Journal of Conflict Resolution*, vol. 7, no. 4 (December 1963), pp. 663–746; E.L.M. Burns, "Can The Spread of Nuclear Weapons Be Stopped?," *International Organization*, vol. 19, no. 4 (Autumn 1965), pp. 851–869; Stanley Hoffmann, "Nuclear Proliferation and World Politics," in Alastair Buchan, ed., *A World of Nuclear Powers?* (Englewood Cliffs, N.J.: Prentice-Hall, 1966), pp. 89–121.

73. See U.S., House, *Nuclear Proliferation: Future U.S. Foreign Policy Implications*, Hearings. Committee on International Relations. Subcommittee on International Security and Scientific Affairs. 94th Cong., 1st sess. (Washington, D.C.: USGPO, 1975), p. 1; Wohlstetter et al., *Moving Toward Life in a Nuclear Armed Crowd?*, pp. 1, 14; Lewis A. Dunn, "Nuclear Proliferation and World Politics," in Joseph I. Coffey, ed., *Nuclear Proliferation: Prospects, Problems, and Proposals* (Philadelphia: American Academy of Politics and Social Sciences, 1977), pp. 29–43; Enid C.B. Schoettle, *Postures for Nonproliferation: Arms Limitation and Security Postures to Minimize Nuclear Proliferation* (London: Taylor and Francis, 1979), p. 14. For a prediction concerning Third World countries only, see Ernest W. Lefever, *Nuclear Arms in the Third World: U.S. Policy Dilemma* (Washington, D.C.: Brookings, 1979), p. 23.

74. Thomas A. Halsted, *Nuclear Proliferation: How to Retard It, Manage It, Live With It* (Aspen: Aspen Institute, 1977); John J. Weltman, "Managing Nuclear Multipolarity," *International Security*, vol. 6, no. 3 (Winter 1981/1982), pp. 182–194; William C. Potter, *Nuclear Power and Nonproliferation: An Interdisciplinary Perspec-

tive (Cambridge, Ma.: Oelgeschlager, Gunn and Hain, 1982), pp. 221–230; Dagobert L. Brito, Michael D. Intriligator, and Adele E. Wick, eds., *Strategies for Managing Nuclear Proliferation* (Lexington, Ma.: D.C. Heath, 1983).

75. Robert S. McNamara, "The Military Role of Nuclear Weapons: Perceptions and Misperceptions." *Foreign Affairs*, vol. 62, no. 1 (Fall 1983), p. 79 (emphasis in original).

2. Sweden

1. See Samuel Abrahamsen, *Sweden's Foreign Policy* (Washington, D.C.: Public Affairs Press, 1957), pp. 67–83; Nils Andrén, *Power-Balance and Non-Alignment: A Perspective on Swedish Foreign Policy* (Stockholm: Almqvist and Wiksell, 1967), pp. 53–72.

2. *Svensk atomenergipolitik, Motiv och riktlinjer för statens insatser på atom-energiområdet 1947–1970* (Stockholm: Industridepartmentet, 1970), pp. 5–6.

3. See O. Gimstedt, "Three Decades of Nuclear Power Development in Sweden," in IAEA, *Nuclear Power Experience* vol. 1 (Vienna: IAEA, 1983), pp. 132–133; Jerome H. Garris, "Sweden and the Spread of Nuclear Weapons: A Study in Restraint" (Ph.D. dissertation, UCLA, 1972), pp. 45–48 (hereafter cited as *A Study in Restraint*). Sweden's uranium deposits were known to be extensive. From the provinces of Närke and Västergötland there were 4.5 billion tons of shale, from which an estimated 150,000 tons of uranium could be extracted, or enough to meet the entire energy consumption of the country for several thousand years. See *Documents on Swedish Foreign Policy*, 1954 (Stockholm: Royal Ministry of Foreign Affairs, 1957), p. 33 (hereafter cited as *DSFP*). See also Sweden, *Foreign Broadcast Information Service*, April 27, 1955 (hereafter cited as *FBIS*). For the correspondence of American efforts to acquire the rights to this supply of uranium from the Swedish government immediately after the end of World War II, see *FRUS*, 1945, vol. 2 pp. 37–40, 45–47, 50–53.

4. For a detailed discussion of R1, see Sigvard Eklund, *Den första svenska atomreaktorn* (Stockholm: Svenska Fysikersamfundets Publikation Kosmos, 1954).

5. Garris, *A Study in Restraint*, p. 50. See also Bertrand Goldschmidt, *The Atomic Adventure* (New York: Pergamon, 1964), p. 82.

6. Garris, p. 77; see also Sweden, *FBIS*, October 22, 1954; *New York Times*, November 27, 1955.

7. *Svensk atomenergipolitik*, p. 8. On this same point, see Garris, *Sweden's Debate on the Proliferation of Nuclear Weapons* (Los Angeles: USC Arms Control and Foreign Policy Seminar, 1972), p. 2 (hereafter referred to as *Sweden's Debate*).

8. See Per Ahlmark, *Den svenska atomvapendebatten* (Stockholm: Aldus/ Bonniers, 1965), p. 21; Garris, *A Study in Restraint*, pp. 92–93. The Swedish words *atomvapen* (atomic weapons) and *kärnvapen* (nuclear weapons) are both used to refer to fission devices. For the sake of consistency, the phrase "nuclear weapons" will be used here, unless "atomic weapons" is cited in an official capacity or in the title of a book.

9. Catherine McArdle Kelleher, *Germany and the Politics of Nuclear Weapons* (New York: Columbia University Press, 1975), p. 53.

10. See Bernard Brodie, "Nuclear Weapons: Strategic or Tactical?," *Foreign Affairs*, vol. 32, no. 2 (January 1954), pp. 217–229; William W. Kaufman, ed., *Military Policy and National Security* (Princeton, N.J.: Princeton University Press, 1956), especially

pp. 102–136; Henry A. Kissinger, *Nuclear Weapons and Foreign Policy* (London: Oxford University Press, 1957), especially pp. 132–202; Robert E. Osgood, *Limited War: The Challenge to American Strategy* (Chicago: University of Chicago Press, 1957), especially pp. 234–284.

11. Raymond L. Garthoff, *Soviet Strategy in the Nuclear Age* (London: Atlantic, 1958), pp. 156–157.

12. Major defense studies expressing the views of the supreme commander (and the Military Council) are normally designated ÖB, followed by the year of issue.

13. The following is based on interviews with General Stig Synnergren, Sven Andersson, and a senior official at the Ministry of Defense. All interviews were conducted during the first two weeks of November 1983.

14. "ÖB-Utredningarna 1954," *Kontakt med Krigsmakten*, no. 9–10, 1954, p. 281.

15. *Ibid*, p. 284. See also the 1954 fall issue of *Militäer Tidskrift*, Sweden's official military publication, for a further example of Swedish military thinking on nuclear weapons at this time.

16. Stig H:son-Ericson, *Kuling längs kusten* (Stockholm: Bonniers, 1968), p. 50.

17. Sweden, *FBIS*, November 3, 1954.

18. *New York Times*, March 10, 1955; Sweden, *FBIS*, March 14, 1955. For information on Sweden's political parties, see Nils Andrén, *Government and Politics in the Nordic Countries* (Stockholm: Almqvist and Wiksell, 1964), pp. 166–174.

19. Sweden, *Riksdagens Protokoll*, 1955, Andra Kammaren, no. 80, B1, p. 80. Cited in Garris, *A Study in Restraint*, p. 107.

20. Garris, *ibid.*, p. 110; Garris, *Sweden's Debate*, p. 5.

21. After the 1958 election the Agrarian Party changed its name to the Center Party.

22. See *Sveriges socialdemokratiska kvinnöforbunds kongressprotokoll* (Stockholm: 1956).

23. Barbro Alving, "Atombomben och samvetet," in *Nej! till svenska atomvapen* (Stockholm: Tiden, 1959), p. 54. This volume was a collection of essays of opponents of Swedish nuclear weapons.

24. See speech of Minister of Defense Torsten Nilsson, in Sweden, *Riksdagens Protokoll*, 1956, Andra Kammaren, no. 2, B1, p. 43. Cited in Garris, *A Study in Restraint*, p. 117. See also, Sweden, *FBIS*, January 25, 1956; *New York Times*, January 12, 1957.

25. *Riksdagens Protokoll*, Ar 1954 Forsta kammaren, no. 21, p. 7.

26. Garris, *A Study in Restraint*, p. 115.

27. "ÖB-Utredningarna 1957," *Kontakt med Krigsmakten*, no. 10–12, 1957, p. 294; see also, Kungl. Maj:ts proposition no. 110 ar 1958, pp. 24–26.

28. *Ibid.*, pp. 294–295.

29. *Ibid.*, p. 294.

30. *Ibid.*

31. *Ibid.*, p. 295.

32. Garris, *A Study in Restraint*, pp. 170–171.

33. Kungl. Maj:ts proposition no. 110 ar 1958, pp. 56–57.

34. *Ibid.*, pp. 92–93. Andersson had succeeded Nilsson as defense minister in March 1957.

35. Garris, *A Study in Restraint*, pp. 222–223; *New York Times*, October 5, 1958.

36. *DSFP*, 1958, pp. 26–27; *New York Times*, November 27, 1958.

37. See UN General Assembly, XIII Session, First Committee, 946th Meeting, October 13, 1958, pp. 22–23.

38. Ahlmark, Den svenska atomvapendebatten, p. 23.

39. Garris, A Study in Restraint, p. 135.

40. Agreement for Cooperation Between the Government of the United States of America and the Government of Sweden Concerning Civil Uses of Atomic Energy, signed and entered into force, January 18, 1956. 7 UST 39; TIAS 3477; 240 UNTS 413.

41. See Amending Agreement of January 18, 1956, signed August 3, 1956; entered into force March 12, 1957. 8 UST 569; TIAS 3775; 279 UNTS 332; Amending Agreement of January 18, 1956, as Amended, signed April 25, 1958; entered into force June 2, 1958. 9 UST 569; TIAS 4035; 316 UNTS 364; Agreement Between the United States of America and Sweden, Amending the Agreement of January 18, 1956, as Amended, signed July 20, 1962; entered into force September 6, 1962. 13 UST 1898; TIAS 5143; 460 UNTS 306.

42. For an overview of Sweden's civilian nuclear energy program at this time, see Holger Lundbergh, "Sweden's Atomic Energy Program," Bulletin of the Atomic Scientists, vol. 15, no. 5 (May 1959), pp. 219–220; and E.G. Malmlöw, "Atomic Power in Sweden," Bulletin of the Atomic Scientists, vol. 19, no. 2 (February 1963), pp. 44–46. The industrial basis for a nuclear weapons option for Sweden is discussed in Jan Prawitz, "A Nuclear Doctrine for Sweden," Cooperation and Conflict, no. 3 (March 1968), pp. 184–186.

43. For the 1956 election results, see Garris, A Study in Restraint, p. 142.

44. See Andrén, Government and Politics, p. 174; Sweden, FBIS, October 15, 1957. The compulsory supplementary pension scheme was passed, 115 votes to 114, in May 1959. See The Times, May 15, 1959.

45. Aside from the Prime Minister, the other members of the committee were Östen Undén, Sven Andersson, Olof Palme, Nancy Eriksson, Lars Larsson, Bo Siegbahn, Richard Sandler, Per Edvin Skiöld, Inga Thorsson, Elisabet Sjövall, Fridolph Thapper, Sture Lantz, Åke Zetterberg, Kurt Ward, Kaj Björk, and the party group leaders in the Upper and Lower Chambers of the Riksdag.

46. Neutralitet, Försvar, Atomvapen (Stockholm: Tiden, 1959), p. 113.

47. Ibid., p. 117.

48. Tage Erlander, Tage Erlander, 1955–1960 (Stockholm: Tiden, 1976), p. 97.

49. Interview with Sven Andersson, Stockholm, November 1, 1983.

50. Garris, A Study in Restraint, p. 276. These precautions stand in contrast to the lack of oversight by the French governments during the Fourth Republic. See Lawrence Scheinman, Atomic Energy Policy in France Under the Fourth Republic (Princeton, N.J.: Princeton University Press, 1965).

51. From 1960 to 1962, Sweden's defense expenditures jumped from $564 million to $690 million, an increase of over 18 percent. See Jerry Wilson Ralston, "The Defense of Small States in the Nuclear Age, The Cases of Sweden and Switzerland" (Ph.D. dissertation, University of Geneva, 1969), p. 234.

52. Interviews with Tage Erlander, Sven Andersson, Nils Andrén, Stockholm, the first two weeks of November 1983.

53. Erlander switched his view some time in 1958. Interview, Tage Erlander, Stockholm, November 2, 1983.

54. Erlander, Tage Erlander, p. 94.

55. Gunnar Jervas, Sweden and Nuclear Weapons (Stockholm: National Defense Research Institute, 1982), p. 8. Ingemar Dörfer earlier supported this interpretation. See Dörfer, System 37 Viggen (Oslo: Universitetsforlaget, 1973), p. 90.

56. Ralston, "The Defense of Small States," p. 234.

57. See, for example, Sweden, Riksdag, Riksdag Protokoll, no. 17, Andra Kammaren, May 15, 1959, pp. 37–40.

58. See Per Edvin Skiöld, ed., Svenska Atomvapen (Stockholm: Tiden, 1959). An anti-nuclear-weapons book appeared the following month. See Ernst Wigforss, Atomvapen (Malmö: Framtiden, Arbets debattforum, 1959).

59. The following analysis is based on interviews with Tage Erlander, Sven Andersson, and Olof Palme.

60. Cited in Garris, A Study in Restraint, pp. 258–259 (emphasis added).

61. Erlander, Tage Erlander, p. 83. The minutes of the Atomic Weapons Committee are deposited at Bommersvik, the headquarters of the Social Democratic Party. Access to these documents, which have never been examined by Swedish scholars, was personally promised to me by Prime Minister Palme in November 1983. It was explained that there would be some delay in order to locate the documents, which were in storage. After many unsuccessful requests to the prime minister's office, I was informed indirectly that I would not be allowed to look at the minutes. The reason given was that their contents were critical of Moscow's policies and pointed in their assessment of the Soviet threat to Scandinavia. It was felt that public release would be embarrassing to Sweden.

62. For an excellent analysis of this issue, see Tomas Ries, The Nordic Dilemma in the 1980s: Maintaining Regional Stability Under New Strategic Conditions, PSIS Occasional Papers no. 1 (Geneva: Graduate Institute of International Studies, 1982).

63. Andrén, Power-Balance, p. 180.

64. Sweden, FBIS, February 17, 1960. See also, DSFP, 1960, p. 76.

65. Nuclear Weapons Acquisition:

	June 1957	Oct. 1958	June 1961
Yes	40%	29%	21%
No	36%	51%	56%
Don't Know	24%	20%	19%

Stig Lindholm and Lars Sjöberg, "Opinionsmätningar Rörande Svenska Kärnvapen" (Opinion Polls Concerning Swedish Nuclear Weapons), in Svenska Kärnvapenproblem (Stockholm: Utrikespolitiska Institutet, 1965), pp. 232–233.

66. This information was common knowledge throughout FOA, and was made available to the prime minister, the defense minister, and the foreign minister. Interview with a senior official at the Ministry of Defense, Stockholm, November 1, 1983. This study is briefly referred to in Jan Prawitz, "Sweden—A Non-Nuclear Weapons State," in Johan Jørgen Holst, ed., Security, Order, and the Bomb (Oslo: Universitetsforlaget, 1972), p. 70.

67. DSFP, 1954, p. 26.

68. Speech by Prime Minister Erlander, DSFP, 1959, p. 46.

69. Neutralitet, Forsvar, Atomvapen, p. 108.

70. For Sven Andersson's remarks, see Sweden, Riksdag, Riksdagens Protokoll, 1958, B Riksdag, Andra Kammaren, no. B7, p. 108. For Olof Palme's speech, see Garris, A Study in Restraint, pp. 209–213. For Tage Erlander's comments, see Sweden, FBIS, November 12, 1958.

71. A/Res/1664 (XVI), December 5, 1961. A discussion of the Undén Plan can be

found in Katarina Brodin, "The Undén Proposal," *Cooperation and Conflict*, no. 2, (1966), pp. 18–29. Sweden's conditions for joining such a nonnuclear club are outlined in *DSFP*, 1962, pp. 87–90.

72. *DSFP*, 1963, pp. 57–59.

73. The United States, the Soviet Union, and Britain agreed to the Partial Test Ban Treaty on August 5, 1963. Sweden signed the treaty one week later and ratified it on November 20, 1963.

74. A/PV. 1319 (prov.), p. 27.

75. ENDC/PV. 288, pp. 11–13.

76. ENDC/PV. 195, August 30, 1967.

77. ENDC/PV. 363, pp. 6–7; ENDC/215; ENDC/PV. 373, p. 5.

78. ENDC/PV. 363, p. 7; ENDC/215; ENDC/PV. 373, p. 5.

79. For a discussion of Sweden's attitude toward the NPT, see Gertrud Svala, "Sweden's View of the Nonproliferation Treaty," in Andrew W. Cordier, ed., *Columbia Essays in International Affairs*, vol. 6 (New York: Columbia University Press, 1971), pp. 94–115; see also, George Quester, "Sweden and the Nuclear Nonproliferation Treaty," *Cooperation and Conflict*, no. 1 (1970), pp. 52–64.

80. Karl E. Birnbaum, "Sweden's Nuclear Policy," *Survival*, vol. 7, no. 9 (December 1965), p. 315.

81. Nils Andrén, "Sweden's Security Policy," *Cooperation and Conflict*, no. 3/4 (1972), pp. 138–139.

82. Östen Undén, "Spridning av Kärnvapen," *Arbetet*, February 22, 1967. Cited in Garris, *A Study in Restraint*, p. 353.

83. *ÖB 62: Riktlinjer for krigsmaktens forsatta utveckling* (Stockholm: Försvarsstaben, 1962), pp. 80–81.

84. *ÖB 65: Utredning om det militära försvarets forsatta utveckling* (Stockholm: Försvarsstaben, 1965), p. 94.

85. *Ibid*.

86. Birnbaum, "Sweden's Nuclear Policy," p. 314.

87. *ÖB 65*, pp. 94–95.

88. *Ibid.*, p. 95.

89. "Säkerhetspolitik och försvarsutgifter: Betänkande av 1965 års försvarsutredning," *Statens Offentliga Utredningar* 1968: 10 (Stockholm: Försvarsdepartmentet, 1968), p. 138. This argument is interesting given the vocal insecurities often expressed by America's NATO partners over fears of the United States "decoupling" its security from that of Europe.

90. *Ibid.*, p. 139.

91. See Alva Myrdal, *The Game of Disarmament* (Manchester: Manchester University Press, 1977), p. 87.

92. See A/C.1/PV. 1579, pp. 23–27.

93. Robert S. McNamara, University of Michigan commencement address, Ann Arbor, June 16, 1962, in *DOSB*, vol. 47, no. 1202 (July 9, 1962), pp. 64–69. McNamara was directing his remarks specifically toward France, but his admonition was noted in Sweden.

94. Oliver Clausen, "Sweden Goes Underground," *New York Times Magazine*, May 22, 1966.

95. Gimstedt, "Three Decades of Nuclear Power Development in Sweden," p. 133. See also, *Svensk atomenergipolitik*, pp. 43–51.

96. *Agreement for Cooperation Between the Government of the United States of America and the Government of Sweden Concerning Civil Uses of Atomic Energy.* Signed July 28, 1966; entered into force September 15, 1966. 17 UST 1176; TIAS 6076; 603 UNTS 61. Due to difficulties, work on the Marviken plant terminated on May 27, 1970. It was converted to an oil-fueled power station in 1974.

97. Garris, *A Study in Restraint*, p. 326.

98. For an examination of Sweden's territorial defense planning, see Adam Roberts, *Nations in Arms* (London: Chatto and Windus, 1976), pp. 84–123.

99. Christer Larsson, "Svenska Kärnvapen Utvecklades Fram Till 1972!," *Ny Teknik*, No. 17 (April 25, 1985). For Swedish news coverage of this and related developments, see *Dagens Nyheter*, April 26, 1985; *Svenska Dagbladet*, April 26, 1985; *Expressen*, April 27, 1985; *Dagens Nyheter*, April 28, 1985.

100. The above information was derived from interviews and correspondence during 1985 and 1986 with senior officials in the Swedish Defense Ministry.

3. South Korea

1. An excellent examination of this period of Korean history is Soon Sung Cho, *Korea in World Politics, 1940–1950* (Berkeley: University of California Press, 1967).

2. Harry S Truman, *Years of Trial and Hope, 1946–1953* (Suffolk: Hodder and Stoughton, 1956), p. 343.

3. Cho, *Korea in World Politics*, pp. 233–236.

4. The text of Acheson's speech can be found in *DOSB*, vol. 22, no. 551 (January 23, 1950), pp. 111–118. General MacArthur and Senator Tom Connally also issued public statements during this period which raised questions over the American commitment to South Korea. See Cho, *ibid.*, pp. 260–261.

5. This agreement was only a cease-fire, not a peace treaty. It was officially between the United Nations Organization and the PRC-DPRK. South Korea was not a party. The text of the Armistice Agreement can be found in United Nations (Security Council), Doc. S/3079, August 7, 1953. The Eisenhower administration seriously entertained using nuclear weapons to end the Korean War. See *Foreign Relations of the United States, 1952–1954*, vol. 15, Korea, Parts 1 and 2 (Washington, D.C.: USGPO, 1984), *passim*.

6. For a brief discussion of the establishment of the ROK and DPRK as distinct legal personalities under international law, see James Crawford, *The Creation of States in International Law* (Oxford: Clarendon Press, 1979), pp. 281–284.

7. "Informal Remarks in Guam with Newsmen," July 25, 1969, *Presidential Papers of the United States: Richard M. Nixon, 1969* (Washington, D.C.: USGPO, 1971), p. 549. See also *U.S. Foreign Policy for the 1970s: A New Strategy for Peace* (Washington, D.C.: USGPO, 1970).

8. *DOSB*, vol. 73, no. 1905 (December 29, 1975), pp. 913–916.

9. U.S., Senate, *U.S. Troop Withdrawals from the Republic of Korea*, January 9, 1978. Report. Committee on Foreign Relations. 95th Cong., 2d sess. (Washington, D.C.: USGPO, 1978), p. 44. See also Joo-hong Nam, *America's Commitment to South Korea: The First Decade of the Nixon Doctrine* (Cambridge: Cambridge University Press, 1986).

10. Charles A. Sorrels, *Planning U.S. General Purpose Forces: Forces Related to Asia*, Congressional Budget Office (Washington, D.C.: USGPO, 1977), p. 50.

11. William E. Griffith, *Peking, Moscow, and Beyond*, Washington Paper 6 (Beverly Hills: Sage, 1973), p. 52.

12. Richard L. Sneider, "Prospects for Korean Security," in Richard H. Solomon, ed., *Asian Security in the 1980s* (Cambridge, Ma.: Oelgeschlager, Gunn and Hain, 1979), p. 117.

13. U.S., ACDA, *World Military Expenditures and Arms Transfers, 1970–1979* (Washington, D.C.: USGPO, 1982), p. 65.

14. For a greater discussion of these events, see Donald S. Zagoria and Janet D. Zagoria, "Crises on the Korean Peninsula," in Stephen S. Kaplan, ed., *Diplomacy of Power: Soviet Armed Forces as a Political Instrument* (Washington, D.C.: Brookings, 1981), pp. 357–411.

15. *DOSB*, vol. 76, no. 1971 (April 4, 1977), p. 307.

16. During congressional hearings in September 1974, Senator Stuart Symington publicly revealed that the U.S. maintained nuclear weapons in South Korea. See U.S., Joint, *Proliferation of Nuclear Weapons*, Hearings. Committee on Atomic Energy. 93rd Cong. 2d sess. (Washington, D.C.: USGPO, 1974), p. 17. At a press conference in June 1975, Secretary of Defense James Schlesinger confirmed that the U.S. had stationed tactical nuclear weapons in the ROK. *New York Times*, June 21, 1975; *Washington Post*, June 21, 1975. For differing estimates of the number of American nuclear arms in the ROK, see *Boston Globe*, July 10, 1977; Russell Spurr, "Korea, 1978," *Far Eastern Economic Review*, May 26, 1978, p. 51; Stuart E. Johnson, *The Military Equation in Northeast Asia* (Washington, D.C.: Brookings, 1979), p. 47.

17. A discussion of the merits and liabilities of the withdrawal plan are beyond the scope of this chapter. For an official explanation of the Carter administration policy, see the testimony of Michael Armacost, Deputy Assistant Secretary of Defense, in U.S., Senate, *Department of Defense Authorization for Appropriations for Fiscal Year 1980. Part 4: Manpower and Personnel*, Hearings. Committee on Armed Services. 96th Cong., 1st sess. (Washington, D.C.: USGPO, 1979), pp. 1454–1460. For arguments in favor of the withdrawal scheme, see Franklin B. Weinstein, "The United States, Japan, and the Security of Korea," *International Security*, vol. 2, no. 2 (Fall 1977), pp. 68–69. For arguments against the withdrawal plan, see Donald S. Zagoria, "Why We Can't Leave Korea," *New York Times Magazine*, October 2, 1977; Frank Gibney, "The Ripple Effect in Korea," *Foreign Affairs*, vol. 56, no. 1 (October 1977), pp. 160–174. For an even-handed treatment of the Carter administration policy, see Larry A. Niksch, "U.S. Troop Withdrawal From South Korea: Past Shortcomings and Future Prospects," *Asian Survey*, vol. 21, no. 3 (March 1981), pp. 325–341. A greater understanding of the historical context of this issue is provided by U.S., Senate, *Korea: Report to the President submitted by Lt. Gen. A.C. Wedemeyer, Sept. 1947*. Print. Committee on Armed Services. 82d Cong., 1st sess. (Washington, D.C.: USGPO, 1951).

18. President Carter's original plan called for $1.9 billion in foreign military credits and grant military aid to the ROK, along with the transfer of $800 million worth of American equipment already in South Korea. *U.S. Troop Withdrawals*, p. 3.

19. See Barbara W. Tuchman, *Stilwell and the American Experience in China, 1911–1945* (New York: Bantam, 1972), pp. 585–586. In addition to the period just prior to the Korean War, there was an even earlier example of American reluctance to defend Korean interests: from the outbreak of the Sino-Japanese War in 1894 to the signing of the Taft-Katsura memorandum in 1905. See John Chay, "The First Three Decades of American-Korean Relations, 1882–1910: Reassessments and Reflections," in Tae-

Hwan Kwak et al., eds., *U.S.-Korean Relations, 1882–1982* (Seoul: Kyungnam University Press, 1983), pp. 15–33.

20. *Mutual Defense Treaty Between the United States of America and the Republic of Korea*, October 1, 1953. TIAS 3097.

21. Sorrels, *Planning U.S. General Purpose Forces*, p. 58.

22. *Agreement Between the IAEA, the Government of the Republic of Korea, and the Government of the United States of America for the Application of Safeguards.* Signed January 5, 1968; entered into force January 5, 1968. 19 UST 4404; TIAS 6435; 637 UNTS 123. Amended by 24 UST 829; TIAS 7594. Signed November 30, 1972. The nuclear materials and equipment that Canada supplied to the ROK were similarly safeguarded.

23. George Quester, *The Politics of Nuclear Proliferation* (Baltimore: Johns Hopkins University Press, 1973).

24. Article X(2) stipulated: "No material, including equipment and devices, transferred to the Government of the Republic of Korea or to authorized persons under its jurisdiction by purchase or otherwise pursuant to this Agreement, and no special nuclear material produced through the use of such material, including equipment and devices, will be used for atomic weapons, or for research on or development of atomic weapons, or for any other military purpose." *Agreement for Cooperation Between the Government of the United States of America and the Government of the Republic of Korea Concerning Civil Uses of Atomic Energy*. Signed November 24, 1972; entered into force March 19, 1973. 24 UST 775; TIAS 7583.

25. For an examination of the development of South Korea's nuclear energy program, see Young-sun Ha, *Nuclear Proliferation, World Order, and Korea* (Seoul: Seoul National University Press, 1983), pp. 81–109.

26. Joseph A. Yager, "The Republic of Korea," in Joseph A. Yager, ed., *Nonproliferation and U.S. Foreign Policy* (Washington, D.C.: Brookings, 1980), p. 48.

27. Ibid., p. 48; see also Korea Electric Power Corporation, *Electric Power in Korea*, Annual Report, 1982 (Seoul: KEPC, 1983), p. 23.

28. Yager, *ibid.*, p. 49.

29. See *New York Times*, February 1, 1976; see also *U.S. Troop Withdrawals*, p. 4.

30. *The Military Balance, 1976–1977* (London: IISS, 1977), p. 57.

31. *FBIS, Asia and the Pacific*, September 28, 1978. For a discussion of the ROK's domestic defense industry, see *U.S. Troop Withdrawals*, pp. 51–55.

32. In December 1975 the ROK purchased a complete Lockheed facility for manufacturing solid-fuel rocket engines. See *New York Times*, December 17, 1975.

33. Brian Jack et al., *Regional Rivalries and Nuclear Response, Vol. II: The South Korean Case: A Nuclear Weapons Program Embedded in an Environment of Great Power Concerns* (Los Angeles: Pan Heuristics, 1978), pp. 93–96.

34. Albert Wohlstetter et al., *Moving Toward Life in a Nuclear Armed Crowd?* (Los Angeles: Pan Heuristics, 1976), p. 41.

35. Jack, *Regional Rivalries*, p. 72.

36. *Ibid.*; Young-sun Ha, "Nuclearization of Small States and World Order: The Case of Korea," *Asian Survey*, vol. 18, no. 11 (November 1978), p. 1138.

37. Wohlstetter et al., *Moving Toward Life in a Nuclear Armed Crowd?*, p. 41. In an April 1977 report, the U.S. Energy Research and Development Agency (ERDA) predicted that the ROK could develop nuclear weapons within four to six years of a decision to do so. Cited in U.S., Senate, *Nuclear Proliferation Factbook*, Print. Commit-

tee on Governmental Affairs. 96th Cong., 2d sess. (Washington, D.C.: USGPO, 1980), p. 325.

38. Over a four-year span, the cost of acquiring nuclear devices would be under $13 million per year, using Wohlstetter's estimates. This would have been less than 1 percent of the ROK's 1976 defense expenditure of $1.5 billion. See *The Military Balance, 1976–1977* (London: IISS, 1977), p. 57. Moreover, this figure would have decreased as a percentage of the defense budget as South Korean defense expenditures increased through the end of the decade. This assumes that nuclear weapons would not have been traded for savings in other areas of defense; in other words, they would have served as a supplement to, not a substitute for, conventional armaments.

39. *Washington Post*, June 6, 1975. South Korea had earlier entered into negotiations with Belgium for a reprocessing laboratory. After India's May 1974 nuclear explosion the Belgians broke off the talks.

40. See Ha, *Nuclear Proliferation*, pp. 130–133, and pp. 179–181 for a chronology of events relating to the ROK's attempt to obtain a reprocessing plant.

41. Jack, *Regional Rivalries*, p. 74.

42. *FBIS*, April 24, 1975.

43. Ernest W. Lefever, *Nuclear Arms in the Third World, U.S. Policy Dilemma* (Washington, D.C.: Brookings, 1979), p. 86. See *Congressional Record*, H.J. Res. 298, March 10, 1975, p. 5921. See also Kim Sam-o, "Seoul tightens its nuclear grip," *Far Eastern Economic Review*, April 18, 1975, p. 44.

44. Interview, U.S. official, American Embassy, Seoul, May 12, 1983. See also *Washington Post*, January 30, 1976; *New York Times*, February 1, 1976; *Los Angeles Times*, November 4, 1978.

45. Franklin B. Weinstein, "Korea and Arms Control II," in John Barton and Ryukichi Imai, eds., *Arms Control II, A New Approach to International Security* (Cambridge, Ma.: Oelgeschlager, Gunn and Hain, 1981), pp. 174–175.

46. *Washington Post*, June 12, 1975. See also *FBIS*, June 14, 1975.

47. *FBIS*, June 16, 1975.

48. *Washington Post*, June 27, 1975.

49. *Washington Post*, June 26, 1975; *FBIS*, June 30, 1975.

50. *FBIS*, November 11, 1975.

51. *Summary of World Broadcasts, BBC*, "Part 3: The Far East," January 31, 1977.

52. *Washington Post*, May 27, 1977; *FBIS*, May 27, 1977.

53. *Korea Times*, June 30, 1977. Cited in Ha, *Nuclear Proliferation*, p. 129.

54. *FBIS*, April 7, 1978.

55. *FBIS*, August 22, 1977.

56. *FBIS*, June 5, 1978.

57. Weinstein, "Korea and Arms Control II," p. 175.

58. See Gregory Henderson, *Korea, The Politics of the Vortex* (Cambridge, Ma.: Harvard University Press, 1968).

59. The Bank of Korea, *The Korean Economy, Performance and Prospects* (Seoul: Bank of Korea, 1983), p. 11.

60. The Bank of Korea, London, personal correspondence, May 1984.

61. Stephen B. Wickman, "The Economy," in Frederica M. Bunge, ed., *South Korea, a Country Study* (Washington, D.C.: USGPO, 1982), p. 150. For a portrait of the ROK economy, see pp. 109–158. By September 1984 this debt had mounted to $40.1 billion. *Business Korea*, vol. 2, no. 3 (September 1984), p. 17.

62. See Margaret P. Doxey, *Economic Sanctions and International Enforcement*, 2d ed. (London: Macmillan, 1980).

63. Franklin B. Weinstein, "Conclusions and Policy Recommendations," in Weinstein, ed., *U.S.-Japan Relations and the Security of East Asia: The Next Decade* (Boulder, Co.: Westview Press, 1978), p. 309.

64. On this general point, see the speech by Secretary of State Dean Rusk, *DOSB*, vol. 58, no. 1508, May 20, 1968, p. 633; see also David A. Baldwin, "The Power of Positive Sanctions," *World Politics*, vol. 24, no. 1 (October 1971), pp. 19–38.

65. Ralph N. Clough, *East Asia and U.S. Security* (Washington, D.C.: Brookings, 1975), p. 161.

66. *New York Times*, August 21, 1975.

67. *Korea Hearld*, January 28, 1977. Cited as Kwak, et al., *U.S.-Korean Relations*, p. 228.

68. U.S., House, *Hearings on Military Posture and H.R. 11500, Part 3: Military Personnel*. Committee on Armed Services. 94th Cong., 2d sess. (Washington, D.C.: USGPO, 1976), p. 781. See also Richard K. Betts, *Surprise Attack, Lessons for Defense Planning* (Washington, D.C.: Brookings, 1982), pp. 273–281.

69. Jack, *Regional Rivalries*, pp. 82–93.

70. This supply might not have lasted very long. In the 1973 Yom Kippur War, Israel's needs for replacements and spare parts became critical in the first few days of the conflict. See Henry Kissinger, *Years of Upheaval* (London: Weidenfeld and Nicolson, 1982), pp. 491–496.

71. Weinstein, "Korea and Arms Control II," pp. 173–174.

72. Lefever, *Nuclear Arms in the Third World*, p. 90.

73. For a discussion of the reasons China and the USSR have for maintaining the status quo in Korea, see Sneider, "Prospects for Korean Security," pp. 110–111, 132–134.

74. With information reportedly based on satellite photos and intercepted communications on the movements of DPRK military units, the CIA study revealed that North Korea had 41 divisions, not the 28 estimated earlier, with 60,000 more ground troops than before, and 2,600 tanks, up 600 from past calculations. See *New York Times*, January 4, 1979; *Washington Post*, January 14, 1979; *New York Times*, January 21, 1979. It was later claimed in the Japanese monthly *Sentaku* that Peking had played a decisive role in the revised appraisal of North Korea's military strength by providing Washington with information on Pyongyang's force buildup. The information China passed to the U.S. was originally supplied by North Korea itself. Pyongyang had sent it to Peking at the latter's request when North Korea had asked for Chinese military assistance. See *FBIS*, September 4, 1979. In an April 1985 interview, former President Carter admitted that he had "never comprehended fully" the 1979 CIA intelligence estimate. *International Herald Tribune*, April 4, 1985.

75. If the USSR had provided nuclear weapons to North Korea, it would have violated Article I of the NPT. While the PRC was not a party to the treaty, it had stated that it would not lend assistance to any country that wished to acquire nuclear weapons. Further, a leading expert on East Asia had commented that "There is, in fact, no prospect that North Korea could acquire a nuclear weapons capability. China will certainly not equip North Korea with such weapons. . . . It is inconceivable that the Soviet Union would supply either weapons or the manufacturing capability to Pyongyang." Allen Whiting, in Franklin S. Weinstein and Fuji Kamiya, eds., *The*

Security of Korea: U.S. and Japanese Perspectives in the 1980s (Boulder, Co.: Westview Press, 1980), p. 144. For an examination of a possible DPRK nuclear weapons program, see Jack, *Regional Rivalries*, pp. 42–43. North Korea formally acceded to the NPT on December 12, 1985.

76. Sneider, "Prospects for Korean Security," p. 128.

77. This stands in contrast to their detailed discussion of another foreign policy issue, the neutron bomb affair, where the U.S. similarly reversed itself. See Jimmy Carter, *Keeping the Faith, Memoirs of a President* (London: Collins, 1982); Zbigniew Brzezinski, *Power and Principle, Memoirs of a National Security Advisor, 1977–1981* (New York: Farrar, Straus, Giroux, 1983).

78. Cyrus Vance, *Hard Choices, Critical Years in America's Foreign Policy* (New York: Simon and Schuster, 1983), pp. 127–130.

79. U.S., House, *Investigation of Korean-American Relations*, Hearings. Committee on International Relations. Subcommittee on International Organizations. 95th Cong., 2d sess. (Washington, D.C.: USGPO, 1978), pp. 79–80. See also *Los Angeles Times*, November 4, 1978.

80. This is based on a survey of the daily South Korean press coverage in *FBIS*, and the reporting on the ROK in the *New York Times* and *Washington Post*. The text of the suspension announcement is in *DOSB*, vol. 790, no. 2030 (September 1979), p. 37.

81. Interview, U.S. official, American Embassy, Seoul, May 12, 1983. This policy was probably initiated under the Carter administration. See *Boston Globe*, July 10, 1977. On July 28, 1978, the *Boston Globe* reported that American nuclear weapons in the ROK were being gradually removed, and that by 1982 there would be none remaining in the country.

82. *DOSB*, vol. 91, no. 2048 (March 1981), pp. 14–15. For a South Korean view of the summit meeting, see *FBIS*, February 3 and 4, 1981.

4. Japan

1. Herman Kahn, *The Emerging Japanese Superstate* (Englewood Cliffs, N.J.: Prentice-Hall, 1970), pp. 165–166.

2. Donald C. Hellmann, *Japan and East Asia, The New International Order* (London: Pall Mall Press, 1972), p. xi. See also Thomas A. Marks, "The Acquisition of Nuclear Weapons by Japan," *Military Review*, vol. 53, no. 3 (March 1973), pp. 39–48. U.S. air force and navy intelligence officers in 1974 saw "a strong chance that Japan's leaders will conclude that they must have nuclear weapons if they are to achieve their national objectives in the developing Asian power balance." This view was opposed by CIA, State Department, DIA, and Army analysts, on the condition that there was not a rupture of the U.S.-Japan relationship. See CIA, "Prospects for Further Proliferation of Nuclear Weapons," DCI NIO 1945–74, September 4, 1974, p. 2.

3. Kei Wakaizumi, "Japan Beyond 1970," *Foreign Affairs*, vol. 47, no. 3 (April 1969), p. 517.

4. Saburo Kato, "Japan: Quest for Strategic Compatibility," in Robert M. Lawrence and Joel Larus, eds., *Nuclear Proliferation, Phase II* (Lawrence, Kansas: University Press of Kansas, 1974), pp. 183–208.

5. See, for example, U.S., ACDA, "India and Japan: The Emerging Balance of Power and Opportunities for Arms Control, 1970–1975," vol. 2 (New York: Columbia Univer-

sity Press, 1971), pp. 61–73; Kiichi Saeki, "Japan's Security in a Multipolar World," in *East Asia and the World System, Part II: The Regional Powers*, Adelphi Paper 92 (London: IISS, 1972), pp. 21–29; Wayne Wilcox, "Japanese and Indian National Security Strategies in the Asia of the 1970s: The Prospects for Nuclear Proliferation," in *ibid.*, pp. 30–39; Zbigniew Brzezinski, *The Fragile Blossom* (New York: Harper and Row, 1972), pp. 102–105, 110, 137; Masataka Kosaka, "Japan's Nuclear Options," in Geoffrey Kemp et al., eds., *The Superpowers in a Multinuclear World* (Lexington, Ma.: D.C. Heath, 1973), pp. 91–105; Kunio Muraoka, *Japanese Security and the United States*, Adelphi Paper 95 (London: IISS, 1973), p. 27; John E. Emmerson and Leonard A. Humphreys, *Will Japan Rearm?* (Washington, D.C.: AEI for Public Policy Research, 1973), p. 111; James H. Buck, "The Japanese Self-Defense Force," *Naval War College Review* (January-February 1974), pp. 40–54; Monte R. Bullard, "Japan's Nuclear Choice," *Asian Survey*, vol. 14, no. 9 (September 1974), pp. 845–853; John E. Endicott, *Japan's Nuclear Option* (New York: Praeger, 1975), pp. vii-viii, 235, 238; Wolf Mendl, *Issues in Japan's China Policy*, (London: RIIA, 1978), p. 123; Joseph A. Yager, "Japan," in Joseph A. Yager, ed., *Nonproliferation and U.S. Foreign Policy* (Washington, D.C.: Brookings, 1980), pp. 9–46; Yukio Satoh, *The Evolution of Japanese Security Policy*, Adelphi Paper 178 (London: IISS, 1982), p. 38.

6. Japan had embarked on a nuclear weapons project during the Second World War. See Deborah Shapley, "Nuclear Weapons History: Japan's Wartime Bomb Projects Revealed," *Science*, vol. 199, no. 4325 (January 13, 1978), pp. 152–157. Commentary on this article was published in *Science*, vol. 199, no. 4330 (February 17, 1978), p. 728; and *Science*, vol. 199, no. 4335 (March 24, 1978), pp. 1286–1290. See also Yoshio Nishina, "A Japanese Scientist Describes the Destruction of his Cyclotrons," *Bulletin of the Atomic Scientists*, vol. 3, no. 6 (June 1947), pp. 145, 167; Leslie R. Groves, *Now It Can Be Told* (London: Andre Deutsch, 1963), pp. 367–372. Since the information in *Science* had been disclosed earlier, the timing of the Shapley article was thought by some in Japan to be a Carter administration ploy to pressure the Japanese to follow American policy and abstain from reprocessing.

7. *Agreement for Cooperation Between the Government of the United States of America and the Government of Japan Concerning Civil Uses of Atomic Energy*, signed June 16, 1958, entered into force December 5, 1958. 9 UST 1383; TIAS 4133. Three years earlier the United States had agreed to exchange information with Japan on research reactor design, construction, and operation, and to provide six kilograms of U-235 for research purposes. See *Agreement for Cooperation Between the Government of the United States of America and the Government of Japan Concerning Civil Uses of Atomic Energy*, signed November 14, 1955, entered into force February 27, 1955. 6 UST 6119; TIAS 3465.

8. Endicott, *Japan's Nuclear Option*, p. 114.

9. Victor Gilinsky and Paul Langer, *The Japanese Civilian Nuclear Program*, RM-5366-PR (Santa Monica: RAND Corp., 1967), p. 3.

10. See Science and Technology Agency, "White Paper on Atomic Energy," in *White Papers of Japan*, 1969–70 (Tokyo: Japan Institute of International Affairs, 1971), p. 135.

11. See, for example, *International Herald Tribune*, October 25, 1974; *Japan Times Weekly*, March 8 and 9, 1975; *New Scientist*, vol. 68, no. 974, (November 6, 1975), p. 335.

12. *Atoms in Japan*, June 1984.

13. *Atoms in Japan*, May 1972.

14. Thomas L. Neff and Henry D. Jacoby, "The International Uranium Market," MIT Energy Laboratory Report No. MIT-EL 80–014 (Cambridge, Ma.: MIT, 1980), pp. 5.3–5.10.

15. For different views on the controversy between the United States and Japan over the Tokai Mura reprocessing plant, see Japan Atomic Industrial Forum, "Possible Impacts on Japan of the Expected New U.S. Nuclear Policy," April 13, 1977, in U.S., Senate, Nuclear Nonproliferation Act of 1977, Hearings. Committee on Governmental Affairs. Subcommittee on Energy, Nuclear Proliferation, and Federal Services. 95th Cong., 1st sess. (Washington, D.C.: USGPO, 1977), pp. 440–441; Michael Blaker, ed., Oil and the Atom: Issues in U.S.-Japan Energy Relations (New York: East Asian Institute, Columbia University, 1980), pp. 37–95; Ryukichi Imai and Henry S. Rowen, Nuclear Energy and Nuclear Proliferation: Japanese and American Views (Boulder, Co.: Westview Press, 1980); Joseph F. Pilat and Warren H. Donnelly, Nuclear Export Policy of the Reagan Administration: A Summary Analysis and Four Case Studies, CRS Report No. 82–70S (Washington, D.C.: Library of Congress, 1982), pp. II.13–II.17; Richard K. Lester, "U.S.-Japanese Nuclear Relations: Structural Change and Political Strain," Asian Survey, vol. 22, no. 5 (May 1982), pp. 417–433.

16. DOSB, vol. 81, no. 2051 (June 1981), pp. 2–4.

17. Atoms in Japan, November 1981. The full text of the joint communiqué is reproduced here.

18. Financial Times, July 20, 1984.

19. Japan Atomic Energy Commission, Long-Term Program For Development and Utilization of Nuclear Energy (Tokyo: JAEC, 1982), p. 26.

20. It has been calculated that 9 to 22 pounds of plutonium are required to build a nuclear bomb. Mason Willrich and Theodore B. Taylor, Nuclear Theft: Risks and Safeguards (Cambridge, Ma.: Ballinger, 1974), pp. 12–16. Using these estimates, Japan would have been able to construct 8 to 19 nuclear weapons from its first natural uranium reactor. Due to the rapid expansion of Japan's nuclear program, this figure would have jumped to 100 to 245 nuclear weapons by the mid-1970s. A 1977 study estimated that by 1985 Japan would be able to manufacture 300 nuclear weapons per year from the spent fuel collected in its light-water reactors. See Report of the Nuclear Energy Policy Study Group, Nuclear Power Issues and Choices (Cambridge, Ma.: Ballinger, 1977), p. 284. Endicott assigned a greater weapons production potential to Japan for this period. See Endicott, Japan's Nuclear Option, p. 135.

21. See Committee for the Compilation of Materials on Damage Caused by the Atomic Bombs in Hiroshima and Nagasaki, Hiroshima and Nagasaki: The Physical, Medical, and Social Effects of the Atomic Bombings (New York: Basic Books, 1981).

22. Gensuikyo is the shortened form of Gensui baku kinshi Nihon kyokai, which translates as the Japan Council for the Prohibition of Atomic and Hydrogen Bombs. The figure of 40 million signatures is cited in J.A.A. Stockwin, The Japanese Socialist Party and Neutralism (Victoria: Melbourne University Press, 1968), p. 88. For discussion of the Lucky Dragon incident, see Ralph E. Lapp, The Voyage of the Lucky Dragon (New York: Harpers, 1958). For the Japanese reaction, see Herbert Passin, "Japan and the H-bomb," Bulletin of the Atomic Scientists, vol. 11, no. 8 (October 1955), pp. 289–292; and Douglas H. Mendel, Jr., The Japanese People and Foreign Policy, (Berkeley: University of California Press, 1961), pp. 155–168.

23. For a discussion of the 1960 crisis, see G.R. Packard, Crisis in Tokyo: The Security Crisis of 1960 (Princeton, N.J.: Princeton University Press, 1966). See also

Frank Langdon, *Japan's Foreign Policy* (Vancouver: University of British Columbia Press, 1973), pp. 7–21; Richard L. Sneider, *U.S.-Japanese Security Relations* (New York: East Asian Institute, Columbia University, 1982), pp. 26–34.

24. All polling data was translated and provided by the United States Information Agency. Two useful analyses of this question and related defense issues are Douglas H. Mendl, Jr., "Public Views of the Japanese Defense System," in James H. Buck, ed., *The Modern Japanese Military System* (Beverly Hills: Sage, 1975), pp. 149–180; Herbert Passin, "Nuclear Arms and Japan," in William H. Overholt, ed., *Asia's Nuclear Future* (Boulder, Co.: Westview Press, 1977), pp. 67–132.

25. It should be noted, however, that the opposition parties objected to NPT ratification between 1970 and 1975. For an examination of the attitude of Japan's opposition parties to the nuclear weapons issue, see Endicott, *Japan's Nuclear Option*, pp. 78–86, 99. See also J.W.M. Chapman, R. Drifte, and I.T.M. Gow, *Japan's Quest for Comprehensive Security* (London: Frances Pinter, 1983), pp. 125–128. One indication of general disapproval of nuclear armaments was provided when the Diet unanimously passed a resolution criticizing India's May 1974 nuclear explosion. See *FBIS*, May 23, 1974.

26. *Treaty of Mutual Cooperation and Security Between the United States of America and Japan*, signed January 19, 1960, entered into force June 23, 1960. 11 UST 1632; TIAS 4509; 373 UNTS 186.

27. In October 1974, it was reported that a secret agreement was concluded in 1960, without a Japanese text, that permitted the introduction of American nuclear weapons in transit into Japan. See *New York Times*, October 27, 1974. It has also been claimed that a secret understanding between the two countries was reached in 1960, which allowed the U.S. to introduce nuclear weapons into Japan in an emergency or if U.N. forces in Korea were attacked. Cited in Chapman, Drifte, Gow, *Japan's Quest*, p. 122. It is not clear if this refers to the same agreement mentioned above. In April 1987, Japanese searching the records in the U.S. Library of Congress unearthed a February 24, 1966 State Department telegram referring to a secret "transit agreement" that was appended to the 1960 U.S.-Japan security treaty. See *New York Times*, April 7, 1987.

28. See testimony of Rear Admiral Gene R. LaRocque, in U.S., Joint, *Proliferation of Nuclear Weapons*, Hearings. Committee on Atomic Energy. 93rd Cong., 2d sess. (Washington, D.C.: USGPO, 1974), p. 18. For the reaction in Japan, see *Japan Times Weekly*, October 7, 8, 9, 10, 1974; *The Times*, October 8, 11, 1974; *New York Times*, October 8, 13, 1974; *Far Eastern Economic Review*, October 18, 1974, p. 17. A November 1974 poll by Asahi showed that 73 percent of the Japanese people did not believe the government's disavowal of the claim that the U.S. had introduced nuclear weapons into Japan.

29. See *International Herald Tribune*, May 20, 1981; *Japan Times Weekly*, May 23, 30, 1981; *Financial Times*, May 23, 1981. A June 1981 poll by *Asahi* indicated that 79 percent of the Japanese people did not believe the government's disavowal of the claim that the U.S. had introduced nuclear weapons into Japan.

30. See John M. Maki, translator and editor, *Japan's Commission on the Constitution: The Final Report* (Seattle: University of Washington Press, 1980), p. 100. Further examination of Article IX can be found in D.C. Sissons, "The Pacifist Clause of the Japanese Constitution," *International Affairs*, vol. 37, no. 1 (January 1961), pp. 45–59; Wolf Mendl, "The Japanese Constitution and Japan's Security Policy," *Millennium: Journal of International Studies*, vol. 7, no. 1 (Spring 1978), pp. 36–51. The circumstances surrounding how this clause was placed in the Constitution are discussed in

Theodore McNelly, "The Renunciation of War in the Japanese Constitution," *Political Science Quarterly*, vol. 77, no. 3 (September 1962), pp. 350–378.

31. Martin E. Weinstein, *Japan's Postwar Defense Policy, 1947–1968* (New York: Columbia University Press, 1971), p. 81.

32. John K. Emmerson, *Arms, Yen and Power* (New York: Dunellen, 1971), p. 129.

33. *Japan Times Weekly*, June 10, 1967.

34. Langdon, *Japan's Foreign Policy*, p. 31.

35. *Defense of Japan*, 1970 (Tokyo: Japan Defense Agency, 1970), p. 40.

36. *International Herald Tribune*, March 22, 1973.

37. Cited in Gaston J. Sigur, "Power, Politics, and Defense," in Buck, ed., *The Modern Japanese Military System*, p. 187. In October 1984 a Socialist Party member of the Diet alleged that in the early 1970s the Ministry of Defense, then under the guidance of Yasuhiro Nakasone, commissioned a report on Japan's ability to produce its own tactical nuclear weapons from its stocks of plutonium. See *The Guardian*, October 19, 1984. It is notable that this claim was made just prior to the vote in the Diet to elect Prime Minister Nakasone to his second term in office.

38. Kei Wakaizumi, "The Problem for Japan," in Alastair Buchan, ed., *A World of Nuclear Powers?* (Englewood Cliffs, N.J.: Prentice-Hall, 1966), p. 78.

39. *Agreement Between the International Atomic Energy Agency, the Government of Japan, and the Government of the United States of America for the Application of Safeguards by the Agency to the Bilateral Agreement Between Those Governments Concerning Civil Uses of Atomic Energy*, 14 UST 1265; TIAS 5429. Signed September 23, 1963, entered into force November 1, 1963. Extended by 18 UST; TIAS 6388. Signed November 2, 1967, entered into force November 2, 1967. Superseded by 19 UST 5371; TIAS 6520. Signed July 10, 1968, entered into force July 10, 1968.

40. *Agreement Between the United States of America and Japan on Space Cooperation*, 20 UST 2720; TIAS 6735; 720 UNTS 79. Signed July 31, 1969, entered into force July 31, 1969.

41. *Documents on Disarmament*, 1967 (Washington, D.C.: USGPO, 1968), p. 153.

42. A/PV. 1563 (prov.), September 22, 1967, pp. 23–27; A/C.1/PV. 1565, May 10, 1968, pp. 27–41.

43. *Documents on Disarmament*, 1970 (Washington, D.C.: USGPO, 1971), pp. 2–5.

44. The final declaration of the Conference of Non-Nuclear Weapons States is reprinted as UN Doc. A/7277.

45. For a discussion of Bonn's views on the NPT at this time, see Horst Menderhausen, "Will West Germany Go Nuclear?," *Orbis*, vol. 16, no. 2 (Summer 1972), pp. 411–434; see also Catherine McArdle Kelleher, *Germany and the Politics of Nuclear Weapons* (New York: Columbia University Press, 1975), pp. 297–301.

46. Shelton L. Williams, *Nuclear Nonproliferation in International Politics: The Japanese Case*, Monograph Series in World Affairs, no. 3 (Denver: University of Denver Press, 1972), p. 45.

47. George Quester, *The Politics of Nuclear Proliferation* (Baltimore: Johns Hopkins University Press, 1973), p. 45.

48. *Documents on Disarmament*, 1976 (Washington, D.C.: USGPO, 1978), pp. 350–352.

49. See *Review Conference of the Parties to the Treaty on the Nonproliferation of Nuclear Weapons*. Final Document. Part I. NPT/Conf/35/1 (Geneva: United Nations, 1975).

50. John E. Endicott, "The 1975–76 Debate Over Ratification of the NPT in Japan." *Asian Survey*, vol 17, no. 3 (March 1977), pp. 281–282.

51. See, for example, Ryukichi Imai, "The Nonproliferation Treaty and Japan," *Bulletin of the Atomic Scientists*, vol. 25, no. 5 (May 1969), pp. 2–7.

52. *INFCIRC/153, The Structure and Content of Agreements between the Agency and States Required in Connection with the Treaty on the Nonproliferation of Nuclear Weapons* (Vienna: IAEA, 1971).

53. Information on the development and implementation of INFCIRC/153 can be found in Imai, *Nuclear Safeguards*, Adelphi Paper 86 (London: IISS, 1972); SIPRI *Yearbook, 1972* (Stockholm: Almqvist and Wiksell, 1974), pp. 133–157; Benjamin Sanders, *Safeguards Against Nuclear Proliferation* (Stockholm: Almqvist and Wiksell, 1975), pp. 32–43; Benjamin N. Schiff, *International Nuclear Technology Transfer* (Totowa, N.J.: Rowman and Allanheld, 1984), pp. 103–106, 117–120.

54. The United States and Britain agreed in December 1967 to permit IAEA inspection of some of their civilian nuclear facilities. In September 1984, the Soviet Union reversed its position and agreed to open for inspection some of its civilian nuclear installations. On February 21, 1985, the Soviet Union signed an agreement with the IAEA to this effect. See *International Herald Tribune*, February 22, 1985.

55. See *Agreement for Cooperation between the Government of the United States of America and the European Atomic Energy Community (Euratom) Concerning Peaceful Uses of Atomic Energy*, signed November 8, 1958, entered into force February 18, 1959. 10 UST 75; TIAS 4173; 338 UNTS 135. See also Warren H. Donnelly, "Creating a Regional Nuclear Organization: The European Atomic Energy Community (Euratom)," in U.S., House, *Science, Technology, and American Diplomacy*, vol. 1. Print. Committee on International Relations, (Washington, D.C.: USGPO, 1977), pp. 203–225. Euratom's members at this time were Belgium, France, Germany, Italy, Luxembourg, and the Netherlands.

56. See David A.V. Fischer, "IAEA/Euratom Agreement—An Explanation," IAEA *Bulletin*, vol. 15, no. 3 (June 1973), pp. 10–16.

57. Two useful articles on the NPT ratification process in Japan are Daniel I. Okimoto, "Japan's Non-Nuclear Policy: The Problem of the NPT," *Asian Survey*, vol. 15, no. 4 (April 1975), pp. 313–327; Endicott, "The 1975–76 Debate," pp. 275–292.

58. See Endicott, *ibid.*, pp. 289–290; Yager, *Nonproliferation and U.S. Foreign Policy*, p. 27. There have been reports that during the Nixon administration the United States was indifferent to Japan's position on the NPT. See Leslie H. Brown, *American Security Policy in Asia*, Adelphi Paper 132 (London: IISS, 1977), p. 7; Seymour H. Hersch, *The Price of Power: Kissinger in the Nixon White House* (New York: Summit Books, 1983), pp. 148, 380–382.

59. The lower figure is cited by Yoshiyasu Sato, "Japan's Response to Nuclear Developments: Beyond 'Nuclear Allergy,'" in Onkar Marwah and Ann Schulz, eds., *Nuclear Proliferation and the Near-Nuclear Countries* (Cambridge, Ma.: Ballinger, 1975), p. 240. Endicott gave a time-frame of "from nine to eighteen months after project initiation." Endicott, *Japan's Nuclear Option*, p. 140. Muraoka cited the upper figure of twenty-four months. Muraoka, *Japanese Security and the United States*, p. 25. In the early 1970s Imai recommended that Japan ought to have the ability to go nuclear within two years of the decision to do so. See Imai, "The Changing Role of Nuclear Technology in the Post-NPT World: A Japanese View," in Johan Jorgen Holst, ed., *Security, Order, and the Bomb* (Oslo: Universitetsforlaget, 1972), pp. 120–130; see also Imai, "Japan and

the World of SALT," *Bulletin of the Atomic Scientists*, vol. 27, no. 10 (December 1971), pp. 13–16.

60. See, for example, Kei Wakaizumi, "Chinese Nuclear Armament and the Security of Japan," *Journal of Social and Political Ideas in Japan*, vol. 4, no. 3 (December 1966), pp. 69–79.

61. *DOSB*, vol. 51, no. 1323 (November 2, 1964), pp. 612, 613.

62. *Ibid.*, vol. 52, no. 1336 (February 1, 1965), pp. 134–136. See also *DOSB*, vol. 55, no. 1417 (August 22, 1966), pp. 303–311. Tokyo's behavior after the Chinese nuclear test indicated that although the Japanese people were opposed to the U.S. introducing nuclear weapons to the country, they nevertheless wised to be protected by the American nuclear umbrella. This apparent inconsistency could be explained by the Japanese belief that American nuclear weapons would attract a nuclear strike in the event of a full-scale conflict.

63. See Joint Statement of the Goverment of the People's Republic of China and the Government of Japan, September 29, 1972, in *Peking Review*, vol. 15, no. 40 (October 6, 1972), pp. 12–13.

64. For an official Japanese view on this issue, see Ministry of Foreign Affairs, *The Northern Territorial Issue* (Tokyo: Ministry of Foreign Affairs, 1970). See also John J. Stephan, *The Kurile Islands: Russo-Japanese Frontier in the Pacific* (Oxford: Clarendon Press, 1974).

65. *Defense of Japan*, 1979, pp. 32–37. See also U.S., Senate, *United States-Japan Security Relationship: The Key to East Asian Security and Stability*, Report. Committee on Armed Services, 96th Cong., 1st sess. (Washington, D.C.: USGPO, 1979), p. 7. The vulnerability of Japan's air defense was exposed in September 1976 with the defection of a Soviet Mig-25, which penetrated Japanese air space undetected.

66. See *Defense of Japan*, 1976, pp. 17–19.

67. *Defense of Japan*, 1980, p. 49.

68. *DOSB*, vol. 61, no. 1590 (December 15, 1969), pp. 555–558.

69. *DOSB*, vol. 73, no. 1889 (September 8, 1975), pp. 382–384.

70. How these guidelines were developed is explained in *Defense of Japan*, 1979, pp. 187–191. The text of the guidelines is printed in *Defense of Japan*, 1980, pp. 288–294.

71. See *Far Eastern Economic Review*, January 12, 1984, pp. 36–37.

72. *International Herald Tribune*, September 18, 1984.

73. Muraoka, *Japanese Security and the United States*, p. 26.

74. *Ibid.* For an example, see the appeal by Japanese scientists in *Bulletin of the Atomic Scientists*, vol. 31, no. 10 (December 1975), p. 9.

75. Kosaka, "Japan's Nuclear Options," p. 98.

76. Makoto Momoi, "Pax Russo-Americana and Its Theoretical Impact on Japan's Defense Concept," in Robert L. Pfaltzgraff, Jr., ed., *Contrasting Approaches to Strategic Arms Control* (Lexington, Ma.: D.C. Health, 1974), p. 200.

77. Momoi, "Are There Any Alternative Strategies for the Defense of Japan?," in Franklin B. Weinstein, ed., *U.S.-Japan Relations and the Security of East Asia, The Next Decade* (Boulder, Co.: Westview Press, 1978), p. 83. If exploded in any of the other environments it would have violated Japan's obligations under the PTBT. After 1976, any detonation would have violated Japan's obligations under the NPT.

78. *Atoms in Japan*, March 1984. It now appears that the *Mutsu* will have one brief test run and then be dismantled.

79. For a detailed look at the difficulties which would confront a Japanese SLBM

force, see Albert Wohlstetter el al., *Moving Toward Life in a Nuclear Armed Crowd?* (Los Angeles: Pan Heuristics, 1976), pp. 121–142.

80. Momoi, "Are There Any Alternative Strategies," p. 83.

81. See Science and Technology Agency, *Space in Japan*, 1964 (Tokyo: Science and Technology Agency, 1965). For a more recent overview of Japan's space program, see Space Activities Commission, *Space Development Program*, March 16, 1983, xerox supplied by the Embassy of Japan, London.

82. Yager, *Nonproliferation and U.S. Foreign Policy*, p. 24.

83. Robert E. Osgood, *The Weary and the Wary: U.S. and Japanese Security Politics in Transition* (Baltimore: Johns Hopkins University Press, 1972).

84. Momoi, "Pax Russo-Americana," p. 201.

85. Muraoka, *Japanese Security and the United States*, p. 25.

86. Emmerson, *Arms, Yen and Power*, p. 354.

87. J.A.A. Stockwin, *Japan: Divided Politics in a Growth Economy*, 2d ed. (London: Weidenfeld and Nicolson, 1982), p. 270.

88. Momoi, "Pax Russo-Americana," p. 198.

89. Momoi, "Are There Any Alternative Strategies," p. 82.

90. Muraoka, *Japanese Security and the United States*, p. 26.

91. Momoi, "Are There Any Alternative Strategies," p. 83. For a more detailed analysis, see Endicott, *Japan's Nuclear Option*, pp. 179–215.

92. For a critique of the proportional deterrence argument with specific reference to Japan, see Wohlstetter et al., *Moving Toward Life in a Nuclear Armed Crowd?*, pp. 116–120.

93. Buck, "The Japanese Self-Defense Force," p. 51.

94. Roger W. Gale, "Nuclear Power and Japan's Proliferation Option." *Asian Survey*, vol. 18, no. 11 (November 1978), p. 1122.

95. Kazumi Konmi, "The Future of Japan in Terms of National Security," *Asian Survey*, vol. 14, no. 4 (April 1974), p. 367.

5. Israel

1. For a description of the "War of Independence," see Harry Sacher, *Israel: The Establishment of a State* (London: Weidenfeld and Nicolson, 1952); Nadav Safran, *Israel: The Embattled Ally* (Cambridge: Harvard University Press, 1978), pp. 43–64.

2. Shimon Peres, *David's Sling: The Arming of Israel* (London: Weidenfeld and Nicolson, 1970), p. 55.

3. It should be noted that American opposition to the attack on Egypt was partly due to its timing, which diminished whatever propaganda value could have been extracted from the Soviet Union's suppression of the Hungarian revolution in late October and November 1956. For an examination of the Suez War, see Moshe Dayan, *Diary of the Suez Campaign* (London: Weidenfeld and Nicolson, 1965); Anthony Nutting, *No End of a Lesson: The Story of Suez* (London: Constable, 1967); Andre Beaufre, *The Suez Expedition: 1956* (London: Faber and Faber, 1969).

4. See Sylvia K. Crosbie, *A Tacit Alliance: France and Israel from Suez to the Six Day War* (Princeton, N.J.: Princeton University Press, 1974), pp. 161–167.

5. See Michael Bar-Zohar, *The Armed Prophet, A Biography of Ben Gurion* (London: Arthur Barker, 1967), pp. 256–258, 292–294; Peres, *David's Sling*, pp. 144–148.

6. "You may be surprised if I tell you that in our country the dominant memory is

not of military triumph, but of the peril and solitude that preceded [the June 1967 war]. . . . For let it be remembered that the Arab states could be defeated and still survive. For Israel there would be only one defeat." Foreign Minister Abba Eban, April 1968. Cited in Michael Brecher, *The Foreign Policy System of Israel: Setting, Images, Process* (London: Oxford University Press, 1972), p. 93.

7. For an analysis of the "Six Day War," see Walter Laqueur, *The Road to War, 1967: The Origins of the Arab-Israeli Conflict* (London: Weidenfeld and Nicolson, 1968); Randolph S. Churchill and Winston S. Churchill, *The Six Day War* (Boston: Houghton-Mifflin, 1967); Nadav Safran, *From War to War: The Arab-Israeli Confrontation, 1948–1967* (New York: Pegasus, 1969), pp. 266–382.

8. The Khartoum Conference resolution is cited in full, and the conference itself discussed, in *Middle East Record*, vol. 3, 1967 (Jersualem: Israel Universities Press, 1971), pp. 262–266.

9. For an analysis of the October 1973 war, see Insight Team, Sunday Times, *The Yom Kippur War* (London: Andre Deutsch, 1975); Zeev Schiff, *October Earthquake, Yom Kippur 1973* (Tel Aviv: University Publishing Projects, 1974).

10. The text of the Treaty of Peace between the Arab Republic of Egypt and the State of Israel can be found in *DOSB*, vol. 79, no. 2026 (May 1979), pp. 3–15.

11. Fuad Jabber, *Israel and Nuclear Weapons: Present Option and Future Strategies* (London: Chatto and Windus, 1971), pp. 15–23.

12. Bertrand Goldschmidt, *The Atomic Adventure* (New York: Pergamon, 1964), p. 83; Ann Wiliams, *Britain and France in the Middle East and North Africa, 1914–1967* (London: Macmillan, 1968), p. 119. See also Lawrence Scheinman, *Atomic Energy Policy in France Under The Fourth Republic* (Princeton, N.J.: Princeton University Press, 1965), pp. 65–66.

13. U.N., *Official Records of the General Assembly*, Ninth Session, First Committee, 716th meeting, November 15, 1954. Speech by Israeli Ambassador Abba Eban, pp. 335–337. There is some possibility that Eban made this claim for a heavy-water pilot production plant on the basis of false information.

14. Jabber, *Israel and Nuclear Weapons*, p. 23.

15. *Agreement for Cooperation between the Government of the United States of America and the Government of Israel Concerning Civil Uses of Atomic Energy*. Signed July 12, 1955; entered into force July 12, 1955. 6 UST 2641; TIAS 3311.

16. Leonard Beaton and John Maddox, *The Spread of Nuclear Weapons* (London: Chatto and Windus, 1962), p. 170.

17. *Agreement between the IAEA, the Government of Israel and the Government of the United States of America for the Application of Safeguards*. Signed June 18, 1965; entered into force June 15, 1966. 17 UST 750; TIAS 6027.

18. *Ibid.* Signed April 4, 1975; entered into force April 4, 1975. 26 UST 483; TIAS 8051.

19. *Protocol Prolonging the Agreement*. . . . Signed April 7, 1977; entered into force April 7, 1977. 28 UST 2397; TIAS 8554. For a relatively recent look at the Nahal Soreq research reactor, see U.S., House, *Middle Eastern Oversight Trip*, Report. Committee on Science and Technology. 96th Cong., 2d sess. (Washington, D.C.: USGPO, 1980), pp. 38–40. By 1969, the Nahal Soreq reactor had been upgraded to a 5-megawatt capacity. In August 1980 it was reported that its capacity had been increased to 10 megawatts. See "The Middle East's Nuclear Race," Confidential Foreign Report, *The Economist*, no. 1643 (August 13, 1980).

20. Aubrey Hodes, *Dialogue with Ishmael: Israel's Future in the Middle East* (New

York: Funk and Wagnalls, 1968), pp. 229–230; S. Flapan, "Israel's attitude towards the NPT," in Bhupendra Jasani, ed., *Nuclear Proliferation Problems* (Cambridge, Ma.: MIT Press, 1974), p. 277; see also Sylvia K. Crosbie, *A Tacit Alliance*, pp. 120–121, 161–169. The precise terms of the 1957 agreement have never been revealed.

21. See *The Times*, December 12, 1960; *Washington Post*, December 18, 1960.

22. The lower figure is cited in J.C. Hurewitz, *Middle East Politics: The Military Dimension* (London: Pall Mall, 1969), p. 476. The higher figure is cited in *Jerusalem Post*, December 22, 1960.

23. Charles Van Doren, "Iraq, Israel, and the Middle East Proliferation Problem," in U.S., Senate, *Nuclear Nonproliferation Policy*, Hearing. Committee on Governmental Affairs. Subcommittee on Energy, Nuclear Proliferation, and Government Processes. 97th Cong., 1st sess. (Washington, D.C.: USGPO, 1981), p. 152, note. In November 1986, the *New York Times* reported that the United States had shipped four metric tons of heavy water to Israel in 1963. The heavy water is now under IAEA safeguards. Under the terms of a 1959 agreement, Norway shipped twenty-one tons of heavy water to Israel. *New York Times*, November 10, 1986. See also *New York Times*, February 17, 1987, and May 26, 1987.

24. See Leonard S. Spector, *Nuclear Proliferation Today* (New York: Vintage, 1984), pp. 369–370, note 4. For a brief discussion of Israel's domestic uranium reserves, see U.N., *Study on Israeli Nuclear Armament*, A/36/431 (New York: U.N., 1982), p. 11.

25. United Nations, *ibid.*, p. 10.

26. *The Economist*. "The Middle East's Nuclear Race."

27. United Nations, *Study on Israeli Nuclear Armament*, p. 11.

28. Bar-Zohar, *The Armed Prophet*, p. 270.

29. *Ibid.*, pp. 270–273; Shlomo Aronson, *Conflict and Bargaining in the Middle East, An Israeli Perspective* (Baltimore: Johns Hopkins University Press, 1978), pp. 44–45.

30. *New York Times*, July 18, 1970.

31. *Washington Post*, November 9, 1976.

32. Testimony of Abraham S. Friedman, ERDA representative, in U.S., Joint, *Proposals for International Cooperation in Nuclear Energy*, Hearing. Committee on Atomic Energy. 94th Cong., 1st sess. (Washington, D.C.: USGPO, 1975), p. 5.

33. "Note from Embassy of Israel," January 13, 1975, Attached to *Amendment to Agreement for Cooperation between the Government of the United States and the Government of Israel.* . . . Signed January 13, 1975; entered into force March 24, 1975. TIAS 8019. With only three other countries—Portugal, Spain, and South Africa—has the United States explicitly noted its opposition to the use of U.S.-supplied materials and equipment for peaceful nuclear explosions. Earlier, in 1969, Beaton had written that Israel could build nuclear weapons by separating weapons-grade plutonium in its hot labs at Nahal Soreq and Dimona. He did not refer to the fact that the Nahal Soreq facility was already under safeguards. See Beaton, "Why Israel does not need the Bomb," *The New Middle East*, no. 7 (April 1969), pp. 7–11.

34. Robert Gillette, "Uranium Enrichment: Rumors of Israeli Progress with Lasers," *Science*, vol. 183, no. 4130 (March 22, 1974), pp. 1172–1174.

35. *Strategic Survey, 1974* (London: IISS, 1975), pp. 35–36.

36. U.S., Senate, *Senate Delegation Report on American Foreign Policy and Nonproliferation Interests in the Middle East*, Report pursuant to Senate Res. 167 of May 10, 1977. 95th Cong., 1st sess. (Washington, D.C.: USGPO, 1977), p. 3.

37. *IAEA Bulletin*, vol. 19, no. 5 (October 1977), p. 2. The author of this article

attributed the pilot reprocessing plant to Israel without his having any firm evidence. This "bluff" was confirmed when Israeli officials subsequently approached him to ask how he had "discovered" Israel's secret.

38. SIPRI Yearbook, 1979, p. 314.

39. See Peter Pringle and James Spigelman, The Nuclear Barons (New York: Avon, 1981), p. 296. In another book published the same year, Perrin was quoted as saying that the French government "also participated in the building of a plutonium extraction plant." See Steve Weissman and Herbert Krosney, The Islamic Bomb: The Nuclear Threat to Israel and the Middle East (New York: Times Books, 1981), p. 113. See also Bertrand Goldschmidt, The Atomic Complex: A Worldwide Political History of Nuclear Energy (La Grange Park, Il.: American Nuclear Society, 1982), pp. 184–187.

40. Beaton and Maddox, The Spread of Nuclear Weapons, p. 173.

41. New York Times, February 2, 1964.

42. Jabber, Israel and Nuclear Weapons, pp. 56–61.

43. For similar reasons, Egypt later declined the American offer as well. After Cairo ratified the NPT in February 1981, the U.S. Congress agreed to reopen negotiations. In January 1985, the U.S. Export-Import Bank offered $250 million toward the estimated $2 to $3 billion cost of a planned nuclear power plant in Egypt. International Herald Tribune, January 30, 1985. This project now appears to have been postponed indefinitely. For a discussion of the proposed 1974 deals with Egypt and Israel, see U.S., House, U.S. Foreign Policy and the Export of Nuclear Technology to the Middle East, Hearings. Committee on Foreign Affairs. Subcommittee on International Organizations and Movements. Subcommittee on the Near East and South Asia. 93rd Cong., 2d sess. (Washington, D.C.: USGPO, 1974); U.S., Senate, Exports of Nuclear Materials and Technology, Hearings. Committee on Banking, Housing and Urban Affairs. Subcommittee on International Finance. 93rd Cong., 2d sess. (Washington, D.C.: USGPO, 1974), pp. 41–57.

44. For a brief discussion of Israeli civilian nuclear developments during this period, see Michael Burton, "Israel-Nuclear History," in Zivia S. Wurtele et al., Nuclear Proliferation Prospects for the Middle East and South Asia (Los Angeles: Pan Heuristics, 1981), pp. A.22–A.27.

45. Spector, Nuclear Proliferation Today, pp. 139–142.

46. See A/C.1/PV.1576, May 29, 1968, pp. 31–36.

47. See George H. Quester, "Israel and the Nuclear Nonproliferation Treaty," Bulletin of the Atomic Scientists, vol. 25, no. 6 (June 1969), p. 7; Neue Zurcher Zeitung, November 30, 1968. Cited in Sven Hirdman, The Near-Nuclear Countries and the NPT (Stockholm: Almqvist and Wiksell, 1972), p. 29.

48. Quester, The Politics of Nuclear Proliferation (Baltimore: Johns Hopkins University Press, 1973), p. 84. In September 1982, Israel's credentials were not accepted at the IAEA's General Conference because of its bombing of Iraq's Osiraq reactor in June 1981. Israel was reinstated in October 1983.

49. A/C.1/L.700, November 20, 1974. This later became A/RES./3263 (XXIX), and was adopted on Jaunary 7, 1975 by a vote of 128–0–2, with Israel and Burma abstaining. For a brief examination of a Middle East nuclear-weapons-free zone, see William Epstein, The Last Chance: Nuclear Proliferation and Arms Control (New York: The Free Press, 1976), pp. 214–215. In August, 1981, the U.S. announced that it was starting "preliminary diplomatic talks" for a Middle East nuclear-weapons-free zone. Baltimore Sun, August 14, 1981. To date, nothing has emerged from these discussions.

50. A/C.1/PV.2028 (prov.), November 22, 1974, p. 62. See also, Efraim Inbar, *Israel's Nuclear Policy After 1973* (Los Angeles: Pan Heuristics, 1977), pp. 62–66. For a fairly recent examination of a Middle East nuclear-weapons-free zone, see Warren H. Donnelly and Joseph F. Pilat, "Nuclear-Weapon-Free-Zones: Record of the Past and Opportunities in the Middle East," paper prepared for the Core Seminar on Nuclear Proliferation of the International Security Studies Program, Woodrow Wilson International Center for Scholars, Washington, D.C., December 1983.

51. Jabber, *Israel and Nuclear Weapons*, p. 95. See also Victor Cygielman, "Rockets Now-What Next," *New Outlook*, vol. 5, no. 7 (September 1962), pp. 5–8; Leonard Beaton, "A radiological arms race in the Middle East?," *New Scientist*, vol. 17, no. 332 (March 28, 1963), p. 679.

52. Crosbie, *A Tacit Alliance*, p. 159; *New York Times*, July 18, 1970.

53. *New York Times*, October 5, 1974. On Jericho's capability as a nuclear delivery vehicle, see Peter Pry, *Israel's Nuclear Arsenal* (London: Croom Helm, 1984), pp. 95–96; see also *New York Times*, July 22 and 29, 1987.

54. See *Washington Post*, September 16, 17, 18, 1975; see also Inbar, *Israel's Nuclear Policy*, pp. 68–70.

55. *The Military Balance*, 1981–1982 (London: IISS, 1981), p. 52. For a recent assessment of Israeli air force capabilities for delivering nuclear bombs, see Pry, *Israel's Nuclear Arsenal*, pp. 100–107. For a somewhat dated but still useful discussion of possible delivery vehicles for nuclear weapons in the Middle East, see Robert J. Pranger and Dale R. Tahtinen, *Nuclear Threat in the Middle East* (Washington, D.C.: AEI for Public Policy Research, 1975), pp. 23–37.

56. *New York Times*, July 18, 1970.

57. *Evening Standard* (London), October 9, 1970.

58. *Boston Globe*, July 31, 1975.

59. *Washington Post*, March 15, 1976.

60. *Time*, April 12, 1976, pp. 39–40. See also Philip Windsor, "The Middle East and the World Balance," *The World Today*, vol. 23, no. 7 (July 1967), p. 281.

61. *New York Times*, April 29, 1977; *The Times*, May 6, 1977. The fullest account of this incident is Elaine Davenport et al., *The Plumbat Affair* (London: Andre Deutsch, 1978).

62. David Burnham has written that there have been "at least ten separate investigations" of the NUMEC affair by U.S. agencies. See Burnham, "The Case of the Missing Uranium," *The Atlantic Monthly*, vol. 243, no. 4 (April 1979), pp. 78–82. For the first accounts of this incident, see *New York Times*, August 24, 1977; *New York Times*, October 20, 1977.

63. CIA, "Prospects for Further Proliferation of Nuclear Weapons," DCI NIO 1945–74, September 4, 1974, p. 1. In 1975, Acting Assistant Secretary of State for Oceans and International Environmental and Scientific Affairs, Myron Kratzer, testified before Congress that the United States did not have any "evidence" that Israel possessed nuclear weapons or was working on the development of nuclear weapons. See U.S., House, *Oversight Hearings on Nuclear Energy: International Proliferation of Nuclear Technology*, Hearings. Committee on Interior and Insular Affairs. Subcommittee on Energy and the Environment. 94th Cong., 1st sess. (Washington, D.C.: USGPO, 1975), p. 19.

64. *International Herald Tribune*, June 30, 1981.

65. Weissman and Krosney, *The Islamic Bomb*, pp. 114, 117. That France might have provided Israel with information from its nuclear tests had been surmised earlier,

in *New York Times*, July 18, 1970; and Ernest W. Lefever, *Nuclear Arms in the Third World: U.S. Policy Dilemma* (Washington, D.C.: Brookings, 1979), p. 68. The *Time* account of April 1976 alleged that Israel might have conducted a nuclear test in the Negev Desert in 1963. For an Israeli view on nuclear testing, see Y. Harkabi, *Nuclear War and Nuclear Peace* (Jerusalem: Israel Program for Scientific Translantions, 1966), p. 165. There is also the possibility that Israel might have told the U.S. that it had to conduct a nuclear test in order to confirm the reliability of its nuclear stockpile. In order to prevent this development, Washington might have been willing to run the Israeli weapon design through its computers and give the results to Israel. If Israel detonated a nuclear device after August 1977, under the Glenn amendment to the International Security Assistance Act of 1977, the U.S. would have been forced to cut off military and economic assistance to Israel, unless the U.S. President certified in writing to Congress that termination of such assistance would jeopardize U.S. national security.

66. Seymour M. Hersch, *The Price of Power: Kissinger in the Nixon White House* (New York: Summit Books, 1983), p. 214, note. A somewhat different type of report surfaced in May 1985. A Federal grand jury in Los Angeles indicted an American citizen on charges of illegally shipping to Israel between 1979 and 1983 800 high-speed electronic switches, named krytrons, that could be used to control the timing of nuclear detonations. Israel admitted that it had received these devices, which can also be used as timers in strobe lights at airports, in high-speed copying machines, and in explosive geological tests for oil, but maintained that the krytrons were not used for any nuclear purposes. Israel promised to place this pledge in writing, and to return the krytrons. See *New York Times*, May 16, 17, 1985; *Washington Post*, May 15, 16, 1985. Assuming that Israel did acquire the krytrons for its nuclear weapons program, this suggests that Tel Aviv lacked sufficient confidence in the reliability of its nuclear capability and wished to avoid the expense of developing its own devices.

67. Insight Team, *Sunday Times*, October 5, 1986. After the *Sunday Times* published this story, Tel Aviv apprehended Vanunu and brought him back to Israel to stand trial on security offenses. See *New York Times*, October 27, 29, 1986; November 5, 10, 1986. Although there has been speculation that the entire Vanunu affair was intentionally fabricated by Israel, it is unclear why Israel would have felt it necessary to reveal such intimately detailed information as was contained in the *Sunday Times* article.

68. *Jewish Observer*, December 24, 1965. Cited in U.N., *Study on Israeli Nuclear Armament*, p. 17. Part of the uncertainty of this statement is due to the fact that nuclear weapons had already been "introduced" to the Middle East, on board the U.S. Sixth Fleet and probably on Soviet ships in the Mediterranean.

69. *New York Times*, May 19, 1966.

70. *The Times*, December 3, 1974.

71. *Daily Telegraph* (London), December 13, 1974; *The Guardian*, December 18, 1974.

72. *Sunday Times* (London), March 14, 1976.

73. *International Herald Tribune*, September 10, 1976.

74. *New York Times*, February 22, 25, 1980. The original report was based on information contained in a book by two Israeli authors, Ami Dor-on and Eli Teicher, entitled *None Will Survive Us: The Story of the Israeli A-Bomb*. Israeli censors refused permission for the book to be published. See *New York Times*, March 30, 1980. For reports of Israeli-South African military and nuclear cooperation, see *New York Times*,

August 18, 1976; Richard P. Stevens and Abdelwahab M. Elmessiri, *Israel and South Africa: The Progression of a Relationship* (New Brunswick, N.J.: North American, 1977); Zdenek Cervenka and Barbara Rogers, *The Nuclear Axis* (London: Julian Friedman, 1978), pp. 325–328; Robert Manning and Stephen Talbot, "American Cover-up on Israeli Bomb," *The Middle East*, no. 68 (June 1980), pp. 8–12; Peter L. Bunce, "The Growth of South Africa's Defense Industry and its Israeli Connection," *RUSI Journal*, vol. 129, no. 2 (June 1984), pp. 42–49. See also *New York Times*, January 29, 1987.

75. *International Herald Tribune*, June 25, 1981. Israel apparently was not beyond exploiting these rumors to bolster its international arms sales by implying that it might also export its nuclear expertise. See *New York Times*, April 1, 1986.

76. See quote of Nahum Goldmann, in *New Outlook*, vol. 4, no. 5 (March/April 1961), p. 15; Beaton and Maddox, *The Spread of Nuclear Weapons*, p. 180; Flapan, "Israel's attitude," p. 280.

77. Yair Evron, "A Nuclear Balance of Deterrence in the Middle East," *New Outlook*, vol. 18, no. 5 (July/August 1975), pp. 18–19; Yoram Nimrod, "Non-Nuclear Deterrence," *New Outlook*, vol. 19, no. 3 (April/May 1976), p. 39; Merrill A. McPeak, "Israel: Borders and Security," *Foreign Affairs*, vol. 54, no. 3 (April 1976), pp. 437–438.

78. Flapan, "For an Atomic Bomb-Free Middle East," *New Outlook*, vol. 5, no. 4 (May 1962), p. 16; Inbar, *Israel's Nuclear Policy*, p. 74.

79. For a brief analysis of Egypt's nuclear program, see Ernest W. Lefever, *Nuclear Arms in the Third World: U.S. Policy Dilemma* (Washington, D.C.: Brookings, 1979), pp. 74–80. For a discussion of early nuclear efforts by the Arab countries, see Evron, "The Arab Position in the Nuclear Field: A Study of Policies up to 1967," *Cooperation and Conflict*, no. 1 (1973), pp. 19–31; see also Lewis A. Frank, "Nasser's Missile Program," *Orbis*, vol. 11, no. 3 (Fall 1967), pp. 746–757.

80. A detailed examination of the Iraqi nuclear program and the Israeli raid on Osiraq are beyond the scope of this chapter. For the official Israeli position, see Government of Israel, *The Iraqi Nuclear Threat: Why Israel Had To Act* (Jerusalem: Government of Israel, 1981). See also H. Grumm, "Safeguards and Tammuz: setting the record straight," *IAEA Bulletin*, vol. 23, no. 4 (December 1981), pp. 10–14; testimony of Roger Richter, former inspector, IAEA, in U.S., House, *Israeli Attack on Iraqi Nuclear Facilities*, Hearings. Committee on Foreign Affairs. Subcommittee on International Security and Scientific Affairs. Subcommittee on Europe and the Middle East. 97th Cong., 1st sess. (Washington, D.C.: USGPO, 1981), pp. 51–59; U.S., Senate, *The Israeli Air Strike*, Hearings. Committee on Foreign Relations. 97th Cong., 1st sess. (Washington, D.C.: USGPO, 1981); Weissman and Krosney, *The Islamic Bomb*, pp. 227–291; Amos Perlmutter et al., *Two Minutes Over Baghdad* (London: Valentine, Mitchell, 1982); Shai Feldman, "The Bombing of Osiraq—Revisited," *International Security*, vol. 7, no. 2 (Fall 1982), pp. 114–142; Roger F. Pajak, "Nuclear status and policies of the Middle East countries," *International Affairs*, vol. 59, no. 4 (Autumn 1983), pp. 596–600.

81. Yuval Ne'eman, "Conceiving a Balanced Defense for a Budding Nation," in Zvi Lanir, ed., *Israeli Security Planning in the 1980s: Its Politics and Economics* (New York: Pergamon, 1984), p. 13.

82. See James Digby, *Precision-Guided Weapons*, Adelphi Paper 118 (London: IISS, 1975); John J. Mearscheimer, "Precision-guided Munitions and Conventional Deterrence," *Survival*, vol. 21, no. 2 (March/April 1979), pp. 68–76.

83. See, for example, Steven J. Rosen, *What a Fifth Arab-Israeli War Might Look*

Like: An Exercise in Crisis Forecasting, ACIS Working Paper No. 8 (Los Angeles: UCLA, 1977), p. 34. See also, Anthony H. Cordesman, "How Much Is Too Much?," Armed Forces Journal International (October 1977).

84. U.S., ACDA, World Military Expenditures and Arms Transfers, 1972–1982 (Washington, D.C.: USGPO, 1984), p. 31.

85. Cited in Paul Jabber, A Nuclear Middle East: Infrastructure, Likely Military Postures and Prospects for Strategic Stability, ACIS Working Paper no. 6 (Los Angeles: UCLA, 1977), p. 7.

86. Jabber, Israel and Nuclear Weapons, p. 85.

87. William B. Bader, The United States and the Spread of Nuclear Weapons (New York: Pegasus, 1968), p. 91; Lawrence Freedman, "Israel's Nuclear Policy," Survival, vol. 17, no. 3 (May/June 1975), pp. 114–120.

88. Jabber, Israel and Nuclear Weapons, esp. pp. 101–111, 122–141.

89. Shlomo Aronson, Israel's Nuclear Options, ACIS Working Paper no. 7 (Los Angeles: UCLA, 1977), pp. 24–34; Aronson, "Nuclearization of the Middle East, A Dovish View," Jerusalem Quarterly, no. 2 (Winter 1977), pp. 27–44; Feldman, Israeli Nuclear Deterrence: A Strategy for the 1980s (New York: Columbia University Press, 1982).

90. IISS, Sources of Conflict in the Middle East, Adelphi Paper 26 (London: IISS, 1966), p. 44; Jabber, Israel and Nuclear Weapons, p. 136; see also Feldman, ibid., pp. 233–236.

91. Robert W. Tucker, "Israel and the United States: From Dependence to Nuclear Weapons?," Commentary, vol. 60, no. 5 (November 1975), pp. 29–43; see also Mark Bruzonsky and Israel Singer, "Dependent Israel: The Two Options," Worldview, vol. 19, no. 4 (April 1976), pp. 42–47. For a similar assessment of American influence over Israeli policy, see George W. Ball, "How to Save Israel in Spite of Herself," Foreign Affairs, vol. 55, no. 3 (April 1977), pp. 453–471. For an opposite view, see Steven J. Rosen and Mara Moustafine, "Does Washington Have the Means to Impose a Settlement on Israel?," Commentary, vol. 64, no. 4 (October 1977), pp. 25–32; Thomas R. Wheelock, "Arms for Israel: The Limits of Leverage," International Security, vol. 3, no. 2 (Fall 1978), pp. 123–137.

92. Tucker, ibid., p. 41.

93. For Libyan efforts to buy a nuclear bomb, see Mohamed H. Heikal, The Road to Ramadan (London: Collins, 1975), pp. 76–77. See also Leonard S. Spector, Going Nuclear (Cambridge: Ballinger, 1987), pp. 146–159.

94. Jabber, A Nuclear Middle East; Robert E. Harkavy, Spectre of a Middle Eastern Holocaust (Denver: University of Denver Press, 1977), pp. 72–73; Feldman, "A Nuclear Middle East," Survival, vol. 23, no. 3 (May/June 1981), pp. 107–115. For an opposite evaluation of future Arab nuclear weapons acquisition, see Geoffrey Kemp, "A Nuclear Middle East," in John Kerry King, ed., International Political Effects of the Spread of Nuclear Weapons (Washington, D.C.: USGPO, 1979), pp. 61–77.

95. Rosen, "Nuclearization and Stability in the Middle East," in Onkar Marwah and Ann Schulz, eds., Nuclear Proliferation and the Near-Nuclear Countries (Cambridge: Ma.: Ballinger, 1975), pp. 157–184; Rosen, "A Stable System of Mutual Nuclear Deterrence in the Arab-Israeli Conflict," American Political Science Review, vol. 71, no. 4 (December 1977), pp. 1367–1383; Feldman, Israeli Nuclear Deterrence, esp. pp. 66–102.

96. Tucker, "Israel and the United States," p. 39.

97. Jabber, Israel and Nuclear Weapons, p. 140; Tucker, ibid., p. 40; Feldman, Israeli Nuclear Deterrence, pp. 129–141.

98. J. Bowyer Bell, "Israel's Nuclear Option," *The Middle East Journal*, vol. 26, no. 4 (Autumn 1972), pp. 379–388; Avigdor Haselkorn, "Israel: From an Option to a Bomb in the Basement?," in Robert M. Lawrence and Joel Larus, eds., *Nuclear Proliferation, Phase II* (Lawrence: University Press of Kansas, 1974), pp. 149–182; Harkavy, *Spectre of a Middle Eastern Holocaust*, pp. 43–47.

99. Pranger and Tahtinen, *Nuclear Threat in the Middle East*, pp. 46–48; Robert J. Pranger, "Nuclear War Comes to the Mideast," *Worldview*, vol. 20, no. 7–8 (July/August 1977), pp. 41–44.

100. Pranger and Tahtinen, *ibid.*, pp. 44–46; Harkavy, *Spectre of a Middle Eastern Holocaust*, pp. 65–67; Charles Holley, "Can The Arabs Go To War?," *The Middle East*, no. 29 (March 1977), pp. 23–24; P.R. Chari, "The Israeli Nuclear Option: Living Dangerously," *International Studies*, vol. 16, no. 3 (July/September 1977), p. 349.

101. Pranger and Tahtinen, *ibid.*, pp. 42–44; Harkavy, *ibid.*, pp. 59–64; Beaton and Maddox, *The Spread of Nuclear Weapons*, p. 179; Evron, "Israel and the Atom: The Uses and Misuses of Ambiguity, 1957–1967," *Orbis*, vol. 17, no. 4 (Winter 1974), p. 1333; Quester, *The Politics of Nuclear Proliferation*, p. 101; Alan Dowty, "Nuclear Proliferation: The Israeli Case," *International Studies Quarterly*, vol. 22, no. 1 (March 1978), p. 96. For a look at the possible characteristics of an Israeli nuclear force, see Pry, *Israel's Nuclear Arsenal*, pp. 45–85. It has often been suggested that under extreme circumstances Israel would use nuclear weapons to strike at Arab countries, even if this action would not spare the Jewish state from annihilation. To use the term "Masada complex" to describe the psychological motivation for this behavior, however, is historically inaccurate, as the Jewish zealots at Masada committed mass suicide rather than surrender to the Romans.

102. Dowty, "Israeli Perspectives on Nuclear Proliferation," in Johan Jørgen Holst, ed., *Security, Order, and the Bomb* (Oslo: Universitetsforlaget, 1972), pp. 144–145; Freedman, "Israel's Nuclear Policy," pp. 114–120.

103. Bruzonsky and Singer, "Dependent Israel," p. 46; Inbar, *Israel's Nuclear Policy*, p. 47; Quester, "Israel and the Nuclear Nonproliferation Treaty," *Bulletin of the Atomic Scientists*, vol. 25, no. 6 (June 1969), pp. 9, 44.

104. The October 1973 war was held as an example of an Arab strategy of limited battlefield aims. See Inbar, *ibid.*, p. 49; Evron, "Israel and the Atom," p. 1332.

105. Beaton and Maddox, *The Spread of Nuclear Weapons*, p. 178; Flapan, "Israel's attitude," pp. 285–286; Oz Chen, "Reflections on Israeli Deterrence," *Jerusalem Quarterly*, no. 24 (Summer 1982), pp. 36–37.

106. Chen, *ibid.*, p. 35; Harkavy, *Spectre of a Middle Eastern Holocaust*, p. 53; Flapan, *ibid.*, pp. 15–16; Committee for Nuclear Disarmament of the Arab-Israeli Region, "Keep Nuclear Weapons Out of Our Region," *New Outlook*, vol. 9, no. 6 (July/August 1966), pp. 64–65.

107. Quester, *The Politics of Nuclear Proliferation*, p. 96.

108. See Flapan, "Israel's attitude," p. 16; Eliezer Livneh, "Israel Must Come Out for Denuclearization," *New Outlook*, vol. 9, no. 5 (June 1966), pp. 44–47; Evron, "A Nuclear Balance of Deterrence," pp. 15–19; Ciro E. Zoppo, "The Nuclear Genie in the Middle East," *New Outlook*, vol. 18, no. 2 (February 1975), pp. 21–26; Pry, *Israel's Nuclear Arsenal*, pp. 115–116.

109. Jabber, *Israel and Nuclear Weapons*, p. 142; Freedman, "Israel's Nuclear Policy," p. 119; Quester, *The Politics of Nuclear Proliferation*, p. 95.

110. Quester, *ibid.*, p. 94; Beaton and Maddox, *The Spread of Nuclear Weapons*, p. 178; Chari, "The Israeli Nuclear Option," p. 353; Dowty, "Nuclear Proliferation: The Israeli Case," pp. 93–95; Jabber, "Israel's Nuclear Options," *Journal of Palestine Stud-

ies, vol. 1, no. 1 (Autumn 1971), p. 24. If the Soviet Union provided nuclear weapons to any Arab state, this would have violated Moscow's obligations under the NPT.

111. IISS, *Sources of Conflict in the Middle East*, p. 43; Jabber, *ibid.*, p. 8; Sven Hirdman, *The Near-Nuclear Countries and the NPT* (Stockholm: Almqvist and Wiksell, 1972), p. 30.

112. See, for example, Aronson, *Israel's Nuclear Options*, p. 12; Perlmutter et al., *Two Minutes Over Baghdad*, p. 47; see also Charles Wakebridge, "The Syrian Side of the Hill," *Military Review*, vol. 56, no. 2 (February 1976), pp. 20–30.

113. See, for example, Perlmutter et al., *ibid.*, p. 48; Uri Bar-Joseph, "The Hidden Debate: The Formation of Nuclear Doctrines in the Middle East," *Journal of Strategic Studies*, vol. 5, no. 2 (June 1982), pp. 205–227; Harkavy, "Pariah States and Nuclear Proliferation," *International Organization*, vol. 35, no. 1 (Winter 1981), p. 159. This motive was not cited by Sadat in his 1978 autobiography, *In Search of Identity* (London: Collins, 1978).

114. Dowty, "Nuclear Proliferation: The Israeli Case," p. 83; Jabber, *A Nuclear Middle East*, p. 3.

115. See *New York Times*, June 16, 1968; Hodes, *Dialogue With Ishmael*, pp. 235–236; Flapan, "Israel's attitude," p. 285; Nicholas Valery, "Israel's silent gamble with the bomb," *New Scientist*, vol. 64, no. 927 (December 12, 1974), p. 809; Crosbie, *A Tacit Alliance*, p. 189. The 1963 deal for the Skyhawk aircraft has frequently been cited as the first arms transfer from the U.S. to Israel. In fact, four year earlier, Washington had provided Israel with 1,000 recoilless guns. Bar-Zohar, *Ben-Gurion* (London: Weidenfeld and Nicolson, 1978), p. 265.

116. Insight Team, *The Yom Kippur War*, pp. 282–284. See also William B. Quandt, *Decade of Decisions: American Policy Toward the Arab-Israeli Conflict, 1967–1976* (Berkeley: University of California Press, 1977), p. 80, note 10.

117. Evron, "Israel and the Atom," p. 1335; Quester, *The Politics of Nuclear Proliferation*, p. 92. Neither author cites any evidence for this assertion.

118. Haselkorn, "Israel: From an Option," p. 171; Aronson, *Israel's Nuclear Options*, pp. 9, 15; see also Sadat, *In Search of Identity*, pp. 252–259.

119. Evron, "The Arab Position in the Nuclear Field," pp. 19–31; Flapan, "Israel's attitude," p. 285.

120. See Flapan, *ibid.*, p. 285. Flapan provides no examples to support this assertion.

121. In 1968 the *New York Times* reported that in early 1961 President Kennedy had sent an intermediary to Israel with the message that the U.S. Sixth Fleet would lend Israel military assistance in the event of Arab aggression. See *New York Times*, June 16, 1968. Israel and the U.S. have a number of agreements in the field of national security. See *Mutual Defense Assistance, Agreement between the United States of America and Israel*, effected by Exchange of Notes, signed July 1 and 23, 1952; entered into force July 23, 1952. 3 UST 4985; TIAS 2675; 179 UNTS 139. *Memorandum of Agreement between the Government of Israel and the Government of the United States of America Concerning the Principles Governing Mutual Cooperation in Research and Development, Scientist and Engineer Exchange, and Procurement and Logistic Support of Selected Defense Equipment*, signed March 19, 1979; entered into force March 19, 1979. 30 UST 3901; TIAS 9434. *General security of information agreement*, Exchange of Notes July 30 and December 10, 1982; entered into force December 10, 1982. TIAS 10617. On November 30, 1981, Secretary of Defense Caspar Weinberger and then Minister of Defense Ariel Sharon signed a memorandum of understanding for strategic cooperation

in the Middle East. On December 14, 1981, the Israeli Knesset approved a law annexing the Golan Heights. Four days later Washington suspended its participation in the agreement. On December 20, Prime Minister Begin canceled the agreement.

122. On this factor's influence in Israeli policy-making, see Brecher, *The Foreign Policy System of Israel*, pp. 229–233.

123. There has only been one reference to Israel's nuclear capabilities in the Soviet press that was not just a reiteration of Western news reports. This was in *Moskovski Komsomolyets*, in August 1972. See *New York Times*, August 9, 1972. Coming only weeks after Sadat's expulsion of Soviet advisors from Egypt, this article was a fairly transparent attempt to convince Cairo that it needed Moscow's support and military assistance. There was a Novosti report issued in Arabic in December 1985, claiming that Israel had engaged in underground testing of nuclear devices in the Negev Desert and that Israel had accumulated a stockpile of forty nuclear warheads. See *New York Times*, December 26, 1985. This report coincided with Syria's deployment of SAM-2 missiles along the Lebanese border and Israeli demands for their removal. There was also a Hebrew-language report by Radio Moscow warning Israel not to continue development of its Jericho-II medium-range missile. See *New York Times*. July 29, 1987. To be sure, the Soviet press has periodically mentioned Israel, along with other countries such as Pakistan and South Africa, in commentary on upcoming NPT Review Conferences.

6. *South Africa*

1. United Kingdom, *Exchange of Letters on Defense Matters between the Governments of the United Kingdom and the Union of South Africa*, June 1955. Cmd. 9520 (London: Her Majesty's Stationery Office, 1955).

2. For an examination of South Africa's postwar foreign policy, see J.E. Spence, *Republic Under Pressure: A Study of South African Foreign Policy* (London: Oxford University Press, 1965); Spence, *The Strategic Significance of Southern Africa* (London: RUSI, 1970); Spence, "South Africa and the Modern World," in Monica Wilson and Leonard Thompson, eds., *The Oxford History of South Africa*, vol. 2, 1870–1966 (Oxford: Clarendon Press, 1971), pp. 477–527; James Barber, *South Africa's Foreign Policy, 1945–1970* (London: Oxford University Press, 1973); Spence, *South African Foreign Policy in Today's World* (Braamfontein: SAIIA, 1975); Spence, *The Political and Military Framework* (London: Africa publications trust, 1975). References to "South Africa" or "the Republic" in this chapter are intended to mean the white-elected central government.

3. Barber, *South Africa's Foreign Policy*, p. 202.

4. The name of this territory was changed to Namibia by U.N. General Assembly resolution 2372 (XXII) on June 12, 1968. South Africa still refers to it as South West Africa.

5. For a discussion of the Court's ruling, see Ernest A. Gross, "The South West Africa Case: What Happened?," *Foreign Affairs*, vol. 45, no. 1 October 1966), pp. 36–48. For this and other aspects of the South West Africa/Namibia situation, see John Dugard, ed., *The South West Africa/Namibia Dispute, Documents and Scholarly Writings on the Controversy Between South Africa and the United Nations* (Berkeley: University of California Press, 1973); Robert I. Rotberg, ed., *Namibia: Political and Economic Prospects* (Lexington, Ma.: D.C. Heath, 1983).

6. The origins of the term "outward movement" or "outward policy" are discussed in Kenneth W. Grundy, *Confrontation and Accommodation in Southern Africa: The Limits of Independence* (Berkeley: University of California Press, 1973), pp. 229–230. Concerning the policy itself, see Larry W. Bowman, "The Subordinate State System of Southern Africa," *International Studies Quarterly*, vol. 12, no. 3 (September 1968), pp. 231–261; Bowman, "South Africa's Southern Strategy and Its Implications for the United States," *International Affairs*, Vol. 47, no. 1 (January 1971), pp. 19–31; Barber, "White Rule and the Outward Policy," in Adrian Leftwich, ed., *South Africa: Economic Growth and Political Change* (London: Allison and Busby, 1974), pp. 319–342; Sam C. Nolutshungu, *South Africa in Africa: A Study in Ideology and Foreign Policy* (Manchester: Manchester University Press, 1975), pp. 259–295.

7. See John Marcum, *The Angolan Revolution*, vol. 2 (Cambridge, Ma.: MIT Press, 1978). See also Colin Legum, "The Soviet Union, China and the West in Southern Africa," *Foreign Affairs*, vol. 54, no. 4 (July 1976), pp. 745–762.

8. See speech by Secretary of State Henry Kissinger, Lusaka, Zambia, April 27, 1976, in *DOSB*, vol. 74, no. 1927 (May 31, 1976), pp. 672–679. The document upon which Washington's earlier policy toward southern Africa was based is contained in Mohamed A. El-Khawas and Barry Cohen, eds., *The Kissinger Study of Southern Africa, National Security Study Memorandum 39* (Westport, Ct.: Lawrence Hill, 1976).

9. See Republic of South Africa, *White Paper on Defense*, 1977 (Simonstown: South African Navy, 1977).

10. See Notre Dame University commencement address by President Jimmy Carter, May 22, 1977, in *DOSB*, vol. 76, no. 1981 (June 13, 1977), pp. 621–625.

11. See P.W. Botha et al., *Towards a Constellation of States in Southern Africa* (Pretoria: Information Service, RSA, 1980); Reginald Herbold Green, "Constellation, Association, Liberation: Economic Coordination and the Struggle for Southern Africa," in Colin Legum, ed., *Africa Contemporary Record, 1979–1980* (London: Holmes and Meier, 1981), pp. A32–45; Deon Geldenhuys, *The Constellation of Southern African States and SADCC: Toward a New Regional Stalemate* (Braamfontein: SAIIA, 1981).

12. The policy of "constructive engagement" is explained in Chester A. Crocker, "South Africa: Strategy for Change," *Foreign Affairs*, vol. 59, no. 2 (Winter, 1980/81), pp. 323–351. This article was written prior to Crocker's becoming Assistant Secretary of State for African Affairs in the Reagan administration. A rejoinder to this policy is John de St. Jorre, "South Africa: Is Change Coming?," *Foreign Affairs*, vol. 60, no. 1 (Fall 1981), pp. 106–122.

13. Robert E. Harkavy, "Pariah States and Nuclear Proliferation," *International Organization*, vol. 35, no. 1 (Winter 1981), p. 140.

14. Richard G. Hewlett and Francis Duncan, *Atomic Shield, 1947–1952* (University Park, Pa.: Pennsylvania State University Press, 1969), p. 174.

15. Bertrand Goldschmidt, *The Atomic Adventure* (New York: Pergamon, 1964), p. 75.

16. OECD/IAEA, *Uranium Resources: Production and Demand* (Paris: OECD, 1983), p. 251.

17. Margaret Gowing, *Britain and Atomic Energy, 1939–1945* (London: Macmillan, 1964), pp. 333–335; see also pp. 378–383.

18. *Atomic Energy Cooperation for Civil Uses*, Agreement between the United States of America and the Union of South Africa. Signed July 8, 1957, entered into force August 22, 1957. 8 UST 1367; TIAS 3885; 290 UNTS 147.

19. See A.R. Newby-Fraser, *Chain Reaction: Twenty Years of Nuclear Research and Development in South Africa* (Pretoria: AEB, 1979), pp. 50–53, 62.

20. The Safari-1 reactor's operating schedule, with a listing of dates and the quantities of enriched uranium supplied by the U.S., can be found in the U.S., Senate, *The Export Reorganization Act of 1975*, Hearings. Committee on Government Operations. 94th Cong., 1st sess. (Washington, D.C.: USGPO, 1975), pp. 67–69, 99–102.

21. *Agreement Between the International Atomic Energy Agency, the Government of the Republic of South Africa and the Government of the United States of America for the Application of Safeguards.* Signed February 26, 1965, entered into force October 8, 1965. TIAS 5880.

22. See Newby-Fraser, *Chain Reaction*, pp. 115–125.

23. Later in the decade there were allegations that West Germany had provided substantial assistance to South Africa in developing its uranium enrichment process. See *Financial Times*, October 27, 1975; *The Observer* (London), October 5, 1975. An official FRG statement addressing these charges is printed in *Frankfurter Allemeine Zeitung*, October 7, 1975. Three years later, accusations and denials were again exchanged. See Zdenek Cervenka and Barbara Rogers, *The Nuclear Axis: Secret Collaboration between West Germany and South Africa* (London: Julian Friedman, 1978), esp. pp. 51–103. For the FRG's response, see *Fact v. Fiction: Rebuttal of the charges of alleged cooperation between the Federal Republic of Germany and South Africa in the nuclear and military fields* (Bonn: Press and Information Office of the Federal Government, 1978). Although the exact nature of the enrichment process remained a closely guarded secret, some details were revealed by South African scientists attending international conferences. Citations for the papers submitted by the South African scientists can be found in U.N., *South Africa's plan and capability in the nuclear field*. A/35/402 (New York: United Nations, 1981), p. 9, note 27. For a brief explanation of the German Becker nozzle enrichment technique, upon which the South African process was allegedly based, see *Science*, vol. 188, no. 4191 (May 30, 1975), p. 912; Allan S. Krass et al., *Uranium Enrichment and Nuclear Weapon Production* (London: Taylor and Francis, 1983), pp. 137–143. The other two commercial techniques of enriching uranium are by gaseous diffusion and gas centrifuge.

24. South Africa, Parliament, House of Assembly, *Debates*, vol. 29, cols. 55–58, July 20, 1970. For views of this development's potential impact on the nuclear market at this time, see D.S. Greenberg, "South Africa: How Valid the Claim for a Uranium Process?," *Science*, vol. 169, no. 3945 (August 7, 1970), p. 563; see also Mike Muller, The Enriching Politics of South Africa's Uranium," *New Scientist*, vol. 62, no. 896 (May 2, 1974), pp. 252–254. Spence has suggested that the timing of Vorster's announcement may have been motivated by the desire to persuade the Conservative government in Britain that military sanctions against South Africa would not be useful and could even be counterproductive by spurring nuclear weapons development. See Spence, *The Political and Military Framework*, p. 109.

25. *The Times* (London), April 8, 1975.

26. There have been recent reports that Pakistan may now also be able to produce weapons-grade uranium. See *Financial Times*, February 10, 1984; and chapter seven, pp. 236–238.

27. U.N., *South Africa's plan*, p. 10. SWU stands for separative work unit, and is related to the amount of energy required to take 1 kilogram of uranium from one enrichment level to another.

28. See Robert Gillette, "Uranium Enrichment: With Help, South Africa is Progressing," *Science*, vol. 188, no. 4193 (June 13, 1975), pp. 1090–1092.

29. Aldo Cassuto, "Can uranium enrichment enrich South Africa?," *The World Today*, vol. 26, no. 10 (October 1970), pp. 419–427.

30. Robert I. Rotberg, *Suffer the Future: Policy Choices in Southern Africa* (Cambridge, Ma.: Harvard University Press, 1980), pp. 153–154.

31. *Financial Times*, February 15, 1978; Richard E. Bissell, *South Africa and the United States: The Erosion of an Influence Relationship* (New York: Praeger, 1982), p. 116.

32. U.N., *South Africa's plan*, p. 10. On January 31, 1984, South Africa announced that it was willing to resume discussions with the IAEA on safeguards for its semicommercial enrichment plant, but not its pilot enrichment plant. By October 1986, these negotiations appeared to reach an impasse. See *Nuclear Fuel*, October 6, 1986.

33. Gregory Jones, *South African Proliferation Prognosis and U.S. Options*, (Los Angeles: Pan Heuristics, 1977), pp. 8–10. On South Africa's motivation for buying nuclear power reactors, see Renfrew Christie, *Electricity, Industry and Class in South Africa* (London: Macmillan, 1984), pp. 193–194.

34. *New York Times*, May 30, 1976.

35. U.N., *South Africa's Nuclear Capability*, A/39 (New York: U.N., 1984), p. 16.

36. U.N., *South Africa's plan*, p. 14. Cervenka and Rogers allege that a "small working model" reprocessing plant is reported to be in South Africa. Cervenka and Rogers, *The Nuclear Axis*, p. 198.

37. U.N., *South Africa's plan*, pp. 13–14. Pretoria was the party who requested that the spent fuel from Koeberg be reprocessed and stored outside South Africa under IAEA safeguards. David Fischer, *The Spread of Nuclear Weapons: Western Europe's Influence on South Africa* (Brussels: Center for European Policy Studies, 1985), p. 9.

38. See exchange of notes attached to *Amending and extending the agreement of July 8, 1957, as amended and extended . . .*, signed May 22, 1974. 25 UST 1158; TIAS 7845. Under this agreement, South Africa was not released from its obligation even if the U.S. failed to export the nuclear fuel for Koeberg.

39. A personal letter by President Brezhnev was reportedly handed to President Carter on August 6 with this information. A Tass statement was issued on August 8 and printed in *Pravada* and *Izvestia* on August 9. See *Current Digest of the Soviet Press*, vol. 29, no. 32, September 7, 1977, p. 6.

40. *New York Times*, August 21, 1977.

41. *International Herald Tribune*, August 23, 1977; *Daily Telegraph* (London) August 23, 1977; *International Herald Tribune*, August 29, 1977.

42. *New York Times*, August 24, 1977. For further details of this event, see *SIPRI Yearbook*, 1978 (London: Taylor and Francis, 1978), pp. 73–79. For a Soviet perspective, see V.F. Davydov, "Nuclear Threat in the Cape of Good Hope," *Soedinennye Shtaty Amerika (SShA)*, December 1977, pp. 48–49.

43. See testimony of Deputy Assistant Secretary of State Myron B. Kratzer, in U.S., Senate, *U.S. Policy Toward Africa*, Hearings. Committee on Foreign Relations. Subcommittee on African Affairs and Subcommittee on Arms Control, International Organizations, and Security Agreements. 94th Cong., 2d sess. (Washington, D.C.: USGPO, 1976), p. 294.

44. See *International Herald Tribune*, February 17, 1977.

45. Jones, *South African Proliferation Prognosis*, p. 13.

46. See *International Herald Tribune*, August 11, 1977.

47. See testimony of Ronald H. Siegel, in U.S., House, *United States–South African Relations: Nuclear Cooperation*, Hearings. Committee on International Relations. Subcommittee on Africa. 95th Cong., 1st sess. (Washington, D.C.: USGPO, 1978), p. 3.

48. Cited in Spence, "The Republic of South Africa: Proliferation and the Politics of 'Outward Movement,'" in Robert M. Lawrence and Joel Larus, eds., *Nuclear Proliferation: Phase II* (Lawrence, Kansas: University Press of Kansas, 1974), p. 215.

49. Cited in Abdul S. Minty, *South Africa's Defense Strategy* (London: Anti-Apartheid Movement, 1969), p. 8.

50. Spence, "The Republic of South Africa," p. 215.

51. Cited in *SIPRI Yearbook, 1972* (Stockholm: Almqvist and Wiksell, 1972), pp. 315–316. After 1972, a PNE program was no longer mentioned in the AEB's annual reports.

52. Cited in Legum, ed., *Africa Contemporary Record, 1971–1972*, p. B363.

53. This was the location of the purported Kalahari test site. See Christie, *Electricity, Industry and Class in South Africa*, p. 192.

54. *The Times*, July 12, 1974.

55. Cited in Legum, ed., *Africa Contemporary Record, 1975–1976*, p. B598.

56. *International Herald Tribune*, February 17, 1977. Earlier, Prime Minister Vorster was quoted in *Newsweek* (May 17, 1976) as saying: "We are only interested in the peaceful applications of nuclear power. But we can enrich uranium, and we have the capability. And we did not sign the nuclear nonproliferation treaty." After an investigation, the U.S. State Department said that this was not the Prime Minister's exact phrasing, but a contraction of his statements during the course of the interview.

57. *Financial Times*, August 31, 1977.

58. A/C.1/PV. 1571, May 20, 1968, pp. 52–62; see also A/C.1/PV. 1579, June 5, 1968, p. 11. It should be noted that South Africa endorsed U.N.G.A. resolution 2373 (XXII) commending the NPT.

59. The 1967 amendment to the 1957 U.S.–South Africa *Agreement for Atomic Energy Cooperation* covered the possibility of applying safeguards if the Republic exported nuclear power reactors, but not for the export of nuclear fuel. See 18 UST 1671; TIAS 6312; 692 UNTS 428. Nonetheless, Pretoria had given assurances that it would not sell unsafeguarded nuclear fuel. See *ibid*. On January 31, 1984, South Africa pledged to attach IAEA or Euratom safeguards to all its nuclear exports.

60. See *Financial Times*, June 27, 29, 1978; *New York Times*, June 29, 1978; *International Herald Tribune*, June 20, 1978; Fischer, *The Spread of Nuclear Weapons*, pp. 35–36. South Africa continued to be subjected to harsh treatment within the IAEA. In September 1979, the IAEA's General Conference voted to reject the credentials of the South African delegation. The IAEA's Board of Governors later voted to exclude South Africa from the Committee on Assurances of Supply.

61. *Financial Times*, November 6, 1978. This action was required by the 1978 Nuclear Nonproliferation Act, which demanded that full-scope safeguards apply to the nuclear activities of any country receiving U.S. nuclear materials and equipment. While exceptions could legally be made, and indeed were with India, this would have been politically impossible in South Africa's case. Fischer has written that a team of South African lawyers had traveled to Washington and arrived at the conclusion that the Carter administration would not have been able to persuade Congress to permit nuclear fuel exports to South Africa, and that this was a "probable reason" for South Africa's refusal to ratify the NPT. Fischer, *ibid*., p. 44, note 45.

62. See *New York Times*, October 26, 1979.

63. "Note verbale dated November 5, 1979 from the Permanent Representative of South Africa to the United Nations addressed to the Secretary-General," in Inquiry into the reports concerning a nuclear explosion by South Africa: Report of the Secretary-General. A/34/674. November 12, 1979. If the event registered by the Vela satellite was a nuclear explosion, it is curious that it was detonated at night, when it would be more visible. If South Africa was responsible, it would have violated its obligations as a party to the PTBT. Also, the signature recorded by the Vela satellite was characteristic of that from a very low yield nuclear explosion, thereby indicating a surprisingly high degree of sophistication for a country's initial test.

64. Executive Office of the President, Office of Science and Technology Policy, Ad Hoc Panel Report on the September 22 Event, p. 2, xerox provided to the author by Prof. Jack Ruina. See also Philip J. Klass, "Clandestine Nuclear Test Doubted," Aviation Week and Space Technology, August 11, 1980; Science, vol. 209, no. 4456 (August 1, 1980), pp. 572–573.

65. See Guy Barasch, "Light Flash Produced by an Atmospheric Nuclear Explosion," Los Alamos Scientific Laboratory Mini-Review, November 1979; Washington Post, July 15, 1980; Washington Star, August 10, 1980; James Adams, The Unnatural Alliance: Israel and South Africa (London: Quartet Books, 1984), pp. 187–196.

66. See New York Times, February 19, 1981; Washington Post, February 19, 1981; Science, vol. 211, no. 4486, (March 6, 1981), p. 1020.

67. Spence has suggested that the timing of this announcement might have been motivated by the upcoming election in South Africa, and Prime Minister Botha's campaign rhetoric that the Republic was strong enough to independently defend its interests in the world. See Spence, "South Africa: The Nuclear Option," African Affairs, vol. 80, no. 321 (October 1981), p. 442, note 2.

68. Financial Times, April 30, 1981.

69. International Herald Tribune, June 26, 1981.

70. Financial Times, November 13, 1981; International Herald Tribune, November 14, 15, 1981.

71. See Nucleonics Week, November 26, 1981; Daily Telegraph, January 20, 1982.

72. See U.S., Senate, U.S. Policy Toward Africa, Hearings. Committee on Foreign Relations. Subcommittee on African Affairs, Subcommittee on Arms Control, International Organizations, and Security Agreements. 94th Cong., 2d sess. (Washington, D.C.: USGPO, 1976); U.S., Senate, U.S. Policy Toward Southern Africa, Hearings. Committee on Foreign Relations. Subcommittee on African Affairs. 94th Cong., 1st sess. (Washington, D.C.: USGPO, 1976); New York Times, May 22, 1976; Financial Times, May 21, 27, 1976.

73. This is not completely accurate. A 1951 defense agreement between the U.S. and South Africa was still in force. See Mutual Defense Assistance Agreement between the United States of America and the Union of South Africa. Exchange of notes, November 9, 1951; entered into force November 9, 1951. 3 UST 2565; TIAS 2424; 160 UNTS 41. This accord enabled South Africa to receive U.S. military assistance "solely to maintain its internal security [and] its legitimate self-defense." At this writing it is still in force. In addition, the U.S. and South Africa have two other agreements relating to national security: Agreement for the establishment and operation of an OMEGA navigation system monitoring facility. Signed May 17 and June 4, 1982; entered into force June 4, 1982. TIAS 10415; and Memorandum of understanding relating to the operation of the Landsat system, with annex. Signed September 19 and October 19, 1983; entered into force October 19, 1983. TIAS 10797.

74. Richard K. Betts, "A Diplomatic Bomb for South Africa?," *International Security*, vol. 4, no. 2 (Fall 1979), pp. 103–104; Report of the Study Commission on U.S. Policy Toward Southern Africa, *South Africa: Time Running Out* (London: University of California Press, 1981), p. 252.

75. Chester A. Crocker, *South Africa's Defense Posture: Coping with Vulnerability*, Washington Paper 84 (Beverly Hills: Sage, 1981), pp. 65–66; Kenneth L. Adelman and Albion W. Knight, "Can South Africa Go Nuclear?," *Orbis*, vol. 23, no. 3 (Fall 1979), p. 644; Dan Smith, *South Africa's Nuclear Capability* (London: World Campaign against Military and Nuclear Collaboration with South Africa, 1980), p. 23; Robert S. Jaster, "Politics and the 'Afrikaner Bomb,' " *Orbis*, vol. 27, no. 4 (Winter 1984), p. 841.

76. See testimony of Robert Alvarez, in U.S., House, *Resource Development in South Africa and U.S. Policy*, Hearings. Committee on International Relations. Subcommittee on International Resources, Food and Energy. 94th Cong., 2d sess. (Washington, D.C.: USGPO, 1976), p. 69; Ashok Kapur, *International Nuclear Proliferation: Multilateral Diplomacy and Regional Aspects* (New York: Praeger, 1979), p. 255.

77. Adelman and Knight,"Can South Africa Go Nuclear?," pp. 642–643; Pierre Lellouche, "The Garrison States," in William H. Kincade and Christoph Bertram, eds., *Nuclear Proliferation in the 1980s: Perspectives and Proposals* (London: Macmillan, 1982), p. 78; C. Raja Mohan, "Atomic Teeth to Apartheid: South Africa and Nuclear Weapons," in K. Subrahmanyam, ed., *Nuclear Myths and Realities: India's Dilemma* (New Delhi: ABC Publishing House, 1981), p. 137.

78. Jaster, *South Africa's Narrowing Security Options*, Adelphi Paper 159 (London: IISS, 1980), p. 45; Spence, *International Problems of Nuclear Proliferation and the South African Position* (Braamfontein: SAIIA, 1980), p. 9; Adelman and Knight, *ibid.*

79. Crocker, *South Africa's Defense Posture*, p. 64; Adelman and Knight, *ibid.*; Betts, "A Diplomatic Bomb," p. 108.

80. Frank Barnaby, *Nuclear Proliferation and the South African Threat* (Geneva: World Council of Churches, 1977), pp. 13–14; African National Congress, cited in *The Guardian*, October 6, 1975.

81. Adelman and Knight, "Can South Africa Go Nuclear," p. 643; Lellouche, "The Garrison States," p. 78.

82. The plane with this capability was the Hawker Siddeley Buccaneer, although its exact range would depend on the nature of the defenses to be penetrated. By 1980, the Republic had six of these aircraft still in service. See *The Military Balance, 1979–1980* (London: IISS, 1980), p. 54. Among South Africa's more modern aircraft, the Mirage F-1, with a radius of 500 miles, would also have been useful as a delivery vehicle. South Africa had virtually no missile program. See Jones, *South African Proliferation Prognosis*, pp. 14–15.

83. Edouard Bustin, "South Africa's Foreign Policy Alternatives and Deterrence Needs," in Onkar Marwah and Ann Schulz, eds., *Nuclear Proliferation and the Near-Nuclear Countries* (Cambridge, Ma.: Ballinger, 1975), p. 224.

84. *South Africa: Time Running Out*, p. 252.

85. See Alvarez testimony, *Resource Development in South Africa*, pp. 70, 73; testimony of Prof. Ronald Walters, Howard University, in *United States-South African Relations*, p. 22; Cervenka and Rogers, *The Nuclear Axis*, pp. 106, 193–194.

86. Spence, "The Republic of South Africa," p. 230.

87. Siegel, in *United States-South African Relations*, p. 8.

88. Smith, *South Africa's Nuclear Capability*, p. 23.

89. Crocker, *South Africa's Defense Posture*, p. 64.

90. Spence, *The Political and Military Framework*, p. 76; see also Connor Cruise O'Brien, "What Can Become of South Africa?," *The Atlantic* (March 1986), pp. 41–68. After May 1974, the Republic might have also thought it necessary to deter future nuclear threats from India over South Africa's treatment of its 800,000-strong Asian population. India was, after all, the first country to impose economic sanctions against Pretoria, in 1946–1947.

91. Cited in Patrick Wall, ed., *The Southern Oceans and the Security of the Free World* (London: Stacey International, 1977), p. 89.

92. Betts, "A Diplomatic Bomb," p. 101; See also George Quester, *The Politics of Nuclear Proliferation* (Baltimore: Johns Hopkins University Press, 1973), p. 202.

93. U.S., ACDA, *World Military Expenditures and Arms Transfers, 1972–1982* (Washington, D.C.: USGPO, 1984), p. 44.

94. Crocker, *South Africa's Defense Strategy*, p. 17. See also Thomas G. Karis, "Revolution in the Making: Black Politics in South Africa," *Foreign Affairs*, vol. 62, no. 2 (Winter 1983/84), pp. 378–406.

95. Bustin, "South Africa's Foreign Policy Alternatives," p. 222; Betts, "A Diplomatic Bomb," p. 97; M. Hough, *The Political Implications of the Possession of Nuclear Weapons for South Africa* (Pretoria: Institute for Strategic Studies, 1980), p. 7.

96. William Gutteridge, "South Africa's National Strategy: Implications for Regional Security," in Deon Geldenhuys and William Gutteridge, *Instability and Conflict in Southern Africa: South Africa's Role in Regional Security* (London: Institute for the Study of Conflict, 1983), p. 3.

97. *The Military Balance, 1979–1980* (London: IISS, 1980), pp. 48–56.

98. Jones, *South African Proliferation Prognosis*, pp. 16–20. See also R.W. Johnson, *How Long Will South Africa Survive?* (London: Macmillan, 1977), pp. 287–327; L.H. Gann and Peter Duignan, *South Africa: War, Revolution, or Peace?* (Stanford, Ca.: Hoover Institution, 1978), pp. 36–55; Jaster, *A Regional Security Role for Africa's Front-Line States: Experience and Prospects*, Adelphi Paper 180 (London: IISS, 1983), p. 37.

99. Adelman and Knight, "Can South Africa Go Nuclear?," p. 640.

100. See Jaster, *South Africa's Narrowing Security Options*, pp. 12–17.

101. See statement by then Minister of Defense P.W. Botha, in *International Herald Tribune*, May 2, 1977. This figure is now claimed to be above 85 percent. On the effectiveness of the 1977 arms embargo, see Crocker, *South Africa's Defense Posture*, pp. 47–51.

102. *The Military Balance, 1979–1980*, pp. 48–56.

103. Crocker, *South Africa's Defense Posture*, p. 84; Gutteridge, "South Africa's defense posture," *The World Today*, vol. 36, no. 1 (January 1980), p. 27; Hough, *The Political Implications*, p. 8.

104. Spence, *The Political and Military Framework*, p. 79; Hough, *ibid.*

105. Spence, "The Republic of South Africa," p. 228; Betts, "A Diplomatic Bomb," p. 104; Crocker, *South Africa's Defense Posture*, p. 62.

106. Barnaby, in Cervenka and Rogers, *The Nuclear Axis*, p. xv; testimony of Prof. David Apter, Yale University, in *U.S. Policy Toward Africa*, p. 259; *International Herald Tribune*, June 10, 1983. Given the almost nonexistent nuclear programs of the other African countries, it is unclear how great a disincentive to South Africa this would have been.

107. See Robert D'A. Henderson, "Nigeria's Nuclear Potential," in David Carlton and Carlo Schaerf, eds., *The Dynamics of the Arms Race* (London: Croom Helm, 1975), pp. 314–331. See also Ali Mazrui, "Africa's Nuclear Future," *Survival*, vol. 22, no. 2 (March/April 1980), pp. 76–79. Nigeria actually has no significant nuclear activities.

The only black African country to have a nuclear reactor is Zaire; a small TRIGA research reactor was purchased prior to its independence. For past efforts to make Africa a nuclear-free zone, see William Epstein, *A Nuclear-Weapon-Free Zone in Africa?*, Occasional Paper 14 (Muscatine, Iowa: Stanley Foundation, 1977).

108. Bustin, "South Africa's Foreign Policy Alternatives," p. 222; Smith, *South Africa's Nuclear Capability*, p. 23.

109. Spence, *The Political and Military Framework*, p. 79; Spence, "International Problems of Nuclear Proliferation," p. 9; *South Africa: Time Running Out*, pp. 252–253.

110. See U.S., House, *Sub-Sahara Africa: Its Role in Critical Mineral Needs of the Western World*. Report. Committee on Interior and Insular Affairs. Subcommittee on Mines and Mining. 96th Cong., 2d sess. (Washington, D.C.: USGPO, 1980). For a dissenting congressional view, see U.S., Senate, *Imports of Minerals from South Africa by the United States and the OECD Countries*, Print. Committee on Foreign Relations. Subcommittee on African Affairs. 96th Cong., 2d sess. (Washington, D.C.: USGPO, 1980).

111. Spence, "The Republic of South Africa," p. 228.

112. *South Africa: Time Running Out*, pp. 327–329.

113. See David E. Albright, "Soviet Policy," *Problems of Communism*, vol. 27, no. 1 (January-February 1978), pp. 20–39; and especially Bruce D. Porter, *The USSR in Third World Conflicts: Soviet Arms and Diplomacy in Local Wars, 1945–1980* (New York: Cambridge University Press, 1984).

114. Spence, *The Political and Military Framework*, p. 78.

115. For Soviet views of the situation in southern Africa, see A. Gromyko, "Neo-Colonialism's Maneuvers in Southern Africa," *International Affairs* (Moscow), no. 12 (December 1977), pp. 96–102; I.A. Ulanovskaya, *South Africa: Racism Doomed* (Moscow: Znanie, 1978). For a recent Soviet discussion of South African nuclear arms, see B. Asoyan, "Southern Africa: Nuclear Bomb in Pretoria's Hands?" *New Times* (Moscow), vol. 21 (May 1984), pp. 22–23. In addition, the Soviet Union and South Africa engage in numerous sub rosa economic dealings. It cannot be estimated how, or if, this would have affected its policy towards the Republic. See Kurt M. Campbell, *Soviet Policy Towards South Africa* (New York: St. Martin's, 1986), pp. 94–126.

116. Cited in Spence, "South Africa; The Nuclear Option," pp. 447–448.

117. *International Herald Tribune*, October 25, 27, 1977. In May 1979, Thomas Pickering, the Assistant Secretary of State for Oceans and International Environmental and Scientific Affairs, testified in a congressional hearing that South Africa had assured the U.S. that it did not have, nor did it intend to develop, a nuclear explosive device, that the Kalahari site was not a testing ground for nuclear explosions, and that it would not conduct any nuclear tests. See U.S., Senate, *Nuclear Proliferation: The Situation in Pakistan and India*, Hearings. Committee on Governmental Affairs. Subcommittee on Energy, Nuclear Proliferation and Federal Services. 96th Cong., 1st sess. (Washington, D.C.: USGPO, 1979), p. 29–30.

118. *International Herald Tribune*, September 16, 1977.

119. Fischer, *The Spread of Nuclear Weapons*, p. 42, note 27.

120. *Daily Telegraph*, June 3, 1978.

121. *Christian Science Monitor*, December 3, 1981.

122. *The Times*, October 18, 1980.

123. *Paratus*, vol. 33, no. 2 (February 1982), pp. 47–80. The article was by Kent F. Wisner, and originally published in *Survival*, vol. 23, no. 6 (November-December 1981), pp. 246–251.

7. India

1. For a fuller treatment of this conflict and the ensuing diplomatic maneuvers, see Michael Brecher, *The Struggle for Kashmir* (Toronto: Ryerson Press, 1953); Sisir Gupta, *Kashmir, A Study in India-Pakistan Relations* (London: Asia Publishing House, 1966); S.M. Burke, *Pakistan's Foreign Policy* (London: Oxford University Press, 1973).

2. These five principles were mutual respect for each other's territorial integrity and sovereignty, nonaggression, noninterference in each other's internal affairs, equality and mutual benefit, and peaceful coexistence. For the text of this agreement, see *Foreign Policy of India, Text of Documents 1947–64* (New Delhi: Lok Sabha Secretariat, 1966), pp. 198–205. For Nehru's interpretation of this agreement, see *Panchsheel, Excerpts from Prime Minister Nehru's Speeches, 1954–56* (New Delhi: Government of India, 1957).

3. For further discussion of this war, see Allen S. Whiting, *The Chinese Calculus of Deterrence* (Ann Arbor: University of Michigan Press, 1975); Neville Maxwell, *India's China War* (London: Jonathan Cape, 1970). For a viewpoint sympathetic to Nehru's handling of relations with the PRC prior to the 1962 border war, see K. Subrahmanyam, "Nehru and the India-China Conflict of 1962," in B.R. Nanda, ed., *India Foreign Policy: The Nehru Years* (New Delhi: Vikas Publishing House, 1976), pp. 102–130. For a legal analysis of the border dispute by an Indian scholar, see Surya P. Sharma, *India's Boundary and Territorial Disputes* (New Delhi: Vikas Publishing House, 1971).

4. William J. Barnds, *India, Pakistan, and the Great Powers* (London: Pall Mall, 1970), p. 180. For an excellent examination of India's security concerns during its first two decades of independence, see Lorne J. Kavic, *India's Quest For Security: Defense Policies, 1947–1965* (Berkeley: University of California Press, 1967).

5. There had been a demand prior to October 1964 that India manufacture nuclear armaments. In March 1963, in response to India's China war, Ramachandra Bade, a member of the ultranationalist Jana Sangh party, urged in the Lok Sabha (Lower House of Parliament) that India acquire nuclear weapons for self-defense. In addition, according to Ashok Kapur, there had been "an ongoing nuclear debate within India's foreign policy and atomic energy establishments since the mid-1950s at least." Kapur, *India's Nuclear Option: Atomic Diplomacy and Decision-Making* (New York: Praeger, 1976), p. 122.

6. See Shyam Bhatia, *India's Nuclear Bomb* (New Delhi: Vikas, 1979), pp. 89–91.

7. R.K. Nehru, "The Challenge of the Chinese Bomb—I," *India Quarterly*, vol. 21, no. 1 (January-March 1965), p. 10. See also Sisir Gupta, "The Indian Dilemma," in Alastair Buchan, ed., *A World of Nuclear Powers?* (Englewood Cliffs, N.J.: Prentice-Hall, 1966), pp. 57–58.

8. See, for example, Sampooran Singh, *India and the Nuclear Bomb* (New Delhi: S. Chand, 1971).

9. See Gupta, "The Indian Dilemma," pp. 62–63; Institute for Defense Studies and Analyses, *A Strategy for India for a Credible Posture Against a Nuclear Adversary* (New Delhi: IDSA, 1968), p. 4.

10. M.J. Desai, "India and Nuclear Weapons," *Disarmament and Arms Control*, vol. 3, no. 2 (Autumn 1965).

11. M.R. Masani, "The Challenge of the Chinese Bomb—II." *India Quarterly*, vol. 21, no. 1 (January-March 1965), p. 21.

12. Cited in Bhatia, *India's Nuclear Bomb*, pp. 113–114.

13. "Broadcast by H.J. Bhabha over All India Radio on United Nations Day,"

October 24, 1964," in J.P. Jain, ed., *Nuclear India*, vol. 2 (New Delhi: Radiant, 1974), pp. 158–160. 100,000 rupees equals 1 lakh, and 100 lakhs (10 million rupees) equals 1 crore.

14. Roberta Wohlstetter has argued that Bhabha erred on his cost figures because he quoted from a U.S. study which had calculated the expenses to the United States, which had already invested billions of dollars in its nuclear program, of building nuclear explosives for its Project Plowshares. "Needless to say, the cost to India to make a few fission and fusion devices of this sort, starting from where the Indian program was at the time, would have been of another order of magnitude." Wohlstetter, *"The Buddha Smiles": Absent-Minded Peaceful Aid and the Indian Bomb* (Los Angeles: Pan Heuristics, 1977), p. 96 note.

15. Bhatia, *India's Nuclear Bomb*, pp. 115–119; Kapur, *India's Nuclear Option*, p. 17. It should be mentioned that India's armed forces are apolitical; they had no direct influence on the political debate concerning nuclear weapons and never entered the nuclear decision-making process.

16. *Hindustan Times*, October 25, 1964.

17. Bhatia, *India's Nuclear Bomb*, p. 111.

18. *Hindustan Times*, November 10, 1964.

19. Bhatia, *India's Nuclear Bomb*, p. 120.

20. See Bhatia, *India's Nuclear Bomb*, p. 110. The political opposition was divided on the nuclear weapons issue, and lacked political influence in any case because of its weakness relative to the Congress Party. The ultranationalist Jana Sangh Party and the People's Socialist Party (PSP) strongly supported acquisition, Swatantra, which represented the interests of the business community, was split, while the Communist Party opposed nuclear weapons for India.

21. Bhatia, *India's Nuclear Bomb*, p. 122; *Hindustan Times*, November 8, 1964.

22. *Lok Sabha Debates*, vol. 35, 3rd series, November 27, 1964, col. 2287.

23. This statement deserves some qualification. There is some evidence which suggests that Nehru's true beliefs concerning India's nuclear option may have been more complex than they are usually portrayed.

First, before becoming prime minister, Nehru had stated on June 26, 1946 before a public gathering in Bombay: "As long as the world is constituted as it is, every country will have to devise and use the latest scientific devices for its protection. I have no doubt India will develop her scientific researches and I hope Indian scientists will use the atomic force for constructive purposes. But if India is threatened she will inevitably try to defend herself *by all means at her disposal*." Dorothy Norman, ed., *Nehru: The First 60 Years*, vol. 2 (New York: John Day, 1965), p. 264 (emphasis added).

Second, during India's deliberations in the early 1960s over whether or not to base its nuclear energy program on the CANDU heavy-water reactor, which used natural uranium, or the light-water reactor, which used lightly enriched uranium, Bhabha submitted a note to the Indian cabinet justifying the selection of the heavy-water reactor. Nehru wrote on the memo that "Apart from building power stations and developing electricity there is always a built-in advantage of defense use if the need should arise." Kapur, *India's Nuclear Option*, pp. 193–194. Kapur does not give an exact date for Nehru's comment.

Finally, the Indian diplomat Arthur Lall, in a personal letter to Kapur, dated January 15, 1973, wrote: "Nehru's willingness to keep the option open did not mean that he favored development of the bomb by India. He was against it. But he knew the political value of keeping the option open." Kapur, "India's Nuclear Presence," *The World Today*, vol. 30, no. 11 (November 1974), p. 462.

24. *Hindustan Times*, January 8, 1965.

25. There was widespread ignorance at this time, even among elites, of the rudimentary facts of nuclear technology and of India's lack of nuclear sophistication. For example, in the December 14, 1964 session of the Lok Sabha, Lalit Sen, the prime minister's parliamentary secretary, claimed that India was "in a position to make uranium-235 if we want . . . if and when it is decided, we could either use plutonium or uranium-235 [for nuclear weapons]." *Lok Sabha Debates*, vol. 37, 3rd series, December 14, 1964, col. 4654. This statement was at least misleading and at most untrue, as India did not have a uranium enrichment capability and its reprocessing facility at Trombay was experiencing operational problems. Nonetheless, Sen's assertion went unchallenged.

26. Shelton L. Williams, *The U.S., India, and the Bomb*, Studies in International Affairs No. 12 (Baltimore: Johns Hopkins University Press, 1969),p. 38; see also Birla Institute of Scientific Research, *India and the Atom* (New Delhi: Allied Publishers, 1982), p. 62.

27. See Richard G. Hewlett and Oscar E. Anderson, *The New World, 1939/1946* (University Park, Pa.: Pennsylvania State University Press, 1962), p. 288; Margaret Gowing, *Britain and Atomic Energy 1939–1945* (London: Macmillan, 1964), pp. 316, 318. Thorium is found in monazite, a mineral which occurs in beach or river sand deposits. India had an estimated 300,000 to 500,000 tons of monazite at Travancore. Scientists working on the Manhattan Project had at one time believed that thorium, which after irradiation is transformed into the fissile isotope uranium-233, could act as a fuel in atomic reactors.

28. Bhatia, *India's Nuclear Bomb*, pp. 84–85.

29. Memorandum prepared in the Office of the Under Secretary of State (Lovett), September 17, 1948, in *FRUS, General: The United Nations*, vol. 1, part 2 (Washington, D.C.: USGPO, 1976), p. 760.

30. K.K. Pathak, *Nuclear Policy of India: A Third World Perspective* (New Delhi: Gitanjali Prakashan, 1980), p. 44; Dhirendra Sharma, *India's Nuclear Estate* (New Delhi: Lancers Publishers, 1983), pp. 21, 51; David Hart, *Nuclear Power in India: A Comparative Analysis* (New Delhi: Selectbook Service Syndicate, 1983), p. 35.

31. For a later critique of India's three-stage nuclear plan, see Wohlstetter, "The Buddha Smiles," pp. 59–65.

32. Wohlstetter, "The Buddha Smiles," p. 72.

33. It has been claimed that this laxity with respect to safeguards can also be explained by Ottawa's relative novelty in the nuclear export business and its attendant inexperience with devising safeguards or formulating appropriate legal language in the nuclear energy field, and by the lack of any international agency at this time to assist in monitoring nuclear activities. However, at this same time the Canadians were playing a very active role in formulating the provisions of the IAEA statute (which was approved in October 1956), and so could have provided for the transfer of safeguards responsibility to the Agency once the IAEA safeguards system became operative.

According to Kapur, India had agreed to "Canadian inspection related to first-generation use of Canadian-supplied nuclear materials but rejected inspection of all nuclear equipment in a reactor and of all peaceful nuclear projects." *India's Nuclear Option*, p. 109. Warren Donnelly believes that the Canadians had access to the reactor for inspection when Canadian-supplied uranium was present, but the Canadians apparently overlooked the possibility that India might indigenously mine uranium of its own and then fabricate the uranium for the CIRUS reactor. This is what occurred with the 1974 PNE, with the Indians subsequently maintaining that the uranium for CIRUS and the plutonium it produced had not been subject to safeguards. Personal correspondence with the author, October 22, 1986.

34. Cited in Wohlstetter, "The Buddha Smiles," pp. 74–75.

35. Cited in Wohlstetter, "The Buddha Smiles," p. 77. Nehru used the term "atomic colonialism" in the Lok Sabha on July 23, 1957, to refer to this same possibility.

36. Leonard Beaton and John Maddox, The Spread of Nuclear Weapons (New York: Praeger, 1962), pp. 140–141. The construction of the Trombay reprocessing facility was also known as Project Phoenix. India received American assistance in building this plant. Bhabha used the blueprints for the Purex process which had been released by the U.S. Atomic Energy Commission, and an American firm, Vitro International, provided technical advice. Wohlstetter, "The Buddha Smiles," p. 63.

37. Lok Sabha Debates, vol. 44, 2d series, August 10, 1960, col. 2014.

38. See G.G. Mirchandani, India's Nuclear Dilemma (New Delhi: Popular Book Services, 1968), pp. 9–11. This realization also compelled India to establish a new Atomic Energy Commission, which was charged, subject to the prime minister's approval, with formulating policies for the Department of Atomic Energy as well as preparing the department's annual budget. See Bhatia, India's Nuclear Bomb, p. 100.

39. V.K. McElheny, "Electric Power Remains Emphasis of India's Nuclear Energy Program," Science, vol. 149, no. 3681 (July 16, 1965), p. 284. A very sophisticated nuclear device can be constructed with as little as four to six kilograms of plutonium.

40. Bhatia, India's Nuclear Bomb, p. 141.

41. Kapur, India's Nuclear Option, p. 144; see also Sharma, India's Nuclear Estate, pp. 88, 91.

42. Kapur, India's Nuclear Option, p. 195; Paul F. Power, "The Indo-American Nuclear Controversy," Asian Survey, vol. 19, no. 6 (June 1979), p. 577. According to a former senior official in the Indian Atomic Energy Commission, Indira Gandhi was unaware of SNEP and Sarabhai canceled it on his own authority. Interview, Bombay, June 1986. India and Canada signed an agreement for RAPS-II in December 1966. For the texts of the Indian-Canadian agreements on RAPS-I and II, see J.P. Jain, Nuclear India, vol. 2, pp. 132–139, 188–189. For background information on these two reactors, see Hart, Nuclear Power in India, pp. 44–48.

43. Michael Brecher, Succession in India: A Study in Decision-Making (London: Oxford University Press, 1966), p. 127.

44. The most comprehensive treatment of this issue is A.G. Noorani, "India's Quest For A Nuclear Guarantee," Asian Survey, vol. 7, no. 7 (July 1967), pp. 490–502. See also, M.R. Masani, "The Challenge of the Chinese Bomb—II," pp. 26–27. A variation on the topic of nuclear guarantees was provided at this time in a well-known article by Raj Krishna. Krishna recommended a policy of "bifurcated" deterrence, with Indian tactical nuclear weapons being backed by an American and Soviet nuclear guarantee at the strategic level. See Krishna, "India and the Bomb," India Quarterly, vol. 21, no. 2 (April–June 1965), pp. 119–137.

45. Indian Express, April 19, 1967; Times of India, May 6, 1967; The Hindu, May 6, 1967. All cited in Noorani, "India's Quest For A Nuclear Guarantee," pp. 498–499. See also Kapur, India's Nuclear Option, p. 141, note 2.

46. The farthest the Soviet Union would publicly commit itself at this time was Soviet Premier Kosygin's February 1966 proposal "to include in the draft [nonproliferation] treaty an article dealing with the prohibition of the use of nuclear weapons against nonnuclear states, parties to the treaty, which do not have nuclear weapons on their territory." See Documents on Disarmament, 1966, (Washington, D.C.: USGPO, 1967), pp. 9–13. This fell short of being a nuclear guarantee to the nonnuclear countries. In June 1968, U.N. Security Council resolution 255, which was sponsored by the United States, the Soviet Union, and Britain, passed unanimously. This resolution declared that any instance of nuclear blackmail or aggression should be referred to the Security Council for immediate attention. Clearly, this too was not a nuclear guarantee of the type India wanted.

47. U.N. General Assembly resolution 2028 (XX): Nonproliferation of Nuclear Weapons, November 19, 1965. A/C.1/L.344. This resolution's fifth and final principle stipulated that nothing in a nonproliferation treaty should prevent countries from concluding regional treaties for establishing nuclear-weapons-free-zones. For a thoughtful discussion of this resolution from India's perspective, see V.C. Trivedi, "Vertical Versus Horizontal Proliferation: An Indian View," in James Dougherty and J.F. Lehman, eds., Arms Control for the Late Sixties (New York: D. Van Nostrand, 1967), pp. 195–203.

48. See ENDC/PV.298, May 23, 1967, pp. 4–17; ENDC/PV.334, September 28, 1967, pp. 4–16. See also K.K. Pathak, Nuclear Policy of India, pp. 90–120. Indian analysts have subsequently leveled two further criticisms at the NPT. First, it is alleged that the treaty is merely a scheme by the nuclear weapons states, in particular by the United States and the Soviet Union, to limit the number of nuclear powers, and second, that the treaty is based on the flawed assumption that more nuclear weapons states will be dangerously destablizing to the international system. K. Subrahmanyam especially has written on this topic. For two fairly recent examples of his thinking, see K. Subrahmanyam, Indian Security Perspectives (New Delhi: ABC, 1982), pp. 70–82; K. Subrahmanyam, "The Real Proliferation," in K. Subrahmanyam, ed., Nuclear Proliferation and International Security (New Delhi: Lancer International, 1985), pp. 54–64.

49. Kapur, India's Nuclear Option, p. 196; Kapur, International Nuclear Proliferation: Multilateral Diplomacy and Regional Aspects (New York: Praeger, 1979), p. 214.

50. Kapur attributes India's decision not to sign the NPT to "a careful reading of public opinion polls. These polls showed that a majority rejected the NPT and favored an Indian decision toward nuclear weapons." India's Nuclear Option, p. 196. The only public opinion poll from this period of which I am aware was conducted in February 1968 by the Indian Institute of Public Opinion. To the question, "Do you wish India to make an atom bomb?," 73 percent responded "yes," 24 percent "no," and 3 percent "can't say." To the question, "Should India sign the Treaty of Nonproliferation of Atomic Weapons (sic)?," 34 percent responded "yes," 40 percent "no," with 26 percent "no opinion." Monthly Public Opinion Surveys of the Indian Institute of Public Opinion, vol. 13, no. 5 (February 1968), pp. 19, 21. An analysis of this data indicates, first, that a plurality, not a majority, opposed the NPT. Second, it suggests that the respondents did not fully understand either the questions or the significance of their answers, as the 73 percent in favor of India manufacturing nuclear weapons should have corresponded to a percentage higher than 40 percent of people not wanting India to sign the NPT, since India would not be allowed to build nuclear bombs under the terms of the treaty. Throwing further doubt on the accuracy of the polling data was that this was the first

time public opinion had been sought on nuclear issues, and more significantly, that the survey only covered the four cities of Bombay, Calcutta, Delhi, and Madras.

51. A/C.1/PV.1567, May 14, 1968, pp. 56–82.

52. Bhatia, *India's Nuclear Bomb*, p. 141.

53. Atomic Energy Commission, *Atomic Energy and Space Research: A Profile for the Decade 1970–1980* (New Delhi: Government of India, 1970).

54. Article IX of this treaty declares that "In the event of either Party being subjected to an attack or a threat thereof, the High Contracting Parties shall immediately enter into mutual consultations in order to remove such threat and to take appropriate effective measures to ensure peace and the security of their countries." For the complete text of the August 9, 1971, agreement, see *Current Digest of the Soviet Press*, vol. 23, no. 22 (September 1971), p. 5. There is evidence that India and the Soviet Union had earlier contemplated and prepared a joint security treaty. See Robert C. Horn, "Indian-Soviet Relations in 1969: A Watershed Year?," *Orbis*, vol. 19, no. 4 (Winter 1976), pp. 1539–1563.

55. On the 1971 India-Pakistan war, see Robert Jackson, *South Asian Crisis: India-Pakistan-Bangladesh* (London: Chatto & Windus, 1973); see also G.W. Choudhury, *The Last Days of United Pakistan* (London: C. Hurst, 1974).

56. Bhatia, *India's Nuclear Bomb*, pp. 144–145.

57. Interview with a former senior official of the Indian Atomic Energy Commission, Bombay, June 1986.

58. Kapur places the decision date "on or around" February 15, 1974. Kapur, *India's Nuclear Option*, p. 198. Raja Ramanna has said that the prime minister gave her permission "a few months" before May 1974. Interview with Raja Ramanna, Bombay, June 1986.

59. Interview with Raja Ramanna, Bombay, June 1986.

60. Interview with a former senior official of the Indian Atomic Energy Commission, Bombay, June 1986. Interestingly, the size and yield of the Indian device corresponded to the plutonium-based bomb, nicknamed "Fat Man," that the United States had dropped on Nagasaki.

61. See *Nature*, vol. 250, no. 5461 (July 5, 1974), p. 8. The dollar figure is in 1974 U.S. dollars. This figure of course includes only the cost of preparing and detonating the device, and does not include the expense incurred in building the CIRUS reactor and the Trombay reprocessing plant. For an authoritative analysis of India's PNE, see R. Chidambaram and R. Ramanna, "Some studies on India's peaceful nuclear explosion experiment," in *Peaceful Nuclear Explosions IV, Proceedings of a Technical Committee on the Peaceful Uses of Nuclear Explosions* (Vienna: IAEA, 1975), pp. 421–435.

62. See J.P. Jain, *Nuclear India*, vol. 2, p. 332.

63. For two studies of the U.S. peaceful nuclear explosions program, see Ralph Sanders, *Project Plowshares: The Development of the Peaceful Uses of Nuclear Explosions* (Washington, D.C.: Public Affairs Press, 1962); Edward Teller et al., *The Constructive Uses of Nuclear Explosives* (New York: McGraw-Hill, 1968). The latter book is specifically cited by those Indians who maintain that the May 18, 1974 event was simply identical to what the United States was doing in the field.

64. Frank Barnaby, *The Nuclear Age* (Cambridge, Ma.: MIT Press, 1974), pp. 108–110.

65. A notable exception was France, which sent a congratulatory telegram to India. Andre Giraud, the chairman of France's Commissariat à l'Energie Atomique, directed

Bertrand Goldschmidt to draft this telegram. Goldschmidt's first effort was not in Giraud's view sufficiently effusive, so Goldschmidt was asked to try again. The second draft was approved and sent to India without the knowledge of the Quai d'Orsay.

66. See J.P. Jain, *Nuclear India*, vol. 2, p. 334.

67. See Wohlstetter, "*The Buddha Smiles*," passim.

68. See J.P. Jain, *Nuclear India*, vol. 2, pp. 343–345.

69. Interview with A.B. Vajpayee, New Delhi, June 1986. Examples of the Soviet Union's dry, factual reporting of India's PNE can be found in the TASS article reprinted in *FBIS*, May 20, 1974; and in *New Times*, no. 21 (May 1974).

70. Gloria Duffy, *Soviet Nuclear Energy: Domestic and International Policies*, R-2362-DOE (Santa Monica, Ca.: RAND, 1979), pp. 23–24; see also *Washington Post*, December 12, 1976. These types of safeguards are known as "pursuit" and "perpetuity" provisions. David Fischer, the former Deputy Director of the IAEA, states that it was the IAEA that insisted that any reactor into which the heavy water was introduced should remain permanently under safeguards. Personal correspondence with the author, October 12, 1986. The text of the Soviet-Indian heavy-water agreement, published by the IAEA as INFCIRC 260, is contained in Duffy, pp. 108–118.

71. Cited in Wohlstetter, "*The Buddha Smiles*," p. 134.

72. See *Agreements regarding the consolidation and rescheduling of certain debts owed to the U.S. Government and its agencies, with annexes*. Signed at Washington, June 7, 1974; entered into force, June 7, 1974. 25 UST 1547; TIAS 7890. Steven Weissman and Herbert Krosney, *The Islamic Bomb: The Nuclear Threat to Israel and the Middle East* (New York: Times Books, 1981), p. 134.

73. The text of the 1963 US-Indian agreement for cooperation on the Tarapur Atomic Power Station (TAPS) can be found at 14 UST 1484; TIAS 5446. The U.S. Atomic Energy Commission refused to allow the export of future shipments of nuclear fuel for Tarapur until it received an assurance from India that the plutonium from Tarapur would not be used to construct nuclear explosives of any type. On September 17, 1974, Homi Sethna wrote to Dixie Lee Ray, the chairman of the USAEC, that the plutonium at Tarapur "will be devoted exclusively to the needs of the station," which effectively precluded its use for nuclear explosives. The USAEC thereupon resumed exports of the lightly enriched uranium fuel. The letter from Sethna to Ray, along with their previous correspondence on the subject, is reproduced in Wohlstetter, "*The Buddha Smiles*," pp. 205–212.

74. See, for example, the testimony of Acting Assistant Secretary of State for Oceans and International Environmental and Scientific Affairs, Myron Kratzer, for acknowledging Canada's role in India's PNE but making no mention of the part played by the United States, in U.S., House, *Oversight Hearings on Nuclear Energy: International Proliferation of Nuclear Technology*. Committee on Interior and Insular Affairs. Subcommittee on Energy and the Environment. 94th Cong., 1st sess. (Washington, D.C.: USGPO, 1975), pp. 3–28. See also Wohlstetter, "*The Buddha Smiles*," pp. 140–156.

75. Leonard S. Spector, *Nuclear Proliferation Today* (New York: Vintage, 1984), pp. 350–351; see also Hart, *Nuclear Power in India*, pp. 39–44. For a discussion of this and other issues surrounding nuclear fuel for Tarapur, see U.S., Senate, *Tarapur Nuclear Fuel Export*, Report. Committee on Foreign Relations. 96th Cong., 2d sess. (Washington, D.C.: USGPO, 1980). See also A.G. Noorani, "Indo-U.S. Nuclear Relations," *Asian Survey*, vol. 21, no. 4 (April 1981), pp. 399–416.

76. See Robert F. Goheen, "Problems of Proliferation: U.S. Policy and the Third

World," *World Politics*, vol. 35, no. 2 (January 1983), pp. 197–202; *New York Times*, July 30, 1982.

77. Interview with a former senior official of the Indian Atomic Energy Commission, Bombay, June 1986.

78. Interviews with Western diplomats and atomic energy officials, 1985 and 1986.

79. After numerous setbacks, the Kalpakkam fast breeder test reactor was commissioned in December 1985. According to one observer, this facility will perhaps require as much as 150 kilograms of plutonium to operate at full capacity. Spector, *The New Nuclear Nations* (New York: Vintage, 1985), p. 282. For further discussion of this facility, see Department of Atomic Energy, *Annual Report 1985–86* (New Delhi: Government of India, 1986); *Nuclear India*, vol. 24, no. 2 (1985).

80. "Address by Indian Prime Minister Desai before Special Session of the General Assembly devoted to disarmament: Indian Nuclear Policy," June 9, 1978, A/S-10/PV.24 (prov.), pp. 7–10. Before going to the United Nations, Desai had read the text of this speech to his cabinet, which had unanimously endorsed it. Interview with Morarji Desai, Bombay, June 1986.

81. Interview with Morarji Desai, Bombay, June 1986. For a discussion of the Desai administration's nuclear policy, see Kapur, "India's Nuclear Politics and Policy: Janata Party's Evolving Stance," and Bhabani Sen Gupta, "Dilemma Without Anguish: India, Morarji and the Bomb," both in T.T. Poulouse, ed., *Perspectives of India's Nuclear Policy* (New Delhi: Young Asia Publications, 1978), pp. 170–188, and 224–239, respectively.

82. See J.P. Jain, *Nuclear India*, vol. 2, pp. 364–367. This letter was written on June 6, 1974. Prime Minister Gandhi's earlier letter of May 22, 1974 to Prime Minister Bhutto assuring him that India remains "fully committed to our traditional policy of developing nuclear energy resources entirely for peaceful purposes" is reproduced in this same volume, pp. 345–346.

83. See Weissman and Krosney, *The Islamic Bomb*, pp. 43–46. See also Zulfikar Ali Bhutto, *The Myth of Independence* (London: Oxford University Press, 1969), p. 153. For a more detailed look at the Pakistani nuclear program by Indian scholars, see P.B. Sinha and R.R. Subramanian, *Nuclear Pakistan: Atomic Threat to South Asia* (New Delhi: Vision Books, 1980); Brij Mohan Kaushik and O.N. Mehrotra, *Pakistan's Nuclear Bomb* (New Delhi: Sopan Publishing House, 1980); D.K. Palit and P.K.S. Namboodiri, *Pakistan's Islamic Bomb* (New Delhi: Vikas Publishing House, 1979). For a more recent examination, see Kapur, *Pakistan's Nuclear Development* (London: Croom Helm, 1987).

84. Weissman and Krosney, *The Islamic Bomb*, p. 167; Spector, *Nuclear Proliferation Today*, p. 81.

85. *Washington Post*, September 23, 1980; see also Weissman and Krosney, *The Islamic Bomb*, pp. 75–76.

86. On November 14, 1983, a lower Dutch court sentenced Khan in abstentia to four years' imprisonment for his activities at the Urenco facility. The Amsterdam Appeals Court quashed the sentence because the Public Prosecutor's office had failed to serve the summons against Khan. In order to renew its charges, the prosecution would have to issue and serve a new summons. For information on Pakistan's attempts to acquire uranium enrichment technology and information, see Spector, *The New Nuclear Nations*, pp. 22–41; Weissman and Krosney, *The Islamic Bomb*, pp. 161–223.

87. See Shirin Tahir-Kheli, *The United States and Pakistan: The Evolution of an*

Influence Relationship (New York: Praeger, 1982). See also Warren H. Donnelly and Ira Goldman, *Nuclear Weapons: The Threat of Pakistan Going Nuclear*, Issue Brief No. IB79093, Congressional Research Service, June 18, 1981.

88. See U.S., Senate, *Hearing on Nuclear Nonproliferation Policy*. Committee on Governmental Affairs. Subcommittee on Energy, Nuclear Proliferation, and Government Processes. 97th Cong., 1st sess. (Washington, D.C.: USGPO, 1981), p. 18. See also *New York Times*, September 17, 1981.

89. *Nucleonics Week*, November 12, 1981, cited in Spector, *Nuclear Proliferation Today*, pp. 365–366. This was the first time in the IAEA's history that this had occurred. However, David Fischer states that the IAEA continuously applied safeguards at KANUPP, and it is "doubtful whether Pakistan could have diverted enough for one bomb." Personal correspondence with the author, October 12, 1986.

90. *Washington Post*, September 23, 1980. Pakistan also possessed a 5-megawatt lightly enriched uranium research reactor at Rawalpindi. This facility, which had started up in 1965, was under IAEA safeguards and was also too small to produce significant amounts of plutonium for New Labs.

91. Cited in Spector, *Nuclear Proliferation Today*, p. 105.

92. *Washington Post*, February 10, 1984.

93. *Washington Times*, July 26, 1984; Spector, *The Near-Nuclear Nations*, p. 115.

94. See *New York Times*, September 19, 1982; *Washington Post*, February 28, 1983; *New York Times*, June 23, 1984. It should be noted that during the period covered by these news articles, the United States was negotiating with the PRC on a nuclear trade agreement, which was finally initialed by President Reagan in April 1984. Those who wanted to prevent this agreement may have been responsible for leaking the information contained in these articles.

95. Both reports, along with a discussion of other issues relating to Pakistan's nuclear program, are cited in Spector, *Going Nuclear* (Cambridge: Ballinger, 1987), pp. 101–124.

96. See *New York Times*, March 6 and 22, 1987.

97. Interviews with Western diplomatic sources, Indian government officials, and academics, New Delhi, June 1986.

98. Western diplomatic sources interviewed in New Delhi in June 1986 believed that India had not stockpiled any weapons-grade plutonium or nuclear devices. It now appears that these sources may have been partly mistaken. On the basis of his June 1986 interview with a senior Indian atomic energy official, Spector reports that India during 1985 and 1986 separated spent fuel from its Madras I nuclear power reactor to obtain plutonium that was free of bilateral or international safeguards. See Spector, *Going Nuclear*, pp. 83–86.

99. Interview, Morarji Desai, Bombay, June 1986. This was confirmed by A.B. Vajpayee, who was Desai's foreign minister. Interview, New Delhi, June 1986. For a thrilling fictionalized account of an Indian conventional attack on Pakistan's nuclear facilities, see Ravi Rikhye, *The Fourth Round: Indo-Pak War 1984, Future History* (New Delhi: ABC, 1982). On the damage India could inflict on Pakistan if it decided to use nuclear weapons, see Paul Bracken, *The Vulnerability of Pakistan to Atomic Attack*, HI-2448-DP, Hudson Institute, June 8, 1976.

Appendix: Technical Note

1. For a more detailed discussion of these subjects, see Samuel Glasstone, *Source-*

book *On Atomic Energy*, 3d ed. (Princeton, N.J.: Princeton University Press, 1967); David Rittenhouse Inglis, *Nuclear Energy: Its Physics and Its Social Challenge* (Reading, Ma.: Addison-Wesley, 1973); Mason Willrich and Theodore B. Taylor, *Nuclear Theft: Risks and Safeguards* (Cambridge, Ma.: Ballinger, 1974), pp. 10–19; Report of the Nuclear Energy Policy Study Group, *Nuclear Power Issues and Choices* (Cambridge, Ma.: Ballinger, 1977), pp. 389–405; SIPRI, *Nuclear Energy and Nuclear Weapon Proliferation* (London: Taylor and Francis, 1979); Dietrich Schroeer, *Science, Technology, and the Nuclear Arms Race* (New York: John Wiley, 1984), pp. 14–81.

Index